Funding G

WITHDRAWN

Youth

2nd edition

Nicola Eastwood

D1651912

DIRECTORY OF SOCIAL CHANGE

Published by
The Directory of Social Change
24 Stephenson Way
London NW1 2DP
tel: 08450 77 77 07, fax: 020 7391 4804
e-mail: books@dsc.org.uk
www.dsc.org.uk
from whom further copies and a full publications list are available.

The Directory of Social Change is a Registered Charity no. 800517

First published 1997
Second edition 2002
Reprinted 2004

ISBN 1 900360 96 9

British Library Cataloguing in Publication Data
A catalogue record for this book is available from the British Library

Cover design by Linda Parker
Text designed and typeset by Linda Parker
Printed and bound by Antony Rowe, Chippenham

Other Directory of Social Change departments in London:
Courses and Conferences tel: 08450 77 77 07
Charity Centre tel: 08450 77 77 07
Charityfair tel: 020 7391 4875
Publicity and web content tel: 020 7391 4900

Directory of Social Change Northern Office:
Federation House, Hope Street, Liverpool L1 9BW
Policy & Research tel: 0151 708 0136

CONTENTS

INTRODUCTION

The second edition

The first edition of the *Youth Funding Guide* was published in 1997. It was very successful and found its place quickly on the bookshelves of those looking for money to develop their work with young people. This second edition responds to requests for an update and recognises how much has changed in the funding landscape.

Something old, something new, something borrowed ...

The National Lottery is now well established and the rebranded Community Fund remains an important funder of work with young people. What has also appeared on the horizon since the first edition is the New Opportunities Fund and its seemingly elastic capabilities to respond to the government agenda. Real opportunities have been presented here for young people's work, particularly in partnership with schools and learning projects.

The Connexions strategy was at the time of writing very new, and it is unclear how it will affect youth work in the long run. The idea of collective – and partnership – working is now commonplace and this is central to both Connexions and other regional and central initiatives. The first edition of this Guide emphasised the importance of being involved in partnership working, whilst also remaining true to the principles that guide an organisation's work with young people. That has not changed. If anything, the challenge to remain engaged but distinctive is greater as partnership opportunities increase.

The Children's Fund is also new on the block and will have an impact across the country. Only when projects have been funded and completed can the Fund's impact upon the lives of poor children be tested and an assessment made of whether they have been given a louder voice as a result.

Young people's participation

During the writing of the book an election resulted in a second Labour government. There is now a government minister for young people, and a Children and Young People's Unit. There are new opportunities to join up policies that affect young people.

At the time of the election much was said about voter apathy, with particular concerns expressed about the lack of interest shown by young people. It remains to be seen how young people will find their democratic appetite although it is certain that central, regional and local government will be keen to reach young voters and non-voters and will have to try new methods. Youth councils and the Youth Parliament have grown in number and influence and may help close the gap in young people's representation. A relatively new initiative is YouthBanks where young people have responsibility for distributing local funds and have more say in governance.

The reach of the book

This second edition covers England only, as funding arrangements are very different in Northern Ireland, Scotland and Wales. It aims to be as comprehensive as possible in detailing the possible funding sources for those working with young people. It focuses on the work of organisations and does not therefore list funding resources for individual young people.

There are arguments for producing all the information electronically and a significant change from the first edition is the huge expansion in the number of websites listed within the book. For anyone to keep absolutely up-to-date with funding developments, web access is almost essential. However, many groups needing and using this book have limited or no access to internet technology. Some will not know where to point their quivering mouse when confronted with the vast array of information that is on the web. This book will give a valuable start.

Many working with young people are computer conversant and confident; others are not. One practitioner said that their organisation had web access but no-one really knew how to use it. 'When we reported a fault on our computer, the person on the other end of the helpline asked what type of computer we had. We said "cream".'

Inspiration

The Directory of Social Change has always argued that as well as describing grant schemes, funding programmes and partnerships, there should always be illustrative examples of how money is spent and who gets what from whom. This is not just about openness; it is also about inspiration. We hope that by reading about the projects that have been successful in gaining support, there will be a knock-on effect with those looking for funds. 'We could do that', or, 'We are doing that – and better', or, 'Why aren't we doing that?' are questions that all youth organisations can ask when looking at some of the projects described in this book.

Acknowledgements and thanks

As with the first book, there were many people who were more than happy to share their experiences of chasing the money and I've come across many examples of good practice and pioneering work. People have again been generous in sharing their time, expertise, insight and enthusiasm.

I am very grateful to all those who have helped the research for the Guide in any way. To name everyone would be impossible. Special thanks to Sarah Wiggins and John Smyth of DSC for their research and insight, and to Kate Sayer and Philip Kirkpartrick for their comments and illustrations. Carola Adams, Margaret McCloud and Sherri Nickson allowed documents and outlines to be used, and Andre Schott, Paul Lapsely, Tim Williams, Virginia Graham and Miss Judith Portrait greatly helped with the case studies. Ray Fabes, Dave Packwood and Janet Watson were very generous with their time and comments at the beginning of the revision.

As always, I am appreciative of all those who corrected entries and drafts, sometimes at short notice. However, the text and any errors within it remain ours alone.

Conclusion

The research was done as fully and carefully as possible, but there may be funding sources that have been missed and some information may be incomplete or will become out of date. If any reader comes across omissions or mistakes in the book, please let us know so that they can be rectified in future editions. A telephone call to the Research Department of the Directory of Social Change (0151 708 0136) is all that is needed *or* e-mail: north@dsc.org.uk.

And finally ...

It is often said that fundraising is simple but never easy. This Guide explains the rules of the fundraising game as we see them, but it still requires persistence and hard work. However, a successful outcome usually makes it all worthwhile. Good luck!

Nicola Eastwood
January 2002

HOW TO USE THIS GUIDE

The first four chapters of this Guide give you the basic tools to start fundraising and to increase your chances of success. Chapters 5 to 11 detail the funding sources with information on those that support work with young people. You need to think about what you want support for in order to decide who to apply to.

The main sources of support are:

The National Lottery

This supports good causes through its distribution boards. Some of the distribution boards give mainly capital grants (building, equipment etc.); others give revenue grants as well (i.e. salaries and running costs). Youth organisations will be particularly interested in Awards for All, the Community Fund, and the New Opportunities Fund

For further information see Chapter 6

Local authorities

Support for project costs, programme development, equipment, salaries and so on can still be raised from your local authority. Each will be different and there are guidelines for making your approach.

For further information, see Chapter 9

Central and regional government

Some support for youth organisations is available through the Department for Education and Skills. Other departments and grant-giving bodies can help with project costs that meet their clearly defined priorities (e.g. regeneration, rural development, social inclusion).

For further information, see Chapter 10

European money

There are a variety of schemes available from Europe, and young people are often a focus area of the programmes. Programmes usually require matching funding from other sources, and many are tied to geographical areas, economic outcomes or capital projects. Some are aimed specifically at young people (e.g. YOUTH).

For further information, see Chapter 11

Grant-making trusts

These are charities which exist to give money to other charities. Some are particularly interested in children and young people; others in general welfare or education; others in certain geographical areas. Most support salaries and project costs for up to three years; others give small one-off grants for equipment or individuals.

For further information, see Chapter 7

Companies

Company support is extensive and varied. It's not just about cash. Links with a company can secure donations, gifts in kind, professional advice and expertise, profile and sponsorship.

For further information, see Chapter 8

Members, friends, the local community

Many youth organisations survive on membership subscriptions and fundraising from the general public. The public is still one of the largest funders of youth work through sponsored events, buying raffle tickets, attending events, and contributing to collections and subscriptions. It also tends to come with few strings attached. You ignore the public at your peril!

For further information, see Chapter 5

The final section of the book contains two chapters on financial and legal organisation for your group. Both are essential to efficient fundraising.

There is a list of useful addresses and sources of information and an index .

1 GETTING STARTED IN FUNDRAISING

Raising money is a challenge. Sometimes it is frustrating, sometimes it is really enjoyable; sometimes you win, sometimes you don't. It is often rewarding; it is always hard work. Like any game, fundraising has its own rules. This section explains the basic rules and gives you strategies for success.

THE FUNDRAISER

In theory, anyone can be a fundraiser. You don't have to belong to a particular professional body; you don't have to take exams; you don't even have to have done it before. However, it is important that you get the right person to do it. The fundraiser will be saying all kinds of things about your organisation or club and making all kinds of promises on your behalf; if he or she says or does the wrong thing, it will reflect badly on you. So what do you need to be a good fundraiser?

Time

There are few quick fundraising fixes. Getting serious money takes serious time. It may be a year before you get your first big grant. It can certainly take nine months to put in for and receive a Community Fund grant. It may take five years to build up a really big event. Be realistic from the start both about how much time you all have and how much time it will all take.

Commitment

This is one of the most important qualities in any fundraiser. It soon becomes clear to the outsider if people are just going through the motions. Some people can raise fortunes through sheer force of personality or their absolute conviction in what they are doing, even if they break all the fundraising rules.

Stamina and persistence

Fundraising can be a hard and dispiriting business. People who quit easily will not succeed. Those who keep their eyes on the prize are usually successful.

Truthfulness and realism

There can be a temptation to promise the earth in order to get money, or to say what you know the donor wants to hear. This is a recipe for complete disaster.

Even if you get the money this time, you'll be setting yourself up to fail, and the funder will be reluctant to trust you again. Raise money for what you want and for what you know you can deliver. What's the point in having a state-of-the-art facility if you have no money to run it?

Knowledge

This can range from the detail of a current project to the overall aims and mission of the organisation. When talking to potential donors, you must be able to answer their questions. The fundraiser who says: 'I'm never allowed to see the books so I don't know how much money we've got' is on a loser from the start.

Equipment

You will need at least a telephone, an answering machine and a word processor and printer. You don't necessarily have to buy them; you may well be able to borrow or scrounge them from members, supporters, local companies or whoever.

Willingness to ask

Modern fundraising methods often miss out the crucial step of simply asking people for money. Fundraisers may put together strong bids and write good applications, but they also need to ask people for support. One major charity commissioned a piece of research about why people were not supporting them. Was it the charity's image? Was it the cause? Was it donor fatigue? No, it was simply that people had never been asked. We often assume that just because people know we are there and that we need the money then they will dig into their pockets. They may well, but only if we ask them to.

Opportunism

The good fundraiser makes things happen. For example, the difference between an OK event and a really successful one could be the fact that a major celebrity turns up. This always gives an event profile and prestige. Often such people come because somebody knows somebody who knows them. The alert fundraiser breaks into these networks. If a local company is having a really good (or really bad) time, it may be ripe to sponsor an event to celebrate their success (or restore their image and profile). The opportunist gets in there, and first.

Luck

You may just happen to say the right thing at the right time, or bump into someone who could be a really useful contact. For example, a colleague was doing a radio interview about a new youth project. After the broadcast a major funder who happened to be listening rang the radio station to find out more and the funder and project were put into contact with each other. You cannot plan for this. However, you must be ready to make the most of any opportunities.

Say thank you

Remember, getting money is only the start of the process. Once people have given once, they are more likely to give again, but only if you treat them properly. At the very least say thank you. You should also aim to keep them informed of what is going on and turn them from a supporter into a committed supporter.

SIX GOLDEN RULES OF FUNDRAISING

Fundraising is a people business

People do not give to organisations; they do not give to abstract concepts. They give to help people or to do something to create a better world. The fundraiser is the person who shows them how they can make this happen. Always stress the human aspect of your work – how you give people a new chance in life, or enable them to experience things they otherwise wouldn't, or whatever.

Fundraising is about the donor

Too many fundraisers concentrate on what they want to tell the donor ('we do this' or 'we need that'). However, it is absolutely vital that you try and scratch each donor where he or she itches. Match the donor to the cause or activity they want to fund. Always ask yourself: 'Why would this donor want to support us? What are their particular concerns and interests?' For example, a parent who simply wants their child to have an enjoyable evening will give on a totally different basis to a company thinking of its future workforce. Try and get into the minds of the different donors and show that you understand their interests and concerns and are doing something about them.

The more personal the better

Donors like to be treated and appreciated as individuals. So the more personal you can make your approach the better. A face to face meeting is far better than a personalised letter which is far better than a circular letter which is far better than a poster.

Fundraising is selling

Fundraising is about change, about making a difference, not about money. It is a two-stage process. The first thing you need to do is show people there is an important need and that you can do something useful about it. If they agree that the need is important and that something should be done; and if they agree that your organisation is doing something significant to make a difference; and if you can show them how some extra support will help you do something even better – then the second stage of asking for money becomes easy. Fundraising is more about selling an idea that the donor can make a difference than it is about asking for money. Once people have been sold the idea, they will normally want to give.

Giving is a matter of trust

People give money to you on the understanding that you will do certain good things. You need to show that you are capable of doing the work, that the money will actually achieve something, that they can trust you to use their money well. This generally boils down to your credibility. In other words, can you show the donor that you have done things like this really successfully before; that you have really good people to do the work; that you are well-liked and respected throughout the community; that lots of other people trust you to do this work?

It's not all about cash now

Donors also tend to give money to organisations and causes they have heard of. This means that it is not always a case of trying to raise money now. You actually may need to spend time building your relationships, becoming better known, getting on local radio or in the press, obtaining endorsements about the quality of your work from experts or prominent people. All this will help strengthen any fundraising case that you eventually make.

Basically, in the words of the old cliché, fundraising is friend-raising. Try to build and keep your fundraising relationships with the same care as you do your friendships. Get to know your donors personally if at all possible; make them feel a valuable part of things; and try to show that you are as keen to listen to what they have to say as to tell them what you want from them.

Also, you need to think and plan ahead. If you want to approach a local company for support, can you spend time getting to know them and them getting to know you before you actually ask for money? If so, where are you going to meet them? Who is going to introduce you? What are you going to say?

THE STRATEGY

When people start talking about developing fundraising strategies, you immediately assume they are talking about a sophisticated plan that could only be drawn up by a fundraising professional. Nothing could be further from the truth. All a fundraising strategy looks to do is answer four basic questions:

- What do we want?
- Why do we want it?
- When do we need it by?
- How are we going to get it?

This section looks at how to draw up a basic plan that will make your fundraising easier.

Why do we need a strategy?

Why bother having a fundraising strategy? Why don't we just get on with the fundraising? If all you need to do is raise £250 for some equipment, you don't need a strategy other than to get 10 members of the club to do a sponsored event and raise £25 each. However, if you need £100,000 to buy and fit out a new youth centre, you will almost certainly be looking at raising large chunks of money from different sources. You need to know what to expect from each. And if you fail in one area (the Community Fund turns your application down, for example) the whole project may fail.

So how do you develop a basic fundraising strategy? Here's a six stage plan.

1 What do we need money for?

You are going to be asking people for money. Therefore you need to be absolutely clear what you are asking for. 'Equipment' isn't much use as an answer. Exactly what equipment? You need to provide a list. If you didn't get all the money, which pieces would you buy?

2 Why is it important?

It's not enough to say to possible donors 'this is what we want'. You have to show them why it is important, so that they feel their money will be doing something valuable. 'We need a minibus' doesn't get you very far. 'We need a minibus because lots of kids hang around on street corners and get into trouble. We also live in a high crime area. Our youth club gives people something good to do with their time, but people are too scared to come. We want to be able to collect them, bring them to the club safely, enable them to have a good time and drop them off at home again.' This is starting to get somewhere.

3 How much will it cost?

There are basically two kinds of costs:

- capital costs – these are the costs of physical items e.g. buildings, equipment, furniture;
- revenue costs – these are the costs of running your activity, for example, salaries, rent, rates, telephone bills.

You need to be realistic about both these costs. For example, you may want a new all-weather sports pitch (capital expenditure). Fine. The Sports Lottery gives capital grants. So you apply to the Lottery and get your grant. Then what? Who is there to look after it? How will you meet the higher insurance costs? Who will handle the extra membership applications as a result of the new facility? How much will the new high-tech floodlighting cost to run?

You need to think all this through before you write for money. There is no point getting your wonderful new facility only to find that you haven't got the money to run it and so the club has to close. You will also need to explain how you came up with the figures you arrived at. (See Chapter 2 on drawing up a budget for more information.)

You may need two lists:

(a) One-off capital costs

This will include all the costs associated with the building or renovation work you may be undertaking. This will look something like:

Building work	£50,000
Refurbishment	£15,000
Furniture	£10,000
Equipment	£17,500
Architect's fees/	
Quantity surveyor	£12,500
Legal fees	£2,500
Non-reclaimable VAT	£2,500
Fundraising expenses	£2,500
TOTAL	£112,500

Or it could simply be the cost of the minibus i.e.:
Minibus (second-hand)   £10,000

(b) On-going revenue costs

These apply once the capital work is finished. So, the organisation undertaking the above building work may face itself with increased costs e.g.:

	2001 (before the building work)	2002 (after the building work)
Rent/rates	£1,000	£3,000
Heat/light	£1,000	£3,000
Salaries	£25,000	£35,000
Insurance	£500	£1,500
Postage & telephone	£750	£1,500
Maintenance of equipment	£1,000	£3,000

Computer costs	Nil	£1,000
Events/competitions	£100	£2,000
Publicity	Nil	£500
Audit costs	£1,000	£4,000
Bank charges	£200	£750

Other (*this list is not supposed to be comprehensive*)

Similarly, with the minibus, you will need to cover petrol, insurance, repairs, road tax and so on.

Once you know how much you need you can then decide where the extra money is coming from.

4 How much have you got?

You need to ask yourselves:

- Can you contribute to the capital part of the project?
- Have you got enough revenue funding once it is built?

Again, you need to be honest and realistic about this. Things almost always end up costing more rather than less than you think and plan for. If you stake every penny you have on getting the thing done, you may run out of money before the project is completed. However, if you play too safe and look as if you are hoarding money, donors may think you are not committed and not give you support.

Have you got the money for all your day-to-day costs once the fundraising is over? Will you need to employ a caretaker or new youth leader? Will you need to double your membership to pay for this? Do you need an increased local authority grant? Will you get it? Will you need to get your members to run the London Marathon to raise the £10,000 extra a year? Will they do it? Will there be any loss of income while building work is being done (e.g. will you need to close the youth club for six months)? Are there any tax or VAT implications?

If you have money that you can put into the project it is an important sign of commitment and is very attractive to other funders. However, don't commit what you haven't got and make sure you allow for contingencies and overspends.

5 Where is the money coming from?

You need to know *before* you start fundraising where you expect the money to come from. Obviously this can only be an educated guess. You may well end up with something like this:

Management committee donations	£1,000
Management committee fundraising	£5,000
Members' donations	£2,500

Members' fundraising	£12,500
Community Fund	£20,000
Charitable trusts	£14,000
Company support	£1,000
Children's Fund	£4,000

You now know who you expect to give what. If they don't then you need to make plans accordingly. In any case, the different funders will want to know how you expect to raise the money.

The different chapters in this Guide will help you decide where to expect to get your money from.

6 Who is going to do the fundraising?

It is all very well writing lots of plans; unfortunately this doesn't actually get the money raised! The final part of this planning stage is the hardest. This is where your arm-twisting skills will come into their own.

You may be thinking of organising the whole fundraising appeal yourself. This has the major advantage of being absolutely clear about who is doing what because you are doing everything. However, be honest!

- Do you have the time?
- Do you have the expertise?
- Do you have the contacts?
- Do you have active support from the rest of the organisation?
- Do you have the necessary financial information?
- In general, are you the best person to be doing it?

If you are convinced that you can and should organise it all, you may well still need help with administration. For example, if you are organising an event, you cannot be in more than one place at once. You will need to delegate. Equally importantly, you may well need people with contacts.

The most effective way of raising money is through personal contacts. You are much more likely to get money from a friend than from someone who hardly knows you. For example, if you were about to do a sponsored abseil, who would you ask to sponsor you? The same principles apply to other kinds of fundraising.

Therefore, if you want to get sponsorship from local companies, why not try to get a prominent local business person onto your fundraising committee? This means that any requests for their support will come from someone they know and respect (i.e. a fellow company chairman) rather than someone from a youth club whom they have never heard of and have no incentive to support.

Ask around your club. Whose parent, sibling or friend is famous or well-off or well-connected? Ask your staff, management committee, leaders, volunteers.

Is anyone related to the president of the chamber of commerce or the president of the local Rotary club or whoever? Produce a shopping list for the ideal fundraising committee and try to recruit it. For example, you may want:

- a person to chair the committee;
- 2–3 members of the club;
- an events organiser;
- a prominent local businessperson (to raise money from colleagues in local businesses);
- a local notable, active or retired (to make lots of fundraising speeches and appearances);
- a local councillor (to help relate to the local authority);
- a lawyer (to provide services free of charge);
- an accountant (ditto).

Alternatively, you could ask famous people if they want to be patrons, presidents or vice-presidents of the appeal. Presidents are usually figureheads who add credibility to the appeal and feature on the letterhead. However, they would only usually expect to make three or four appearances at key points in the appeal (for example to open an event, present some awards, or receive a significant cheque).

The trick with getting outside people in is to make sure you get what you want from them. There is no point asking your most famous local sports personality to make six appearances in aid of the appeal only to find out that (a) she keeps letting you down at the last moment, or (b) she charges you a fortune for each appearance. The first case severely annoys your sponsors and those attending the event; the second case lands you with costs that you didn't expect, and which may even wipe out the event's surplus. When formally inviting people onto the committee, make it clear in the letter what you expect from them.

Also, avoid the temptation to go for too large a committee. It may be that the committee as a whole never or only rarely meets. If you have busy people they do not have much time; get the best from them.

Once you have done all this basic planning, you are ready to begin to raise money.

> Beware of rhinos – people who are really here in name only

2 HOW MUCH DO WE NEED?
A guide to basic budgeting

Success in raising money depends upon focus, planning and presentation. All of these are involved in drawing up a budget for a project. You want to be confident that what you are asking for is realistic in terms of what the funder can give, but also that you have asked for enough. Surprisingly often, funders say that projects have been under-costed and applicants should have asked for more.

A budget will help your organisation with:
- planning
- accountability
- setting objectives
- directing funders
- raising money for core costs.

WHO SHOULD DRAW UP THE BUDGET?

There is no magic formula or sorcerer's skill in formulating a budget. There are undoubtedly people who cope with figures more confidently than others and hopefully there is at least one person in your organisation who has this expertise. However, the process of budgeting should also involve those who will actually carry out the work as they are likely to have an idea of what will be involved. They will also carry the burden of an under-funded project if the costing is not realistic. Consultation also encourages accountability. Where people have been involved in drawing up targets for income and expenditure they will have more idea of what resources are really available and why they should keep to their forecasts.

WHAT NEEDS TO BE INCLUDED IN THE BUDGET?

How much a project really costs

Before looking at any income that will come to the project, you need to look first at how much the project will cost to run. There are obvious costs and other costs that are hidden. Some items such as equipment may seem easier to fund than others. Do not leave less attractive elements out as these are part of the real cost of running a project. This is an opportunity to apportion core costs to a project and raise money for salaries, running costs, depreciation for instance. (See Chapter 3 on Fundraising for projects.)

Some organisations are nervous about this approach, worrying that funders may be scared off by large amounts that seemed to have been 'smuggled in'. Do not be. A well-received report written by the Association of Chief Executives of Voluntary Organisations (ACEVO) *Funding our future* recommended this approach, calling it 'full project funding'. Funders who have a feel for the business of sifting applications will recognise a realistic project costing when they see one. (If you are applying to funders who you suspect may not appreciate this approach you can explain your figures more fully, or simply present a shopping list of items for them to choose from.) If you ask for too little you may not be able to run the project at all, or if you do, only run it half as well as if you had allocated costs properly.

> One national foundation stated that applicants sometimes seemed to lack confidence to ask for the full sum they needed. This didn't help their case. If the proposal is well thought out and it needs £20,000 rather than £10,000 to see it through, applicants should apply for the full amount.

Having a realistic grasp of how much a project will cost means allowing for:
- capital costs (that is machinery, equipment, buildings etc.);
- running costs (that is salaries, rent, heating, depreciation, decoration etc.).

Whether you are budgeting for a capital item, or the running costs of the project, the processes will be the same.

DRAWING UP A BUDGET – ESTIMATING YOUR COSTS

Capital costs

If you are planning a capital project (an extension to your existing facilities, or a new building for the youth club for example) you need firstly to list all your costs. These may include all or some of the following.

Land and buildings
How much will it cost to buy the land?
How much will it cost to rent office/hall space?

Professional charges
Accountant
Architect
Feasibility studies

Quantity surveyor
Solicitor
Structural engineer etc.

Building costs
Site works before construction
Construction cost (as on contractor's estimate)
Furniture and fittings
Security system
Decoration
Equipment

You should add to this list as necessary. However, these are only the costs of *building* your extension or new hall. They do not show how you will pay for the long-term costs (such as maintenance, heating, lighting, security, insurance and so on). These on-going costs should be included in your revenue budget as below.

> No budget will be 100% accurate. It is your best guess at the time you are planning the project of how much money you will need. You may wish to put in a contingency for unforeseen costs, if you feel this is a sensible precaution. And if at a later stage it appears that your figures are no longer accurate, you can always revise your budget so that it reflects the financial situation as you then know it. Remember though, that you may not be able to get any extra money from a funder to cover this.

The above list also assumes that you will be paying for everything. In fact, a friendly architect may reduce their fees as a donation; you may be able to get your members to paint the hall with donated paint from a local factory, and your furniture may be given by a firm that has recently been refurbished. All this should be taken into account and your budget adjusted as necessary. In some cases when applying to funders it helps your case to show how much you have raised from your own resources. Gifts in kind (such as donated furniture, reduced solicitor's services etc.) should be costed and their financial value recorded.

Revenue costs

These are your main running costs and will include all or some of the following.

Premises
Rent
Rates
Maintenance of the building, inside and outside
Heating
Lighting
Health and safety measures
Security
Insurance
Depreciation of equipment

Administration
Salaries (including National Insurance)
Telephone
Postage
Stationery/printing
Cleaning/caretaking
Book-keeping, audit and bank charges
Training courses
Child care
Volunteers' expenses
Miscellaneous (e.g. travel, tea, coffee etc.)

Project costs

These are the costs of running individual activities or pieces of work which take place in the building or as part of your remit as a youth organisation. Where you can, split your work up into separate units that can be costed individually. You can then look at what a project costs, which includes capital items and revenue costs such as those listed above. By costing projects separately you can keep track of individual project costs; allocate some of your general running costs to projects; and prepare funding applications.

Costing a project – an example

Imagine you are running training courses in video film production (i.e. this is your project). You will have two basic categories of costs – direct and indirect.

The direct costs will include the equipment, publicity and trainer's fees – these are usually fairly easy to identify. The indirect costs (sometimes called support costs or hidden costs) can be harder to pinpoint. They generally include items such as staff time for those not involved on a day-to-day basis in the project (for example manager, admin worker, finance controller), depreciation, use and maintenance of the building (including rent, rates, heat and light), insurance, post, telephone, stationery and other office costs.

A difficult area is how to calculate the central or office costs. Obviously, you cannot work out in advance exactly how many telephone calls you will make, stamps you will need or paper clips you will buy. The best way to come to a reasonable estimate is to try and work out how much of your organisation's time and facilities will be taken up by the project. So if your project will be the

---

Sample budget

Project name: Video Film Production Course

Course duration: two days a week for four weeks. Non-residential.
Number of participants: 28–30 (four groups of about seven members)
Number of tutors: two

Costs:
(a) Equipment:
    Video camera hire   £
    Video cassettes   £
    Editing equipment hire   £
(b) Staff:
    Tutors (i)   £
    Project director (ii)   £
(c) Building use:
    Heating   £
    Electricity   £
    Training room (iii)   £
    Publicity   £
    Office expenses   £
    Caretaking/cleaning   £
(d) Overhead:
    Insurance   £
    Depreciation (iv)   £
    Miscellaneous   £
Total costs   £_____

Notes
(i) Requires two people each working 10 hours per week for four weeks at say £11.50 per hour (i.e. 2 x 10 x 4 x £11.50).
(ii) A part-time post for 2 months @ £..... per month
(iii) 25% of current facilities for 8 days, so allow 25% x 8 x £X room hire per day
(iv) Equipment is usually depreciated over three years so you would need to allow 33% of the purchase price of the equipment each year – this is so that you build into the budget the cost of replacing out-of-date or broken down equipment.

fourth one in the organisation, it takes up the same amount of space as the others and requires the same amount of the manger's supervision time, then it would be reasonable to allocate a quarter of all your central costs to the project. However, if it is only taking up a tenth of the organisation's time and facilities, then allocate a tenth of these costs. Remember, you are not expected to predict things down to the last penny; rather, the funder simply wants to see a sensible way of calculating the full cost of doing this work.

This process may seem daunting, exacting and time-consuming in the beginning. It may also seem a little approximate, particularly where you are allocating overheads to a project. It is worth persevering so that you include a reasonable estimate of the hidden costs as well as the ones you can more easily tie down. In a climate where it is more and more difficult for groups to get funding for the less glamourous parts of their work, it is vital that applicants cost projects appropriately. They must include core costs. This is what full project funding is all about – trying to identify the real cost of the work you are doing.

The process of thinking how much it actually takes to run a project can be sobering, but can also be the way to fund your running costs. Anyway, if you are successful, funders may require detailed accounts of how the money was actually spent to compare this with your initial budget. More and more funders expect to see these central costs included in a budget. They see it as a sign of good management and of a well planned piece of work, rather than the applicant trying to smuggle inappropriate costs into a budget.

DRAWING UP A BUDGET – ESTIMATING YOUR INCOME

Your budgeted costs set out what you need to spend. However, you can only spend money you have earned, raised or borrowed. The other side of a budget needs to show where you intend the money to come from.

Look at each source of income you can expect (for example local authority, subscriptions, fundraising events) and list them as you did your expenditure. You will need to look at where this year's income came from and make a reasonable guess about what will happen next year. Most of this is common sense rather than crystal ball gazing. You can look at opportunities as well as threats to your funding. Is there a new source of trust support that has opened up? Do you have more members this year than you did last year? Do you have a keen new group of parents and helpers? Has your funding been affected by local government reorganisation? Is your three-year grant from the Bootstrap Trust finishing this year?

It is much easier to predict expenditure than income. You obviously need to keep a close eye on both. There is a tendency for expenditure to be higher and income to be lower than budgeted! Monitor your income frequently and carefully. Allow for any shortfall in your expected income quickly. For example, if you had expected to raise £30,000 from the Community Fund to expand your your support service for young homeless people, but your application fails, you then have to make some decisions. Have you got reserves, and do you want to use them for this? Can you borrow the money? Can you raise money through cutting expenditure in other areas? Do you have time to find another funder? Should you abandon the scheme?

When forecasting income it helps to list both definite and hoped for funds.

Source of income	Budget	Certain	Probable	Possible
Local authority	£25,000	£25,000	–	–
Memberships subs (i)	£2,000	£1,200	£600	£300
Trusts (ii)	£5,000	–	£3,000	£2,000
Local companies (iii)	£250	£250	£250	–

Notes

(i) **Membership subs:** Imagine you have 100 members paying £12 each. You can enter £1,200 in the definite column for next year. You estimate you can accommodate more (although you will have to work out any significant increases in expenditure that this will cause). You have a waiting list of around 50, and you predict that they are all likely to join, so enter £600 in the probable column. You also hope that some publicity will bring in an extra £25, but you are not sure, so put £300 in the possible column.

(ii) **Trusts:** Your budgeted £5,000 can be entered in the probable column if you are confident of the trust (e.g. the grant is recurrent). You would put the figure in the possible column if you know less about the trust(s).

(iii) **Local companies:** Similarly with companies, if you have a warm relationship with local businesses, they are represented on your management committee, or if you play golf with the chair of the board, the £250 can go under probable. Otherwise enter under possible.

With your income and expenditure figures you should have a budget worksheet that looks something like the example overleaf.

INCOME VS. EXPENDITURE

Having listed your projected spending and income you will now have an idea of where you stand. This process can give an overview for the whole organisation but can also give the picture for individual projects. You may predict that the money coming in is greater than your anticipated spending. In your understandable euphoria you should check the budget carefully. Have you been too optimistic on your sources of income, or have you missed some areas of expenditure or under costed them?

If your income is below your projected spending you will need to look carefully at the reasons for this. Is the snapshot year you are looking at exceptional in some way? Do you have a large number of one-off start-up costs related to a big project (such as building work, feasibility studies, equipment costs etc.) which will not be repeated in following years, or does the deficit come as a result of regular income failing to match routine expenditure? Wherever there is a shortfall you will have to do some planning immediately. What you should *not* do is adopt any of the following:

- *The ostrich approach:* which is to panic and delay any action by putting your head in the financial sand.
- *The lemming technique:* assume the figures must be wrong, say 'We've always managed before' and carry on regardless. This is a certain recipe for disaster.
- *The 'don't worry, be happy' maxim:* assume that you will be 100% successful in all your fundraising efforts (which is unrealistic) and that costs will also magically all go down. If you sit on your hands and think something will turn up, it almost certainly won't.
- *The wishful thinking strategy:* when in doubt add a nought or two to your income figures and hope that you will be more successful in fundraising than you had first foreseen. If you are going to do this you might as well have not bothered preparing a budget in the first place.
- *The 'dream' on philosophy:* imagine that some money spinner or fundraising event will cover the deficit, but have no idea what this will be. Another approach would be to suggest an appeal to past members when you have never done this before and have no idea what money will be raised.

Instead of being tempted by any of the above, you will need to be realistic, clear thinking and hard headed. Look carefully at the figures, again, and satisfy yourself that all are reasonable. Decide whether the shortfall is short-term or long-term. Look at what you can afford to do, and whether you can manage the deficit by some tweaking, or by more drastic surgery. You may need to scale some things down, or wait a while longer to start other things. You will need to allow for time lags if you are cutting expenditure. The effect will not necessarily be instant. You may have to cut some activities altogether or use successful projects to subsidise other under funded ones. Whatever you decide, make sure that it is realistic and that it is clearly understood within the organisation.

Income/expenditure budget

Date of budget:

Expenditure . . . .

Item . . . .

Cost . . . .
Notes* . . . .

. . . .

Total costs £_____

Income:

Source   Total   ☐ Certain   ☐ Probable   ☐ Possible
Notes* . . . .

. . . .

Total income £_____

Projected surplus/deficit £_____

*Notes: How reliable is this figure? What is it based on? Is it the highest, lowest or average figure?

. . . .

. . . .

. . . .

. . . .

CASH FLOW PREDICTIONS

The final phase of this part of budgeting is looking at your cash flow. This is where you try to forecast when the money will come in, and when it will go out. Will there be any significant changes in costs or income during the year? This is particularly important if you have a large building project where large bills have to be paid. Will you have enough money to cover them?

Budgeting – a five step plan

Step 1 Estimate your costs (these are usually higher than you first think)
Step 2 Estimate your income (this is usually lower than you first think)
Step 3 Predict your cash flow
Step 4 Make adjustments as necessary
Step 5 Implement your budget, monitor it and make it work – it should be a standard item at management committee meetings

Take all the different areas of expenditure that you have listed. Work out in which month each will be paid. For example, salaries are paid evenly throughout the year; rent may be paid quarterly; insurance due in October; deposit for the residential activity week is to be paid in February; the printing bill for the summer arts event is due at the end of June. Once you have done this, try to then allow for the events and items of expenditure that will be extra this year. If you have some flexibility, you may want to plan them in months where other expenditure is relatively low. Once you have done this, total up each month's expenditure.

You should now do the same with your expected income. Again, this may be erratic and difficult to predict. If you have a local authority grant, this may be paid in April; membership subs may be collected throughout the year; Single Regeneration Budget money for your employment skills project may be paid in September; the grant from the European Social Fund may come in September too; and your second year's funding from the Fair Dues Trust is sent after their February trustees' meeting. These are the sources you can predict. There may be others such as the various award schemes that change each year and make planning difficult. If you have a source of money such as a grant from the Youth Justice Board, which is new to your organisation, you will have to spend time becoming familiar with the timing of payments.

By matching the expected monthly spending with the expected monthly income you will spot any gaps where there is little or no money to meet expected bills. You need to plan and take action for this. You may be able to re-negotiate your payment terms for some items. You may need to arrange an overdraft facility. If you are hiring equipment you will want to schedule payments in months that have less expenditure.

Forecasting becomes particularly important if you are planning a large capital project. Some funders will only pay once the work has been completed, so you will have to pay contractors before you get the grant. Some funders will not pay if the work has been started already, and you may have to find money for feasibility studies and surveys before any money is awarded. You need to allow for these.

Having worked out your budget you should now have a good idea of how much you need; what you need it for; and when you need it by. You are now in a position to approach funders.

3 FUNDRAISING FOR PROJECTS

Fundraising is about getting hold of enough money to meet the day-to-day or capital costs of your organisation, plus the resources required for future development. However, it is far easier to raise money for something specific than to appeal for administrative costs or general funds. This is because donors can then match the support they give to some specific piece of work that they are really interested in. They will feel that their money is actually doing something and that they have made a real contribution.

For example, a Save the Children Fund appeal asking for money for rent and rates would not get very far; appeals asking for help with work in Somalia (or wherever) have been really successful.

The same principle applies to your fundraising. Asking for money towards the upkeep of your youth club may (just) work with your local authority; it won't get very far with the BBC Children in Need Appeal. They will only want to fund a particular project or part of your work (for example, your new work with disabled children and young people). Your members (or their parents) will also respond much better to an appeal for one thing (such as a new item of play equipment) than for a generous contribution to your overall expenses.

Thinking of your work in project terms and designing projects which will attract support is the basis of successful fundraising. It is now accepted practice and called 'full project funding' as noted in the report *Funding our future* (ACEVO).

Make your project sound exciting

One of the great advantages with project fundraising is that you can highlight particular areas of your work that will interest the particular person you are writing to. However, make sure you do everything that you can to show that the work is lively, worthwhile and worth funding. The donor's first response is then more likely to be 'Gosh, that sounds good; we ought to be backing that', rather than 'I've had ten applications like that in the last month, and none of them are likely to achieve very much'.

A fundable project should be:

- Specific – an identifiable item of expenditure or aspect of the organisation's work.

- Important – both to the organisation and to the cause or need it is meeting. If there is some long-term impact that will be an added bonus.
- Effective – there should be a clear and positive outcome.
- Realistic – the work proposed should be achievable.
- Good value – the work should be a good use of the donor's money.
- Topical – it should be looking at current issues and concerns.
- Relevant – it should be relevant to the donor and the donor's particular funding concerns.
- Bite-sized – it should not be too large or too small for a donor to support, although the cost might be shared through several smaller grants. If it is too large, it might be broken down further into sub-projects.

HOW TO IDENTIFY A PROJECT

Case study:

Anytown Youth Centre

A range of different things go on at Anytown Youth Centre. They include general activity nights for young people of different ages, after-school clubs for primary-aged children and basic facilities for young people to practice music (used mainly by local rock bands). However, the club needs to generate another £3,000 a year to cover its costs. It also wants to re-lay its main hall floor which (a) is totally unsuitable for wheelchair users and (b) is getting unsafe anyway. This will cost £10,000. The club has £950 in the bank. What can it do?

- Put up the members' subs and hire charges to cover the £3,000 a year deficit. However, many members and groups struggle to afford the current fee and would probably leave if it went any higher. So the club may end up making the problem worse.
- Have a one-off special appeal to members and users. OK, but what about next year?
- Apply to the local authority for a grant. Possible, but most local authorities are heavily strapped for cash.
- Organise an annual major rock festival with a battle of the bands. Fine, but it's a bit ambitious and who is going to organise it?
- Write round to local trusts and companies to fund the deficit. They wouldn't fund it.

Clearly there are problems with all the above strategies. Also, they don't really begin to tackle the floor problem. So, the Centre could try to divide its needs into more attractive projects.

- They could get funding to expand the after-school clubs to secondary school age. This would attract funds from various groups interested in the welfare of children. It could also be run on a fee-paying basis to bring in extra money. They could also try to interest the members in music through the musical facilities they already have.
- They could get funding to recruit new members. For example, they could raise money for new instruments, recording equipment or whatever to get more musicians in who would then pay fees.
- They could bring in adults. For example, they could run a parenting course, sessions on drugs awareness for parents, health and fitness programmes, communicating with your teenager or whatever. All these could be devised with the help of the young people and they could raise the money from a grant-making trust by showing how it's a new and exciting approach to re-building family relationships.
- They could develop specific activities for disabled children, maybe centred on music or a sports league for wheelchair users.
- They could raise money for other future income generators (e.g. social or catering facilities which they could also use to hire the premises out).

There are plenty of other options in addition to the above. However, the advantage of breaking things down into projects is that you can appeal to a wider range of funders. You are no longer restricted just to those concerned for young people. You can apply to people interested in music, health, parenting and family life, disabled people etc. Having done this, the replacement of the floor is a much easier proposition because (i) the building is clearly being used for the benefit of a wide cross-section of the community; (ii) this brings in a number of potential new funders (for example, both the arts and sports lottery funds in the above example), and (iii) you can look at the best way of getting that particular piece of work done (in this case, for example, you may be able to bring in people under a local training scheme for young unemployed adults). You can then hive off some of your central costs into the applications for funding (see below).

By breaking the bigger picture up and dividing it into projects, you can focus on activities (e.g. parenting courses, children with disabilities) rather than your own core needs (money for bills), widen the range of possible funders (you are no longer just about your current users) and force yourselves to be a bit more creative in your fundraising. This has far more of a business look to it than traditional fundraising with costs centres, apportionment of overheads and contingency allowances.

FULL PROJECT FUNDING – HOW TO COST IT

To cost a project properly, you need to include all the direct and all the indirect costs which can reasonably be said to be necessary to the running of the project. This means you should allocate a proportion of your central (or core) costs to the project. The process of costing a project has several stages.

1 Describe the project

Be clear about what the project is. By this, you should identify what the project will do for its users rather than how it will solve your funding problems. For example: 'We will develop our after-schools club (as in the case study above) to include secondary school age children. This will achieve the following: ...'.

2 The direct costs

Write down a list of all the direct costs. For the after-school club these could include:
- staff costs
- extra tables and chairs (for homework)
- pens, paper and exercise books
- kitchen equipment
- drinks and biscuits
- advertising and publicity
- computers and software
- transport.

3 The indirect costs

Write down a list of all the relevant central costs. This is where you need to be more creative in your thinking because you must include all the hidden costs. At this point you are trying to establish how much the project actually costs to run. Please note, you are not trying to fiddle any figures or pretend that you have costs that you really don't. You are simply recognising that the work you do requires a wide range of expenditure.

So, the after-school club cannot run without a building; the building needs heat, light and insurance; the leaders of the club will need the use of a telephone and photocopier; they may need supervision, training and support, and so on.

So your list of indirect costs will include:
- rent and rates
- heat and light
- postage and telephone
- management and supervision of the project
- book-keeping

- insurance
- cost of training courses.

> **There's no such thing as core funding!**
>
> Groups often say they can get funding for 'projects' or for capital spending but not for their administrative or core costs.
>
> To tackle this, the first step is forget the whole notion of 'core costs'. They do not exist. You do not have any costs other than those which are necessary for carrying out your work or 'projects'.
>
> So, you need to:
> - think of your work as a series of projects;
> - build your full overhead costs into each of these activities;
> - recognise that if the overhead costs have not been paid for, the project is not fully funded.
>
> The trick is to include the relevant central costs in each project budget. You can then use the 'glamour' of the project to get the 'unattractive' administrative costs paid for.

4 Costing the costs

Put a figure against all the areas of expenditure. This is pretty straightforward for the direct costs, although make sure you get more than one quote on each cost. The difficulty is how to cost the indirect expenditure. You cannot put a precise figure on this; all you can do is be reasonable. You should try and work out what proportion of the central costs the project needs.

So, say the Youth Centre as a whole is currently used for 40 hours a week and you intend to run the after-school club for 10 hours a week. This means it will then be in the building 20% of the time. Say that it will occupy half the Centre's rooms. Putting these two figures together you can then say that it takes up 10% of the Centre's building costs. So allocate 10% of all the rent, rates, heat, light, postage, telephone etc. to the after-school project.

Say you have one Youth Centre manager who has responsibility for all the activities in the building. You will need to work out how much time this person will spend supervising the after-school project and allocate the salary and national insurance costs accordingly. So, for example, if the manager works a 35-hour week and will spend on average six hours per week on the after-school project, allocate 17% of the salary and national insurance to that.

You will also need to work out an allocation for the caretaker, cleaner, administrator or any other salary costs associated with the Centre and the project.

5 Is it reasonable?

Ask yourself: 'Does the total figure look reasonable?' Is it too high or too low? Does it look real value for money? Many of the costs you will put down (such as a premises) are effectively impossible to put a precise figure on , so the budget is flexible. You may need to juggle the final total a bit. The key thing is that you can justify how you have arrived at those figures if a funder pushed you on it.

And finally ...

You now have to decide who will pay for what. Are you going to ask one funder for the whole amount for the project? Are you going to ask various funders? Are you going to allocate some of your own money to the project (for example 10% of your local authority grant)? Whatever you do, remember:

- apply to a funder who is interested in your kind of work;
- ask for an amount they can conveniently give;
- stress the benefits of the project and show how it is real value for money.

4 PREPARING AND WRITING A GOOD FUNDRAISING APPLICATION

The fundraising application is the point of contact between you who needs the support and those who can give it to you. It is the opportunity to sell your idea to someone who has the means to make it happen. The more you can help funders do a difficult job, the more they may be inclined to help you. This help may be a cash donation, sponsorship of an event, gifts for a raffle, time and expertise from a member of staff, equipment or whatever. Your task is to make them interested enough in your ideas to want to support you.

Some cautionary words

Writing applications is not a science. You may write the clearest, brightest, most engaging application that fits all the funder's criteria, and yet still not be successful. You may not even get a photocopied rejection slip, let alone an explanation of why you did not get a grant. On the other hand you may know of people who break all the 'rules' and yet their spidery illegible scrawl and rambling prose brings in thousands regularly. There is no easy explanation for this and you should not take it personally. Don't give up; keep trying.

There are many ways of asking. You can ask face to face; you may make a presentation to a group or meeting of supporters; you may use the telephone. Wherever possible, make a personal contact. It is amazing how few people are asked personally for money, and often this would be the best approach. Ask yourself whether it is possible to discuss the application with the funder before you write to them. Where it is a possibility, contact them first, so that the application itself confirms a discussion you have already had rather than being a 'cold' mailing.

The most likely approach to the funding bodies outlined in the rest of this book, however, is by writing a letter or filling in an application form. This chapter will look at what to include in an application letter, and also how to improve your presentation.

Most of the effort of application writing goes into condensing a full account of the project and organisation into a description of around 1,000 words, one to two sides of A4 or, at worst, a 3cm x 14cm box on an application form. This makes good sense from the funder's point of view. They have many applications to look through and cannot spend time reading and interpreting vast amounts of information, however interesting and worth while.

SOME KEY POINTS

- You cannot tell funders everything; there is not enough time and they would not listen. Many application letters are far too long. Put yourself in your reader's place. Would you persevere through long pages of information about an organisation you knew little or nothing about? A general rule would be one and a half sides of A4 maximum for a letter to a grant-making trust, and one side maximum to a company. Proposals to local authorities and central government departments may give you more space – on the whole, officials will be more used to reading long project descriptions. This should not be an excuse for wasted waffle. You should still keep to a clear, positive and succinct style.

Two approaches
If you were a funder, which approach would excite you enough to read on?

a) *The wolf from the door appeal*
The Dire Straits Youth Association desperately needs support. Any help would be gratefully received. The neighbourhood where the group meets is a very deprived area lacking most facilities. The youth group was started five years ago, and has often struggled to keep going. If it does not secure funding it will be forced to close. The association has had its core-funding reduced in successive years and now finds itself with a funding deficit. If your organisation could make some contribution to the group, however small, it would assist its continuation, and ensure that local young people at least have something to do. Without your support, the group may have to close.

b) *The leading the horse to water appeal*
The Dire Straits Youth Association has met for the last five years. We run sports competitions, volunteering projects with other local charities, as well as weekly events where young people can meet regularly. Our leaders are local people who give their time freely. Some have gone on to complete youth work qualifications. Local businesses, schools, colleges, the police and the local authority all have links with us. The popularity of the group means that we now need your help with our new bus project. This will take our activities out to young people who cannot travel to us. I have included a list of equipment that we need for the bus. Is there something you would like to donate or help to fund?

- In your letter, select and concentrate on your main selling points, emphasising those which will be of most interest to the particular person/supporter you are writing to.
- Don't ask funders to support your organisation. Instead, ask them to support the people you help, the work you do, and preferably, a specific project.
- Believe in what you are doing. Be upbeat. Positive messages are more inviting than negative ones. Take the approach of the Tina Turner song: 'We're simply the best'. If you do not believe in what you are doing why should potential supporters? Too many applications strike a defensive note and end up apologising for their work. Don't go in for shroud-waving where you focus on the gloomy consequences of not getting the money. Paint an exciting picture of all the things that will happen when you do get the money. You want to enthuse people, not resort to emotional blackmail.

THE INGREDIENTS OF A GOOD APPLICATION

Before you put pen to paper, or finger to keyboard, you need first to have prepared thoroughly. Ideally, the application should be the quick part of the process; just as in Chinese cooking, more time should be spent in preparing the ingredients than in producing the final dish. These should be selected carefully for quality, consistency and their contribution to the overall presentation.

Most funders (including members of the public) receive thousands of requests each year; think carefully about how you can make your application stand out from the crowd. At very least you should be aware of the traps which could prevent your application getting the attention it deserves.

You will need to make a number of key points which will catch the readers attention, arouse interest in the work, and 'sell' your proposal. Ask yourself:

- Why on earth should anyone want to support us?
- What is so important about what we are doing?

In other words what is unique about your work? What is different? Why is it necessary? What will it achieve? And why should this particular donor want to support it? You should try your answers and application out on a friend who does not work in the same field and has no knowledge of your work. One funding adviser who regularly reads two page summaries of projects before they go forward for full assessment says that they're sometimes none the wiser as to what the organisation is doing, or what the project is about. Funders need to feel they know the context you're working in and what you're trying to do. You need to reassure them by presenting a context they can understand. An outsider's view can tell you whether you are assuming too much of your reader, whether you need more or less information to make your case, and when you have got it about right.

Six essential elements of an application

- Who you are
- The need you meet
- The solution you offer
- Why you should do it
- The amount you need
- The future you have

1 Who you are

The funder wants to know what kind of organisation they are dealing with. How long have you been going? What are your key activities? What have you done that has been especially brilliant? What have been some of your major successes? In other words, can you show the funder that you are reliable, respectable and someone they would want to be associated with?

2 The need you meet

All voluntary organisations exist to meet a particular need, to make society better in some way. You need a brief and clear explanation of the need or the problem that you exist to deal with. How widespread is it? Is it local or does it have regional, national or international implications? If it is local, what special features of the community make it special or interesting to support? Point to who will be helped by your work, which can be a wider group than just the young people involved in the project. Emphasise any elements that are special or unique in the need you are trying to meet. Can you explain the problem however complex, in one or two sentences?

> Is the problem we are addressing worse than others?
> or,
> Is the solution we are offering better than others?

Show how important and urgent the need is. You may want to highlight what would happen if you were not doing anything about the problem. Do not be over-emotional; this is an opportunity to give your reader assurance that something constructive can be done. However, do not undersell yourself or assume that 'everybody knows this is a problem'. If people do not think there is a need to meet or problem to solve, they will switch off. If they think that it is not very pressing, they will find something else that is urgent. If they do not think that you understand the problem they will assume you cannot solve it either. You need to do the following:

- describe the problem;
- support this by evidence;
- say why this is important.

3 The solution you offer

Once you have established the need and said how important it is to do something about it, you then need to show that you can offer a particular solution. For example: 'We will provide peer education by visiting 15 schools, colleges and groups of young people in our area. We will speak to 700 young people and aim to recruit a further 20 counsellors from these sessions. We will produce an outreach and information pack that will be distributed to each school, college and youth group in the area.'

Be clear

When making your case avoid laziness in your arguments. It is a common fault of applications that they state the obvious and rely on circular reasoning. For instance, if you are asking for money to build a hall, the temptation is to argue: 'The problem we have is that there is no meeting hall for the young people in our community. Building a hall would solve the problem.' A funder would reasonably want to know 'Why?' If you don't identify a need you cannot offer a solution.

You need to point to the actual or expected results of your work, and how these will be measured (often referred to as outputs and monitoring). This may be for instance, how many young people will attend; how leaders will be attracted and trained from the local community; how resources will be shared with other groups; how an information pack will be distributed to local schools.

Be realistic

Make sure that what you want to do is workable, that it can be done in a reasonable time, by you, and that it gives value for money. Don't promise what you can't deliver. If anything, err on the side of modesty, and then you can broadcast the additional benefits that come from the project when the work is finished. You should define clearly how you will overcome any problems that may come as a result of running the project (for a school homeworking club: safety, adult supervision, accountability, links with school etc.).

Support your case

Good arguments to support your case would be to look at other communities where a similar project has led to visible benefits for young people (for example in the personal development of the young people, their integration into the community, enhanced opportunities for sport and art, access to courses and education, or reduced vandalism and crime). You could point to a survey that shows how young people would use your facilities, or the results of an outreach project that reflect young people's use of time and shared resources. You may also want to refer to how the facility will be used to benefit the wider community.

In short, the donor should now be saying: 'I can see there is a real problem and the project would certainly make things better'.

4 Why you should do it

You now need to establish your credibility. Why should you be the group to run the project? Why should the funder trust you? What is different about the way that you do things? How effectively will you manage the project?

Sell your case

Think about your plus points. Do you use volunteers creatively? Do your leaders come from the local community? Do they participate in leadership training qualifications? Do they have a story to tell that would interest a funder? There must be something about your group or your work that is attractive and fulfilling to those who help. By training local leaders, for example, you have given the community a vital resource, and encouraged people to discover commitment and talents that may otherwise have been left unused. This builds credibility for a group by showing commitment to all in the community, not just a lucky few.

Success breeds success

Do you have examples of media coverage that give positive images of your work? Have any of your young people achieved something as a result of your activities? Have you helped raise money for other causes in a committed and imaginative way? Has your group or an individual gained an award or recognition for a scheme or achievement? A report in the local paper can help to support your case. Do you have a 'Local Boy/Girl Makes Good' story? Has your group produced a celebrity? Do you have a famous former member who regularly supports events each year? Positive publicity can show the spectacular results of working with young people and the importance of what you do. They can also establish that you are here to stay, with a record of making things happen.

Are you successful in raising money from other sources? Do you have a mixture of supporters from a number of sectors? Do you have good working relationships with agencies, local business, schools, local authorities etc.? What have these partnerships achieved? Financial stability will impress any funder; this is one of the keys to establishing trust. The more diverse and secure your funding portfolio is, the more likely you are to be entrusted with other grants. Strong links with other groups and organisations give a good indication of how integrated you are, and further proof of how much added value your activities bring to the community. Funding your group may bring knock-on benefits to other groups you work with.

Generally, can you show that your work is good value for money, and are you more cost-effective than the alternatives? What makes you the right people to be meeting this need? Is your approach an example of good practice that could be copied and applied elsewhere?

You should be able to come up with a number of good reasons why you should be supported. The more you can do this, the more credibility you have. The more credibility you have, the more likely the donor is to trust you with their money. Success breeds success, and funders will be attracted to a confident upbeat approach. Your plus points will all help to sell your case, so make them clearly and confidently in your application.

5 The amount you need

Funders are keen to know about the project first and the value of the work being done. But you also need to tell them very clearly what it costs and how much you expect them to give. Some applications tail off when it comes to asking for money. There is no need. By now you should have made a good case for someone to support you, and proved that you can be trusted with their money. This is the point of the letter after all, and if you're too embarrassed to ask for the money, there is little point in sending it off. There are different ways to ask for what you want, and you should think about the type of funder you are applying to.

Where you are asking a funder for a small amount, or where you think they would like to see some obvious benefit from their donation, you can produce a shopping list. This can be very effective when raising money from companies. You can suggest an item from the list that you think the supporter would like to pay for. You can give a range of items with costs starting at a level that all those you are writing to can afford (see below). However, by including more expensive items you hopefully persuade them to give more. Also, you are giving them something specific to pay for which many donors like. If you are looking for gifts in kind rather than cash this is the best way to give supporters an idea of what you want. (There is further guidance on gifts in kind in Chapter 8, Winning company support.)

Shopping list for 'Schools at play' project

Equipment	Cost
12 Cones	£ 2.42 each
6 Footballs	£ 4.95 each
4 Corner flags and poles	£ 8.75 each
4 Nets	£ 18.50 pair
Centrahoc set	£ 42.50
Mini cricket set	£ 43.95
Short tennis set	£ 60.50
Parachute pack	£ 89.50
Earthball	£102.50

6 The future you have

Make sure that you emphasise your long-term viability. This underlines your credibility and why funders should support you. If your future is not at all sure, funders may think their money would be better used elsewhere. Show how the project will be funded once the grant has been spent. Where you are applying for money for a new facility, who will pay for its running costs once it is opened? How will you continue a project when the three-year grant has finished?

How to ask for money

Fraser Falconer, Regional Coordinator, Scotland BBC Children in Need Appeal

- State clearly how much the overall project will cost (for example 'We are looking to raise a total of £30,000').
- Give the funder a clear idea of how much you expect them to contribute. You can do this in one of three ways:

  (i) Ask for a specific amount (i.e. 'I am therefore writing to ask you for £2,000').

  (ii) Show how much other trusts have given (e.g. 'BBC Children-in-Need have already given us £2,000'). This will indicate that you expect a similar amount from the trust you are currently writing to.

  (iii) Show how many trusts you are writing to (e.g. 'I am therefore writing to you and eight other major trusts to ask for a total of £10,000'). This gives the trust a pretty good idea of how much you expect them to give (i.e. around £2,000), but gives them flexibility to give more or less than this.

- Show where the rest of the money is coming from (i.e. 'The overall project will cost £30,000. We expect to raise £15,000 from our members and supporters; £5,000 from other fundraising events and £10,000 from grant-making trusts. I am therefore writing to you and eight other major trusts to ask for a total of £10,000'). This will give the trust more confidence that you know what you are doing and you can raise the necessary money.

What to say in the application letter

Now that you have done your research and pulled all your selling points together you need to put them into some kind of order. There are no golden rules for writing proposals, no perfect letters of application. What works for the club down the road will not necessarily work for you. Inject your own personality and approach as far as possible. The following is a structure that many have found to work, and this can be a starting point for your own letter.

1 Project title

This can be really effective, especially if it is catchy and quickly describes what you want to do.

2 Summary sentence

This is the first bit of the application to be read. It may be the last! It tells the reader what the application is about and whether it is likely to be relevant to them. 'I am writing to you to ask for a donation towards the cost of ...' is a reasonable start. Keep it short and to the point.

3 The introduction: who you are

Many applications say little or nothing about who the organisation is; they just go on about what they want. Assume that the reader knows nothing about you. What would they need to know to trust you with their money? You need to show you are good, reliable, well-used and well-liked – in three or four sentences.

4 The problem: why something needs to be done now

Now you move onto the problem you want to solve, and why it is important that something is done now. Remember, people are basically interested in what you do rather than who you are. Do not ask people to support you; ask them to support your work and the people you help.

The X Factor: the plus points that give you an edge

Write down as many selling points for your group as you can. Below are some possible categories which may help you to see the strengths of your group.

- People (What's different, good, or extraordinary about your members, helpers, workers etc.?)

  _____

  _____

- Pounds and pennies (What's sound and bankable about your finance? What's successful about your fundraising?)

  _____

  _____

- Personal achievements (Has anyone achieved something notable through your activities? Have your members or volunteers gained experience, qualifications, employment, training etc. through being part of the group? Do you have a local, regional or national profile?)

  _____

  _____

- Partnerships (Who have you linked up with? What has been achieved?)

  _____

  _____

The X Factor: the plus points that give us an edge

- Publicity (Have you had any coverage in the local press? Have you been successful at recruiting new members and leaders through outreach?)

  _____

  _____

- Perseverance (Do you have a good track record? How long has your group been running?)

  _____

  _____

- Performance (Has your group developed activities or projects that have been adopted and taken off elsewhere? What are you 'Simply the Best' at?)

  _____

  _____

We meet the following need(s) _____

The needs we meet are particularly important because _____

Our solution is new and ground-breaking because_____

We are different/unique because _____

Our other strengths are _____

If we did not exist then _____

Funders are keener to support success stories rather than failures. You need to be confident of your successes to show how you stand out from the crowd. List your five greatest successes in the past five years (and select one that's appropriate for an application letter):

1 _____

2 _____

3 _____

4 _____

5 _____

And finally, to build your confidence further in preparation for the application letter, complete this tie-breaker in twenty words or fewer:

'We are the best there is in our work with young people because ...'

_____

_____

_____

_____

5 Your proposals: what you intend to do about the problem

You now need to show what you intend to do and how you intend to do it. Make sure you include your targets (outputs) and you will reach them. If you are having problems with this part, maybe you could try predicting what the club will be like in two years' time and how things will have changed.

6 Why you should do it

By now you have stated who you are, the need you want to meet and how you are going to do it. Now you need to show why you are the best people to do it. Assume your reader is saying: 'This is all very well but how can I trust this group to deliver on this?' This question will partly be answered by how good and clear your solutions to the problem are. However, you should also establish the credibility of your club. Use your plus points to show your ability, professionalism and good track record to get the job done well. Quotes, especially from those benefiting from what you do, or those who have previously used your services are always helpful here.

> Remember to ask first if the funder has an application form to fill out. There is no point sweating blood to get the perfect letter of application written only to find out that you have to redo the whole thing on an application form. If you are unsure about the information required on the form, contact the funder for clarification if you can. With an application form there will be more scope for this than with a letter. Sort out all the problem areas on the form before you ring, and go through each in one phone call. This will save time for you and the funder.

7 The budget: how much you need

This is how much you intend to spend on the project. It includes direct costs and overhead costs. (See Chapter 3 on Fundraising for projects and Chapter 2 on How much do we need? A guide to basic budgeting for further details.)

8 Funding plan

You need to show the funder where you intend to get the money from. It may be that you are asking this funder for the whole amount, or you may be getting it from a variety of sources. Therefore, you need to say something like: 'The total cost of this project is £50,000. Our local authority have agreed to give us £5,000, and this will be matched by European money of £5,000. We aim to raise £10,000 from local supporters, £20,000 from the Community Fund, and £10,000 from grant-making trusts.'

You also need to show how you intend to meet the longer-term costs (see Chapter 1 on Getting started in fundraising for more information).

9 The rationale: why the funder might be interested and what their role is

It can help to have a final rallying call before you sign off to leave the reader feeling positive and enthusiastic. There are many reasons why the donor may be interested:

- you are running a good project which is right at the heart of their stated policies and priorities;
- you have already received support from them and this further grant will allow you to build on that success;
- there is a personal contact which it will pay to highlight;
- there is a particular benefit to the donor which you want to stress. (This is especially the case with companies who will want to see a business or public relation return on their money.)

Sometimes, people sum up on a negative note: 'Wouldn't it be a tragedy if all this good work came to an end' or, 'If we don't raise £30,000, the project will have to close.' Avoid this kind of thing at all costs. You've made a good, convincing case with positive reasons for supporting your work. There is no reason to assume you will not get the money, so be positive.

Start making sense – a guide to writing simply

- Keep sentences short and to the point. Develop a news style that cuts out long complicated sentences. Look at line spacing, point size and font selection.
- Keep paragraphs short. Look at the layout critically. Would it entice you to read further. Are you put off by long sections of text? If you are, your reader will be as well.
- Avoid jargon. You may understand what you are talking about; outsiders generally will not. Explain acronyms.
- Be direct; do not waffle. Use as few words as possible. It adds to the 'readability' of your application, and keeps the length down.
- Use personal pronouns such as 'we', 'our', 'you' and 'your' rather than 'The organisation/association', 'the users' etc.
- Use strong verbs and tenses, rather than weaker ones like the passive. 'Our young people work closely with local schools' reads better than 'Local schools have become involved with the activities organised by the young people in the club.'
- Weed out waffle and waste. Say something sincerely, simply and succinctly.
- Re-read and rewrite.

10 The signatory: who puts their name to the application

This could be anybody, for example, the project leader, the director, the fundraiser, the chairman of the management committee, an appeal patron. Whoever signs it must:

- **Appear sufficiently senior**. This shows you are treating the application seriously.
- **Be knowledgeable**. The funder may well ask for more information. The person who signs the letter should be able to tell them what they need to know, including the overall financial position of the organisation. If the name on the letter cannot give this information it appears that the application has not been well organised, and the project not well thought through. If you have a patron who signs the letters but does not know about the day-to-day running of the project, you should include the contact details of someone who will be able to answer more detailed questions.
- **Be available**. Again, if the funder wants more information they don't want to have to leave a whole series of messages before they get the details they need to make a decision.
- **Be open**. Leave your potential supporter with plenty of opportunity to talk to you, find out more, or visit. Many will decline your invitations to come and look at the work or meet the young people, but people like to be asked.

What do you send with the application letter?

If the funder has an application form you must fill it out following its instructions. However, if you are writing an application letter, you should send the following supporting materials:

- A set of your most recent accounts, or a budget for the year if you are a new organisation.
- A budget for the particular project you are wanting support for, including estimated income and expenditure.
- An annual report (if you have one). If you have not done so before, think about your annual report as a fundraising tool. It does not have to be a dry as dust account of the last year with minimal information on what you do. It can say as much about your activities and success stories as you want it to.

You can also enclose anything else that will support the application (for example newsletters, press cuttings, quotes sheets, videos, photos, drawings, letters of support from famous people). However, do not rely on these extra bits to get you the money. They will not compensate for a hopeless letter. Assume that the funder will only read your letter and the financial information (budget and accounts). They should be able to get the complete picture from these. If in doubt, ask yourself:

- Is this relevant to the application? Is it absolutely essential or a nice extra?
- Will it help the funder to make a decision in our favour?

- Can I afford to send all this?
- Does it present the right image? (Is the additional material so glossy that it implies you are a rich organisation? Can you get publicity material sponsored?)

Remember, everything is for a fundraising purpose. If the accompanying information does not help the application, do not include it. It is definitely not a case of never mind the quality, feel the width.

What do you do with the letter?

There are two main strategies.
1 Send it out to all relevant funders all at once. This is the most common technique. It has the advantage of getting the appeal up and running and you will know reasonably quickly where you stand.
2 It may well be better to send the application out in stages. Write to a few of your key supporters first and see if they will lead the appeal (i.e. give you a grant which then encourages others to do the same). When some of these have committed themselves to supporting you, then write to the rest saying that firstly, you have already raised £10,000 of the £20,000 needed, and secondly, that X, Y and Z funders gave it to you. You may want to write something like: 'We are writing to you and six other key supporters to raise the money we need.'

Money tends to follow money. The more you raise, the easier it is to raise more. Highlight any money that has already been raised or pledged. Sending applications out in stages usually improves your chances because you concentrate initially on those most likely to support you. Then you widen the net to include those who don't know you as well but will take their cue from other funders' confidence in you. However this approach is more time consuming and needs more planning. Have you got the time to do this? It may not be the remedy for crisis funding where you are desperate to get money in as soon as possible.

What to do after the letters have been sent

You should keep a simple record of what you have sent where. It will help you keep track of applications and to know how supportive each funder is. Note also the supporting materials you have sent, or the events you have invited funders to.

Apart from this, mostly you can do nothing except wait for a yes or no. You can ring to check that the application has arrived, but you do not want to seem to be hassling or pressurising people. Different types of funders will have different expectations of this. Some local authority officers for instance will discuss how your application is progressing; others such as some trusts or companies will not welcome any follow-up contact at all. They will not have the time or inclination to answer your enquiries, however general.

The bare bones application letter

Note, there is no such thing as a model application letter. Write your letter in the way that best suits you and the work you are doing. Be yourself and let your work be seen in its best light. However, here is one skeleton outline that will help you develop fundraising muscle in the right places.

Dear .... (*wherever possible use the name of the correspondent. If you do not know it, make every effort to find out, and get the spelling right*)

I am writing on behalf of .... seeking funding towards the cost of ....
.... was set up in .... by .... to do ....
Major initiatives have included ....

I am writing about our .... project. The need we are meeting is particularly important because ....
We know the project will be effective because ....
We know we are the best people to do this work because ....

The project will cost £......... We intend to raise the money as follows:........
As you are interested in .... (*location, funding criteria etc.*) I am therefore writing to you for ....
At the end of the grant we expect the project will be funded by ....

If you require further information, or you wish to discuss the application, or you would like to visit and see the work, please contact me on ....

Yours sincerely,

....

This is a possible structure for a letter. Use it as a checklist to make sure everything that is relevant to the application has been included.

Don't forget: Use headed notepaper, include your charity number (if you have one) and sign the letter.

If you get a positive response, write to say thank you immediately and put these people on your mailing list for the future. Keep them informed of your progress. Note any conditions on the grant that have to be met (e.g. sending a written report to the funder each year) and make sure you keep to them. If there is any variation in what you have been given the money for, and what you are actually going to do, you should inform the funder and check this is acceptable. (This is particularly the case with grant-making trusts.) You will want to go back to those who have supported you for help in the future. Keep them interested in your progress and how the money has been spent to help young people. If individuals have benefited, personal accounts and progress reports can be an easy and friendly way of keeping the funder interested and enthusiastic about what their money has helped to achieve.

It is perfectly possible to send those funders still considering your appeal a further letter to update them on progress. The letter can be quite short, saying: 'We understand you are still considering our application about ... However, you may be interested to know that we have so far raised £10,000 of the £20,000 we need. This has come from ... Please contact me if you need any further information about the project.'

IF AT FIRST YOU DON'T SUCCEED ...

Do not be afraid to go back to people who turned you down, unless they have said they would never support your kind of work. There are many reasons why you might not have got money: they may have funded something similar the previous week; they may have run out of money; they may have had a deluge of brilliant applications and yours was next on the list; they may have never heard of you before. Go back next year with a different proposal, and the next year and the next year.

Your application letter

Your application letter should tell any reader everything they need to know about your appeal in a short space of time. Assume they will not read anything else you send, and then answer the following:

- Will they have a clear idea of who you are, what you want, why you want it?
- Will they see what good it will do, what you expect from them, where else the money will come from, and what happens when their support has finished?

Before you send the letter, give it to a friend who knows little or nothing about your project. After reading the letter quite quickly, if your friend cannot answer the above questions, nor will your potential supporter be able to.

Thinking about different supporters

In following chapters there are details on who might support you and their reasons. You will have to take into account what each funder will be looking for and why. A company, for instance, will be looking at the commercial possibilities of linking up with you; what is good for their business. They may look for more tangible benefits in the short term than say, a trust or local authority. Read each of the chapters that cover the funders you are hoping to approach for tips on how to apply.

And finally ...

A major grant-making trust states in its guidelines: 'A thoughtful and honest application always stands out in the crowd! Tell us clearly what the problem is, and how your project will do something about it. Give us relevant facts and figures, please don't use jargon, and don't be vague. You don't need to promise the moon just tell us what you can realistically achieve. Your budget should show that you've done your homework and know what things cost.

'A thoughtful and honest application isn't a hurried and last minute dash to meet our deadlines with something dreamed up overnight. It is a serious and sincere attempt by your organisation to use its experience and skill to make a positive difference where it is needed.'

Applications checklist

- Does it have a personal address? (If it's the 'Dear Sir/Madam' variety, don't bother until you have more information on the supporter. Check the spelling of the person's name and the funder you are writing to.)
- Does the first paragraph catch the reader's attention?
- Are you clear about what you want and why you want it?
- Is your work likely to be interesting to the donor?
- Is it clear how much the donor is expected to give? Is this reasonable?
- Is the application nicely presented? Does it attract the eye with short paragraphs and no spelling mistakes?
- Does it back up what it says with good supporting evidence?
- Is it positive or upbeat? (If it's gloomy and negative; think again.)
- Does it take account of guidelines published by the donor? Does it make a connection with the supporter's interests?
- Is it written in clear, plain English, or does it use lots of long sentences full of qualifying clauses and jargon?
- How long is the application? 1½ sides of A4 is plenty for a trust; one side for a company. Remember it does not have to say everything, but it has to say enough.
- Crucially, is the application appropriate? A brilliant letter to the wrong people will not get support.

5 RAISING SUPPORT FROM THE PUBLIC

THE PUBLIC PURSE

In all fundraising the best questions to ask at the start are: 'What do we want to do?' 'What do we need to do it?' and 'Where is the best place to get it from?' Although this book sets out the governmental, corporate and charitable sources of money that you can apply to, by far the biggest giver is the general public. There was a time when groups raised money largely by asking those involved with the group, their nearest and dearest, and anyone else who would turn up, to support a jumble sale or car wash. Now, the emphasis is more upon honing the application letter and polishing up your presentation skills to appeal to a major funder. However, the general public is a vital resource and you should not neglect it. While you are chasing the grant, do not forget to woo the public. Put bluntly, if you decide not to bother with raising money from the public, you are immediately ruling out about a third of the money available to charities.

Anyone who wants to raise money should keep in mind that whilst grants are important, getting the public to support your group can be more so. It can be far more effective in terms of time and money to fundraise say £800 for a digital camera and computer equipment from the local community rather than applying to a trust or company. This means 400 people giving £2; 300 giving around £2.70; 200 giving £4; 80 giving £30, 20 giving £50, or a combination of these amounts. It also helps to make your case to other funders if you have a well established track record of successful fundraising from the public. Fundraising can bring good publicity to raise the profile of your group locally. However, it is also a lot of work, and you need to assess the scale of any proposed event, the help you can rely on and its expected return.

> Even when you've raised core funding for your organisation, it makes sense to continue to raise money from the local community. It heightens your profile and nurtures local links, giving your project deeper community roots and a strong local identity.

This chapter will give some pointers to planning, some money-making possibilities, and some pitfalls to avoid.

There are all sorts of reasons why people support and give to good causes.

- *They are already involved with and sympathetic to the cause.* Parents, helpers organisers and patrons for instance. These are usually the most dedicated fundraisers and donors. You should not have to convert them to your cause, they should already be tuned in to what you are doing and its importance.

- *They have been involved in the past.* Former members, old boys and girls networks, and people who have benefited from the club. Occasional reunions, particularly if combined with an anniversary, can be a way of focusing their financial support. Past members will still have some affection for the club, and hopefully, fond memories; they will want to support the present activities.
- *They know someone involved with the work.* The life-blood of sponsored events is the network of extended family and friends connected with those taking part. They will not necessarily know anything about the club, but they may want to support the individual.
- *They think the organisation is worth supporting because of the work it is doing.* This is an appeal to those in the high street, who do not have any personal contact with your organisation but value the work that you do. Your activities may tie in with their interests in some way such as health promotion, education, job prospects, social skills, crime prevention.

Case study:

Fitzrovia Youth In Action

A London community football project that helped to regenerate a rundown area was founded and led by a group of young people. Having played football on an area that had been neglected and vandalised, the local young people decided to clean up the playing space and win the support of the local community in the process. A great deal of time was spent in winning people to the cause and creating local enthusiasm for the idea of a safe and attractive playing area as a community resource. Winning support from the public is not just about raising money, but also includes gaining people's time, contacts, expertise and goodwill.

Fitzrovia Youth in Action has attracted numerous large supporters to the project over a number of years, but has continued to raise money from the local community. One year they raised £37,000 from a large number of small donations and small, largely local grants. Those leading the fundraising felt that support from local businesses and the local community meant that the project stayed close to its mission of bringing young people and local residents together in a positive way to help improve their community.

Contact: Andre Schott, Fitzrovia Youth in Action, 52 Maple Street, London W1P 5GE Tel. and Fax: 020 7636 5886

- *Where the organisation has had recent press coverage* and people want to help, for example, Ranulf Fiennes polar walk to help those with muscular dystrophy, or Ian Botham's charity walks for those with leukaemia
- *The heart-string factor* which is probably the most unmeasurable of all. In all fundraising this has to be handled with care, and with young people you may want to think carefully about the kind of image you want to promote.

There may be more than one reason why people connect with a cause. Some of the runners in the London Marathon for example will represent any or all of the above motivations. Planning any fundraising should first take into account the support networks your group is immediately in touch with. You can then look at the wider audiences who may be attracted to the event and your cause.

Creating Support

Those at the very heart of what you are doing, such as family, friends, workers and the young people themselves are your most enthusiastic supporters. They are the people nearest the action and the foundation of any fundraising effort. Next in line will be previous members and organisations and agencies that your group has links with. These can include schools, sports clubs, arts venues which you use, as well as local dignitaries. These people do not know your group so well, but they have some affinity with it, as well as an interest in seeing it prosper.

You can also appeal to the wider community such as those you have business links with. (Is there a travel company you use regularly? Who do you bank with?) One youth group arranged with a local restaurant where the youth leader had links to run a cheap themed food evening on the days when the café would have been shut. They provided the labour, marketed the event to family, friends and supporters and took the profit. The business provided the venue and advice.

Finally, you can organise events in the high street or shopping precinct such as bag-packing at a supermarket or money-spinning events such as a Christmas present-wrapping service. These will bring in people who know nothing about your group but are attracted by the activity. If you think creatively about venues, activities and audiences you can increase your chances of success.

Ten of the most popular fundraising events
(*although not necessarily the highest earners*)

Sponsored events
Street collections
Jumble-sales
Fairs
Coffee mornings
Discos
Raffles
Car washes
Auctions
Bring and buy sales

Working with young people gives a ready and responsive group of volunteer fundraisers. Young people are often the most enthusiastic about raising money on behalf of others. They can also be energetic in taking part in imagination-grabbing fundraising events for their own group.

Making the most of the membership

Where you are a membership organisation, your members and volunteers are a vital resource. The young people themselves may have more time than money, and it is important to harness both resources. Members, volunteers and staff can give:

- time
- money
- help
- advice
- contacts
- experience
- energy
- enthusiasm.

You should also remember to review membership subscriptions regularly.

Local fundraising

There are a number of local bodies to approach for support who might consider raising money on your behalf. A number of these have a youth focus and all have a local dimension. Distinctive appeals which would be attractive to raise money for work best, as do requests for small amounts of money . Someone within the organisation to promote your cause also helps. Some will welcome presentations. Local groups include:

- Lions
- Rotary Clubs and Rotoract
- Round Table
- Soroptimists
- Inner Wheel
- Chambers of Commerce
- Women's Institutes
- Student rag committees
- Masons
- Trade unions
- Young Farmers' Clubs
- Local police and fire brigades
- Faith communities: churches, synagogues, mosques, temples and gurdwaras

FUNDRAISING EVENTS

Before organising your event you need to be sure of why you are asking people for money. It will help to decide which event and the way it will be run if you have considered why people will want to give. As mentioned above people give for a number of reasons which can be simplified to four:

- they like the *organisation*
- they like the *people*
- they like the *cause*
- they like the *event*.

Make sure you know who the event is aimed at and that it will be attractive to them.

Once you have decided on your event you then need to answer some key questions. A small team of people can help to think through these points and share the organising load.

- Why are you doing this? Is the event attractive in itself, or is it the cause?
- What are the risks to you in organising this event? (How easily could it go wrong? How much money do you stand to lose?)
- Who are you raising the money for, yourselves or for an outside cause?
- Who will organise the event(s)?
- Who will come to the event(s)?
- What is the local competition likely to be, especially around certain times of year?
- Where will it be held?
- Is it safe?
- Do you need permission?
- How much money do you hope to raise?

This last question becomes increasingly important the higher your initial outlay is. It will be no good to you or your group if you organise the best screen-printing tee-shirt design competition ever if you cannot guarantee customers for the product. Young people may learn much in the process about team-work, creativity, organisation and marketing, but if your group is seriously out of pocket, or even goes bust in the end, you may wonder whether it was worth it. Remember too, that all outside events are at the mercy of the weather and you should make contingency plans.

> **There are basically two kinds of fundraising event:**
> - ticket events where money is raised through ticket sales
> - participation events where money is raised through sponsorship of those taking part.

One fundraiser has suggested that any event should have three figures for the amount of money that is to be raised, all targeted at a particular audience:

- What you think the event will raise (say £1,500);
- What you tell your management committee it will raise (say £1,200);
- What you tell supporters you hope to raise. ('We are hoping to raise £1,000. Help us reach this total.' When the total is reached early on, there should be enough momentum to raise the remaining £500.)

There is also much to be said for starting small and increasing in confidence if you are new to event fundraising. People sometimes start too ambitiously with very grand schemes. You should do what you know you and your group can achieve and build from your success. Organising a bring and buy sale may not have the appeal of a music festival in the park, but will be easier to run and have fewer risks attached. Who knows, if you really catch the fundraising bug, you could run the local answer to Live Aid next year.

Case study:

Foot and Mouth and the naked truth about fundraising

Suffolk Young Farmers' Club (YFC) bared all in their determination to beat the Foot and Mouth restrictions on county shows where they usually fundraised. Following the example of the famous Rylstone Women's Institute alternative calendar, Suffolk YFC produced their own version and got down to basics with the Naked Truth Calendar for 2002. They also had extensive publicity and managed to shift a few calendars too.

Contact: Suffolk YFC, Tel: 01473 785547, e-mail: suffolk-yfc@totalise.co.uk

---

Sponsored events – a guide

Getting someone to be sponsored for doing something is the most common way that groups and individuals raise money from the public. It is easy to see the advantages:

- easy and quick to organise;
- easy to contact supporters;
- reaches a potentially large number of different donors through personal contact;
- uses participants who are members of the group and helps the group's identity;
- fun – hopefully;
- little initial outlay;
- almost unlimited number of activities that can be sponsored;
- can raise large sums of money;

- can be used to focus on areas of interest: for example, overnight lock-in in unheated church hall for the homeless; fast for famine relief; litter swoop for the environment.

With imagination and enthusiastic volunteers, you can take a sponsored event and do something different with it. People may yawn at yet another sponsored swim or walk (although they will probably support it because they know the person doing the event) but if you can give the activity a new twist you build new enthusiasm for the event itself. Sitting in a bath of jelly or baked beans (or both) will grab the attention of people who may not know the participant or the cause. They may not care about, or even like the cause but will stop to give money if they laugh in the process. Holding the event in a shopping centre or a school hall will attract maximum publicity. The humiliation or exhibitionist factor increases with the publicity, as does the number of pounds donated.

Publicity can also be increased if the event is even slightly off the wall. A group of teenagers which regularly raises money for famine relief by fasts, bike rides, car washes and the like, also looks to more alternative events to heighten their profile. They have sponsored carol singing in June, and hold marathon beach parties in December. Not only does this maintain the momentum of long-term fundraising, but also keeps their own interest from flagging. This is an important factor when young people are doing the hard work of raising money where interest and enthusiasm can seep away quickly. Youth workers will need to be quick-footed and have a few different ideas for events to keep interest high.

> The history of event fundraising is littered with grand failures where groups tried to organise too much too soon, and assumed that initial enthusiasm would become sustained commitment. Be ruthlessly realistic about the numbers involved, possible disasters and public apathy before you give something the go ahead.

Publicity

Attractive publicity materials can give any event an added boost and place it firmly within a youth context. Comic Relief which organises the Red Nose extravaganza is among the leaders in the field here. Even something as mundane as the humble sponsorship form is given the Red Nose treatment (see below).

The effect is to give sponsors a laugh, jazz up the image of the event and to encourage a certain approach to raising money. It also appeals to their vanity. A previous sponsor form allowed sponsors to choose a title when sponsoring such as: The Divine …, The Luscious …, The Galactically Clever …, The Youthful yet Mature …, The Rippingly Torsoed …, The Deeply Fanciable …, and so on. Comic Relief aims to put the 'fun' into fundraising, and there is no reason why

Red Nose Supa mega sponsorship form

Dear Fabulous Sponsor,

First, thanks a million, million times. And then a million more. Second, before you fill in your donation details please just read the message on the back of this form – your donation could be worth 28% more at no extra cost to you! Nothing could be easier!

Please sponsor me (name) _____

To (event) _____

The very generous promising person's name	Full address including post code	Total amount sponsored	Total received	Very important box. Please tick if you would like Comic Relief to reclaim the tax on your donation. Costs you nothing, earns us lots.
The fabulous _____	_____	____	___	_____
The fabulous _____	_____	____	___	_____
The fabulous _____	_____	____	___	_____
The fabulous _____	_____	____	___	_____
The fabulous _____	_____	____	___	_____
The fabulous _____	_____	____	___	_____
Etc …				

Fabulous total raised £ _____

The official bit you fill in when you've collected the cash!

Name _____
Address _____
_____
Postcode _____
Telephone _____
Signed _____
Parent/Guardian if under 18
Total Amount Enclosed _____

Please return this form and all the money raised to your local Event Organiser or directly to:

Comic Relief 2001, Ernst & Young, PO Box 678, London EC4A 1NT

Comic Relief is a registered charity, number 326568

Big it Up – your donation could be worth 28% more!

It's brilliant! Every time you make a donation to Comic Relief we can increase it by 28%. How? For every £1 you give, providing you are a UK taxpayer* , we get an extra 28p from the Treasury – because the government doesn't want to feel it has taxed you on money you are giving to a good cause. So that's why we're asking you to tick the little red box on the right when you write down your full name and address on this form. Please, please do it. If this gorgeous scheme had been in place last Red Nose Day, we would have made something like an extra £4 million. With your help we can Big it Up.

* You must have paid as much tax (or more) as the 28% of your donation that we are getting back. But unless you're giving us thousands of pounds, that's very, very, likely!

your own sponsored event cannot do this as well. Remember that attractive does not necessarily mean expensive. A catchy phrase and an arresting appeal can work as well as a form printed in three colours. The sponsorship form should include all the relevant information, including your charity registration number if you have one. You can also take advantage of the Gift Aid scheme by incorporating a tick box and explanation. (See Chapter 13 on Tax and VAT.)

Sponsorship incentives for participants

Usually, people look at the incentives to give money from the donor's point of view, but you should also consider how to encourage those participating in the event and asking for sponsorship. This is particularly important for younger children who may be easily discouraged if they only have two or three names filled in on their forms. It will not matter to them if these have given £10 each. To young children it will be the number of names on the form rather than the size of the gift that impresses.

You may want to mark in some small way the participants who raise the most money, have the most names, or even have the most imaginatively decorated sponsor form. To preserve harmony you may want to make this a team effort where older participants can help the younger ones. You do not want to excite too much competition, or you will probably encourage some creative accountancy and find the whole cast of Eastenders signed up on each form. Sponsored events can become cut-throat; but it can be good to show participants that they will have something to see for their efforts.

The world's biggest, smallest, zaniest ...

The appeal of appearing in the Guinness Book of Records is legendary. Record attempts have to be safe, so razor-blade swallowing is now out, as are fat pet records. Young people will almost always be excited by the chance of being record breakers. It does not have to be high wire walking or underwater chess either. If you attempt to construct the largest drink can chain, or write the largest Christmas card in the world to some high profile personality and get it sponsored, you may get local press coverage and photographs as well as adding to your funds, even if you don't make the record.

For information on how your record-breaking attempt will be assessed, contact: www.guinnessworldrecords.com, or, Records Research Services, Guinness World Records, 338 Euston Road, London NW1 3BD Tel: 0870 241 6632; Fax: 020 7891 4501

Incentives for sponsors

One of the largest incentives for sponsors may be that they will not be asked for money again for some time. It will help your fundraising generally, and events involving the public specifically, if there is some sense of planning to your campaigns. 'They're always asking for money' is one of the most off-putting reputations an organisation can have. Even if it is largely unfounded it can be very hard to shake off. If you draw up a calendar of events that evenly spaces those that will be specifically asking people for money it will help you and those that want to support you to concentrate their energy and financial support.

Many organisations use a shopping list of items to help people give away their money. It helps the sponsor feel their contribution is important and people generally like giving money to buy things which can be seen. Organising a fundraising event is probably not the time to raise money for core costs such as a manager's salary or the MOT for the mini–bus. There are no doubt spectacular exceptions to this rule, but by and large you will be more successful if you are raising money for equipment or a specific activity or trip that directly benefits the young people. You might try something like the following:

Dear Beloved Sponsor, welcome to our sponsor form. *In-Tents Youth Club* is raising money to buy some camping equipment for their summer camp. We are running a sponsored sleeping bag olympics on 1st April. With the money that you generously give we aim to buy:

Camping equipment:
3 x tents, 1 x ground sheet, 1 x gas stove and 1 x mallet.
All this will help 50 young children have the summer holiday of their lives!
Thanks for your help.

Or, alternatively, you may want to say what each £5 donated can buy:

Arts equipment:
Blank video tapes for a film project
Entrance tickets to local festival
Face-paints for drama workshop

Sports equipment:
Table tennis balls

General equipment:
Leaflets to promote a summer activity week.

Helping people to give

The public are no different from other donors when it comes to wanting to be told how to give and even how much. Many will not have much idea when handed a sponsor form of how much they should give. The following will lead them by the hand and help to maximise their donations.

- Sponsors will usually look at the names already on the list and what they have given. Participants can ask their most generous supporter to sign the form first. This is more likely to be a mum or dad, or grandparent, rather than a younger brother or sister. Other sponsors will follow their lead. They may not pledge as much, but they will not want to be significantly lower either. They are signing their names to the form and do not want to appear too mean. If the number of sponsors is likely to be high you may want to distribute the large donors throughout the form.
- Give donors the option of sponsoring the number of units as well as a total amount. (It is always a good idea to give a total amount, rather than sting the sponsor after your group's Herculean triumphs. If the sponsor has pledged 10p a bounce, an enthusiastic claim for £25 after 250 bounces may be a bounce too far.) You should also think about the type of unit – 10p a kilometre for instance will generate more income than 10p a mile.
- As mentioned above, you might want to offer a small prize for the person who has the most names, or the biggest total. This can be an incentive for the sponsor as well as the participant but should only be token. Certificates or badges to be presented may well be enough.

Do the right thing – do you need a licence?

The regulatory hurdles you will have to clear will depend upon the event you are running. It is also worth doing a risk assessment on your event. The Health and Safety Executive (*Information line: 08701 545500; website: www.hse.gov.uk*) can give guidelines.

Depending on the event you are running you may have to consider the following:

- Bye-laws – check with the local authority's leisure and recreation department, or other authorities such as rivers, waterways, footpath, coastal, heritage and so on.
- Car boot sales – contact the licencing office of the local authority for guidance.
- First aid, fire and police regulations – contact the appropriate body.
- Food hygiene and safety – contact environmental services at the local authority for guidance.
- Health and safety – check all aspects of your activity with the local authority and the local health and safety office.
- Liquor licence – contact the local Magistrates Court (Clerk to the Licensing Justices)

- Lotteries – small, one-off events will not need a licence. Those brave enough to compete with the National Lottery and organise ticket sales over a longer period of time (social lotteries) should apply to the licencing office of the local authority. The Gaming Board of Great Britain also has information on regulation (*Enquiry line: 020 7306 6269; website: www.gbgb.org.uk*).
- Public entertainment licence – contact the licencing office of your local authority.
- Public liability insurance – check with your insurer.
- Safety certificates – where you are organising fairground rides, motorised tours, balloon rides or the like you need to apply for appropriate licencing. The leisure and recreation department, environmental services or the licencing office can give guidance.
- Street closures – you need to apply for a Street Closure Order from the local authority.
- Sunday trading – contact the local authority to find out the current regulation.

A sponsored event checklist

1 Check the event is safe and appropriate for those taking part and those who will be asked to sponsor. The event should be irresistible but not irresponsible.
2 Get parents'/guardians' permission to go ahead.
3 Get permission from any appropriate local bodies e.g. police, local authority, schools, residents.
4 Talk to the media about coverage. Look for celebrities to take part.
5 Look at possibilities for any elements of the event to be sponsored e.g. donations of prizes, sponsorship of printing, tee-shirts, drinks etc.
6 Design and print sponsor forms. Detail amounts and units, where the money is to go and what it will buy.
7 If the event is a marathon event or a 24 hour relay club activity, organise a rota and sign up participants.
8 Organise the day; first aid, stewards, refreshments, signposting, equipment and information.
9 Tidy up afterwards.
10 Thank everyone who took part. Give prizes if necessary.
11 Collect money and chase up the reluctant.
12 Publicise the amount of money collected and tell those who gave what the money has bought.

Celebrities

Working with someone famous can help to raise the profile of your event or your organisation. There are a number of advantages to attracting a 'name' to your cause:

- increased media coverage, locally and nationally;
- more people may come to an event;
- other funders may attend a celebrity event;
- morale boost for those participating and organising the event;
- positive role model for young people;
- may be able to obtain discounted rates or items from suppliers;
- may have contacts and links with other groups and 'names'.

If you do not already have a celebrity connected with your fundraising, look at whether you have a patron, notable trustees or any famous names who once had a connection with your organisation. Did the local soap star now made good once attend the youth group? Does the olympic hurdler from your patch owe her start to your group's activities or facilities? Celebrities will rally to your cause if they:

- like and trust the group and agree with what you are trying to do;
- have some connection with you;
- like the event.

Ten tips on working with the famous

1 Think about your audience.
2 Choose someone your audience knows and likes.
3 Choose someone who is sympathetic to your cause, ideally someone with first hand knowledge, and who has a connection with your organisation.
4 Contact any celebrity well in advance of any event.
5 Be very clear about what you want their involvement to be.
6 Offer to pay expenses (mileage, materials, meals, accommodation etc.) and budget accordingly.
7 Brief them well, and advise them about any press coverage.
8 Make sure those who will be meeting and introducing them know what to do.
9 Don't overrun, unless they initiate it.
10 Say thanks, and keep them in touch with what you are doing.

As with everything else in fundraising, you need a mixture of the tried and trusted, together with the new and eye-catching. Delia Smith may be a little tired of being asked to contribute to fundraising cookbooks, but if she likes what you are trying to do she may still send a recipe for you to include.

In general, fundraising from the public is one of the most exciting ways of raising money. It can be a lot of fun. Remember, though, start small, start early, be realistic and make sure you have contingency plans for when things go wrong!

Planning events
Checklist – how to organise an event
Lancashire Community Futures (a community council) has produced a checklist to cover planning, preparation and running a village event. You can adapt the following to your own activity, but remember this cannot cover all eventualities and you should use this as the start for your planning, rather than the last word.

If you are thinking of holding an event, a logical approach to the planning process will always produce a better organised, safer and more enjoyable event.

This list has been designed to be a step by step guide and checklist, taking an organising committee through all the stages necessary in planning a wide range of community events.

The list follows the logical order of event planning, starting with:

1 Feasibility – the following points should be considered to ascertain the feasibility of your event before planning starts.
   - What type of event are you planning?
   - Why are you holding it?
   - When will you hold it? will it clash with other events?
   - Where will you stage it, safely?

2 Once you are satisfied that the event is feasible, the next stage is to PLAN IT.

3 After deciding that your idea is sound, and getting committee approval, the final task is to appoint an overall event co-ordinator – who has overall control – and an organising committee.

Organising a community event

Planning

Agree the date of the event, and set realistic timetables for preparation. Consider the main areas of planning. The Outline Plan for your event should cover the areas listed below:

Safety	Assigned	Finalised
Insurance	☐	☐
Risk assessment	☐	☐
Health & safety	☐	☐
Safe site	☐	☐
Occupier's Liability Act	☐	☐
Health & Safety at Work Act	☐	☐
Other ...		

Budget		
Draft budget & contingency	☐	☐
Break even point	☐	☐
Sponsorship/grant aid	☐	☐
Costs/sales	☐	☐
Trade/concessionaires	☐	☐
Re-instatement deposit	☐	☐
Other ...		

Publicity		
Sponsors' requirements	☐	☐
Trade adverts	☐	☐
Advertising costs	☐	☐
Publicity material costs	☐	☐
Other ...		

Programme	Assigned	Finalised
Time/date – other local events	☐	☐
National events	☐	☐
Holidays	☐	☐
Legal considerations –		
Food hygiene	☐	☐
Planning permission	☐	☐
Licences – alcoholic drinks	☐	☐
Music/dance	☐	☐
Personalities/guests	☐	☐
Other ...		

Site		
Mains services	☐	☐
Car parking	☐	☐
Access to/from	☐	☐
Marquee hire	☐	☐
Reinstatement	☐	☐
Other ...		

Staffing
Numbers required
Paid
Volunteers
Other ...

Preparation

Having planned the event and agreed the timetable for preparation. You must assign tasks to members or sub-groups, and arrange dates for their completion. For larger events, sub-committees for each area of preparation e.g. safety or publicity, should be set up. The event committee must meet regularly to make sure everything is going to plan – or to iron out any problems. Members of the organising committee should take responsibility for individual areas. Completion dates should be set.

	Assigned	Completed
Safety		
Signs	☐	☐
Barrier hire	☐	☐
First aid personnel	☐	☐
PA systems/radio	☐	☐
Public liability	☐	☐
Other ...		

Budget		
Costs – services	☐	☐
Staff	☐	☐
Site	☐	☐
Equipment	☐	☐
Suppliesv	☐	☐
Income – sponsorship	☐	☐
Admission charge	☐	☐
Trade stands	☐	☐
Advertising on site/programme	☐	☐
Tickets/programme sales	☐	☐
Insurance	☐	☐
Other ...		

Publicity		
Radio/TV what's on	☐	☐
Programmes	☐	☐
Press release	☐	☐
Sponsors' requirements	☐	☐
Handbills	☐	☐
Posters	☐	☐
Photographer	☐	☐
Other ...		

Programme

	Assigned	Completed
Start/finish times	☐	☐
Food hygiene	☐	☐

Organising a community event

Planning permission ☐ ☐
Insurance – high risk activities ☐ ☐
Specific items ☐ ☐
Third party claims ☐ ☐
Consequential loss ☐ ☐
Cancelled event ☐ ☐
Damage to site ☐ ☐
Weather insurance ☐ ☐
Catering bars ☐ ☐
Other ...

Site
Sign posting ☐ ☐
Site plan ☐ ☐
Electricity/water ☐ ☐
Toilets – disabled access ☐ ☐
First aid post ☐ ☐
Lost children area ☐ ☐
Seating – fire/safety regulations ☐ ☐
Car park –
Disabled/vehicle recovery ☐ ☐
Other ...

Staffing
Recruitment – parking, tickets, ☐ ☐
Officials, catering, security ☐ ☐
Uniforms/bibs ☐ ☐
Expenses/meal tickets ☐ ☐
Troubleshooters ☐ ☐
Other ...

On the Day

Arrive Early – earlier than you think you'll need. Ensure individual members know their delegated tasks. Check all tasks have been completed. Run through the event and the volunteer jobs. Event co-ordinator should not be tied to one job, but should be free to assist and troubleshoot where necessary.

Safety	Assigned	Checked
PA/radios & coded messages	☐	☐
Marshals – bibs	☐	☐
Barriers – secured	☐	☐
Signs – Keep Out, Exit etc.	☐	☐
First aid post – signposted	☐	☐
Experienced personnel	☐	☐
Fire fighting equipment	☐	☐
Police	☐	☐
Electrician	☐	☐
Other ...		

Money		
Float	☐	☐
Prize money/cheques	☐	☐

Organising a community event

Secure cash boxes
Tickets – start no.
End no.
Other ...

Publicity
To the event signs
Programmes on sale
Radio/TV on the day
Banners/flags
Reporters/photographers
Other ...

Site	Assigned	Checked
Car Park – security disclaimer		
Toilets – clean – check regularly		
- well positioned – accessible		
lost children area – staffed		
- signposted		
Seating – set out		
– checked – anchored		
Electrical supply/generator		
Water/drainage		
Catering outlets – clean & priced		
Bars – plastic glasses –		
clean & priced		
Other ...		

Staffing
Easily Identified
Briefed/Specific Duties
Given Meal Tickets/Expenses
Other...

After the Event
THANK YOUR TEAM BUT TRY TO MAINTAIN MOMENTUM TO ENSURE THAT
ALL POST EVENT JOBS ARE COMPLETED. DISCUSS PROBLEMS AND HOW
THE EVENT COULD BE IMPROVED NEXT YEAR. START PLANNING NOW!

Return Site to Original Condition
Extra Litter Collection
Thank You Letters
De-briefing
Press Release/Photographs
Bank Money – Prepare Accounts

REMEMBER – THIS LIST CANNOT COVER ALL EVENTUALITIES. SPACE HAS
BEEN LEFT FOR YOU TO FILL IN THE INDIVIDUAL REQUIREMENTS SPECIFIC
TO YOUR EVENT

*Produced by: Lancashire Community Futures, 15 Victoria Road, Fulwood, Preston
PR2 8PS Tel: 01772 717461*

Fundraising ideas are plentiful. A number of websites have ideas for events and activities, and tips on how to run them, including Children in Need which produces an A to Z of ideas at: www.bbc.co.uk/cin The following are some to get you started:

A–Z of fundraising ideas

A is for...   Antiques, Arts and Crafts, Auction, Anything Annual

B is for...   Birthday Cakes, Barbecues, Bingo, Buy-a-Brick, Bazaars, Beach Parties, Breakout, Book Fairs

C is for...   Concerts, Cookies, Carol Singing, Car Washes, Car Boot Sales, Coffee Mornings, Cookbooks, Caption Competitions, Calendars

D is for...   Duck (plastic) Racing, Dinner Party, Dutch Auction, Discos, Dance Marathons

E is for...   Exhibitions, Eating, Everything Extreme (lowest, highest, fastest, slowest etc.), Eating baked beans (or similar) with a cocktail stick)

F is for...   Fasts, Fetes, Fairs, Festivals, Face Painting, Fashion Shows, Fun Runs, Foam Party

G is for...   Garden Parties, Gardening, Growing (bulbs, plants, vegetables etc.), Guess the Weight, Gang Shows

H is for...   Haircuts, Horse Races, Highland Games

I is for...   It's a Knockout, Italian Evening

J is for....   Jumble Sales, Jam Making, Junk Mail/Newspaper Collection

K is for...   Karaoke, Knitting, Kite Making

L is for...   Lunches, Lotteries, Line Dancing, Limbo Competition

M is for...   Marathons, Merchandise, Meals on Heels, Mammoth Markets, Matchbox Challenge

N is for...   Newspaper Recycling, Naming (dolls, teddies, animals etc.), Nearly New Sales

O is for...   Olympics, Open House, Old Time Music Hall, One Hundred Club, Open Gardens, Obstacle Course

P is for...   Promise Auction, Performances, Post, Parachute Jump, Pick a Straw or Lollipop, Pet Show, Press-ups

Q is for...   Quizzes, Quilts

R is for...   Raffles, Rallies, Races

S is for...   Something Sponsored, Swimathons, Show (art, craft, fashion etc.), Scavenger Hunts, Sales, Stalls, Smartie® Tube Filling, Slow Bike Race, Stocks

T is for...   Three Peaks, Tournaments, Tombolas, Talent Competition, Treasure Hunts, Teddy Bear's Picnic, Table Sales

U is for...   Unusual, Unwanted Gift Sales

V is for...   Vouchers, Valeting (car)

W is for...   Wine-tasting, Welly Wanging, Walks (guided, ghostly, sponsored etc.)

X is for...   Xmas (parties, fairs, cards etc.)

Y is for...   Yodelling (sponsored, competition)

Z is for...   Zoological, Zany

6 RAISING MONEY FROM THE NATIONAL LOTTERY

> ## Lottery programmes covered in this chapter
> - Awards for All (A4A)
> - Community Fund
> - Local Heritage Initiative (LHI)
> - New Opportunities Fund – activities for young people; and out of school childcare
> - New Opportunities Fund – Green Spaces and Sustainable Communities
> - Regional Arts Lottery Programme (RALP)
> - Sport England Lottery Fund

HOW NATIONAL LOTTERY MONEY IS DISTRIBUTED

The National Lottery has been very successful in raising money for good causes and many voluntary organisations invest a substantial part of their fundraising energy into getting a grant from one of the five Distribution Boards. Around 94% of the population has bought at least one lottery ticket, whilst around 65% participate regularly. Original income projections have now been revised upwards and by 2001, £14 billion had been directed towards 'good causes'. When the National Lottery was launched in 1993, five good causes were announced that were to benefit from the proceeds:

- the arts
- charities
- heritage
- sport
- projects to mark the millennium.

In 1998, the sixth good cause, the New Opportunities Fund, was created to support education, health and the environment using additional money created by the introduction of the Wednesday draw, and then subsequently money that had been previously directed towards marking the millennium. There is a grant distribution scheme for individuals (and outside the scope of this book) unLTD, which has received a transfer of £100 million from the Millennium Commission to contribute to an endowment which will support individuals in social enterprise.

National Lottery income is divided between the five lottery distribution boards which are independent of each other, and theoretically independent of government. These are:

- Community Fund (previously known as the National Lottery Charities Board) which receives 16.7% of National Lottery income for good causes;
- the Arts Councils which receive 16.7% of good cause income;
- the Sports Councils which receive 16.7% of National Lottery income;
- the Heritage Lottery Fund which receives 16.7% of income;
- the New Opportunities Fund which receives the greatest share of National Lottery good cause income totalling 33.3%.

SMALL GRANTS PROGRAMME

Awards for All

1st Floor, Reynard House, 37 Welford Road, Leicester LE2 7GA
Tel: 0845 600 2040 (for application information)
Website: www.awardsforall.org.uk
Contact: Daisy Powell, Information Officer

Awards for All is an excellent scheme for introducing organisations to the Lottery. It is a cross-distributor lottery programme supported by the Arts Council of England, the Community Fund, the Heritage Lottery Fund, the New Opportunities Fund, and Sport England. The programme aims to make small grants to local organisations that may have little or no experience of applying for lottery funds. Around three quarters of applicants to the programme are applying for lottery funding for the first time.

Awards for All gives grants of between £500 and £5,000 to organisations with an income of less than £15,000 a year. Eligible groups must be constituted and not-for-profit. Individuals, statutory authorities (apart from parish councils and schools) and bodies established to fundraise for them are not eligible.

The programme is simple in its approach and gives the broadest possible outlines of what can be funded. This allows groups to apply under a wide range of activity headings. The programme aims to fund activities by small groups which: 'involve more people in a wide range of community activities; are open to everyone; are well organised and planned; and benefit the community'.

Examples of activities include:
- staging an event, activity or performance
- running training courses
- setting a pilot project
- running a conference or seminar
- special repairs or conservation work (apart from places of worship with listed status)
- start-up costs
- publicity materials
- professional fees
- research costs
- equipment and materials
- transport costs
- volunteers' expenses.

Awards for All will not fund:

- general running costs
- activities benefiting an individual only
- activities which promote a strong religious belief
- endowments
- loan payments
- second hand vehicles
- foreign trips
- projects with high ongoing maintenance costs.

Projects combining arts, heritage, sports education, health, the environment and other community activities are encouraged. The programme also has a particular regional focus determined by each of its nine regional offices. In a number of these (such as the North East, the East and West Midlands and the South West) young people are part of the regional focus. Priorities will change over time and organisations should contact their regional office (listed below with the areas they cover) or look at the Awards for All website for current information.

Where a project does not come under one of the regional priorities the following advice is given by the regional offices:

'Don't worry ... The regional priorities help us to reach groups or areas that have not been as successful in attracting Awards for All funding. This does not exclude groups that fall outside this focus – and similarly it does not guarantee that we will fund projects that meet the criteria. The most important aspect of the project is how well it meets the programme aims. But where we get more applications than the programme can fund we will use the regional focus as a 'tie-breaker' among similar applications ... If your group does not fit into one of our target groups, don't worry – we won't automatically turn you down.'

Examples of awards to young people's projects

- Harrogate Young People's Theatre – £3,500 for theatre hire and scenery costs to stage a young people's production;
- Hamilton Young People's Community Forum – £1,000 to hire a gym and sports equipment, and to pay for a sessional arts worker and materials to develop sports and arts activities for young people;
- Tudhoe Young People's Group – £2,210 for a programme of workshops and outings;
- Young People's Caribbean Carnival (Waltham Forest) – £5,000 to promote and develop the carnival by workshops and costume production;
- Young Bristol – £4,400 for leaders' qualifications in canoeing, sailing, mountain biking, powerboating, powerboat safety and first aid;
- Fleckney Club for Young People – £4,400 toward topsoil and recovering costs for a BMX track and display and launch party;
- 1st Millbrook Scout Group – £5,000 for blinds and to improve hall acoustics;
- 1st Newquay Scout Group – £4,568 for a computer, camping/climbing gear and headquarters equipment;
- 4th Erith Guide Company – £1,664 for an activity holiday;
- Whittlesey Scout and Guide Joint Committee – £5,000 for roof and gutter replacement on their headquarters;
- Woodcraft Folk SW region – £3,200 to research existing resources and to identify volunteer skills and needs.

Applications: Application forms are available from the website or by telephoning 0845 600 2040. Applicants are asked to give details of an independent referee to support the application. The application will first be assessed by an awards officer who will look at the following:

- how the group is managed;
- how the application fits the aims of the programme, such as: supporting community activity, extending access and participation, increasing skill and creativity, improving the quality of life and how the application fits the regional focus;
- who benefits from the activity;
- whether the budget is appropriate and realistic;
- what the group is contributing to the activity such as cash or in kind contributions

The assessor may telephone both the applicant and the referee for more information on the project and the organisation. Following assessment, the application is then passed to a joint regional committee representing all the involved lottery distributors for a final decision.

Decisions are made within three months of the application being received, and where successful, payments are made within a month of the decision being announced. The award must be spent within 12 months of the payment being made.

Unsuccessful applicants will be contacted with an explanation of the main reasons as to why the application was turned down. Unsuccessful applicants can reapply to the programme at any time.

Successful applicants will be asked for an End of Grant Report when the project has been completed. Those who are successful can apply for further support once their initial grant has been completed, but it should not be for exactly the same project as before.

Regional offices
Regional office staff can give help and advice on how to prepare and submit applications.

East Midlands (Derby, Derbyshire, Leicester, Leicestershire, Lincolnshire (apart from North and North East Lincolnshire), Northamptonshire, Nottingham, Nottinghamshire)
City Gate East, 2nd Floor, Tollhouse Hill, Nottingham NG1 5NL
Tel: 0115 934 9304 **Fax:** 0115 948 4435
Minicom: 0115 948 4436

Eastern (Bedfordshire, Cambridgeshire, Essex, Hertfordshire, Luton, Norfolk, Peterborough, Southend, Suffolk, Thurrock)
2nd Floor, Elizabeth House, 1 High Street, Chesterton, Cambridge CB4 1YW
Tel: 01223 449009 **Fax:** 01223 312628
Minicom: 01223 352041

London (Barking and Dagenham, Barnet, Bexley, Brent, Bromley, Camden, City of London, Croydon, Ealing, Enfield, Greenwich, Hackney, Hammersmith and Fulham, Haringey, Harrow, Havering, Hillingdon, Hounslow, Islington, Kensington and Chelsea, Kingston-upon-Thames, Lambeth, Lewisham, Merton, Newham, Redbridge, Richmond-upon-Thames, Southwark, Sutton, Tower Hamlets, Waltham Forest, Wandsworth, Westminster)
9th Floor, Camelford House, 89 Albert Embankment, London SE1 7UF
Tel: 020 7587 6600 **Fax:** 020 7587 6610
Minicom: 020 7587 6620

North East (Darlington, Durham, Hartlepool, Middlesbrough, Northumberland, Redcar and Cleveland, Stockton-on-Tees, Tyne and Wear)
6th Floor, Baron House, 4 Neville Street, Newcastle upon Tyne NE1 5NL
Tel: 0191 255 1100 **Fax:** 0191 233 1997
Minicom: 0191 233 2099

North West (Blackburn, Blackpool, Cheshire, Cumbria, Greater Manchester, Halton, Lancashire, Merseyside, Warrington)
Ground Floor, Dallam Court, Dallam Lane, Warrington WA2 7LU
Tel: 01925 626800 **Fax:** 01925 234041
Minicom: 01925 231241

South East (Bracknell Forest, Brighton and Hove, Buckinghamshire, East Sussex, Hampshire, Isle of Wight, Kent (apart from Bromley and Bexley) Medway Towns, Milton Keynes, Oxfordshire, Portsmouth, Reading, Slough, Southampton, Surrey (apart from the boroughs of Croydon, Kingston-upon-Thames, Richmond-upon-Thames, Sutton) West Berkshire, West Sussex, Windsor and Maidenhead, Wokingham)
3rd Floor, Dominion House, Woodbridge Road, Guildford, Surrey GU1 4BN
Tel: 01483 462900 **Fax:** 01483 569893
Minicom: 01483 568764

South West (Bath and NE Somerset, Bournemouth, Bristol, Cornwall, Devon, Dorset, Gloucestershire, Isles of Scilly, North Somerset, Plymouth, Poole, Somerset, South Gloucestershire, Swindon, Torbay, Wiltshire)
Beaufort House, 51 New North Road, Exeter EX4 4EQ
Tel: 01392 849705 **Fax:** 01392 253105
Minicom: 01392 490633

West Midlands (Herefordshire, Shropshire, Staffordshire, Stoke-on-Trent, Warwickshire, West Midlands, Worcestershire)
8th Floor, Edmund House, 12-22 Newhall Street, Birmingham B3 3NL
Tel: 0121 200 3500 **Fax:** 0121 212 3081

Yorkshire and Humberside (East Riding of Yorkshire, Kingston-upon-Hull, North Lincolnshire, North East Lincolnshire, North Yorkshire, South Yorkshire, West Yorkshire, York)
3rd Floor, Carlton Tower, 34 St Pauls Street, Leeds LS1 2AT
Tel: 0113 224 5300 **Fax:** 0113 244 0363
Minicom: 0113 245 4104

MAIN GRANTS PROGRAMME

ARTS

Regional Arts Lottery Programme (RALP)

Contact the regional arts boards. Details below.
Website: www.arts.org.uk

The Regional Arts Lottery Programme (RALP) is managed by the ten Regional Arts Boards (RABs). The programme aims to increase:

- access to the arts
- education through the arts
- production and distribution of the arts
- investment in artists
- development sustainability of arts organisations.

Each of the ten English Regional Arts Boards has its own set of priorities for RALP, and a number of regions include developing the arts for young people as one of these. It is essential that organisations thinking of applying to RALP consult their RAB to discuss their planned application. Contact details can be found below.

Grants for projects

Arts project grants range between £2,000 and £30,000, and most grants are likely to be in the £5,000 to £20,000 range. Awards to arts projects are generally one-off grants, occasionally, longer term projects over two to three years are supported

Examples of arts project grants

- Wise Thoughts received £13,700 for its project Arts for Herts. The performance and visual arts residency worked with young people from ethnic minorities to promote greater understanding of HIV and AIDS.
- Chester Youth Fringe received £6,900 for its Sunday in the Park to showcase young local talent and to bring together professional artists and young people. The project includes community based workshops in music and visual arts.

Grants for capital

Capital grants can support costs such as equipment, vehicles, musical instruments, access improvements, refurbishment of arts buildings and public art. Grants range from £2,000 up to (exceptionally) £100,000. Most awards are less than £30,000.

Examples of capital grants

- Manor Residents Association received £7,900 to support its Youth Music Collective. The RALP grant was used to buy guitars those under 16 years old. Outon Manor is one of the most deprived areas in the country, and over 30 young people benefited from

weekly music tuition.
- Villages In Action received £28,900 for its Digital Express programme for young people between 14 and 25 in Devon. The grant included buying a range of capital items including a camera, projector, digital video equipment, a computer and a printer.

Grants for organisational development for arts organisations

Grants can support a range of organisational development activity for arts organisations including business planning, training, restructuring, marketing, artistic development, relocation and dealing with debts. Awards range from £2,000 to £30,000 and additional information about the applicant organisation is likely to be required.

National arts organisations applying for organisational development funding will need to show how they meet one of the national priorities detailed in the RALP application pack.

Example of a grant for organisational development

The National Association of Youth Theatres received £33,800 towards relocation costs. The grant funded the costs of new marketing activities following NAYT's move to Darlington, improvements to services to members and new office equipment. A freelance artist was also contracted to design the new office interior.

Assessment

Applications are assessed against the following criteria:
- the quality of artistic and educational activities including plans for artists' involvement;
- the public benefit of the project

including access, marketing plans, the effect on the public, and value for money;

- the ability and commitment of the organisation to manage the proposal;
- how the proposal meets the aims of the programme and adds to regional or national priorities;
- the financial effect of the proposal and its effect on the organisation in the future

RALP will not fund:

- film production;
- activities or events which are not open to the general public (except for institutions such as prisons or old people's homes);
- activities which duplicate existing provision;
- project costs already covered by existing funding;
- fundraising events;
- prizes and bursaries;
- second-hand equipment (there are a small number of exceptions and a separate guidance note is available);
- ongoing running costs of organisations, equipment or buildings;
- applications from organisations distributing profit, unless there is clear benefit to the public.

Applications: Organisations can apply for one type of award or a combination of all three. Applications will be processed and assessed by the RAB where the project is to take place. National organisations will be assessed by the RAB in which they are based.

The website of England's Regional Arts Board has individual pages for each region, as well as guidance notes and an application form. The regional websites contain full details of each RAB's local priorities for RALP. Application forms

and guidance notes are also available by telephoning each RAB, and early contact is advised.

Separate guidance notes are available on:

- organisational development
- musical instruments and second-hand equipment
- buying vehicles
- access
- artists' fees

There are no deadlines for applications. Decisions are taken within four months of a completed application being received.

Regional Arts Boards contact details

East England Arts
Tel: 01223 454400
E-mail: info@eastern-arts.co.uk

East Midlands Arts
Tel: 01509 218292 **Fax:** 01509 262214
E-mail: info@em-arts.co.uk

London Arts
Tel: 020 7608 6100 **Fax:** 020 7608 4100
Minicom: 020 7608 4101
E-mail: info@lonab.co.uk

North West Arts
Manchester Office
Tel: 0161 834 6644 **Fax:** 0161 834 6969
Minicom: 0161834 9131

Liverpool Office
Tel: 0151 709 0671 **Fax:** 0151 708 9034
E-mail: info@nwarts.co.uk

Northern Arts
Tel & Minicom: 0191 255 8500
Fax: 0191 230 1020
E-mail: info@northernarts.org.uk

South East Arts
Tel: 01892 507200 **Fax:** 01892 549383
E-mail: info@seab.co.uk

South West Arts
Tel: 01392 218188 **Fax:** 01392 433503
Website: www.swa.co.uk

Southern Arts
Tel: 01962 855099 **Fax:** 01962 861186
E-mail: info@southernarts.co.uk

West Midlands Arts
Tel: 0121 631 3121 **Fax:** 0121 643 7239
E-mail: info@west-midlands-arts.co.uk

Yorkshire Arts
Tel: 01924 455555 **Fax:** 01924 466522
Minicom: 01924 438585
E-mail: info@yarts.co.uk

CHARITIES AND GOOD CAUSES

Community Fund

St Vincent House, 16 Suffolk Street,
London SW1Y 4NL
Tel: 0845 791 9191 (for application
forms and preliminary enquiries),
020 7747 5299 and regional offices for
more detailed information
Fax: 020 7747 5299
E-mail: enquiries@community-fund.org.uk
Website: www.community-fund.org.uk
Contact: Earl Newman, Senior
Information Officer, and regional
offices (details below)

Community Fund is the operating name
of the National Lottery Charities Board.
It aims 'to give grants to groups that help
meet the needs of those at greatest
disadvantage in society and improve the
quality of life in the community'. The
budget available for distribution in 2001/
2002 was £288 million. To date, £2.1
billion has been awarded to over 46,000

projects since the National Lotteries
Charities Board started in 1995.

The Community Fund supports projects
that:
- help people or communities overcome
  problems which prevent their
  participation in economic, social and
  community life;
- help people facing disadvantage which
  is severe, long-term, difficult to tackle
  or who face a combination of needs;
- try to prevent, or reduce as far as
  possible, future disadvantage.

As well as support for projects which
directly benefit people, there is also
support for projects which develop
voluntary and community organisations
and facilities. Projects that introduce new
ways of working in the voluntary and
community sector are also supported.
There are regional funding priorities for
each of the nine regions in England, and
details of these are available from the
regional offices (see below).

From mid 2001 the community
involvement and poverty and
disadvantage programmes were merged
into a single Main Grants programme.
Grants range from £500 up to £500,000
for England-wide applications. The
average size of grant is currently around
£100,000 over three years, and the usual
maximum is £300,000.

The funding priorities for the Main
Grants programme will apply until April
2002. These are:
- black and ethnic minority
  communities;
- developing capacity in advice and
  advocacy organisations;
- disabled people's groups;
- volunteering projects for marginalised
  groups;

- refugees and asylum seekers;
- projects tackling economic decline.

The funding priorities may change following the publishing of the strategic plan in Spring 2002 which will cover the period 2002–2007.

Grants are currently given for:
- one, two or three year projects;
- capital or revenue costs (or both); and
- part or total funding of a project.

Examples of grants given to good causes involving young people

- £179,900 over one year to 1st Dickleburgh Sea Scout Group, South Norfolk to construct a purpose-built, energy-efficient new building to replace the existing run-down sea scout hut.
- £16,500 over one year to Albrighton Scouts and Guides, Wolverhampton to build a climbing wall and buy dinghies to develop teambuilding activities.
- £12,350 to Fovant Youth Club, Salisbury to carry out repairs and renovations to the club building which provides the only social and recreational facility for local children.
- £273,900 over three years to Christ Church Youth and Community Centre, Bootle to develop an after-schools club, a lifestyles club for older people, a young men's group and a local radio broadcast. The grant covers the salaries of a centre manager, administrative assistant and an activities officer and associated running costs.
- £231,300 over three years to Just Drop-in Youth Info and Advice Limited, Macclesfield to refurbish the advice centre, professional fees, rent, office equipment and the salary of a new, full-time centre co-ordinator.
- £196,500 over three years to the Methodist Youth Club of Nailsea, North Somerset for the salaries of one full-time and two part-time detached youth workers, a minibus to use as a mobile resource unit and running costs of a street-based support, referral and advice service.
- £74,100 over one year to Mullion Youth Club, Kerrier towards refurbishing the youth centre, installing a computer suite and building a skate park.
- £263,970 over three years to Warwickshire Association of Youth Clubs for the salaries of two full-time and five part-time posts, office equipment, training and travel expenses, and general running costs. The award follows a previous grant and continues the work of the volunteer development officer to train and support volunteers in youth groups and youth services.

Assessment of applications

There are two stages to the assessment process. When an application is first received the following are assessed:
- the legal eligibility of the organisation (that it is properly constituted, not-for-profit, charitable) and that it is permitted to carry out the activity that is being applied for;
- the health of the organisation's finances;
- the use and extent of the organisation's free reserves;
- how the proposed project meets the Community Fund's general funding policies;
- whether the applicant organisation is applying for itself and not another organisation;
- any previous grants given and the use made of them, and whether the organisation currently holds a grant;
- whether the application is complete;

- where the application is from a consortium, the eligibility of each of the members;
- where the organisation is a branch of another organisation, if it falls within the Community Fund's policies;
- whether the application has been made by the organisation and not by a professional fundraiser;

- where the application involves higher and further education, whether the lead applicant is an eligible voluntary organisation;
- that the project's costs are reasonable;
- where the proposed activity covers all four UK countries, that there is enough evidence to show that people will benefit in each country;

Making the most of assessment – 10 tips from an assessor

1   Remember that not all assessors are familiar with projects involving young people. Don't assume too much knowledge on their part of what you are trying to do and how you are proposing to do it.

2   Have all the relevant documentation to hand. If an assessor rings and you do not feel prepared with the necessary information, ask for another more convenient time when you will be better organised. Ask what information they will be looking for so that you have everything to hand. An assessment call is lengthy. It will save you time and stress, and make the assessor's life easier, if you are organised and prepared.

3   If the assessor is making a personal visit, make sure that the person conducting the tour and answering the questions is briefed and knows the content and details of the application well.

4   Remember that assessors are human. There is no need to go overboard, but make sure they feel welcome. Cocktails and canapés are too much, but coffee and biscuits will probably be welcome.

5   Be open and honest. Don't go over the top or try to paper over the cracks. If your organisation is perfect, why do you need the money anyway?

6   See the assessment as a discussion not an interrogation.

7   Use friendly, jargon-free language. Be straightforward in your answers.

8   If your proposal is for a minibus, building or a salary, you may need to supply copies of any supporting documentation to the assessor if they do not have them.

9   Keep a record of what you've been asked for. This will help you after the assessment to make sure you've fulfilled your side of things. At key points in the conversation, ask the assessor to reflect back his or her understanding of what has been said. This will avoid misunderstandings.

10   At the end of the assessment, don't be afraid to ask questions about anything you're unsure of. It should be a two-way process, and this is your chance to gain some first-hand knowledge about what happens next, when you can expect to hear, or anything else that is needed.

- that there is sufficient evidence that the project can achieve what the application says it can;
- that the project is additional to statutory provision and funding.

Where the application satisfies the first set of assessment criteria, the application moves to the second and final stage. This will seek to establish whether:

- the organisation is well managed and the finances are in order;
- that the project has been planned well and will meet an identified need;
- that the organisation's procedures are in line with good practice.

For projects costing £200,000 or more, there is a personal visit from a Community Fund assessor. (In addition, 5% of applications for projects under £200,000 are randomly selected for a visit.) Assessments for other applications are made by a telephone call, which can last up to two hours. The application is assessed by a points system which covers the following questions:

- Is the organisation well managed and financially sound?
- Does the project have clearly defined objectives and a thorough and reasonable project plan that can be monitored and reviewed?
- Is the budget accurate and reasonable?
- Does the project meet a clearly defined need?
- Does the organisation and project reflect the different backgrounds and circumstances of the community they serve and do they involve service users in decision making?
- How far does the project help meet the needs of those at greatest disadvantage and improve the quality of life of the community?

- Does the primary focus of the project meet one or more of the country or regional funding priorities, and if so, how? (Where a project does not come under one of the funding priorities, it can still be assessed against the other criteria to be considered for a grant.)

Applications for projects costing up to £60,000

In mid 2001 a programme for smaller grants was introduced to make it easier for all organisations of whatever size to apply for support. It will cover the whole of the country by mid 2002.

The programme supports projects where the total cost is between £500 and £60,000 (where building work is not more than £30,000). It has the same aim as the Main Grants programme which is to help disadvantaged people and improve the quality of life in local communities. Regional funding priorities will be the same as for the Main Grants programme. The application form is shorter than the one for the Main Grants programme and there are no assessment visits. Assessment is carried out by telephone. There are four assessment criteria which are similar to the Main Grants programme:

- Is your organisation financially sound and well managed, and do you have the necessary procedures and experience to deliver the project successfully?
- Is there a real need for your project and is your project meeting that need?
- Are your project costs and plans for carrying out the project accurate and reasonable?
- Does your project meet any of the funding priorities for the country or region where the people who will benefit live? If so, how?

There is a separate application pack for the small grants programme available from the website or by telephoning the enquiry line. This new programme will be quicker in its processing of applications. A decision should be reached and communicated within four months of receiving completed application.

Business plans

Where the total costs of the project are for £200,000 or more, applicants need to submit a business plan which relates to the project rather than the organisation. The Community Fund's application pack includes helpful information on what to consider and include in the preparation of a business plan.

'A business plan is a document which explains:
- why a project is needed;
- how a project will work;
- how a project will be managed;
- what the beneficiaries will gain;
- how you will measure achievements;
- what the project will cost and how you will fund it; and
- why your organisation should do the project.

We ask these questions on the application form, but a business plan should cover these areas in more detail. A business plan is likely to include:
- a one-page summary;
- your organisation's aims and objectives and how the project fits into these;
- a description of the project to be delivered;
- an analysis of the need, with figures of service users;
- a survey of similar or related services or projects provided by other organisations;
- the project's aims and objectives;
- a work plan for year one including objectives, method of achievement, and a target to be achieved within a set timetable;
- details of how you will monitor your achievements;
- a project management structure;
- a budget and cash flow forecast for each year;
- a fundraising plan with important dates;
- a marketing plan with important dates;
- a summary of your organisation's track record of delivering similar projects; and
- staff requirements, including the skills of the main people involved in the project.'

From the Community Fund application guidance 2001

Funding for deprived areas

Further funding for 50 of the most deprived areas of England was announced in mid 2001. £150 million over three years, made up of £50 million from the New Opportunities Fund (NOF) and £100 million from the Community Fund, has been allocated from existing lottery distribution budgets to help under-invested areas. In particular, it will focus on those areas where application for funds have been lower, and the aim is to improve both the number and quality of applications. There will be continuing discussion around which 50 areas it will be most appropriate to direct the additional funds to. Within these areas the main funding priorities of the Community Fund will apply, and the application process will be as rigorous as for other areas. At the time of writing it had not been decided what type of awards were likely to be made and the balance between NOF and Community Fund type projects.

Applications: Application forms for the Main Grants programme and that for projects up to £60,000 can be downloaded from the website or by telephoning the enquiry line. Applicants who are considering applying for land and buildings (excluding rental costs) must also obtain a property applications booklet which is also available from the website or by telephone. There is no closing date for applications. the Community Fund will not make retrospective grants or cover costs incurred before its grant is paid. Therefore, leave plenty of time (at least six months for the main programme) between sending off the application form and project start date.

Regional offices

There are nine regional offices which can help with enquiries and give guidance about applications.

East Midlands

City Gate, East Block, 2nd Floor, Tollhouse Hill, Nottingham NG1 5NL
Tel: 0115 934 9300 **Fax:** 0115 948 4435
Minicom: 0115 948 4436
E-mail: enquiries.em@community-fund.org.uk

Eastern

Elizabeth House, 2nd Floor, 1 High Street, Chesterton, Cambridge CB4 1YW
Tel: 01223 449000 **Fax:** 01223 312628
Textphone: 01223 352041
E-mail: enquiries.ea@community-fund.org.uk

London

Camelford House, 89 Albert Embankment, London SE1 7UF
Tel: 020 7587 6600 **Fax:** 020 7587 6610
Minicom: 020 7587 6620
E-mail: enquiries.lon@community-fund.org.uk

North East

6th Floor, Baron House, 4 Neville Street, Newcastle upon Tyne NE1 5NL
Tel: 0191 255 1100; **Fax:** 0191 233 1997;
Minicom: 0191 233 2099;
E-mail: enquiries,ne@community-fund.org.uk

North West

Dallam Court, Dallam Lane, Warrington WA2 7LU
Tel: 01925 626800 **Fax:** 01925 234041
Minicom: 01925 231241
E-mail: enquiries.nw@community-fund.org.uk

South East
3rd Floor, Dominion House, Woodbridge
Road, Guildford, Surrey GU1 4BN
Tel: 01483 462900 **Fax:** 01483 569893
Minicom: 01483 568764
E-mail: enquiries.se@community-
fund.org.uk

South West
Beaufort House, 51 New North Road,
Exeter EX4 4EQ
Tel: 01392 849700 **Fax:** 01392 491134
Textphone: 01392490633
E-mail: enquiries.sw@community-
fund.org.uk

Yorkshire and the Humber
3rd Floor, Carlton Tower, 34 St Pauls
Street, Leeds LS1 2AT
Tel: 0113 224 5300 **Fax:** 0113 244 0363
Minicom: 0113 245 4104
E-mail: enquiries.yh@community-
fund.org.uk

West Midlands
8th Floor, Edmund House, 12–22
Newhall Street, Birmingham B3 3NL
Tel: 0121 200 3500 **Fax:** 0121 200 3500
Minicom: 0121 212 3523
E-mail: enquiries.wm@community-
fund.org.uk

England
1st Floor, Reynard House, 37 Welford
Road, Leicester LE2 7GA
Tel: 0116 258 7000 **Fax:** 0116 255 5162
Minicom: 0116 255 7398

The England-wide team considers
applications which are:
▪ across the whole of England;
▪ or those covering more than one
  English region;
▪ or those covering England and one or
  more other UK country.

HERITAGE

Local Heritage Initiative

The LHI Team, The Countryside
Agency, John Dower House, Crescent
Place, Cheltenham GL50 3RA
Tel: 0870 9000 401(Information line)
E-mail: lhi@countryside.gov.uk
Website: www.lhi.org.uk
Contact: Alison Lammas

The Heritage Lottery Fund has allocated
£8 million to a regional scheme, the
Local Heritage Initiative (LHI), which is
administered by the Countryside Agency
and supported with a further £1 million
from the Nationwide Building Society.
The Heritage Lottery Fund has promised
continued funding for the initiative until
2010.

The scheme aims to 'help local groups
to investigate, explain and care for their
local landscape, landmarks, traditions and
culture.' It covers rural and sub-urban
areas in England, but not the centres of
large towns.

Examples of projects that could be
eligible for LHI support include:
▪ natural heritage – such as restoring
  local streams for wildlife and access
  and cleaning up reed beds
▪ built heritage – such as repairing and
  restoring small local features such as
  milestones
▪ archaeological heritage – such as
  surveying and the interpretation of
  local features and mapping out local
  heritage trails or researching local place
  names
▪ industrial heritage – such as making
  industrial heritage sites safe for public
  access
▪ customs and traditions – such as
  creating local commemorations of

important people, places, events and activities and recording local history, traditions and customs

LHI grants pay for such costs as:
- investigative work into local heritage;
- material and labour costs for conservation or restoration;
- improvement of public access to heritage assets;
- specialist advisers;
- archive costs;
- activities to involve the wider community particularly young people;
- essential equipment;
- legal advice and training for volunteers;
- volunteer insurance costs specially associated with LHI projects.

Grants will not cover:
- work carried out before the application and grant offer has been made;
- expert advice given by the applicant or group members (although this can count as in-kind help);
- items that only benefit an individual;
- routine maintenance and one-off repair projects.

The LHI gives grants of between £3,000 and £15,000 to cover 60% of the costs of a project. The remaining 40% can be raised by cash, in-kind support, volunteer time or a combination of these elements.

The LHI states: 'We are not specifically targeting schools and youth groups, but there is a big involvement from this sector within the communities we have funded'.

Previous grants have included two projects working with children and young people. Otterburn YMCA was awarded £15,000 towards recreation and education activities at Otterburn Hall. The Derbyshire Childcare Clubs

Network received a grant of £2,990 to support local history and heritage work in its clubs. Each club for children aged four to 12 received a grant of £100 to initiate heritage projects.

Applications: Application forms as well as information sheets on planning and running heritage projects are available from the website or by telephoning the information line.

There are no application deadlines, and the turnaround of applications is around three months (except in the summer months) from receiving the completed application form.

NEW OPPORTUNITIES FUND

New Opportunities Fund – Education

Heron House, 322 High Holburn, London WC1V 7PW
Tel: 0845 000 0121
Textphone enquiries 0845 602 1659
E-mail: education@nof.org.uk
Website: www.nof.org.uk

In 1998, a sixth distribution board covering education, health and the environment, was added to the other five supported by income from the National Lottery. The New Opportunities Fund (NOF) is the distributing body that has responsibility for awarding grants under this expanding sixth cause.

The fund supports sustainable education, environment and health projects that will:
- improve the quality of life for people throughout the UK;
- address the needs of those who are most disadvantaged by society;

- encourage community participation;
- complement relevant local and national strategies and programmes.

It works with national, regional and local partners from the public, private and voluntary sectors. There are a number of programmes, and the current initiatives most likely to support projects involving young people are:

- **education** – out of schools hours childcare
- **environment** – green spaces and sustainable communities.

The New Opportunities Fund has introduced a raft of programmes and initiatives, largely in response to governmental concerns. The expectation is that this will continue and the fund's programmes will be used to meet government policy objectives. The fund's activities are continually expanding (the New Opportunities Fund is projected to be administering up to a third of all National Lottery income by 2002) and organisations working with young people are likely to see more opportunities for support under future initiatives. The website has regularly updated information.

In summer 2001 the New Opportunities Fund announced the activities for young people programme. This was not an open application programme and closed in September 2001. It built extensively on a DfEE pilot scheme to run summer activity schemes with outdoor adventure, sports and arts for those leaving school at 16. The fund has allocated £38.75 million over three years until 2004 to fund summer activity schemes in the 47 Connexions areas. The schemes are accredited and linked to the Connexions Service in offering advice and guidance through personal advisers in job, training and education options, particularly focusing on those at risk of not participating in post-16 training or work opportunities.

Contracts were awarded to the summer activity partnerships and were not part of an open application process. NOF suggests that other '... organisations can become involved by working with the summer activity partnerships to help them deliver projects, identify the target young people or provide further training or employment opportunities.'

The activities partnerships are most likely to be lead by the Connexions Service where it is established, or by local authorities, with partners drawn from educational establishments, career services, welfare and youth services and activity providers. The fund states: 'The partnerships hope to deliver a mixture of residential and non-residential activities during the summer months to those school leavers who are likely to become out of touch with education, training and employment opportunities. Activities might include performing and visual arts, outdoor adventure, sports, volunteering, multi-media and website projects. Each young person will have a dedicated personal adviser, who will help them to develop their future plans and contribute to activities that focus on employment skills, careers guidance and personal development.'

Partnerships will not have funds that they can allocate to voluntary organisations helping to implement the activities. Voluntary organisations are more likely to have a contracting relationship with the partnership where they contract to supply services or undertake pieces of work. Applications for support can only to be submitted by the lead organisation of the summer activity partnership in each of the 47 Connexions areas. The fund suggests three possible routes for voluntary organisations to be involved: helping partnerships deliver projects; helping to identify and recruit young people for projects; and by providing further training or employment opportunities. The point of contact for organisations working with young people will be the Connexions Service in their area (see page 307) or by visiting the website at: www.connexions.gov.uk

Education – out of school hours childcare

Various initiatives to date under the New Opportunities Fund's education strand have been supportive of organisations working with young people. Two previous programmes – out of school learning activities, and community access to lifelong learning – both awarded a number of grants to young people's projects. Both these programmes are now closed.

The remaining programme, out of school hours childcare, is half way through its distribution programme. Whilst much of the income has been directed towards schools, a number of young people's projects have also been awarded grants. These include:

- £32,000 to J K Youth Forum, Luton, for 30 after school places and 50 holiday places for children aged between three and fourteen.
- £10,800 to Shavington Youth Club, Crewe, for 16 before-school and eight after-school places for children aged between three and fourteen years.
- £49,000 to Sandwich Youth Club, Kent, for 50 after-school places and 50 holiday places for eight to fourteen year olds. The scheme will benefit a

local junior school and two secondary schools.

There is a total of £198.5 million available in England until 2003. The types of schemes which will be supported are:
- holiday playcare schemes, in schools, community centres or the workplace;
- wrap around childcare such as an additional hour beyond an after school learning club;
- integrated childcare and learning schemes. These should link in with at least one school's aims and development plans although they do not have to based there;
- activity based out of school hours childcare, particularly for children aged 11 – 16, to develop and explore their recreational interests, build self-esteem and improve skills.

What the New Opportunities Fund will support

Childcare grants will support expenses such as:
- start-up costs of groups and organisations (which may include registration and initial running costs);
- running costs to provide new childcare places at existing schemes;
- small capital projects, such as equipment, or premises refurbishment.

Grants to single providers are for a minimum of £500, and can be for up to £50,000 for new childcare places, by either setting up a new service or by expanding existing provision. There are two ways of applying: an individual approach from a single provider, or a consortium application through an Early Years Development and Childcare Partnership (EYDCP). For a grant to cover a one year scheme providers can apply individually. Where schemes are to

---

Business plans

The application should include a business plan. The New Opportunities Fund suggests that this should include:

- your organisation's aims and objectives
- how many places you will be providing and how you know they will be needed
- how many staff you will need to employ;
- your timetable for the project
- how much it will cost and how much parents will be expected to pay;
- other sources of funding and plans to secure long-term sustainability
- how you plan to monitor the project

---

extend for two or three years, the approach must come through a consortium. There can be advantages to applying within a partnership, which include help with preparing the bid, as well as business support, training and development funding. Information is available from the fund's website or by telephoning the enquiry line.

Unfortunately, most grants will be for one year only. To be eligible for longer term funding, the proposed provision must be in an area that has been designated as particularly disadvantaged, which are the 5% most deprived wards in England. A list of areas is available from the fund. Any application for continuation funding in the second and third year must show that the application is for new places. Details and an application form are available on the website or by telephoning the enquiry line.

In all applications it must be clear how the places that are created help to meet the aims of the local childcare partnership and fit in with local strategic plans. Organisations working with young people must demonstrate:

- how their proposals will link to local schools

- how parents will be served
- sustainability
- the support of the local community
- accessibility
- good quality childcare
- value for money
- equal opportunities
- how the childcare is additional to existing provision
- monitoring systems
- compliance with statutory obligations for working with children.

Successful out of school childcare applications will display a number of strengths. These include:

- clear planning (of demand for places, beneficiaries and time-scales)
- good market research which anticipates parents' needs
- strong links with schools
- sensible business planning and realistic income/expenditure projections
- reliable and compliant monitoring systems
- credibility within the community
- sound management

To be eligible, organisations need to request an application form by 31 March 2003. These, together with guidance notes are available from the website or by telephoning the enquiry line. Completed application forms must be returned by 15 April 2003, for the proposed project to start by 30 September 2003. Decisions on awards should be made in June 2003.

Submitted applications are assessed and further information may be requested by telephone. There is not an assessment visit. The fund will take into account the view of the local childcare partnership when making a decision to award the grant or not.

New Opportunities Fund – Green Spaces and Sustainable Communities

Heron House, 322 High Holburn, London WC1V 7PW
Tel: 0845 000 0121
Textphone enquiries 0845 602 1659 (individual award partners, contact details below)
E-mail: greenspaces@nof.org.uk
Website: www.nof.org.uk

A total of £97 million in England is available under this programme to support projects in urban and rural areas which help communities 'understand, improve or care for their natural environment, focusing on disadvantage'. The programme supports initiatives and activities which contribute to:

- recreational green space and playing fields
- children's play space
- making green space more accessible for communities
- sustainable communities.

Grants are distributed through five award partners in England. These agencies are funded for up to five years to distribute grants to individual community projects which aim to improve the local environment. Programme priorities have been agreed with each award partner, and the emphases are as follows:

- Barnardos' – children's play space;
- BTCV, Countryside Agency, English Nature – making green spaces more accessible for communities;
- Royal Society for Nature Conservation – sustainable communities;
- Sport England – recreational green space and playing fields.

Award schemes with opportunities for those working with young people

Barnardo's and the Children's Play Council
Through their Better Play scheme, Barnardo's and the Children's Play Council give grants of between £2,000 and £100,000 to local groups and voluntary organisations developing local play opportunities for children and young people. Grants are largely for revenue costs. There is a quicker application process for those applying for £10,000 or less.

Grants in the first round were given towards projects lasting up to three years and totalled over £2.3 million to around 100 projects in England and Wales. Details of individual awards were not available at the time of writing. In April 2002, a second round will be open for applications for projects lasting up to two years, and in the final round in 2003, projects will be funded for one year. The general helpline or website will further details of the application process as they are announced.

BTCV

BTCV runs the People's Places scheme which supports the creation and renovation of green spaces. Projects should actively involve people from the local community, with a particular emphasis on areas where there is disadvantage or little access to green spaces. BTCV will distribute around 1,000 awards over five years in grants ranging between £3,000 and £10,000. Training is available to help groups with project planning. At the time of writing no details of awards were available.

English Nature

English Nature's scheme Wildspace! distributes grants to projects which help local communities improve, care and enjoy their local environment. Part of the programme is aimed at local authorities and those with responsibility for local nature reserves. There is also support for wildlife trusts and community organisations, particularly in disadvantaged areas that do not have access to natural open spaces. Grants of between £5,000 and £25,000 can be given for project costs (and will be for up to 75% of the total costs); grants of up to

£20,000 are available to employ community liaison officers and grants of up to £25,000 can be given to buy land.

The Countryside Agency

The Doorstep Greens programme aims to help local communities in urban and rural areas to create or transform 200 green spaces into community greens. Applications are particularly welcomed from projects in disadvantaged areas and those involving 'multi-purpose' open spaces. Grants range between £10,000 and £15,000 and can be over five years. Regional advisers can help to develop projects and advise on partnership working. At the time of writing no details of awards were available.

Applications:

Barnardo's and the Children's Play Council Better Play scheme is closed until April 2002. For further information, guidance and an application pack, contact: 0845 0000 121; website: www.barnardos.org.uk

BTCV People's Places scheme is an open application process running over five years. Applicants should contact BTCV to register an interest and submit their

Strengthening your application

- Allow plenty of time for the planning the project and filling in the application form.
- Prepare a business plan, whatever the scale of the activity.
- Management of the project is vital. Develop a simple management structure to explain who will do it.
- Explain the project clearly without jargon. Don't assume the assessing officer will know anything about your area and its needs.
- Make sure everyone who needs to be has been consulted. Partnerships are time-consuming and you need to allow time for this.
- Provide evidence to support your proposals.
- Answer all the questions.

proposal for an initial check for eligibility. Where eligible, BTCV will support the application through a mentoring process. It is anticipated that the period of assessment between the two stages will last around six months.

For further information, guidance and an application pack, contact 01491 821 600; website: www.btcv.org

English Nature Wildspace! scheme will run for six years, with all grants to be awarded by 2006. The grants panel will make decisions on awards three times each year. Application packs are available by contacting 01733 455415; website: www.english-nature.org.uk

The Countryside Agency Doorstep Greens scheme has a two stage application process. Stage 1 must be received and checked before applicants can move to stage 2. There is no deadline for applications.

Application packs are available by contacting 0845 000121; website: www.countryside.gov.uk

Applicants can apply to more than one award partner scheme at any time.

SPORT

Sport England Lottery Fund

Sport England Lottery Fund,
Community Projects Capital Fund,
PO Box 649, London WC1H 0QP
Tel: Lottery Line: 0845 7649 649
Website: www.sportengland.org

Sport England is the brand name for the English Sports Council and is a distributor of lottery funding for sport in England. It aims to increase participation in sport, especially amongst young people and also to help with the development of talented performers. It supports local projects under the Community Projects Fund and there is a World Class Fund for élite sports performers.

A total of around £200 million a year will be available from 2002, of which the Community Projects Fund (CPF) will total £150 million. This fund supports the building of new sports facilities, improving existing facilities and buying sports equipment. Funds are now also available for applicants before they have to incur design costs in the development of facilities.

The CPF has three main elements:
- Awards for All (A4A)
- Community Projects Capital Fund
- Community Revenue Programme.

Awards for All (A4A)

Small projects awards (grants of between £500 and £5,000) are given to schools and voluntary groups. awards are given towards new activities to help with the capital and revenue costs of a project. Priority is given to areas of deprivation, schools, disabled people, women and girls, people on low incomes and ethnic minority groups. Funding is allocated to regions according to population and relative economic deprivation. Decisions are made locally and are distributed by Awards for All. (See above.) This is a good place to start for groups looking to develop sports activities and for gaining confidence in applying for lottery funds. (See page 68)

Community Projects Capital Fund

Capital awards of over £5,000 are available to support 'community provision for all' which is aimed at increasing participation in sport. Up to 65% of the total capital project cost may be applied for, although school projects

Recent sports grants to voluntary youth organisations

- £1,550 to Banktop Youth Forum, Blackburn for equipment and kit to establish a football team to take part in a local league;
- £4,930 to Croyland Youth Centre, Enfield for a ballcourt goal unit;
- £4,044 to Crewe and District Youth Centre for equipment and coaching fees to develop table tennis;
- £5,000 to Brick Lane Youth Development, Tower Hamlets for sports activities for those using the club and young women using the drop-in centre;
- £1,100 to Parchmore Church Youth and Community Centre, Croydon to buy and repair sports equipment for those using the youth club;
- £4,282 to West Berkshire Federation of Voluntary Youth Workers for canoe and kayak equipment and training for members;
- £4,125 to Youth Federation for Cheshire, Halton, Warrington and Wirral.

or those in priority areas may apply for up to 80% and 90% respectively.

Priority is given to schemes which benefit young people, women, people form ethnic minority communities and those on low incomes. The Priority Areas Initiative (PAI) is used to focus resources on areas of need. Those eligible for the capital awards may be eligible to apply to the Priority Areas Initiative for further funding for up to 90% of the total project costs. The priority areas are the 20% most deprived areas in England; a list is available from Sport England. The majority of potential beneficiaries of the proposed activity must come from one of these areas for the project to be eligible.

The School Community Sport Initiative (SCSI) covers applications for community sports facilities on school sites. Projects may apply for up to 80% of the total project costs.

Applications under the Community Projects Capital Fund can be considered where:

- the applicant is a bona fide organisation that exists for the public good and community benefit;

- the proposed activity covers a sport recognised by Sport England;
- the project costs more than £5,000;
- the applicant can raise at least 35% matching funds from non-Lottery sources (this is relaxed under the Priority Area Initiative, and School Community Sport Initiative);
- the activity leads to a significant increase in participation or a measurable improvement in sporting standards.

Community revenue programme

Revenue awards of over £5,000 are available to help tackle social exclusion in sport. The programme includes the Active Communities Development Fund and Sport Action Zones as well as school sport co-ordinators and active sports.

Active Communities Development Fund (ACDF)

The ACDF is a further revenue programme which aims to increase participation in four target groups: ethnic communities; people with disabilities; women and girls and people on low incomes. The Sports Lottery Fund has allocated investment to the fund of £7.5 million in 2001/2; £9 million in 2002/2003 and up to £15 million in following years. Projects attracting support from the fund will be innovative, community-led, involving a partnership approach, linking with other funding programmes, strategic and sustainable into the future.

Support is likely to be given for:
- salaries of full, or part-time community sports workers to increase participation;
- development funds usually attached to an outreach worker;
- providing expert advice;
- education and training activities to increase local groups' capacity to provide sporting opportunities.

Further details and an initial bid form are available from Sport England regional offices. The first round of awards from the fund were made in the summer of 2001. Four rounds of awards will be made each year.

Example of an Active Communities Development Fund grant

Kings Cross and Brunswick Neighbourhood Association (KCB) received £127,100 Camden United Football Project which will pay for a sports worker to enable girls and women the Bangladeshi, Somalian and refugee local communities to become involved in sport. There are 120 different languages spoken in the area and before the football project started in 1995 the area had numerous inter-racial tensions.

The football project enable young people from many different cultures to play football together and there was a noticeable decline in racial hostility. After being funded on a hand to mouth basis the ACDF grant will help to make the

project more secure. By adding cricket, basketball, tennis and Kabadi to the football programme 800 more people will participate in the sports programme. The KCB project worker stated: 'This project will work with members of all the communities and engage them with the planning, programming and publicising of the sports activities. We will show them the positive role that sport can play within society. We aim to use sport as a tool to offer advice and training on health, education, citizenship, drugs , housing, crime and employment.'

The total cost of the project is around £206,600. Non-Lottery support has been given by Camden Youth Service, Kings Cross Partnership, local mosques and schools, local tenants' associations Metropolitan Police, and the SRB board.

Sports Action Zones

There are also 12 Sports Action Zones which have been identified as areas of need. These will increase to 30 by July 2002 following the submission of bids in September 2001. Details of the zones are available from Sport England. There are a range of opportunities attached to the zones, and contact should be made with the zone manager for further details of local provision.

Applications:

Awards for All
Application forms are available from the website www.awardsforall.org.uk or by telephoning 0845 600 2040. (See page 70 for details.)

Community Capital and Revenue Programmes
An information pack containing application forms and the list of priority areas is available by contacting the Lottery Line on:0845 7649 649. Pre-application advice is available by

completing the Intent Form (contained in the information pack) and sending it to Sport England Lottery Fund, FREEPOST Sport England. Consultation forms are also provided to be sent to organisations that know your sport or your area. These are then returned to Sport England by the organisations and should provide supporting evidence for your project. Advice and help with applications is also available by contacting the Lottery Line: 0845 7649 649. Completed applications should be sent to the PO Box 649 address above.

The Active Communities Development Fund An Initial Bid form, together with further details of the fund are available from the regional Sport England regional offices:

East
Tel: 01234 345222 **Fax:** 01234 359046

East Midlands
Tel: 0115 982 1887 **Fax:** 0115 945 5236

London
Tel: 020 8778 8600 **Fax:** 020 8676 9812

North East
Tel: 0191 384 9595 **Fax:** 0191 384 5807

North West
Tel: 0161 834 0338 **Fax:** 0161 835 3678

South East
Tel: 0118 948 3311 **Fax:** 0118 947 5935

South West
Tel: 01460 73491 **Fax:** 01460 77263

West Midlands
Tel: 0121 456 3444 **Fax:** 0121 456 1583

Yorkshire
Tel: 0113 243 6443 **Fax:** 0113 242 2189

The Community Fund, however, is about to change the elaborate application and assessment system that the sector has become familiar with in the last decade. From January 2004 in Scotland, and probably from later in 2004 in the rest of the UK, that whole system is being scrapped for almost its exact opposite! There will be a very short outline proposal to start with, followed by a chance to work out a full application in co-operation with Community Fund staff. This application will concentrate on just two criteria (neither of them numerically scored): How far do the promised outcomes of your project meet the Community Funds priority of meeting the needs of those at greatest disadvantage in society? And what is the likelihood of your achieving them?

In the longer term, Community Fund grants may also be affected by their enforced merger with the New Opportunities Fund, but the continuation of existing funding streams is being guaranteed for some time into the future, so any such changes will only be long term.

7 RAISING MONEY FROM GRANT-MAKING TRUSTS

One of the main sources of support for work with young people is that given by grant-making trusts. Not so long ago trust money would be a fairly exotic flower in the youth funding greenhouse. Now it is a central source of income, looked at and tapped into by the majority of those working with young people. To get the most from your links with trusts and to improve your applications you need to know how the trust world works and what trusts are looking to give money for.

This chapter gives a listing of trusts interested in supporting young people, often with significant grants. The list is not definitive, as there are too many to detail in this book. There are many potential supporters of young people among grant-making trusts, and many will be interested in your work even if they have no stated preference for supporting youth organisations. This chapter looks at how you can strengthen your approach and how to make the most of the wide variety of grant-making trust resources that are available. It should be read along with Chapter 4 on Writing a good fundraising application.

HOW ARE TRUSTS RUN?

Trustees
The key players in the trust game are the trustees. They are responsible for running the trust and, crucially, making the grant decisions. They meet every month, every three months, once a year or whenever there are enough applications to make it worthwhile – it depends on the trust.

Staff
Most of the larger trusts have paid staff to administer the trust. They may have a full or part-time Secretary, Clerk or Director (the name varies). These people are not trustees, so they do not make grant decisions. However, they receive all correspondence, may visit applicants or request more information, and make recommendations to trustees about whether a project is good or not. However, the trustees always have the final say on what is and is not supported.

Policies
Most larger trusts will have grant-making policies. These will say what kinds of activity they support (for example environmental charities, projects for ethnic

minorities), where they support them (for example throughout the UK, only in Merseyside, or within five miles of the town hall), what kinds of grants they like to give (capital or revenue) and what they will definitely not support. Trusts with such policies almost never give grants outside their stated policy. If you do not fit the criteria, do not apply.

Written applications

Most trusts receive written applications; sometimes by a form, often by letter. On the basis of these applications they decide who they will give a grant to and for how much. Some trusts, however, do not consider any applications at all, rather they go out and find the projects they want to support. There is nothing wrong with this. However, when a trust states that it does not respond to applications or that it only supports projects known to the trustees, unless you have a personal contact with one of the trustees, leave the trust alone.

Most grant-making trusts are swamped with applications. They could easily give their money four or five times over on the basis of applications they already receive. This does not mean that you should not apply, but rather that you will have to put time and effort into making a good application to an appropriate trust. So how do you decide who to apply to and how do you go about it?

WHAT KIND OF GRANTS DO TRUSTS GIVE?

Cash

Most trusts simply make cash donations. These vary in size depending on the annual income of the trust. However, most grants from national trusts will be in the £500 to £10,000 range, although some give up to £1 million. In the listing of trusts at the end of the chapter, examples of grants given to youth organisations by trusts range from £200,000 to the headquarters of a mainstream youth organisation down to £200 for equipment for a very local group. Small local trusts may give as little as £10.

Short-term/pump priming

Most grants are given for one to three years. A handful of enlightened trusts may venture beyond the three year watershed and invest significantly in an organisation over a longer period. Trusts do not see their role as paying for core services for a long period of time; rather, they like to kick start new and exciting projects into life and then expect someone else to take on the long-term funding. Once you have come to the end of your trust grant, it will rarely give more money for the same thing. However, you can go back for funding for a different project. Therefore, unless you are new or very small, do not ask trusts to support your organisation as a whole, rather ask them to support a particular piece of work or meet a specific need.

Revenue and capital

Trusts will give grants both for revenue (salaries, rent, rates etc.) and for capital (such as building and equipment costs). Some will consider funding the core costs for an organisation, others will look for a clear project outline to support. If you are applying for revenue costs, try to show how the project will be self-funding once the trust money runs out. If it is for a capital project, show how well the facility will be used and how the running costs will be met.

Innovation/difference

One of the most important parts of any application to a grant-making trust is where you show what is new about your proposed project. What makes it stand out from the crowd? Is it a brand new project? Are you moving into a new area? Do you have a new approach to a problem? Are you reaching a new group (for example, homeless young people at risk, or those truanting from school)? Are you using new ways to solve old problems (for example, using sport or the arts to empower young people with few skills, or using peer group education to teach about health)? Are you giving disadvantaged people new skills (for example, encouraging local people from deprived communities to take part in youth leader training)? Do your activities break down barriers in communities in new ways (for example, organising sports events to bring divided communities together)?

Not statutory

Grant-making trusts will not fund things that they see as the responsibility of the state (i.e. that central or local government should be funding). Just because the state is cutting back on its commitments, it does not mean that trusts will automatically step in. Trust funding is certainly not a substitute for lost local authority funding.

WHICH TRUSTS GIVE MONEY TO WORK WITH YOUNG PEOPLE?

A large number. Trusts may respond to your application if your activities are educational, have social welfare objectives, or just because you work with children and young people and they want to support that. It might also be that you are within a geographical area of interest, such as a town, county, region or even parish. Even if they do not have a stated priority to give to young people's activities, your work may still be eligible. A number of trusts have 'General charitable purposes' as a broad description of their grant-giving. Your project will fit here as well as any other, unless they have drawn up a list of beneficiaries which remains unchanged from one year to the next. Where a trust gives to support education, you may be eligible if you work with, say, those who have been excluded from school or you have an innovative approach to vocational training. Similarly, where a trust is concerned with the environment, your young people's project to create urban green areas may fit snugly with their stated interests.

The best known trusts receive the most applications. It is also the case that the large national trusts have the most money, unless you are very fortunate to live and work in the area where a very large local trust operates. Generally, it pays to find local trusts first to apply to, as these will have geographical limitations on the number of organisations that they can help.

A great deal of local giving is done on a friendship basis where trustees give to projects they know and like. Sometimes they give to the same organisations year in year out. If so, try to work your way onto their list. You should make a real effort to get to know local trustees personally. At least you can send them regular information.

You can find out about local trusts by:
- Word of mouth. Ask around your management committee, leaders, parents or neighbouring groups. Where someone has been successful with a local trust, build on their experience.
- Your local or regional association headquarters if you have one may have details of trusts in the area.
- A local Council for Voluntary Service. The address of the nearest will be in the telephone book.
- Local directories of trusts. These are produced locally by Councils for Voluntary Service and nationally by the Directory of Social Change (see Useful addresses and sources of information).
- The local press. Some trusts advertise their applications procedures and closing dates through local papers or community networks. Donations to local organisations may be covered in news stories.

In recent years some areas have started large local trusts from scratch. These community trusts/foundations raise money from industry and other grant-giving bodies to then distribute in the local area. Children and young people will be a natural area of interest, and you should let them know what you are doing, and find out how they can support you. In some areas community foundations have also become more prominent as the local body responsible for part of the Children's Fund distributions. (For further details, see Chapter 10.)

National trusts

Where there is no local trust that works in your area you will have to throw your funding net wider to include national trusts. These usually have more money but are the most heavily applied to. They also tend to be narrower in

The ten largest trust givers to young people's work

The following trusts and foundations have stated an interest in supporting work with children and young people. Their priorities differ greatly within this field. All have entries included in the listing at the end of chapter. Some have specified a grant amount for children and youth or youth; with others, we have estimated a figure. For those trusts that have specified their grant total for children and youth, some will include their support of individuals as well as organisations.

	Grant total	Grants to children & youth or youth	Year
1 BBC Children in Need	£20,000,000	£20,000,000	1998/1999
2 Comic Relief	£7,800,000 (UK)	£4,000,000	1999/2000
3 The Prince's Trust	£5,000,000	£5,000,000	1999/2000
4 Henry Smith's Charity	£23,780,000	£2,290,000	2000
5 John Lyon's Charity	£2,082,000	£2,082,000	2000/2001
6 Rank Foundation	£7,400,000	£2,000,000	2000
7 Help a London Child	£881,000	£881,000	2000
8 Church Urban Fund	£3,400,000	£872,000	1999/2000
9 Tudor Trust	£26,000,000	£841,000	1995/1996
10 Garfield Weston Foundation	£30,000,000	£350,000	1999/2000

their focus. Circular letters to them almost always fail; carefully targeted applications to relevant trusts have a much greater chance of success.

WHO TO APPLY TO AND HOW TO DO IT

The crucial question in deciding whether or not to apply to a trust is: 'What do we and the trust have in common?' What you want to do must meet with what the trust is seeking to fund. This may be in terms of geography, where you and a local trust operate in the same area. There may be a particular target group (for example young people, older people, those with disabilities, or disadvantaged people) who you want to involve in your activity and the trust wants to help. The activity itself may be an area where the foundation has a long-standing interest (such as increasing the leadership skills of young people). As in most fundraising, the motto with charitable trusts might be: 'Only connect'.

With this is mind, you should do the following:

- *Read Chapter 4 on Writing a good fundraising application.* The six key elements of an application are all highly relevant to trusts. It helps to be clear about all the information you need to put in before you start your serious planning.

- *Devise one or a series of projects that you need money for.* Unless you are very new or very small, it is unlikely that a trust will support your entire organisation. Rather they will want to support a particular piece of work that fits in with their specific interest. Hence the emphasis on projects. Also, make sure you can show them how your project fits into their grant-making policies.
- *Work out what is new about this work.* Trusts are not interested in picking up the tab to meet existing costs; they want to see something new about a project. Does it give new opportunities to needy young people? Does it try to solve a long-standing problem in a new and exciting way? Is it developing a new service in that town, village etc? If there's nothing new about the project, your chances of raising significant trust monies are remote.
- *Decide how the project can be funded in the long term.* Trusts generally only give grants for up to three years, but they like to see long-term benefits. You will need to persuade them that you can pay for the work once their funding has run out.
- *Maximise the impact of your personal contacts.* Ask around your organisation, your management committee, staff, members, members' families, supporters, anyone! Does anyone know any charity trustee or trust administrator personally? If so, get them to make contact with the trust and see how the land lies. Personal applications are always the best!
- *Look through the guide books, this one and others.* There are various trust directories to look at and the local CVS will have details of them. DSC publishes an extensive range.
- *Get hold of the guidelines published by the trusts themselves.* Read them carefully and address the points they raise in your application. For example, if the guidelines ask how the project will be evaluated, you need to give them a clear idea.
- *Where the trust has paid administrators, you can ring them to discuss your application* (for example, would it be eligible, do you have to be a registered charity, when would it be considered, do you need to fill out an application form?). Most of the larger trusts are prepared to have a preliminary chat over the phone. However, if you get the impression that they don't want to talk, don't push it.
- *Write to the trusts you have identified.* The letter should not be more than two sides of A4. In this letter you should state clearly:
  - who you are
  - what you do
  - why it is important
  - what you need
  - what it will achieve
  - where you will get the money from.

You should also send a budget for the particular project, a set of accounts for the organisation as a whole, an annual report and maybe one or two other documents to support your application.

The above is the most basic strategy. The following should help you stand out from the crowd.

Evaluation

Evaluation and monitoring are here to stay. Some trusts ask for nothing from an organisation following a grant being given. A large number of the major foundations ask for a narrative report and some ask for detailed analysis of the project and the difference it has made. A handful may have monitoring requirements that look similar to those of the European Social Fund. Applicants should take this into account. You may find yourself expending considerable time and effort in securing a grant, and then expending further energy in extensive monitoring requirements for what it is a relatively small sum of money. A condition of one grant scheme which awarded £2,700 to a project was the completion of 20 pages of monitoring information.

- *Build contacts.* You will probably be able to identify 10 or 15 key trusts who you have a good chance of getting support from, maybe now or maybe in the future. If you can, warm them up by sending some information before you actually write to them for money. This could be your annual report, some press coverage or a newsletter. The main purposes are: (a) to show yourselves in a positive light; (b) to try and get your name known before you write for money, and (c) to show that you are committed to a longer-term relationship with the trust. Many trusts complain that the only time they hear from people is when they want money. They actually like to know how things are going. From time to time some of the major trusts may seek out projects to support. If they already know about you, you will feature more prominently on their grant-making radar.

  Supporting material does not need to be fat and glossy. Most trusts are run by busy people with little time to wade through long project descriptions. A letter saying: 'In May, 2001, you supported us with ..., and we are now able to report that ...' is all you need. Remember, this is not an appeal letter; you are not asking for money. Be brief, upbeat and informative. Practice writing your update on a postcard to keep the length down. Send the trust this kind of information once or twice a year. If you don't know trust people personally, this is the next best thing.

> ## Tips for applying to a grant-making trust
>
> One national grant-making foundation gives the following guidance to those applying for grants:
>
> 'In making your application it is important to realise that yours is one of many competing for limited resources. It is helpful to us if your application is:
> - Clear, concise and to the point – say what you do or propose to do, how much it will cost and how it will impact on your clients.
> - Be transparent, open, direct. Do not try to hide what you want funds for in the guise of something else.
> - Be realistic – don't just pick a figure out of the air and work your project/ programme around it.
> - Start with need, justify the need and outline a tangible response to meeting the need that makes sense.
> - We have found that projects are very strong in telling us about their aims and objectives, but weak in telling us what they do and how it impacts on young people and children.'

- *If the project is new or unknown to the trust*, get well-known sponsors or supporters to say how well-run the project is and how much needed it is. This helps create a bridge between you and the trust.
- *Offer to visit the trust to explain your work*, or better still try to get them to come and see you. Put them on your VIP list for events you may be running. They probably will not come, but they might. If they do, you will be half way to getting a grant so long as you take time to show them round, introduce the kind of people they want to meet and generally get them enthusiastic about what you are doing. Most organisations put all their energy into writing the application. Some energy could also be put into meeting face to face with grant-making trust personnel.
- When you do get a grant, remember this is the beginning of the relationship not the end. Keep them informed of how things are going (they will probably ask for information anyway). Always try to be positive and upbeat. If you get one grant and spend it well, you have got a good chance of getting another grant for something different later on.

Presenting your case

For foundations without application forms, you need to present your case clearly in an application letter of no more than two sides of A4. In many cases it is all the trust has to go on to make a decision. One significant supporter of work with young people suggests: 'Tell the story simply; who you are; what you are going to do, how you are going to do it; who's going to do it; what difference it will make is vital for us; and how much it will cost. Documents such as annual reports, a recent set of audited accounts, and details of other funding that has been raised should be attached, but this is supporting material. Do not rely on it. The star of the show needs to be the case you make in the letter. Pass the letter to someone who doesn't know your organisation. If they still don't know what you do by the end of the letter, you've written the wrong letter.'

Some dos and don'ts when writing to trusts

Do

- Plan a strategy
- Plan ahead
- Select a good project
- Believe in what you are doing
- Select a target
- Write an application tailored to the needs of the trust you are approaching
- Use personal contact
- Prepare a realistic and accurate budget for the project
- Be concise
- Be specific
- Establish your credibility
- Keep records of everything you do
- Send reports to keep trusts informed
- Try to develop a partnership or long-term relationship
- Say thank you

Don't

- Send a duplicated mail shot
- Ask for unrealistic amounts
- Assume trusts will immediately understand the need you are meeting
- Make general appeals for running costs
- Use jargon
- Beg

GRANT-MAKING TRUSTS SUPPORTING ORGANISATIONS WORKING WITH YOUNG PEOPLE

The following list of 90 foundations includes large grant-making trusts that have made young people a priority in their grant distribution. As stated at the beginning of the chapter, a large number of general trusts could have been included. For instance, the Northern Rock Foundation is a large giver to a number of different areas of the voluntary sector mainly in North East England as well as Scotland, Cumbria, Yorkshire and the north west of England, but as it does not have a specific youth focus it is not detailed here. (Guidelines are available from: 0191 284 8412; website: www.nr-foundation.org.uk) Similarly, the Lloyds TSB Foundation for England and Wales is a large national giver but without a priority for youth projects. Grants for organisations working with young people may be available under other parts of its general programmes for the voluntary sector. (Information is available from: 020 7204 5276; website: www.lloydstsbfoundations.org.uk)

The list details those trusts that each year give £20,000 or over to organisations working with young people and who have a national, or significant regional or local presence. Inevitably, a large number of the local trusts are based in London, but there are also local foundations operating in other parts of the country.

One community foundation – the Community Foundation serving Tyne and Wear and Northumberland – has been included, largely because of its interesting work in developing grant-making by young people through the YouthBank initiative. However, all community foundations will be open to applications from organisations working with young people in the local area; some will make them a priority in their grant-giving. They also play a central role in distributing part of the Children's Fund. (See Chapter 10 for further details.) Community foundations now cover around 70% of England. Details of your nearest community foundation can be obtained from the Community Foundations Network 020 7422 8611; www.community foundations.org.uk; or through your local council for voluntary service.

29th May 1961 Charitable Trust

Social welfare, general, with an interest in the Midlands, London and the South of England

c/o Macfarlanes, 10 Norwich Street, London EC4A 1BD
Tel: 020 7831 9222 **Fax:** 020 7831 9607
Correspondent: The Secretary

Income: £3.5 million (1999/2000)
Grant total: £3.1 million (1999/2000)
Grants to youth: Est. over £150,000 (1999/2000)

The trust makes over 300 grants a year, mostly between £1,000 and £5,000 although they can be up to hundreds of thousands of pounds. Grants are mainly given to both national and local organisations working in the Midlands, London and the south of England. In 1999/2000 only £10,000 in total was given to the north of England. Most grants are repeated from year to year, with perhaps less than 20% of the grant total available for reallocation in a given year.

The trust has six categories of giving, including: 'Art, leisure and youth projects'. Grants totalling £917,000 were made in this category in 1999/2000, including one of the largest: £100,000 to the Federation of London Youth Clubs. Other awards included £55,000 in two grants to the Warwickshire Association of Boys' Clubs: £10,000 each to Raleigh International and St Chad's Children's and Young People's Activities; £7,500 to Avenues Youth Project and £7,000 each to Coventry Boys' Club, the National Federation of Young Farmers Clubs and Outward Bound Trust. Other grants included £5,000 to Warwickshire Scout Council and Youth Clubs UK; £3,000 each to Northamptonshire Association of

Youth Clubs and Streetwise Youth; and £2,500 to Duke of Edinburgh's Award.

Grants are only given to registered charities, and no grants are given to individuals.

Applications: To the secretary in writing enclosing a copy of the most recent accounts. Trustees meet in February, May, August and November.

Adint Charitable Trust

Children, medical and health, with some preference for London

BDO Stoy Hayward, 8 Baker Street, London W1M 1DA
Tel: 020 7486 5888
Correspondent: D R Oram, Trustee

Income: £351,000 (1998/99)
Grant total: £279,000 (1998/99)
Grants to youth: About £100,000

A large proportion of grants made by this trust either go to organisations working in the London area or to UK organisations based there. Grants range from a few hundred pounds to tens of thousands. Several organisations have received payments for a number of years.

Beneficiaries have included: Children's Centre Fund (£18,000); Croydon YMCA (£10,000); Surrey Association of Youth Clubs (£2,500) and Whizz Kidz (£500).

Grants can be made to registered charities only and in no circumstances to individuals.

Applications: To the correspondent, in writing only. There is no particular form in which applications are required; each applicant should make its own case in the way it considers best. The trust states that they cannot enter into correspondence.

The Lord Austin Trust

Social welfare

c/o Martineau Johnson, St Phillip's House, St Phillip's Place, Birmingham B3 2PP
Tel: 0121 200 3300
Correspondent: David L Turfrey and Miss Lucy Chatt

Income: £180,000 (1999/2000)
Grant total: £148,000 (1999/2000)
Grants to youth: £51,000 (1999/2000)

One of the trust's main areas of giving is to organisations concerned with the 'care, maintenance, education and upbringing of poor children'. It listed grants to 'young people' as totalling £51,000 in its accounts. No further information on the size of grants or the number of beneficiaries was available.

Applications: In writing to the joint correspondents, D L Turfrey and Miss Lucy Chatt. The trustees meet twice a year to consider grants.

The Philip Barker Charity

General in Cheshire

1a Rothesay Road, Curzon Park, Chester CH4 8AJ
Correspondent: Mrs M G Mather

Income: £87,000 (1999/2000)
Grant total: £96,000 (1999/2000)
Grants to youth: £43,000 to young people's charitable work (1999/2000)

The trust was set up in 1990. It has recently decided to increase its focus on local charities, whilst also supporting individual young people undertaking 'adventurous gap year activities' with recognised UK charities, such as the Project Trust and Raleigh International.

A grants list was not included with the trust's accounts for 1999/2000, so it is not clear what type of young people's charitable activities were supported. Previous grants have included £6,000 to Scout Association (Huntington) to re-roof its hut.

In the case of individual grants, awards are only made to individuals sponsored by registered charities.

Applications: In writing to the correspondent.

The BBC Children in Need Appeal

Welfare of disadvantaged children

PO Box 76, London W3 6FS
Tel: 020 8576 7788 **Fax:** 020 8576 8887
E-mail: pudsey@bbc.co.uk
Website: www.bbc.co.uk/cin/
Correspondent: Martina Milburn, Director

Income: £20 million (1998/99)
Grant total: £20 million (1998/99)
Grants to youth: Est. over £600,000

This charity was set up by the BBC to distribute the proceeds of its annual appeal of the same name. (At the time of writing it had raised £12,895,900 on the day of the 2001 appeal.) It aims to make a positive difference to the lives of disadvantaged children and young people (aged 18 and under) throughout the UK. Grants start from a few hundred pounds, and can sometimes go up to £75,000 or more.

The four main categories of children being helped are:
- Children living in poverty and deprivation, for whom life is a struggle; with many spending their childhood in run-down homes, in drab and hopeless

environments. Some children experience temporary homelessness. (Grant total: £8.7 million)

- Children suffering from illness, distress, abuse or neglect. Many of these children are 'invisible'. They may be confined to home or hospital through illness; they may be in care; or they may have become quiet and withdrawn through grief, neglect or abuse. (Grant total £4.9 million)
- Children with mental or physical disabilities. Children with disabilities need extra help to join in with chosen activities. Some are profoundly disabled from birth or from an accident and are totally dependent on constant care from others. (Grant total £4.5 million)
- Children with behavioural and psychological disorders. These children are often labelled 'difficult'. Their behaviour makes it difficult to fit in, and they are often rejected and desperately unhappy. (Grant total: £0.7 million)

The charity welcomes applications from properly constituted not for profit groups. These include: self help groups, voluntary organisations and registered charities. Salary and revenue grants are for up to three years but rarely for amounts over £25,000. For the following, only one year grants are given:

- capital projects
- seasonal projects e.g. holiday playschemes
- holidays and outings
- equipment and welfare funds.

Organisations may hold only one grant at a time from the BBC Children in Need Appeal.

The trust makes an annual grant of £500,000 for the Family Welfare

Association, to provide emergency grants for individual children in need. In 1998/99 there were 40 other large grants of over £70,000 up to £122,000. These included:

- £95,000 over three years to Tullochan, for the part running costs, including salaries, of a project organising weekly activities for 10 to 12 year olds;
- £80,000 over three years to Artillery Youth Centre for the salary and ongoing costs of a senior youth worker;
- £77,000 over three years to YMCA Mountain Ash for a project worker, sessional support, and running costs;
- £74,000 over three years to Govanill Youth Project for the salary and ongoing costs of a full-time worker and sessional staff;
- £72,000 over three years to Dash Ogwr for the salary of a young people's worker plus running costs;
- £72,000 over three years to Shaftesbury Society, for the salary and ongoing costs of a community development worker to work with 9 to 13 year olds living on three estates in Bradford;
- £72,000 over three years to Getaway Girls, for the part-time salaries of two youth workers, one working with Asian girls and one with African Caribbean girls.

Medium-sized grants included:

- £2,800 to Aiming High Project for the costs of an activity programme for young ethnic women;
- £2,700 to Queens Park Bangladesh Association for a weekly youth worker for a youth development project;
- £2,600 to Dolphin Youth Group for the hiring and operating costs of tail lift ambulances.

Small grants included:

- £300 to Seymour Hill Youth Club for buying new equipment for children under 16.

The appeal does not consider applications from private individuals or the friends or families of individual children. In addition, grants will *not* be given for:

- trips and projects abroad
- medical treatment or medical research
- unspecified expenditure
- deficit funding or repayment of loans
- projects which take place before applications can be processed (this takes up to five months from the closing dates)
- projects which are unable to start within 12 months
- distribution to another/other organisation(s)
- general appeals and endowment funds
- the relief of statutory responsibilities.

Applications: Comprehensive application forms and guidelines are available from the address above and on the website. There are two closing dates for applications: 30 November and 30 March. Organisations may submit only one application and may apply to only one of these dates. Applicants should allow up to five months after each closing date for notification of a decision. (For summer projects applications must be submitted by the November closing date or they will be rejected because they cannot be processed in time.)

The Bedford Charity

Education, welfare and recreation in Bedford and its neighbourhood

Princetown Court, Pilgrim Centre, Brickhill Drive, Bedford MK41 7PZ
Tel: 01234 369500 **Fax:** 01234 369505
E-mail: grants@harpur-trust.org.uk
Correspondent: Tony Bickerstaffe, Chief Executive

Grant total: £418,000 to organisations (2000/01)
Grants to youth: £46,000 (2000/01)

The trust makes around 80 grants a year, averaging about £5,000 each, in Bedford and its neighbourhood. Generally around £100,000 a year is set aside for a substantial contribution to a 'major project' with a value of £500,000 or more.

In 2000/01 beneficiaries included: Youth Action Bedfordshire for a co-ordinator's salary, and Bedford Sea Cadets towards the refurbishment of their centre.

No grants are given to organisations or individuals outside the borough of Bedford, unless the organisation supports a significant proportion of residents of the borough.

Applications: On a form available from the correspondent.

Benham Charitable Settlement

General, with an interest in Northamptonshire

Hurstbourne, Portnall Drive, Virginia Water, Surrey GU25 4NR
Correspondent: Mrs M Tittle, Managing Trustee

Income: £158,000 (1999/2000)
Grant total: £163,000 (1999/2000)

The trust's policy is to make a substantial number of relatively small grants to registered charities working in many different fields – including charities working with children and young people.

The trust has been particularly supportive of a major local youth organisation, the Northamptonshire Association of Youth Clubs. The trust's 2000/01 annual report stated: 'In recent years the settlement has made a series of substantial donations, exceeding £1.6 million, to the Northamptonshire Association of Youth Clubs'. In 2000/01 the award to this organisation was £35,000.

Five other organisations received grants of over £1,000 in the year, totalling £31,000. Youth organisations to benefit from smaller grants included: Kettering District Scout Council (£500); Sea Cadets (£400); and Northampton St Albans Scout Group (£350).

No grants are given to individuals.

Applications: In writing to the correspondent. The trust regrets that it cannot send replies to all applicants, nor will they accept telephone calls. It states: 'Applications will be dealt with promptly at any time of year, but no charity will be considered more than once each year (repeated applications are automatically ignored for twelve months).'

Percy Bilton Charity

Disabled, young or older people

58 Uxbridge Road, London W5 2TL
Tel: 020 8579 2829 **Fax:** 020 8567 5459
Correspondent: Mrs Wendy Fuller, Administrator

Income: £636,000 (2000/01)
Grant total: £616,000 to organisations (2000/01)
Grant to youth: £193,000 to youth welfare causes and youth groups (2000/01)

Grants are made to organisations working with disabled people, youth and older people and range from £2,000 up to a usual maximum of £20,000; generally awards are for less than £5,000.

In the area of youth work, grants can be made:

- to provide assistance to alleviate the problems facing young people who are educationally or socially underprivileged, disadvantaged or marginalised
- to encourage young people into education, training and employment away from crime, substance and alcohol dependence, unemployment and educational deprivation
- to provide facilities for recreational activities and outdoor pursuits for young people who are underprivileged or disadvantaged.

Grants are normally only for building projects or for items of capital expenditure. Larger grants in 2000/01 included:

- £10,000 to Highbury Vale-Blackstock Trust in London towards refurbishing a building and providing services including a youth club;
- £3,000 to 198 Gallery in London towards a computer training

programme for 16 to 18 year olds from ethnic minority backgrounds;

- £2,200 to Abingdon Motorcycle Project, Oxfordshire, towards protective clothing for motorcycle maintenance and riding sessions for young people aged 13 to 17 years who are at risk of offending or exclusion from school.

Smaller grants included a number of youth organisations:

- Acorn Centre Youth Project in Edinburgh received £500 towards programme development materials;
- four scout groups received grants of £300 to £460 each, towards camping equipment, tents, chairs and a metal storage container;
- £420 to Youth Point in Leeds towards posters;
- Alliance Youth Works in Northern Ireland received £400 towards play equipment;
- Beechfield Youth Club in North Devon received £300 towards board games and sports equipment.

The charity will *not* consider:

- donations for general funding/circular appeals;
- the arts (theatre, dance groups, etc.);
- running expenses (for the whole organisation or for projects);
- salaries or office equipment/furniture;
- minibuses and motor vehicles;
- playschemes/summer schemes;
- holidays/residentials or expeditions for individuals or groups;
- trips, activities or events;
- centres or village halls predominantly for wider community use;
- community sports/play area facilities;
- pre-schools or playgroups (other than for special needs groups);
- church/church hall refurbishment or repair (including disabled access);
- schools, colleges and universities (other than special schools);
- welfare funds for the distribution of grants to individuals;
- hospital equipment;
- projects which have already been completed;
- research of any kind;
- minor building/conversion works.

Applications: Applications for small grants should be addressed to the Small Grants Committee; all other correspondence should be directed to the charity administrator, as above. Where applicants are uncertain about the eligibility of their appeal, they can contact the charity either in writing, giving a brief outline, or by telephone.

How to apply for main funding
The charity does not provide application forms. Applicants should include the following in their appeal:

1 A brief history and outline of the charity.
2 A description of the project and its principal aims.
3 Details of funding: i) For equipment appeals, provide a list of items required with costs. ii) Provide a budget for the project, including details of funds already raised and other sources being approached. iii) State cost or costs involved for building/refurbishment projects – itemise major items and professional fees (if any).
4 Submit building or other plans. Does the project have all relevant planning consents?
5 Dates when construction/refurbishment is to commence and be completed.

6 State whether the project has ongoing revenue funding.

7 Plans for monitoring and evaluating the project.

8 Enclose a copy of the latest annual report and accounts.

In the case of major building/refurbishment appeals, applicants are asked to apply after 75% of the funding has been secured, as offers are conditional upon the balance being raised within one year.

The trust requires grants to be taken up within 12 months of the offer.

For a small grant (£500 or less) applicants should supply the following:

1 Brief details of the organisation.

2 Outline of the project and its principal aims.

3 Cost of the item/s required. Reference from one youth organisation that you work with, or a Voluntary Service Council.

4 A copy of the latest accounts.

The board meets quarterly to consider applications, normally in March, June, September and December. It may take up to three months for the application to be considered. Since the charity receives more applications than it can fund, inevitably some will be unsuccessful. However, applicants who are unsuccessful may reapply after 12 months of the initial decision. Where applicants are successful, they should allow at least one year from the date of payment before reapplying. On-site visits or meetings may be required for larger applications. A report must be submitted within one year after the grant is paid describing the activities resulting from the project. If requested, photographs must be supplied free of charge to the charity.

The Sydney Black Charitable Trust Limited

Young people

6 Leopold Road, London SW19 7BD
Tel: 020 8947 1041
Correspondent: M B Pilcher, Secretary

Income: £73,000 (1998/99)
Grant total: £40,000 (1998/99)
Grants to youth: Possibly £40,000 (1998/99)

The trust provides support to youth organisations. The annual report also stated that support is given to religious, medical and other institutions, such as those helping people who are disadvantaged or disabled. Further details of the type of activities the trust supports were not available.

Applications: In writing to the correspondent. This trust is administered together with two other Black charitable trusts.

Isabel Blackman Foundation

General, in Hastings and St Leonards only

13 Laton Road, Hastings, East Sussex TN34 2ES
Tel: 01424 431756
Correspondent: R A Vint, Secretary

Income: Est. £200,000 a year
Grant total: £186,000 (2000/01)
Grants to youth: £4,700 (2000/01)

Set up in 1966, the trust has several aims, including the support of youth organisations. The trust looks to help those who can demonstrate they are also helping themselves. Five grants were made under the heading 'Youth clubs and organisations' in 2000/01, although the amounts given in each category appear to vary each year. Grants were £2,000 to Hastings and Bexhill Youth Service; £1,000 each to Hastings Sea Cadets and 6th Hastings (Blacklands) Scout Group; £280 to 3rd and 4th Hastings Guides, £250 to Elim Youth Club and £200 to an individual.

Grants are considered only for people and organisations within Hastings and St Leonards.

Applications: In writing to the correspondent. The trustees meet bi-monthly to consider applications.

The Booth Charities

Welfare, health, education, in Salford

Midwood Hall, 1 Eccles Old Road, Salford, Manchester M6 7DE
Tel: 0161 736 2989 **Fax:** 0161 737 4775
Correspondent: Mrs L J Needham, Chief Executive

Income: £1.4 million (1999/2000)
Grant total: £1.1 million (1999/2000)

The Booth Charities are a group of at least 10 local trusts supporting disadvantaged people in Salford. Together they provide a wide range of support, including pension payments to individuals, grants to local charities and facilities such as almshouses, day centres and holiday camps for children from poor families.

This entry focuses on Humphrey Booth the Elder's and Grandson's Charities, whose main activity is to maintain and repair the Sacred Trinity Church in Salford, but who also make grants to organisations ranging from

hundreds to tens of thousands of pounds. Most grants appear to be for capital purposes, but revenue funding is also provided, including running costs and salaries and bursaries for health and youth workers. The largest amounts seem to go to projects where the charities' contribution is significant and to some where individual trustees have personal connections.

Part of the charities' main objects are stated as 'giving youth and young children of the city the opportunity to benefit educationally; and from contrasting teamwork experiences not otherwise open to them'. In 1999/2000, beneficiaries included:

- 43rd Salford Scouts to help maintain their premises;
- Salford Boys America Fund to enable inner city boys to participate in an exchange visit;
- Oakwood School Youth Club towards the cost of providing a part-time project worker for young people with physical and learning disabilities.

Applications: In writing to the correspondent.

The Bridge House Estates Trust Fund

Welfare in London

PO Box 270, Guildhall, London EC2P 2EJ
Tel: 020 7332 3710 **Fax:** 020 7332 3720
E-mail: bridgehousetrust@ corpoflondon.gov.uk
Website: www.bridgehousegrants. org.uk
Correspondent: The Chief Grants Officer

Income: £35 million (1999/2000)
Grant total: £15.5 million (2000/01)

The trust concentrates its giving in five broad areas including under the heading 'Children and young people'. The trust says it 'views young people as a major resource, whose potential can be wasted if not nurtured and supported'. In 2000/01, 54 grants totalling £2.9 million were made in this category. In all cases priority is given to projects in areas of deprivation, with the overall aim of improving the lives of people who live in the capital, and especially those who suffer the highest levels of poverty and disadvantage.

Whilst the greatest number of awards are made to organisations working in the inner London boroughs, grants are given to groups in each of the 33 London authority areas and the trust promotes its grant programme in areas receiving the fewest awards. In exceptional cases the trust may fund outside these priority areas.

The trust has also started a pilot small grants programme applicable to all the London boroughs, but on a three year cycle (11 of the boroughs each year). In 2000/01 there were 288 grants, ranging from £500 to £5,000 and totalling £900,000. In 2001/02 a budget of £1 million was allocated to the second phase.

The trust received 489 applications to its main grants programme during 2000/01, and of these, 52% of applications were successful. The average grant was £62,000, compared to the average request of £80,000. Of these grants, 53% were for revenue over two or three years; 21% were for revenue for one year; and 16% were one-off capital donations.

Under the heading of 'Children and young people', the trust states: 'We aim to:

- support children and young people to develop their potential
- encourage the active involvement of young people in society
- support young people in crisis to re-establish their lives positively.'

'We have identified three themes:
i) Preventative work with children and young people (aged 5–16). This includes work with families, individuals and groups, particularly: work preventing homelessness or drug and alcohol misuse; advice, counselling and information services; life skills and personal development projects; work breaking cycles of violence, abuse, crime and mental illness.
ii) Work promoting the active involvement of young people (aged 11–18). We want to encourage work through: enabling young people to realise their potential; encouraging young people to take responsibility; involving young people actively in their communities, including inter-generational work; developing personal and emotional skills, especially in the areas of parenting, lifeskills and relationships.
iii) Young people in crisis (aged 16–21). Applications are welcome from: projects tackling drug and alcohol problems and homelessness; groups supporting young parents, young carers or those with mental health problems; projects offering fresh opportunities to those who are living in poverty or deprivation.'

'We wish to encourage the following principles of good practice:
- the principle of involving young people in the planning and delivery of services

- projects aiming to give young people the opportunity to participate actively in society.'

Grants are given to children and young people under the small grants programme, through, for example: activity programmes; youth work; scouts, guides and other 'uniformed groups'.

Applications addressing the needs of marginalised or disaffected young people are particularly welcome.

Grants made in 2000/01 included those to:

- Voice for the Child in Care, £130,000 towards the salary and support costs of a service helping young people who have run away from home;
- County Scout Council of Greater London South West, £46,000 towards the salary and project costs of developing increased access to scouting;
- Emmanuel Youth Club, £3,600 towards salary costs of a part-time youth worker over 42 weeks;
- 15th Bromley (Bickley & Widmore) Scout Group, £3,500 towards a new heating system;
- West London Sports & Youth promotion, £3,500 to organise and run regular sports events for young people living in deprived housing estates in North Westminster.

The trust *cannot* fund:

- political parties
- political lobbying
- non-charitable activities
- statutory or corporate bodies where the body involved is under a statutory or legal duty to incur the expenditure in question
- grants which do not benefit the inhabitants of Greater London.

The trust *does not* fund:

- individuals
- grant-making bodies to make grants on its behalf
- schools, universities or other educational establishments
- other statutory bodies
- medical or academic research
- churches or other religious bodies where the monies will be used for the construction, maintenance and repair of religious buildings and for other religious buildings and for other religious purposes
- hospitals.

Grants *will not* usually be given to:

- organisations seeking funding to replace cuts by statutory authorities;
- organisations seeking funding to top up on underpriced contracts.

Applications: Applications must be submitted on an application form (which is available from the trust, or can be downloaded from the website) with accompanying documentation. Applications sent by fax or e-mail will not be considered. The form is a substantial eight-page document. It includes a full page summary 'request for funding' which will be copied to trustees. Applications from unincorporated bodies, unless they are registered charities, will not be considered unless a registered charity has agreed to receive and account for any grant that may be awarded.

Applications are considered by the trust fund committee and the form may be included in the papers for a committee meeting. Applicants should ensure that the completed form provides a sufficient summary of what is proposed without the need for any other information to be attached. All applications will be acknowledged. Before the application is considered by the committee it will have been assessed; the assessor may need to visit the applicant organisation. The trust says, 'If you need someone to talk to about your application, please get in touch with the grants unit. We will be happy to discuss it with you'.

The Burton Breweries Charitable Trust

Young people and leader training, in Burton, East Staffordshire and South Derbyshire district (including a small area of north west Leicestershire)

Gretton House, Waterside Court, Third Avenue, Centrum 100, Burton-on-Trent, Staffordshire DE14 2WQ
Tel: 01283 740600 **Fax:** 01283 511899
E-mail: info@burtonbctrust.co.uk
Website: www.burtonbctrust.co.uk
Correspondent: B E Keates, Secretary

Income: £35,000 (1999/2000)
Grant total: £30,000 to organisations and individuals (1999/2000)
Grants to youth: £30,000 to organisations and individuals (1999/2000)

The trust supports organisations and individual young people aged 11 to 25, and also supports individuals of any age participating in youth leadership training. Grants to youth organisations may be made annually, for up to three years, to enable an organisation to achieve a specific objective. Only in exceptional circumstances will a grant exceed £5,000 in any one year. Grants to individuals will not be more than £500.

Awards will *not* be made for the direct benefit of educational establishments financed by the local authority. However, voluntary groups within such establishments, or those using their facilities, may be considered for support. Trustees concentrate on major projects reasoning that most youth organisations should be able to afford minor items out of their own funds, although this does not preclude minor items from being considered. Where the application is for part funding of a project, the trustees will require the organisation to show that the remaining funds can be raised.

In October 2001 the trust's website listed examples of previous grants: £22,000 towards a 17-seater minibus presented to East Staffs Youth Forum; £1,500 to Burton Venture Trust for improvements to climbing equipment; £1,000 to Burton Youth for Christ – Compact 2000 Club; and £500 to Burton-on-Trent Asian Girls'/Women's Activity Group towards recreational activities.

Beneficiaries must be aged between 11 and 25; other age-groups are excluded. Organisations and individuals living or, in full-time education, outside the beneficial area are not supported.

Applications: In writing to the correspondent. The trustees meet in February, June and October, and applications should be submitted in January, May and September. Further information is available on the website.

The Carnegie United Kingdom Trust

Community service, arts, heritage

Comely Park House, Dunfermline, Fife KY12 7EJ
Tel: 01383 721445 **Fax:** 01383 620682
Website: www.carnegieuktrust.org.uk
Correspondent: John Naylor, Secretary and Treasurer

Income: £1.7 million (2000)
Grant total: £1 million (2000)
Grants to youth: £65,000 (June–October 2001)

The trust makes grants between £1,000 to £50,000 for up to three years in a limited number of fields. The trust reviews its grant-making policies every five years to identify new needs as they arise. A new quinquennial policy was launched in April 2001 and is outlined in the Quinquennial Grants Policy Guidelines 2001–2006. The three policy areas are:
- rural community development: village initiatives and village halls;
- creativity and imagination;
- young people: active and constructive participation.

The third policy is the only one of the three which is not new for this quinquennium. The trust states 'The policy is open to registered charities and voluntary organisations but not to statutory bodies or those which are funded predominantly from statutory sources.'

Priority will be given to proposals which:
- have well-structured evaluation built in from the start;
- demonstrate or help to develop standards for active participation (draft

suggested standards are available from the trust);
- build capacity for the longer term by progressive experience and the training of young people and by the development of adult support workers.

'Each proposal should include many of the following characteristics:
- allows young people to exercise personal and social responsibility;
- involves young people in devising and managing the proposed programme;
- improves the relevance and fitness of services available to young people;
- prepares young people for participation in a democracy and a civil society;
- engages young people in their community and wider society;
- provides a creative and educational process which improves social and communication skills;
- exposes other generations to the reality of young people's lives today.'

Grants to young people's organisations in 2001 included those to:
- Article 12 in Scotland (£15,000) to extend the organisation geographically and to help it to become independent;
- Children's Rights Alliance for England (£10,000) for the Young People Translation Unit to translate information about public policy and proposed legislation into accessible high quality young people friendly terms;
- Penumbra (£15,000) – young people's mental health peer education project in Scotland
- Youth Action Cambridge (£15,000) for their young people's executive power project, to engage, train and support young people to take up positions of genuine authority and responsibility with local and countywide decision-making bodies;

- YWCA (£10,000) for their project, Young Women's Voices, to encourage, train and support young women to participate fully in decision-making within the YWCA and the wider community.

Grants are *not* made in response to:
- general appeals
- closed societies
- endowment funds
- debt clearance
- individuals
- replacement of statutory funding.

The following were specifically excluded during the quinquennium, 1996–2000:
- restoration, conversion, repair and purchase of buildings
- formal education – schools, colleges and universities
- sports
- research or publications, conferences and exhibitions (except in special circumstances where trustees wish to initiate certain work)
- community business initiatives
- animal welfare
- medical or related healthcare purposes
- holidays, adventure centres and youth hostels
- residential care, day-care centres and housing
- conciliation and counselling services
- care in the community
- pre-school groups and playschemes
- arts centres, professional arts companies and festivals, including performances and workshops
- pipe organs in churches and other buildings
- environmental matters, including displays and trails
- libraries.

The trust does not usually accept another application from the same organisation within 12 months from the date of the decision in the case of a rejection, or completion in the case of an award.

Applications: Application is usually by letter, except for proposals to the Voluntary Arts – information network, Independent Museums – volunteer development and Village Halls programmes. All applications should be directed to the secretary. Applicants should not approach individual trustees.

All applications need to include the information listed below:
- Brief description of the organisation – its history, work budget, management and staffing.
- Last annual report, audited accounts, the main part of the constitution, charity registration number and committee membership.
- Description of the project including its purpose; time scales incorporating any milestones during the programme; expected outcomes; number of people who will benefit; and how the project will be managed.
- Amount requested from the Carnegie UK Trust.
- Budget for the project, including details of funds already raised and other sources being approached.
- How the work will continue after the trust's grant has been completed – plans for monitoring and evaluating the project: the trust attaches great importance to this.
- How information about the project and associated learning will be shared with others in the field.
- Contact name, address, telephone and fax numbers. These should normally be for the person directly responsible for the work, not the fundraiser.

The application letter should be signed by the senior person responsible, such as the chair or the director. Applications can be submitted at any time, and are acknowledged on receipt.. Deadlines for applications are 30 January for the March trustees' meeting, 30 April for the June meeting and 30 September for the November meeting. The trust aims to inform applicants of trustees' decisions by the end of the month in which the meeting is held. However, the volume of applications received and the need for assessment may mean consideration is delayed.

Early preliminary submissions are particularly welcome so that a comprehensive application can be presented to the trustees. Enquiries about trust policy and a possible application are invited by telephone to the secretary or administrator. Applications within guidelines which are being considered for a grant may be followed up with enquiries for further information and by a visit from a trust representative.

The Chippenham Borough Lands Charity

General in Chippenham

32 Market Place, Chippenham, Wiltshire SN15 3HP
Tel: 01249 658180 **Fax:** 01249 446048
E-mail: cblc@lineone.net
Correspondent: Mrs M Roynon, Administrator

Income: £391,800 (2001)
Grant total: £230,093 (2001)

The objects of the charity are:
- to help people who are elderly, sick, disabled or in need and live in the parish of Chippenham;
- to benefit people living in the parish of Chippenham and its neighbourhood, or any section of those people, through providing or helping to provide facilities for recreation or other leisure-time occupations, where that provision is charitable;
- to promote any other charitable purposes, whether or not covered above, for the benefit of those living in the parish of Chippenham.

In 2001, a total of 183 individuals and 58 organisations were given awards. All schools in Chippenham are well supported by the charity. Organisations working with young people supported included: Wiltshire Youth Theatre (£4,000); Young People's Theatre Group (£2,000); Pewsham Youth Club (£2,000); the Youth Offending Team (£1,000); St Andrews Youth Club (£200) and Chippenham Youth (£250).

Anyone outside Chippenham is *not* supported by the charity.

Applications: In writing to the correspondent.

The Church Burgesses Educational Foundation

Education, youth in the City of Sheffield

c/o Dibb Lupton Alsop, Fountain Precinct, Balm Green, Sheffield S1 1RZ
Tel: 0114 283 3268
Correspondent: Sue Marshall, Charities Administrator

Income: £305,000 (1999)
Grant total: £337,000 (1999)
Grants to youth: Est. £90,000 (1999)

The trust supports 'education (including social and physical training) of persons under 25 who or whose parents are resident in the City of Sheffield and who are in need of financial assistance'.

Beneficiaries included: YMCA (£27,000); Youth Associations South Yorkshire (£8,000); South Yorkshire Clubs for Young People and the local scouts group (£7,000 each); YWCA (£6,000); Sea Cadets (£5,500); YWCA Young Mothers Project (£4,000); Dyslexia Association (£3,000) and the local guides association (£2,000).

Grants were also made to parish-based youth work with 14 grants totalling £30,000, and ranging between £130 and £7,000. Beneficiaries included St Leonard's for a youth worker (£7,000); St John the Baptist, Owlerton (£6,700), Leo's Out of School Club (£3,000); St Hilda's Youth Club (£1,200); St Mark's, Broomhill (£700) and St James' Holiday Club, Woodhouse (£150).

Applications: In writing to the correspondent. Trustees meet four times a year in January, April/May, July/August and October. Applications should be sent in December, March, June and September, for the respective meetings.

The Church Urban Fund

Welfare, Christian development in disadvantaged urban areas in England

1 Millbank, London SW1P 3JZ
Tel: 020 7898 1000 **Fax:** 020 7898 1601
E-mail: enquiries@cuf.org.uk
Website: www.cuf.org.uk
Correspondent: Chief Executive

Income: £2.5 million (2000)
Grant total: £3.4 million (1999)
Grants to youth: £872,000 mostly to young people (2000)

The fund gives grants to community-based projects tackling disadvantage, poverty and marginalisation in Urban Priority Areas (UPAs) throughout England. Its projects fall into seven areas, one of which is youth/children. Grants are normally up to a maximum of £30,000, but most are for less than £10,000.

There are three types of grant: project grants, development grants and small grants.

Project grants
These are made in four grants rounds each year specifically to projects in UPAs with the aim of helping specific communities face their local challenges. Any project with a charitable purpose that is able to raise part of the required money from other sources and is linked to the anglican church may apply for a grant. Grants can be one-off payments covering building expenses or may be paid over several years to cover the salary of a worker. To apply for a grant, contact your diocesan CUF coordinator (through the local diocese). Guidelines for completing the application form are available through the website or by contacting the CUF coordinator through the diocesan offices.

Development grants
The development programme works in partnership with faith communities and statutory and voluntary projects. It supports effective and radical thinking, within the church and outside it, on tackling powerlessness, racial discrimination, physical decay, social disintegration and poverty. To apply for a development fund grant, applicants should read the guidance thoroughly.

Guiding principles:
- Proposals must clearly demonstrate benefits to communities experiencing urban deprivation.
- Proposals should involve partnerships with other agencies. These may be of other faith communities, or statutory or voluntary bodies.
- There should be a strategic dimension which seeks to have an impact on the church and the wider community, alongside a theological dimension which seeks to increase the prophetic impact of the church.
- There should be a clear evaluative element, an intention to produce outcomes that can be models for others, and a process for disseminating insights and experience.
- Proposals should demonstrate the distinctive contribution of faith communities to urban community development and regeneration.

Small grants

The small grants programme has two components: small initiatives and project support. Awards are up to £2,000 and applicants may apply at any time, receiving an answer as soon as the request is processed.

To be eligible for these grants, a project must demonstrate church involvement, be serving an urban priority area and be engaged in urban regeneration. All applications must be made on the appropriate form and submitted via the diocese along with relevant documentation and the recommendation of the diocesan bishop. For more information, contact your diocesan coordinator or the grants unit.

Small initiative grants

Specific work up to a maximum of £2,000. These grants assist communities, particularly the most disadvantaged, that do not feel ready or able to take on full-scale projects but nevertheless want to engage in work on a smaller scale that involves urban regeneration. This could include pilot work to test the need and the community's wish to become involved, or specific short term work such as youth and children's initiatives.

Project support grants

Grants are available for social audit/ architect fees, project development, and project evaluation.

Social audit grants

Stage 1: Social audit. Maximum £2,000. Research into the social need of the area, including consultation with the church and wider community.

Stage 2: Architect study. Maximum £1,500 (or 50 per cent of total costs) towards architect's fees, with evidence of match funding.

Project development grants: maximum £2,000

The involvement of local people and project users is fundamental to CUF's aims. These grants could be used to involve local people in committee structures, project start-ups, ideas generation and the like. Part of the grant may be used to provide childcare facilities during training.

Project evaluation: maximum £500

Grants are available for independent, external evaluations of projects that have been supported by CUF for three years and wish to apply for a continuation of their grant.

Grants to children and young people (2000)

Grants of £24,000 and above were made to 14 organisations and were listed in the accounts. The remaining grants in this category totalled £512,000. The larger grants were:

- £30,000 to Streetlevel Youthworker in Hackney;
- £30,000 to Christ Church Parish Youth Project in Upper Armley;
- £27,000 to M13 Youth Project;
- £27,000 to Clapham Churches Youth Project;
- £27,000 to All Saints Young People's Project.

Of the remaining grants most were to youth projects, for example: Elizabeth's Youth Project, Earlham; Parish Youth Worker, Dogsthorpe; and Warren Park Youth Initiative, Havant.

The following are *not* supported: payments for stipendiary clergy; projects and activities for which full funding is normally available from the church commissioners, dioceses, local authorities, statutory bodies or organisations for the conservation of historical buildings; charitable grants to individuals; direct support of other grant-making institutions; and capital support for voluntary aided schools eligible for statutory funding.

Applications: Check with the fund whether a project falls into one of the supported areas, and request a formal application form. All applications for grants are first of all sent to the diocesan bishop, who must approve the application before it is sent to the trustees. The bishop will also indicate the priority of projects in relation to the long-term plan for the diocese. Field officers also visit every applicant to help with applications. The grants committee meets in March, June, September and December; applications have to be sent over two months in advance. Contact the fund for details of exact dates and of the relevant diocese contacts.

The City Parochial Foundation & Trust for London

Social welfare in London

6 Middle Street, London EC1A 7PH
Tel: 020 7606 6145 **Fax:** 020 7600 1866
E-mail: info@cityparochial.org.uk
Website: www.cityparochial.org.uk
Correspondent: Bharat Mehta, Clerk

Income: £6.2 million (1999/2000)
Grant total: £5.6 million (1999/2000)

The City Parochial Foundation
The foundation's policies for 2002–2006 are: 'Generally, any organisation applying to us for funding should:

- be a registered charity (or have applied for charitable status), an Industrial and Provident Society or a Friendly Society;
- be open to all members of its community;
- involve its service users as much as possible in the overall control and the management of the organisation;
- be committed to sharing information, good practice and findings from its work with other organisations;
- be open to learning from the experience of other organisations;
- work jointly with other organisations as much as possible.

'We welcome applications from all organisations working with poor Londoners who are experiencing discrimination, isolation or violence, but we particularly encourage applications from organisations that work with, or are aiming to work with, the following:

- black, asian and minority ethnic communities
- disabled people

- established communities, often predominantly white, in areas of long-term poverty
- lesbians and gay men
- refugees and asylum seekers
- young people aged 10 to 25.'

Youth groups working with young people aged 10 to 25 years are eligible to apply for a grant if they work in one of the following three areas:
- providing advice, information and individual advocacy – especially those organisations that are user-led or those that encourage user involvement, participation, and which lead to user empowerment;
- developing, promoting and providing education, training and employment schemes;
- attempting to develop initiatives that tackle violence and hate crimes against the target groups.

Youth organisations previously supported by the trust include:
- The Pedro Club which received a grant towards an out-of-school learning and support centre;
- Downside Settlement, which runs activities such as cross-country running, adventure weekends and provides sports training, was funded for running costs;
- Fourth Feathers Youth Club was given a grant towards refurbishment and redevelopment of the club;
- Youth Works Hackney, which helps young people to be involved in the regeneration of the physical, social and economic environment was supported with a grant towards the Project Manager's salary.

The Trust for London
The trust's guidelines are broader than those of the City Parochial Foundation,

and grants are targeted at small, new and emerging organisations with an emphasis on self-help. 'So, if young people in an area got together to develop a project, say about mutual support as young refugees, or to tackle issues around drugs on an estate, etc. then the trust could consider funding it.'

The trust's policies for 2002–2006 centre on support for organisations which:
- benefit local people and communities in London;
- are charitable, but not necessarily registered charities;
- help local communities to identify and tackle local problems;
- do work that might be used to teach others;
- local people and communities have set up to help themselves;
- are open to all members of their community;
- are set up to tackle a specific issue.

Grants are given to: identify needs and deliver services; gain access to training opportunities; organise meetings, conferences, seminars and events which identify problems, raise awareness, explore solutions, or promote good practice.

Funding can be used for: everyday costs and overheads, including the cost of heating, lighting, telephone calls, postage, rent and council tax; one-off capital costs for buying equipment; the costs of paying for sessional and part-time staff. (The trust does not fund full-time staff either in full or in part.)

Funding can be up to a maximum of £10,000 per year, and support is given for up to three years.

Organisations approaching the trust for help must:
- have a constitution or a set of rules that govern their activities;

- be run by a group of people who may be called the trustees or the management committee;
- have their own bank or building society account where two named people from the trustees or management committee have to sign all the cheques;
- be able to provide financial statements for the last year, for example, independently examined financial statements, or audited accounts. (If the organisation is very new, a copy of the most recent bank or building society statement will do.)

The trust is particularly keen to fund work with:
- black, asian and minority ethnic community organisations;
- organisations providing creative educational activities for children and young people, including supplementary and mother-tongue schools;
- organisations run by disabled people for disabled people, including people with learning disabilities, people living with HIV or AIDS, and people with mental health problems;
- refugee and migrant groups;
- self-help groups, for example: children and family groups; estate-based organisations; lesbian and gay groups; older people's groups; organisations set up to tackle a specific issue; women's groups; youth groups.

In 1999/2000 grants included:
- £10,000 to Christ Gospel Ministry – Future Generation Youth Club;
- £8,000 to Bangladesh Youth Forum (Newham);
- £7,000 to Health Initiatives for Youth – UK;

- £5,000 each to African Youth Trust and Turkish Youth and Community Association;
- £4,000 to Ethio Youth England;
- £3,000 each to Andover Youth and Community Trust and Supporting African Youth Development;
- £700 to SPEC Jewish Youth and Community Centre.

The City Parochial Foundation does *not* give grants for the following:
- endowment appeals
- individual members of the public
- major expenses for buying or building premises
- medical research and equipment
- organisations currently receiving funding from Trust for London
- to replace public funds
- trips abroad.

Trust for London does *not* give grants for:
- distribution by umbrella bodies
- general appeals
- holiday playschemes
- individual members of the public
- major expenses for buying or building premises
- part of a full-time salary
- replacing spending cuts made by local or central government
- research
- trips abroad.

Applications: Application guidelines for the foundation and trust are very similar. They are available from the address above, and from the website. (The guidelines are available in braille; in large print; on audiotape; or in a format designed for people with learning disabilities. Contact the foundations for these.)

Field officers are available to help with an application, and applicants can discuss their proposal before applying; contact the trust and foundation on the number above. Applicants should first read the guidelines and check the eligibility of their organisation and how the work fits into the grant-making priorities detailed above.

Stage 1: Where the work does fit the guidelines applicants should send us written details of the planned work and funding needs (on no more than two sides of A4 paper) along with: the organisation's constitution; the most recent financial accounts; and the most recent annual report if available.

Stage 2: Where the foundation or trust feel that the planned work fits into their grant-making priorities, a field officer will arrange to discuss the application further.

Stage 3: Once the applicant and the field officer have discussed the application, the applicant organisation can submit a full written application on no more than three sides of A4 paper in a format that the field officer has given.

Where the application is for the trust, the field officer will give the applicant a form to fill in. The full application must be received before the relevant deadline listed below.

Stage 4: The field officer presents the application to the grants committee, which makes the final decision.

Stage 5: Applicants are told about the decision in writing after the foundation's trustee board meeting.

Applicants need to contact the foundation or trust at least three months before the relevant deadline. The foundation's grants committee meets four times a year in January, April, July and

October. The deadlines for receiving completed applications are: 31 January for the April meeting; 15 April for the July meeting; 15 August for the October meeting; and 15 November for the January meeting.

The trust's grants committee meets four times a year in March, June, September and December. The deadlines for receiving completed applications are: 31 January for the March meeting; 15 April for the June meeting; 31 July for the September meeting; 15 October for the December meeting.

Applications are completed when applicants have met with a field officer, staff have no further questions to raise, and all the necessary information has been received.

The Clothworkers' Foundation and other Trusts

Clothworking, general

Cloth workers' Hall, Dunster Court, Mincing Lane, London EC3R 7AH
Tel: 020 7623 7041
Correspondent: Michael Harris, Secretary

Grant total: £3.9 million (2000)
Grants to youth: Est. £150,000 (2000)

Grants are over £1,000 and seldom for more than £50,000. Awards are generally given for capital expenditure and in a wide range of fields. Grants are made by means of single payments, except in the case of the more substantial grants, which may be made in up to five annual instalments. Preferential consideration is given to appeals received from self-help organisations and to charities requiring pump-priming for development and more extensive fundraising initiatives. There is also a preference cause supporting textiles and related activities.

Grants to young people's causes included:

- £30,000 to Raleigh International towards its youth development programme;
- £25,000 to Northamptonshire Association of Youth Clubs, towards replacing an accommodation building;
- £22,000 to National Association of Clubs for Young People, towards a nationally accredited awards programme for young people related to their involvement in their youth club;
- £10,000 to 1st Wellington Scout Group, towards building improvements;
- £7,500 to Coventry Boys' Club towards replacing a mini-bus;
- £4,000 to The Pedro Club, towards its outdoor pursuit facilities.

Charitable support is *not* given:

- if it may go in direct relief of state aid or in the reduction of financial support from public funds;
- directly to organisations or groups which are not registered charities;
- in response to applications by, or for the benefit of, individuals;
- by means of sponsorship for individuals undertaking fundraising activities on behalf of any charity;
- towards the general maintenance, repair or restoration of cathedrals, abbeys, churches or other ecclesiastical buildings, unless they have an existing and long-standing connection with The Cloth workers' Company, or unless they are appealing for a specific purpose which is considered to be of outstanding importance in relation to the national heritage;

- to schools/colleges in the primary, secondary or tertiary sector of education (whether public or private), unless they have an existing and long-standing connection with The Clothworkers' Company;
- to organisations or groups whose main objects are to fund or support other charitable bodies.

There is little support for major national charities or for their local branches. Normally the foundation does not support charities whose accounts disclose substantial financial resources and which have well-established and ample fundraising capabilities. With certain limited exceptions, the foundation does not make annual subscriptions or recurring grants to charities.

Applications: Initial telephone enquiries are welcomed. The Clothworkers' Foundation does not issue application forms. However, all applicants must complete a data information sheet, which should accompany the written application/appeal. The following should be included:

1 Applications from registered charities should be made in writing on the applicant charity's official headed notepaper. Ideally, the appeal letter itself should be no longer than two and a half pages of A4.

2 Detailed costings or a budget for the project or projects referred to in the appeal letter should form a separate appendix or appendices to the appeal letter and should provide the fullest possible financial details.

3 The latest annual report of the applicant charity, together with the latest available full audited accounts, including a full balance sheet should also

accompany the written application. In the written application letter, applicants should:

- Introduce the work of the applicant charity; state when the charity was established; describe its aims and objectives; and define precisely what the applicant charity does and who benefits from its activities.
- Comment upon the applicant charity's track record since its inception, refer to its notable achievements and successes to date, and give an interesting synopsis of the organisation.
- Describe the project requiring funding fully, clearly and concisely, and comment on the charity's plans for the future.
- Provide full costings or a budget for the project/projects to include a detailed breakdown of the costs involved.
- Give details of all other applications which the applicant has made to other sources of funding, and indicate precisely what funds have already been raised from other sources for the project.
- All applicants are, of course, perfectly at liberty to request a precise sum of money by way of grant. However, it can be more beneficial for the applicant to concentrate on providing accurate and detailed costings of the project concerned, thereby enabling the foundation to make its own judgement as to the level of financial support to be considered.

Applicants can greatly help their cause by concentrating on clarity of presentation and by providing detailed factual information. The foundation will then do its utmost to ensure that the application receives the fullest and most careful consideration.

Trustees meet regularly in January, February, May, July, October and December. The committee's recommendations are then placed before a subsequent meeting of the governors. Accordingly, there is a rolling programme of dealing with and processing applications and the foundation prides itself on flexibility. A decision may take up to twelve weeks and all applicants are notified of the outcome by letter. Successful applicants are normally barred from reapplying for the next five years.

Comic Relief

Community-based charities

5th Floor, 89 Albert Embankment, London SE1 7TP
Tel: 020 7820 5555 **Fax:** 020 7820 5500
E-mail: ukgrants@comicrelief.org.uk
Website: www.comicrelief.org.uk
Correspondent: The UK Grants Team

Income: Over £50 million (2001)
Grant total: £10.6 million in Africa; £7.8 million in the UK (1999/2000)
Grants to youth: £4 million (1999/2000)

Comic Relief derives its revenue from the Red Nose day fundraising event that it stages with BBC television every two years. 'Comic Relief aims to reach the poorest and most disadvantaged communities to help them take control of their lives and find solutions to the problems they face.' The extent of grantmaking depends entirely on the fundraising success of each Red Nose day. Grant-giving programmes operate on a two year cycle, each with five 'rounds' of applications.

Over 400 grants are currently made in a full two year cycle of the UK programme, with an average award of over £20,000, and with few grants being for less than £2,000. 10% of the money is allocated for grants of less than £5,000. Awards are made towards capital or revenue costs and may be single payments or made over three years. Buildings are a very low priority.

The trust states: 'We make grants to voluntary organisations and self-help groups throughout the UK. We give particular attention to parts of the UK which often miss out on funding, especially towns and cities outside London, and rural areas. We welcome applications from both small local grassroots projects as well as larger organisations.'

'Any work we fund must be charitable. If your group is not a registered charity, but the work you are planning to do has charitable aims, we can pay funds through a registered charity.'

'We are especially keen to hear from groups, in the areas that we support, who are very disadvantaged or find it particularly hard to get funding. So we welcome applications that specifically benefit the following:

- people from black and ethnic minority groups
- women
- lesbians and gay men
- people who live in rural areas, and towns and cities outside London.'

'To apply, these groups must fall within one or more of our grant-making programmes.'

Grants up to £5,000

This programme is only open to small, local organisations with a turnover of up to £100,000. The maximum is £5,000, and priority is given to applications for core and equipment costs.

Grants over £5,000

This programme is open to any voluntary organisation that works within the grant-making programmes. Grants are given for running costs for up to three years, and will not usually be for more than £30,000 each year. However the trustees might give more to projects which show new ideas or will make a major impact.

Applicants can contact the Grants Team to discuss their project before applying.

Supporting young people grants programme

'We welcome applications from organisations which provide services to young people aged 11 to 25 who are experiencing severe difficulties and need intensive support. Examples of the issues we will support include:

- drug and alcohol misuse
- homelessness
- mental ill health
- violence, abuse and sexual exploitation
- criminal justice
- young carers
- 'looked after' young people
- bullying and harassment.

We are especially keen to hear from projects that tackle the range of problems young people may face. We do not expect services to be managed by young people, but we will look closely at how far groups consult young people in developing their services.

We cannot fund general youth or prevention work. The Supporting young people programme is intended to support projects working with young people who have already slipped through the net and need intensive help and support.'

During 2001 to 2003 we will put aside some of the grant money to two special programmes:

- drug services for young people from black and minority ethnic communities;
- promoting young people's participation in decision making.'

In 1999/2000 grants included:

- £15,000 to Trinity Youth Association in Northumberland;
- £13,000 to London Youth; £10,000 to Young People Taking Action in Suffolk;
- £5,400 to Southwick Neighbourhood Youth Project in Tyne and Wear;
- £5,000 to Teme Valley Youth Group in Shropshire;
- £1,500 to Basement Youth Trust in Hereford & Worcester.

For UK grants, in general, the following are not funded:

- academic research
- general appeals
- schools, colleges and hospitals
- individual people
- promoting religion
- trips abroad, holidays and outings
- services run by statutory or public authorities
- medical research or equipment
- minibuses
- sporting activities
- general youth or prevention work.

The charity also notes that it does not fund social clubs or activities for the elderly.

Applications: (For UK grants only)

Grants up to £5,000
On an application form available from the correspondent, who should also be contacted for details of deadlines.

Grants over £5,000
There is a two stage application process: 'At stage 1 you fill in the summary form, giving basic details about your work. This will give us enough information to decide whether you should send us a full application or not ... As well as assessing your application against the requirements of the individual programme, we will take the following into account:

- the size of your organisation – we want to fund both small and larger organisations;
- the ages of people who will benefit from our funding;
- the benefit to groups who face particular disadvantage (women, people from black and minority ethnic communities, lesbians and gay men, and people living in rural areas);
- how involved the project users are in the planning and management of the organisation;
- how the work influences policy or changes the lives of disadvantaged people;
- how we are spreading our funding throughout the UK.

'Once we have received all the summary forms we will draw up a shortlist of applications for Stage 2. If your application qualifies, we will send you our full application pack.

'We cannot consider another application until you are in the last nine months of your funding from us.' There are five grant-making cycles for grants over £5,000, spread throughout the year.

The Community Foundation serving Tyne & Wear and Northumberland (formerly Tyne & Wear Foundation)

Social welfare, general in Tyne and Wear and Northumberland

Cale Cross House, 156 Pilgrim Street, Newcastle upon Tyne NE1 6SU
Tel: 0191 222 0945 **Fax:** 0191 230 0689
E-mail: general@community foundation.org.uk
Website: www.community foundation.org.uk
Correspondent: Maureen High, Senior Grants Administrator

Income: £5.8 million (2000/01)
Grant total: £3.3 million to organisations (2000/01)
Grants to youth: Est. £828,000 (2000/01)

The foundation manages over 80 funds to support community development in the region. Most grants are for £2,500 or less, with a few grants of up to £100,000, some over two or three years.

Through the Readman Foundation, one of the foundation's funds, grants are awarded to individual young people and to voluntary organisations that give young people the opportunity to help themselves. The Readman Foundation is especially keen to support black groups undertaking projects that will make a difference and encourage talents of young people in ways that would help their future careers.

The YouthBank is another grantmaking fund run by and for young people, and was set up in 1999.

Examples of grants made in 2000/01 are given below.

The Readman Foundation
118 grants to organisations totalling £159,000, including those to: Longbenton Youth Project (£9,000); Northumberland Scouts Council (£5,000); and Pelaw Youth Centre (£3,900).

YouthBank
20 grants totalling £3,122, including: £800 to Air Training Corps; £750 to Who Cares? North East and £740 to Wansbeck Young People's Forum.

Grants given from other funds
£15,000 to Trinity Youth Association; £9,400 to Pelaw Youth Centre; £2,500 each to Balliol Youth Centre and Northumberland Clubs for Young People and £1,000 to Outdoor Trust.

The foundation does *not* normally make grants for the following purposes:
- sponsorship and fundraising events;
- small contributions to major appeals;
- large capital projects;
- endowments;
- political or religious groups;
- work which should be funded by health and local authorities;
- projects outside our area … unless funding is made available by one of its supporters from funds they have contributed to the foundation.

Applications: Applicants should use the latest grant guidelines, which can be obtained by telephone or e-mail, or from the website. Community Foundation staff welcome telephone calls to discuss an application at any stage.

Applicants need only make a single application to the foundation, whose staff will match the application to the most suitable fund(s). Applications are acknowledged within two weeks and applicants may be contacted by staff for further information or to arrange a meeting. Decisions are made by grants panels and/or donors and ratified by the board of trustees; applicants usually know the outcome within three months. Those who are not awarded a grant will be sent a standard letter and invited to telephone if they wish to discuss the matter further.

The Construction Industry Trust for Youth

Building projects benefiting young people

Construction House, 56–64 Leonard Street, London EC2A 4JX
Tel: 020 7608 5184 **Fax**: 020 7608 5001
E-mail: city@thecc.org.uk
Website: www.charitynet.org/~city
Correspondent: The Administrator

Income: £55,000 (2000)
Grant total: £68,000 (2000)
Grants to youth: £68,000 (2000)

The trust will consider supporting any youth organisation for building projects benefiting: students, people who are unemployed or disadvantaged by poverty, and those living in both rural and urban areas. Individuals under 25 can be considered for sponsorship for training in the construction industry. Grants for building projects will only be given to organisations which have no restrictions as to colour, class, creed or sect and only for the provision of permanent buildings for the use of youth between the ages of 8 and 25 years or for sponsorship in training disadvantaged young people under 25 who wish to enter the construction industry.

Grants range between £2,000 and £5,000, and are one-off for buildings, or for up to three years for training. No grants are given for equipment, furniture, maintenance, repairs, decorating, transport or running costs. Training outside the construction industry and associated trades and professions is not considered.

Applications: In writing to the correspondent for an application form, with an outline of the request.

The Ernest Cook Trust

Educational aspects of conservation and rural environment, youth, arts and crafts and architecture, related research

Fairford Park, Fairford, Gloucestershire GL7 4JH
Tel: 01285 713273 **Fax**: 01285 711692
E-mail: grants@ernestcooktrust.org.uk
Website: www.ernestcooktrust.org.uk
Correspondent: Mrs Antonia Eliot, Awards Administrator

Income: £1.8 million (2000/01)
Grants total: £629,000 (2000/01)
Grants to youth: Est. £20,000 (2000/01)

The trust makes grants for educational purposes to various causes, including youth organisations, in particular to projects in areas of urban deprivation. Under the Youth heading, the trust's guidelines say: 'Support for education and training in this category includes work that helps young people to lead fulfilled lives while remaining sensitive to the needs of others and which increases their chances of employment'.

Grants are made to charitable and not-for-profit organisations. 'The trust believes that small grants are often as beneficial as large grants and there is therefore no minimum or maximum grant size. Single grants are awarded but in exceptional circumstances grants up to a maximum of three years are considered'.

In 2000/01 56 grants were made under the Youth heading. A list of beneficiaries was provided by the trust, they included schools, museums and other causes outside the scope of this guide. Youth organisations supported included: Northleach Youth Club (£6,000 towards the appointment of a trainee youth worker); Cirdan Sailing Trust (£5,000 towards its bursary scheme); Pedro Club (£5,000 towards setting up a newsletter project), Downside Clubs (£1,000 towards swimming teaching aids) and Kilkeel Bridge Association (£1,000 towards buying equipment for a youth club).

Medicine, health or social work projects are not supported, and grants are not awarded for work overseas, or for building work, agricultural colleges, sports and recreational activities. Awards are not made retrospectively. General appeals are not normally supported. Funds are rarely committed for community projects, or for publications. The trustees also avoid schemes where their input would simply replace funds customarily provided from public sources. The trust very rarely funds individuals. Support for wildlife trusts and for farming and wildlife advisory groups is largely restricted to those based in counties in which ECT owns land (Gloucestershire, Buckinghamshire, Leicestershire and Dorset).

Applications: A leaflet is available outlining how to make an application in the first instance. 'The trustees consider most grant applications at meetings in March and October, having a further mechanism for the making of grants smaller than £2,000 at more frequent intervals. Applications for the two main meetings must be finalised by 31 January and 31 August. There is no application form but applicants are asked to focus their request on a specific educational need and to present clear and concise proposals on a maximum of four sides of A4 paper. The enclosure of an sae will ensure acknowledgement of an application.'

Cripplegate Foundation

General, in Cripplegate/Islington, London

76 Central Street, London EC1V 8AG
Tel: 020 7336 8062 **Fax:** 020 7336 8201
E-mail: david@cripplegate.org.uk
Correspondent: David Green, Clerk

Income: £1.1 million (2000)
Grant total: £910,000 to organisations (2000)
Grants to youth: Est. over £60,000 (2000)

The foundation will consider applications for many different purposes, including providing core funding. It will only support groups working in the following areas of London: the ancient parish of St Giles, Cripplegate, London, the former parish of St Luke Old Street as constituted in 1732 (broadly speaking, the southern part of Islington and the north of the City of London), and now extended to include the Islington Council wards of Barnsbury, Bunhill, Clerkenwell, Canonbury East, Canonbury West, St Mary, St Peter and Thornhill.

The trust supports organisations that:
- address an identified need in the area of benefit;

- address a need not covered by other local projects;
- which draws in funds and resources from elsewhere;
- which provide a benefit at a reasonable cost per head.

The trust identifies the needs of young people aged from 0–25 years, as a high priority. Grants towards work with young people include:

- £20,000 to Crown & Manor Boys' Club towards the costs of repairs to youth club building;
- £11,000 to Blessed Sacrament Church towards the running costs of an after-school club and youth group;
- £5,000 to Community of Refugees from Vietnam towards the cost of one year pilot project for new after-school activities for the Vietnamese community in Barnsby;
- £4,600 to Islington Bangladesh Association towards the costs of a young Bengali women's group;
- £2,500 to St John's Youth Centre towards the cost of their fitness room;
- £500 to Times Boxing Club towards equipment.

Grants are *not* given to:

- national charities and organisations, or organisations outside the area of benefit, unless they are carrying out a piece of work in the area of benefit;
- schemes or activities which would be regarded as relieving either central government or local authorities of their statutory responsibilities;
- grants to replace cuts in funding made by the local authority or others;
- medical research or equipment;
- national fundraising appeals or appeals to provide an endowment;

- advancement of religion and religious groups, unless they offer non-religious services to the local community;
- animal welfare;
- retrospective grants;
- commercial or business activities;
- grants for concerts or other events held in the Church of St Giles-without-Cripplegate;
- grants for students at City University.

Applications: Application forms can be obtained from the correspondent. They are also available as a Microsoft Word document, which can be supplied on receipt of a formatted 3.5 inch floppy disk, or by e-mail. However, the foundation will not accept completed application forms submitted by e-mail. The foundation welcomes a preliminary approach by telephone from charities, organisations or individuals who are unsure how to complete their application form or want information on whether they are eligible for a grant. Contact Kristina Glenn, Grants Officer, or David Green, the Clerk to the Governors.

Before an application goes to the governors an applicant will normally be visited and applicants should allow time for this when applying. Application forms are required to be returned at least six weeks before the meetings. Applications for less than £25,000 are considered at grant committee meetings in January, April, July and October. Applications for £25,000 or more are considered by the full board in March, June and December.

The Harry Crook Foundation

Education, elderly, homelessness, youth, in Bristol

Veale Wasbrough, Solicitors, Orchard Court, Orchard Lane, Bristol BS1 5WS
Tel: 0117 925 2020
Correspondent: D J Bellew

Income: £107,000 (1999/2000)
Grant total: £358,000 (1999/2000)

The foundation was established in 1963 by Dr Harry Crook, who endowed it with shares in his Kleen-E-Zee Brush Co. Ltd, famed for its door to door brush salesmen. The trustees 'consider it their duty to maintain and support those causes which were dear to Harry Crook's heart ... by supporting charitable causes which serve the city of Bristol or its immediate environs, or which are personally known to the trustees'.

The foundation's report states it is mainly concerned with elderly, homeless, education and youth charities. It can also make grants to support other specific projects, and small donations for a wide range of charitable purposes.

Grants were broken down by the trust into four categories, shown here with examples of grants.

Annual commitments: £66,000 (27 grants between £400 and £8,000) Beneficiaries included Avon Outward Bound Association; Bristol School for Young People and Duke of Edinburgh Awards Scheme.

Discretionary grants of £5,000 and over: £259,000 (seven grants between £5,000 and £208,000) Bristol 5 Club for Young People was among the beneficiaries.

Discretionary grants under £5,000: £31,000 (40 grants between £500 and £2,500) Recipients included Avonside Strategic Board for Young Enterprise.

Adventurers: £2,200 (12 grants between £100 and £500) Beneficiaries included: Avon Venture Scouts; Crosslinks; Hartcliffe Club for Young People; Student Partnership Worldwide and Uganda Expedition.

Applications: In writing to the correspondent. The trustees meet twice a year in November and July, but applications can be sent at any time as there is a sifting process prior to the trustees meetings.

Baron Davenport's Charity

Almshouses/hospices/residential homes, children and youth, in the West Midlands

Portman House, 5–7 Temple Row West, Birmingham B2 5NY
Tel: 0121 236 8004 Fax: 0121 233 2500
E-mail: baron.davenport@virgin.net
Correspondent: J R Prichard, Secretary

Income: £969,000 (2000)
Grant total: £575,000 (to institutions, 2000)
Grants to youth: £109,000 (2000)

The charity gives grants in a number of areas including, organisations helping children and young people up to 25 years of age. In this category, grants of over £2,500 were listed with the accounts for 2000, and included £7,500 to Stonehouse Gang, Birmingham, and £5,000 to Duke of Edinburgh's Awards – Midlands area. The other grants in the list included a number to organisations that help children and young people with learning and physical disabilities and life inhibiting/threatening illnesses. Most grants are for £1,000 or less.

Applications: In writing to the correspondent, accompanied by the latest accounts. Distributions take place twice a year at the end of May and November and applications should be received at the charity's office by 15 March or 15 September. All applications are acknowledged and those not within the trust's objects are advised. Organisations will normally only receive one grant in a year.

Duchy of Lancaster Benevolent Fund

Youth and education, general in the North West

Duchy of Lancaster Office, 1 Lancaster Place, Strand, London WC2E 7ED
Tel: 020 7836 8277 **Fax:** 020 7836 3098
Correspondent: F N J Davies, Secretary

Income: £900,000 (1999/2000)
Grant total: £303,000 (1999/2000)
Grants to youth: £88,000 to youth and education (1999/2000)

Grants given by the trust are mostly for amounts under £1,000, which are not listed in the accounts. Of the 82 grants listed, all, except two of £20,000 each, were for between £1,000 and £5,000. The charity supports organisations in Lancashire, Greater Manchester and Merseyside, but also in others 'where the Duchy has historical links (such as landed interests and the presentation of church livings)'. From the grants lists these appear to include Pontefract and Leicester.

In the Youth and education category, 123 grants were made, of which 23 were for between £1,000 and £5,000. Grants included: The Prince's Trust (£5,000); Fleetwood Gym Boys Club and Fleetwood Youth Forum (£2,500 each); Ocean Youth Trust (£2,000); Lancashire Youth Clubs Association (£1,500); and 5th Sefton Sea Scouts (£1,000).

Applications: To the correspondent, at any time.

Dulverton Trust

Youth and education, welfare, conservation, Christian religion, general

5 St James's Place, London SW1A 1NP
Tel: 020 7629 9121 **Fax:** 020 7495 6201
E-mail: trust@dulverton.org
Correspondent: Major General Sir Robert Corbett, Trust Director

Income: £2.8 million (2000/01)
Grant total: £3 million ((2000/01)
Grants to youth: Est. £300,000 (2000/01)

Grants vary between £1,000 and £125,000. Though most grants go to national projects, there is an increasing interest in regional or local projects. Awards are made towards capital or revenue costs, and are normally one-off payments.

Youth and education continues to be the largest single category supported by the trust, accounting for over one third of the grants by value. This reflects the priority placed by the trustees on assisting the development of young people, particularly those suffering from disadvantage.

Examples of grants in 2000/01 included: £31,000 to Duke of

Edinburgh's Award Scheme; £28,000 to Church Lads' and Church Girls' Brigade; £25,000 each to Taste for Adventure and West Yorkshire County Scout Council; £18,000 to Youth Clubs UK; £16,000 to Raleigh International; £13,000 to Outward Bound; and £10,000 each to GAP Activity Projects and Norfolk Youth Projects.

The trust is seldom able to support appeals:

- from the broad fields of medicine and health, including drug addiction and projects concerning people who are mentally and physically disabled;
- from within the Greater London area or Northern Ireland.

Also generally excluded are:

- projects concerning museums, churches, cathedrals and other historic buildings;
- the whole field of the arts;
- projects for schools, colleges and universities;
- expeditions.

Grants are made only to registered charities and never to individuals.

Applications: A written application, preferably restricted to two sheets of paper, should be addressed to the Director, although initial enquiries are welcomed by telephone to establish the eligibility of a proposed appeal. Applications should include the registered charity number, a brief description of the background and aims of the charity, the circumstances and specific aims of the project for which funds are sought and details of any funding already secured. A copy of the most recent annual report and accounts should also be enclosed. Trustee meetings are held four times a year in January, May, July and October.

The John Ellerman Foundation

Health, welfare, art and conservation, for national organisations only

Aria House, 23 Craven Street, London WC2N 5NS
Tel: 020 7930 8566 **Fax:** 020 7839 3654
E-mail: postmaster@ellerman. prestel.co.uk
Website: www.ncvo-vol.org.uk/jef.html
Correspondent: Eileen Terry, Appeals Manager

Income: £4.9 million (2000/01)
Grant total: £4.1 million (2000/01)
Grants to youth: Est. £100,000 (2000/01)

The foundation aims to support a broad cross-section of charities doing work of national significance, in four categories including 'Community Development and Social Welfare'. This category covers grants to youth work.

The trust makes about 100 grants a year, nearly all are between £10,000 and £100,000, to national organisations only (although they do not need to be large) for core, project or capital costs. Grants can be over one, two or three year periods. There is a particular interest in innovation and in cooperation between charities (of which the foundation believes there to be too many).

Youth projects receiving grants of £15,000 each included: Federation of London Youth Clubs; Raleigh International; Sea Cadet Association; Welsh Association of Youth Clubs and Youth Clubs UK.

Grants are made only to registered charities, and are not made for the following purposes:

- medical research

- for or on behalf of individuals
- individual hospices
- local branches of national organisations
- 'friends of' groups
- education or educational establishments
- religious causes
- conferences and seminars
- sports and leisure facilities
- purchase of vehicles (except for those used for aid transport)
- the direct replacement of public funding
- deficit funding
- domestic animal welfare.

Circulars will not receive a reply. The foundation cannot make donations to the continents of America south of the USA.

Applications: In the first instance, send a letter of not more than two pages of A4 without enclosures. From this, trustees will decide whether they want to invite a formal application. If so, an application form and further details will be sent. All letters will receive a reply. The trust is happy to discuss potential applications by telephone; ask for the appeals manager. The trustees meet regularly throughout the year and there are no deadlines.

The Essex Youth Trust

Youth, education of people under 25 in Essex

Gepp & Sons, 58 New London Road, Chelmsford, Essex CM2 0PAJ
Tel: 01245 493939 **Fax:** 01245 493940
Correspondent: P Douglas-Hughes, Clerk

Income: £365,000 (1998/99)
Grant total: £313,000 (1998/99)
Grants to youth: Est. Over £65,000 (1998/99)

This trust comprises four charities and the combined objects are the education and advancement of people under the age of 25. Preference is given to those who are in need owing to 'being temporarily or permanently deprived of normal parental care or who are otherwise disadvantaged'. Grants are given to individuals in accordance with the objects of the trust.

The trust's 1998/99 annual report states that while it is 'still discovering where the need for funds is most essential', it anticipates a continuing commitment to make grants to 'organisations which seek to diminish the use of drugs amongst young people'.

In 1998/99 55 grants were made, mostly one–off. Grants to youth groups included: £18,000 to Colchester Youth Service; £15,000 to Frenfield Boys Club; £10,000 to Barking and Dagenham Young Persons Project 2000; £5,000 each to Basildon Boys Club and Essex County Scout Council; £3,100 to Dockland Scout Programme; £3,000 to Epping Forest Youth for Christ; £2,500 to Frenford Clubs and £2,000 each to Metropolitan Police Volunteer Cadet Force and Teen Talk.

Applications: On a form available from the correspondent.

The Eveson Charitable Trust

General in Herefordshire, Worcestershire and the West Midlands, including Birmingham and Coventry

45 Park Road, Gloucester GL1 1LP
Tel: 01452 501352 **Fax:** 01452 302195
Correspondent: Alex D Gay, Administrator

Income: £2.3 million (2000/2001)
Grant total: £2.9 million (2000/2001)
Grants to youth: Est. over £110,000
(2000/2001)

Most of the trust's grants are given to
registered charities, and the average size
of awards in 2000/01 was £8,400. One
of the trust's areas of giving is to 'children
in need whether disadvantaged or
physically or mentally handicapped'.

Its grants were divided into the
following three categories in the 2000/
01 accounts:

- Accommodation: includes grants to
organisations providing non-health
related accommodation and respite/
holiday accommodation (£260,000 in
grants in 2000/2001). Grants in this
category included £5,000 to
Birmingham Federation of Clubs for
Young People and £3,000 to
Birmingham PHAB Camps towards
holidays that integrate young people
with and without disabilities.
- Healthcare (£694,000 in grants)
- Social care and development: includes
organisations providing human and
social services to a community or
target population, such as services for
young people (£1.9 million in grants).
Grants in this category included:
£20,000 to Basement Youth Trust in
Ross-on-Wye, in two grants towards
the running costs of this charity which
supports disaffected young people;
£15,000 to The Children's Society
towards the running costs of the Youth
Link Project in Birmingham helping
vulnerable young people who are on
the streets; £10,000 to Endeavour
Training towards their work with
disadvantaged young people in
Birmingham and Solihull; £5,000 to
All Saints Youth Project, Birmingham,

towards the running costs of youth
work in Kings Heath; and £2,900 to
Bangladesh Community Development
in Birmingham, towards sports and
recreational activities for disadvantaged
young people.

Grants are not made to individuals, even
if the request is submitted by a charitable
institution.

Applications: The trustees meet
quarterly, usually at the end of March and
June and at the beginning of October
and January. Completed applications
must be received at the trust's office at
least six weeks before the meeting at
which it is to be considered. Applications
can only be considered if they are on the
trust's simple form, Application for
Support which can be obtained from the
correspondent. The form must be
completed and returned together with a
copy of the latest accounts and annual
report of the organisation.

Where applications are submitted that
fall clearly outside the trust's grant-giving
priorities, the applicant is advised that the
application cannot be considered and
reasons are given. All applications that are
to be considered by the trustees are
acknowledged in writing. Applicants are
advised of the quarterly meeting at
which their application is going to be
considered. Trustees' decisions are given
in writing soon after these meetings.

The Esmée Fairbairn Charitable Trust

Social development, arts and heritage, education, environment

11 Park Place, London SW1A 1LP
Tel: 020 7297 4700 **Fax:** 020 7297 4701
E-mail: info@esmeefairbairn.org.uk
Website: www.esmeefairbairn.org.uk
Correspondent: Margaret Hyde, Director

Income: £39 million (2000)
Grant total: £24.1 million (2000)
Grants to youth: Est. £170,000 (2000)

The trust does not restrict the types of grant it is prepared to make, but 'will concentrate increasingly on revenue projects, with capital projects being accorded low priority'. Grants are often of a substantial size and given over a three year period. Repeat grants are also occasionally made. Many grants are for core costs. The trust, however, also makes grants below £10,000 as 'they can make a real difference to so many organisations'.

The foundation gives grants which benefit young people aged 11 to 25. However, it does not have a specific programme for this group and applicants should refer to the guidelines under each heading. Listed mainly under the social development heading, grants made in 2000 to youth organisations included:

- £94,000 to Youth Culture Television Foundation, towards media and technical training over two years for deprived 11 to 19 year olds
- £30,000 to Hangleton & Knoll Project, towards the cost of continuing work over three years
- £22,000 to 42nd Street, towards the funding of a lesbian, gay and bisexual young people's project

- £15,000 to Consett YMCA towards funding evening and weekend activities for disaffected young people.

Smaller grants made under the social development heading, included:
- £9,000 to Belle Vue Sports & Youth Centre;
- £8,300 to West Lothian Youth Action Project;
- £5,000 to Shropshire Youth Association;
- £4,000 to Ash to Adderley Rural Youth Project ;
- £2,500 to Shard End Youth Centre.

The trust will *not* fund:
- individuals;
- applications from organisations which have applied within the previous 12 months;
- work which has already taken place;
- work which does not directly benefit people in the UK;
- work which directly replaces statutory funding;
- medical research;
- standard health services and day/residential care;
- animal welfare;
- expeditions and overseas travel;
- endowment funds;
- general appeals or circulars.

Applications: All applicants should first obtain the trust's guidelines (send an sae to the trust or see the trust's website). Applications for grants up to £5,000 should be made on the trust's application form available from the trust.

Applications for grants over £5,000 should be in the form of a letter with supporting information. The following information is required:
1 A brief description of the organisation, its work, management and staffing structure, and current budget.

2 A description of the purpose of the project for which funds are required, the amount sought from the trust, who will manage the project, the project start/finish dates and the results expected.

3 A budget for the project, details of funds already raised and other sources being approached.

4 How the organisation intends to monitor and evaluate the project.

5 The plans for sharing information about the project and learning with others in the field.

6 The most recent annual report and audited accounts.

7 The organisation's charitable status, including the charity's registration number.

8 The contact name, address and telephone number.

Both kinds of application can be made at any time of the year. The process of dealing with an application, from receipt to communicating the trust's decision, can take between two and six months. Once the application has been considered the trust does not usually accept another application from the same organisation within 12 months from the date of the decision.

Ford of Britain Trust

General in areas where the Ford Motor Company has a presence

Room 1/602, Eagle Way, Brentwood, Essex CM13 3BW
Tel: 01277 252551
Correspondent: The Director

Income: £694,000 (2000/01)
Grant total: £490,000 (2000/01)
Grants to youth: £56,000 (2000/01)

The trust supports organisations in the areas where the Ford Motor company is based namely South Wales, Northern Ireland, Merseyside, Southampton, Midlands, Essex and East London. 11% of grants are given to youth causes, which covers grants to schools and youth groups that are registered charities and have a written constitution.

The trust mainly makes one-off grants for specific items or equipment, rather than for running costs. Grants range from a few thousand pounds (up to about £5,000) to a few hundred pounds. Applications for revenue costs are rarely considered. No grants are given to individuals, research, overseas projects or for travel.

Applications for new Ford vehicles are considered when two-thirds of the purchase price is available from other sources. Vehicle grants are not usually more than £1,500, but registered charities may be able to arrange a reduction from the recommended retail price. Grants are not available for second-hand vehicles.

A grants list was not included with the trust's accounts and further details of grants were not available.

Applications: In writing to the correspondent. Applications should include the following:

- purpose of the project
- whom it is intended to help and how
- why the project is important and necessary
- how the project is to be carried out
- the project's proposed starting time and time of completion
- total cost of the project
- how much has been raised so far, sources of funding obtained and expected

- examples of fundraising activities by the organisation for the project
- the amount being asked for.

A brief outline of the background of the charity is appreciated. Where appropriate, copies of accounts should be provided. Trustees meet in March, July and November each year. Applications are considered in order of receipt and it may take several months before an application is considered. The trust receives many more applications than it can help.

The Charles S French Charitable Trust

Community projects, disability, children and youth, with an interest in north east London and south west Essex

169 High Road, Loughton, Essex
IG10 4LF
Tel: 020 8502 3575
Correspondent: R L Thomas, Trustee

Income: £201,000 (1999/2000)
Grant total: £162,000 (1999/2000)
Grants to youth: £52,000 (1999/2000)

The trust has a policy of supporting primarily local charities which help children and the local community, and have been mainly in north east London and south west Essex. Grants to youth organisations account for 32% of the trust's total grantmaking. A list of beneficiaries was not provided by the trust.

The trust only gives grants to registered charities.

Applications: In writing to the correspondent, including a copy of your latest accounts.

J Paul Getty Jr Charitable Trust

Social welfare, conservation

1 Park Square West, London NW1 4LJ
Tel: 020 7486 1859
E-mail: BOBTPGT@aol.com
Correspondent: Ms Bridget O'Brien Twohig, Administrator

Income: £1.6 million (2000)
Grant total: £1.3 million (2000)
Grants to youth: £249,000 (2000)

The trust says it 'aims to fund projects to do with poverty and misery in general, and unpopular causes in particular, within the UK'. The emphasis is on self-help, building esteem, enabling people to reach their potential. The trustees favour small community and local projects which make good use of volunteers.

Over 100 new grants are made each year, mostly for revenue costs over three years (except for a number of smaller awards of hundreds rather than thousands of pounds). Grants are typically for amounts between £5,000 and £30,000 (over three years). Priority is likely to be given to projects in the less prosperous parts of the country, particularly in the north of England, and to those which cover more than one beneficial area.

Grant priorities included the following for young people:
- young people in need of support because they are homeless or have addiction or mental health problems;
- young offenders, or young people who have dropped out and are getting into trouble;
- communities which are clearly disadvantaged trying to improve their lot, particularly projects to do with helping young people in the long-term.

Grants in the youth category included a number for workers' salaries made over three years, such as those to: Impact, Bradford (£17,000 in 2000); Prince's Trust East Durham Project (£13,000); Wyborn Youth Trust, Sheffield (£11,000); Himmat Project, Halifax – working with Asian young people (£10,000); Youth Matters, Torquay (£8,000); and Dawlish Action for Youth – youth café (£5,000).

Other grants to youth organisations included: £15,000 to Powerpoint Youth Project, Portsmouth, for running costs; £10,000 each to Community Campus '87 in Stockton on Tees towards capital and Lyme Regis Development Trust for set-up costs for a new youth café; £5,000 to Streets Ahead, Worcester, towards a young people's' club's running costs; and £2,500 to XAS Club, Wakefield towards young people's activities.

The trustees do *not* generally consider applications for the following:

- elderly
- children
- education
- research
- animals
- music or drama (except therapeutically)
- conferences and seminars
- medical care (including hospices) or health
- medical equipment
- churches and cathedrals
- holidays and expeditions
- sports or leisure facilities (including cricket pitches).

Residential projects or large building projects are unlikely to be considered. The trustees do not support national appeals or grant-giving trusts such as community trusts. Headquarters of national organisations and umbrella organisations are unlikely to be considered, as are applications from abroad. No applications from individuals are considered. Past recipients are not encouraged to apply. The project must be a registered charity or be under the auspices of one.

Applications: A letter no more than two pages long is all that is necessary at first, giving an outline of the project, a detailed costing, the existing sources of finance of the organisation, and what other applications, including those to statutory sources and the Community Fund (formerly the National Lottery Charities Board), have been made. Applicants should also say if they have applied to or received a grant previously from the trust. Videos, tapes or bulky reports should not be sent, and they will not be returned. Annual accounts will be asked for if the application is going to be taken further.

The project will be visited before an application can be considered by the trustees. This may mean a delay, as it is only possible to visit a small part of the country between each quarterly trustees' meeting, and three months is the least it can take to award a grant. Some small grants of up to £1,000 can be made without a visit, but only for specific purposes. Applications can be made to the administrator at any time, and all letters of appeal will be answered; applicants should confine themselves to two pages in the first instance.

The G C Gibson Charitable Trust

Churches, health, welfare, general in East Anglia, South Wales, Scotland

Deloitte & Touche, Blenheim House, Fitzalan Court, Newport Road, Cardiff CF2 1TS
Tel: 029 2048 1111
Correspondent: Karen Griffin

Income: £565,000 (2000/01)
Grant total: £620,000 (2000/01)

About 150 grants a year are given to a broad selection of charitable causes, often in East Anglia, South Wales or Scotland. Grants are generally between £1,000 and £5,000 and are usually repeated.

The organisation has supported work within a range of charitable fields, but as the trust does not categorise them it is difficult to discern the trust's priorities. One of the five or so better funded charitable fields is perhaps youth/education. Although grants are made to beneficiaries for one year at a time, once a charity has been awarded a grant the trustees are likely to continue to make awards to that charity provided they are happy with how the money is used, and they are very happy that such grants should go towards core running costs. Some organisations have received regular grants from the trust for as long as 20 years.

Occasionally grants are made on an explicitly one-off basis, usually for a capital project. Co-funding arrangements will also be considered, and the trustees have awarded several grants in conjunction with the National Lottery/Community Fund. Particularly in the case of lesser-known charities, the trustees tend to look favourably on applications from charities that are recommended by someone they know.

Beneficiaries are frequently well-established national charities; about 10% have 'royal' or 'national' in their titles. The great majority of grants are for £1,000, £2,000 or £3,000. Only registered charities will be supported.

Applications: In writing to the correspondent in October/November each year; trustees meet in December/January. Successful applicants will receive awards during January. Organisations that have already received a grant can reapply describing how the previous year's grant was spent and setting out how a further grant would be used. In general, less detailed information is required from national charities with a known track record than from small local charities that are not known to the trustees. Owing to the volume of applications, it is not possible to acknowledge each application, nor is it possible to inform unsuccessful applicants.

Simon Gibson Charitable Trust

General

Wild Rose House, Llancarfan, Vale of Glamorgan CF62 3AD
Tel and Fax: 01446 781004
E-mail: bryan@marsh66.fsnet.co.uk
Correspondent: Bryan Marsh, Trustee

Income: £480,000 (1999/2000)
Grant total: £483,000 (1999/2000)
Grants to youth: £70,000 (1999/2000)

The trust was established in 1975 by George Simon Gibson, son of George Cock Gibson whose trust appears above. Around 100 mostly small and recurrent grants are made each year to a broad range of charities. Beneficiaries are often UK charities, or local organisations in Norfolk, Suffolk, Cambridgeshire, South Wales or Central London.

In 1999/2000 the majority of the 127 awards ranged between £1,000 and £3,000 with nearly half for £2,000. Grants included those to: Sea Cadets and Youth Clubs UK (£4,000 each); Drive for Youth and Guide Association, Cambridgeshire (£2,000 each); and First Exning Boy Scouts Troop (£1,000).

No grants are given to individuals.

Applications: In writing to the correspondent; the trust has no application forms. Telephone calls are not welcomed. The trust acknowledges all applications but does not enter into correspondence with applicants unless they are awarded a grant. The trustees meet in May and applications should be received by March for consideration at that meeting.

The Goldsmiths' Company's Charities

General, London charities, the precious metals craft

Goldsmiths' Hall, Foster Lane, London EC2V 6BN
Tel: 020 7606 7010 **Fax:** 020 7606 1511
E-mail: the.clerk@thegoldsmiths.co.uk
Website: www.thegoldsmiths.co.uk
Correspondent: R D Buchanan-Dunlop, Clerk

Income: £2 million (1999/2000)
Grant total: £1.8 million (1999/2000)
Grants to youth: £35,000 (1999/2000)

This entry covers three of the charities of the Goldsmiths' livery company in London: John Perryn's Charity; the General Charity; and Goldsmiths' Charitable Donation Fund. 300 grants a year are given to support a broad range of causes, which are London-based or national charities only.

Most grants are of between £1,000 and £2,000, with a maximum of around £50,000, and are mainly for revenue costs. Half of the beneficiaries in any one year receive grants repeated over three years.

The trust's annual report writes about its grants to youth causes as follows: 'grants have been made towards psychotherapy for children, counselling and research into adolescent breakdown. … a high proportion of grants have also been made to youth associations and activities, and it is encouraging that there is a wide range of youth organisations, and more particularly volunteers, devoted to developing the talents and sense of adventure in young people from disadvantaged backgrounds and to discovering new ways of doing this …'

In 1999/2000 grants to youth groups and organisations ranged between £500 and £5,000. They included: £5,000 to Federation of London Youth Clubs towards the costs of training programmes; £2,500 to Endeavour Training towards long-term support for young people; £2,000 each to Churches together in Clapham for the salary of a youth development worker and Shadwell Basin Outdoor Activity Centre towards a canoeing programme for younger and less-skilled members, and £1,500 each to Pedro Club for the refurbishment costs at the Marlow site and St John's Youth Centre for the youth development project.

Grants are not given to: medical research; memorials to individuals; overseas projects; animal welfare.

Applications: Charities applying for general charitable support should apply on an application form available from the correspondent. The following should be included:

- an outline of the current work and experience of the applicant organisation including details of staffing, organisational structure and use of volunteers;
- the organisation's most recent annual report, if one is published;
- a detailed budget for the proposed activity;
- the organisation's most recent audited accounts (or financial report required by the Charities Act);
- the methods by which the success of the project will be evaluated;
- the income/expenditure projection for the organisation for the current year;
- other grant-making organisations appealed to for the same project and with what result;
- preference for a single or annual grant for up to three years.

Trustees meet monthly except during August and September.

Grantham Yorke Trust

General in the West Midlands, in particular the Birmingham area

Martineau Johnson, St Philips House, St Philips Place, Birmingham B3 2PP
Tel: 0121 200 3300
Correspondent: David L Turfrey & Lucy Chatt

Income: £244,000 (1999/2000)
Grant total: £210,000 to organisations (1999/2000)

The trust gives grants for education and relief-in-need to individuals and to local organisations, particularly youth organisations in Birmingham and the West Midlands.

Grant information was not available for 1999/2000. In 1998/99 the trust gave grants totalling £316,000, made up of £223,000 to organisations and £93,000 to individuals. Large grants included: £5,000 each to Birmingham Community Association Youth Project and Dodford Children's Holiday Farm.

Youth beneficiaries in previous years have included: Birmingham Young Volunteers; St Martin's Youth & Community Projects; Birmingham Pakistan Scout Development Project; Intercity Camp Trust; Sikh Community & Youth Service, Guide Association – Woodlarks Camp; Rubery Youth Marching Band and Shard End Youth Centre.

Applications: In writing to the correspondent.

The Great Britain Sasakawa Foundation

Links between Great Britain and Japan

43 North Audley Street, London W1Y 1WH
Tel: 020 7355 2229 **Fax:** 020 7355 2230
E-mail: gbsf@gbsf.org.uk
Website: www.gbsf.org.uk
Correspondent: Michael Barrett, Chief Executive

Income: £657,000 (2000)
Grant total: £512,000 (2000)
Grants to youth: About £30,000

The foundation supports youth exchanges to strengthen links between the UK and Japan. Grants are normally between £500 and £3,000. Roughly three quarters of the beneficiaries are based in the UK and few receive recurrent awards.

Grants for youth exchanges are administered through Connect Youth International, and enquiries should be directed to this agency.

Grants are not given to individuals applying on their own behalf. The foundation can, however, consider proposals from organisations which support the activities of individuals, provided they are citizens of the UK or Japan. No grants can be made for the construction, conservation or maintenance of land and buildings.

Applications: Youth exchange and school applicants should submit their application to Connect Youth International, The British Council, 10 Spring Gardens, London SW1A 2BN, whose Japanese Exchange Programme is supported by the foundation, aims tot encourage exchanges in both directions. (Further information on the work of Connect Youth International is on page 289.)

The Alfred Haines Charitable Trust

Christian, health, welfare, with a preference for the West Midlands

Dale Farm, Worcester Lane, Sutton Coldfield B75 5PR
Tel: 0121 323 3236 **Fax:** 0121 323 3237
E-mail: ahct@quothquan.org
Correspondent: The Trustees

Income: £92,000 (1998/99)
Grant total: £156,000 (1998/99)
Grants to youth: £24,000 (1998/99)

The trust prefers to support specific projects and concentrates on helping smaller charities based in Birmingham and the immediate surrounding area.

Grants are generally one-off, although projects may be funded annually for up to three years. The trust prefers to make grants towards specific items and does not give to large appeals. Projects overseas or outside the West Midlands, whether Christian or not, will only be considered where the applicants are known to a trustee or are recommended by someone known to a trustee who has first hand knowledge of the work.

In 1998/99 no grants list was provided by the trust, but the number of grants and grant totals were given under seven headings. Under the heading 'Youth work, workers and support activities (including salaries, expenses of voluntary workers, educational literature)', 25 grants were made totalling £24,000. In the past grants have been for between £100 and £5,000.

Support is *not* given for:
- activities which are primarily the responsibility of central or local government or some other responsible body;
- animal welfare;
- church buildings – restoration, improvements, renovations or new ones;
- environmental – conservation and protection of wildlife and landscape;
- expeditions and overseas trips;
- hospitals and health centres;
- individuals, including students (On the rare occasions that individuals are supported, the person has to be recommended by someone known to the trustees and the funding should be of long-term benefit to others.);

- large national charities; it is unusual for the trust to support large national charities even where there is a local project;
- loans and business finance;
- medical research projects;
- overseas appeals (see above);
- promotion of any religion other than Christianity;
- school, universities and colleges;
- purely evangelistic projects.

Applications: In writing to the correspondent, including: a brief description of the activities of the organisation; details of the project and its overall cost; what funds have already been raised and how the remaining funds are to be raised; a copy of the latest accounts including any associated or parent organisation; and any other leaflets or supporting documentation

Trustees meet bi-monthly to consider written applications for grants. Replies are only sent where further information is required. No telephone calls or correspondence will be entered into for any proposed or declined applications. Successful applicants are required to complete an official receipt and produce a report on the project, usually after 10 months. Successful applicants are advised to leave at least 10 months before applying for further support.

The W A Handley Charitable Trust

General, in Northumberland and Tyneside

c/o Ryecroft Glenton, 27 Portland Terrace, Newcastle upon Tyne NE2 1QP
Correspondent: The Secretaries to the Trustees

Income: £399,000 (1999/2000)
Grant total: £362,000 (1999/2000)
Grants to youth: £83,000 to children and youth (1999/2000)

The trust's policy is as follows: 1) Grants will be in response to applications from within the Northumberland and Tyneside area and from national charities either operating within or where work may be expected to be of benefit to the Northumberland and Tyneside area. Grants will not usually be made outside these areas. 2) Grants will commonly be in response to appeals directed towards: crisis funding; pump-priming finance; operating expenses; alleviation of distress. 3) Grants will be made out of income and may take the form of recurrent or single payments. Grants will not normally be made out of capital. 4) Grants to youth and uniformed groups will be made to the local umbrella group where possible rather than to individual clubs and associations.

In 1999/2000 40 grants were given to youth/children, totalling £83,000. The trust has a regular list of 124 charities which received £141,000 in total. The other £222,000 was given to 35 of the 419 organisations which applied to the trust. Beneficiaries of one-off grants included those to Chester-le-Street Sea Cadet Corp (£3,400) and Balliol Youth Centre and Wayout in Gateshead

(£1,000 each). Among the regular beneficiaries, grants ranged from £500 to £3,000, although most were for £1,000 or less. Recipients included Big Lamp Youth Project; Durham Scout County Association; North Tyneside Girl Guides; Northumberland Association of Boys' Clubs and Tyneside Youth for Christ.

No grants are given to individuals.

Applications: In writing to the correspondent. Grants to registered charities only. Grant distributions take place at the end of March, June, September and December.

William Harding's Charity

Education, welfare in Aylesbury only

c/o Parrott & Coales (Solicitors),
14 Bourbon Street, Aylesbury,
Buckinghamshire HP20 2RS
Tel: 01296 318500
Correspondent: J Leggett

Income: £571,000 (1998)
Grant total: £702,000 (1998)
Grants to youth: £57,000 (1998)

The trust supports a range of causes for the benefit of the residents of Aylesbury in Buckinghamshire. Grants to youth organisations in 1998 included £11,000 to Aylesbury Youth Action, and £6,500 to Youth Concern to support two groups

meeting at UpTown Coffee Bar. No support is given to 'persons and organisations not based in Aylesbury Town.'

Applications: In writing to the correspondent.

The Harris Charity

Young people

Richard House, 9 Winckley Square,
Preston PR1 3HP
Tel: 01772 821021 Fax: 01772 259441
Correspondent: P R Metcalf, Secretary

Income: £118,000 (2000/01)
Grant total: £66,000 to organisations (2000/01)
Grants to youth: Est. £30,000 (2000/01)

The trust helps young people under 25 who live in the county of Lancashire, with a preference given to the borough of Preston.

Organisations helping children from 0 to 25 years are supported. Grants to organisations were listed in the 2000/01 accounts under the headings set out in the chart below.

Grants included:
- £3,000 to Chorley District Scout Council towards a security fence around the scout centre;

The Harris Charity – grants 2000/01			
	Preston area	Lancashire area	2001 total
Charitable	£6,000	£16,000	£22,000
Educational	£13,000	£3,900	£17,000
Recreational – scouts, youth clubs etc.	£7,600	£8,300	£16,000
Recreational – sports, playgroups etc.	£9,400	£2,400	£12,000
Totals	£36,000	£30,000	£66,000

- £2,000 each to 46th Preston (Notre Dame) Scout Group towards four tents; Lancashire Youth Clubs Association towards an information library database and Lonsdale District Scout Council towards furnishings and a disabled toilet;
- £1,300 to Foxton Youth and Community Centre towards a floor and ceiling storage cupboard;
- £880 to Penwortham St Teresa's Junior Football Club towards football strips;
- £200 to Young Enterprise Preston towards a presentation evening.

Grants were also given to individuals for activities such as organised trips, music, sport and educational equipment.

Applications: Application forms can be obtained from the correspondent. Appeals received before 31 March are considered by July each year. Appeals received before 30 September are considered the following January.

The Haymills Charitable Trust

Education, medicine, welfare, youth, in the UK, but particularly the west of London and Suffolk, where the Haymills group is sited

Empire House, Hanger Green, Ealing, London W5 3BDl
Tel: 020 8991 4309
Correspondent: W Ferres, Secretary

Income: £132,000 (1999/2000)
Grant total: £80,000 to organisations (1999/2000)
Grants to youth: £55,000 to 'Youth and welfare' (1999/2000)

The trustees' report states: 'the trustees regularly review their policy, aiming to make the best use of the funds available by donating varying amounts to projects which they believe are not widely known and thus are likely to be inadequately supported. Their main support is to registered charities operating in areas known to them, especially those lying in and to the west of London and in Suffolk'.

Grants fall into four main categories, including a youth category, where support is given for training schemes to assist in the education, welfare and training of young people. In 1999/2000 grants totalling £85,000 were made to organisations and six individuals. Beneficiaries included Middlesex Young People's Club and Raleigh International (£3,500 each) and Greater London Central Scout County (£500).

The trust states 'No personal applications for support will be considered unless endorsed by a university, college or other appropriate authority. Each year, a limited number of applicants can be considered who can show that they are committed to further education and training preferably for employment in the construction industry'.

Applications: In writing to the correspondent, but see note above. Trustees meet at least twice a year, usually in March and October. Applications are not acknowledged.

The Charles Hayward Foundation

Welfare and health, medical research, overseas

Hayward House, 45 Harrington Gardens, London SW7 4JU
Tel: 020 7370 7063/7067
Correspondent: Mark Schnebli, Administrator

Income: £2.1 million (2000)
Grant total: £1.6 million (2000)
Grants to youth: Est. £85,000 (2000)

This is a new charity formed from the merger of the previous Hayward Foundation and the Charles Hayward Trust. Grants, generally ranging from £1,000 to £50,000, are given mainly for capital costs for welfare and health, medical research and overseas.

The following organisations are eligible to apply for grants: UK-based registered national and regional charities, smaller local charities, churches and religious organisations, partnerships, community organisations, and mutual welfare societies which are responsible for their own management, finances and fundraising.

The trust informed us that its grant making to youth organisations is in many ways a peripheral part of its work. According to our calculations, youth grants account for 5% of the trust's total grants. In 2000 grants were made under the Youth and early intervention category to the following youth organisations:

- Welsh Association of Youth Clubs, Cardiff: £22,000 towards a youth achievement award scheme in the Merthyr area;
- St Nicholas's Church, Beverley: £18,000 towards a new youth room in a church community centre;
- Spiral Trust, Bournemouth: £10,000 towards furniture and fittings for a youth drop-in centre;
- Youth Aid, Lewisham: £10,000 towards refurbishing a young people's drop-in and information centre;
- Barcaple Christian Outdoor Centre: £7,500 towards buying a barn for indoor sports;
- Keyhold Trust, Wales: £5,000 towards the conversion of a hay barn to a drama studio;
- Newquay Christian Centre, Cornwall: £5,000 towards converting a church hall to accommodation for young people;
- Perdiswell Young People's Club: £5,000 towards an extension for a youth club building.

Further grants were made to youth groups under the 'Small grants and miscellaneous' heading, for example: £1,000 to Darlaston Boys' Club; £800 to Chichester Youth Adventure Trust and £100 to Stanton under Bardon Youth Club in Leicester.

Grants are *not* made:
- to individuals;
- for ongoing revenue expenditure;
- to pay off loans;
- for fundraising activities, transport, travel, holidays, bursaries, general repairs, computers, video or sound equipment, church restoration, academic chairs or endowment funds;
- to replace government or lottery funding or towards activities which are primarily the responsibility of central or local government or some other responsible body;
- to other grant-making organisations;
- to organisations that restrict their benefit to one section of society;

- to animal welfare organisations;
- sports clubs.

Organisations that have large reserves or endowment funds and well established funding streams are given a lower priority.

Applications: Applications should be made in writing to the correspondent. Applicants should send an initial short résumé of the project, together with a set of the latest audited accounts. The foundation can then advise as to whether more information is required. This initial application should not exceed three sides of A4 paper, excluding enclosures.

All applications will receive an acknowledgement. However, as there is often a waiting list, and trustees meet only four times a year to consider applications, applicants may have a wait of several months before they receive a decision. Please note that there are always many more applications than the foundation is able to fund out of its limited resources. On average, 1 in 20 applications are approved by the trustees. Applicants should read the guidelines very carefully, as the trust warns that inappropriate applications waste time.

Information required

- *Name and location of organisation* – The official name of the organisation and its location.
- *Contact details* – Give the name and position of the person submitting the application, contact telephone number and address.
- *Description of organisation* – Provide a description of your present work and the priorities you are addressing.
- *Quantify the scale of your operation* – how many people do you help and how?
- *Description of proposed project* – Describe the project you are undertaking,

detailing the number of people and groups who will benefit and how. Specify how life will be improved for the target group.
- *Project cost* – Give a breakdown of the costs for the full project. Capital and revenue costs should be kept separate. For a capital project, include only information on the capital costs.
- *Funds raised and pledged* – Give a breakdown of the funds raised to date towards your target, separating capital and revenue, where applicable. Include the amount of any of your own funds or reserves going into the project, and any money you intend to borrow.
- *Outstanding shortfall* – Specify the amount of money you still need for capital and revenue separately.
- *Timetable* – State the timetable for the project; when it will start and be finished.

Enclosures and other information required

Please enclose with your application:
- One recent set of full audited accounts. Include accounts for connected organisations. If applicable and relevant to the size of your project, please also provide further information, as follows:
- A summary of how you are going to evaluate the success of the project, and how you will report this back to the foundation.
- An annual report.
- References, recommendations or letters of support.
- Explanation of how you will fund the ongoing costs of your project.
- Floor plans, drawings, or pictures (no larger than A3).
- A list of any other funders who are actively considering making significant contributions.

- A prospectus or business plan for the project.
- Progress of any planning or statutory requirements required for your project to proceed.

Applications are accepted at any stage and are prioritised according to project timetable and suitability. Applicants are advised to write as soon as they have accurate details of their project. Applicants can discuss the project before writing to the foundation and applicants by contacting Mark Schnebli or David Brown on 020 7370 7063 or 020 7370 7067.

The Hedley Foundation

Youth, health, welfare

9 Dowgate Hill, London EC4R 2SU
Tel: 020 7489 8076 **Fax:** 020 7489 8977
Correspondent: P T Dunkerley, Secretary

Income: £1.2 million (1999/2000)
Grant total: £996,000 (1999/2000)
Grants to youth: Est. £100,000 (1999/2000)

The trust gives over 250 grants a year, the majority being for between £1,000 and £5,000. Most are for capital costs such as building refurbishment or to purchase equipment, but larger amounts (particularly when for £10,000 or more) are more likely to be for revenue or project funding, occasionally over a period of three to five years.

The foundation has four funding priorities including one for young people covering their education, training, health and welfare (currently about half the foundation's budget). A grants list was only available for 1998/99 when the largest grants went to the Outward

Bound Trust (£30,000, project costs) and Fairbridge (£20,000, 'voluntary sector coalition'). Other grants to youth organisations included £10,000 each to Cumbria Association of Youth Clubs (annual donation); GAP Activity Projects (2nd of 3 annual donations); Raleigh International (3rd and final donation) and the YMCA (building redevelopment); £6,500 to Prince's Trust Volunteers (team funding); and £5,000 to Old Moat Youth Outreach Project (equipment).

Grants are made only to registered charities. No grants are given to:
- overseas charities
- individuals, under any circumstances
- national and very large appeals.

Applications: The trustees meet about every six weeks, so applications receive prompt attention. They should be accompanied by the latest available accounts, and a note of the present state of the appeal and its future prospects; in the case of buildings, it should also outline plans and details of planning status. For community schemes it would be helpful to have a brief description of the community, its history, present make-up and aspirations, what is going for and against it and so on, to put flesh on the application. Trustees individually have visited many charities to which the foundation might make or had made grants.

Help a London Child

Children in Greater London and a few surrounding areas

c/o Capital Radio, 29–30 Leicester Square, London WC2H 7LA
Tel: 020 7766 6203 **Fax:** 020 7766 6195
E-mail: adam.findlay@capitalradio.com
Website: www.capitalfm.com
Correspondent: Rich Hornsell, Allocation Manager

Income: £1.1 million (2000)
Grant total: £881,000 (2000)
Grants to youth: £124,000 (2000)

This is an annual charity appeal run by a London commercial radio station. It makes a large number of small grants each autumn to London children's charities. The charity is keen to support a wide range of activities and projects including holidays and outings in the UK, equipment, music, arts and drama.

In 1999/2000 grants were made totalling £124,000 under the 'youth' heading, which covers grants to clubs and centres focused on children over eleven years old, including scouts and guides and adventure playgrounds. The average size of a grant is £2,000, and only very rarely is a grant of more than £5,000 awarded.

The charity describes its grantmaking as follows: 'HALC invites applications from any group. If you are not a registered charity, you can still apply, but you must have your application endorsed by a registered group willing to accept the grant on your behalf. 'The HALC panel look favourably on projects that directly benefit children. Successful projects should illustrate how the money will go directly to the children involved rather than on administration.'

Reapplications are encouraged; of groups awarded grants in 1999, 29% applied again in 2000, of which 77% were successful. Organisations can be funded repeatedly for three years or more as long as they can show new aspects of the project and, particularly, how the previous grant has enabled the project to develop. After this, the guidelines say that 'projects applying for a fourth year in a row will be given less priority than other applicants'. If applicable, applicants are advised to show how the project would maintain funding in future years if a repeat application were not successful.

In 1999/2000 grants in the youth category included: £3,600 to The Tower Youth Club Summer Project 2001; £3,500 to Avenues Unlimited towards residential experiences for young people; £2,500 to Westminster House Youth Club towards the continuation of summer scheme expansion; £2,300 to Cambridge House and Talbot Young People's Project towards Hi-Light Youth Group; £2,000 to 1st Langley Scouts ASC Memorial Fund towards a climbing wall at a camp site; £1,500 to Abbey Wood Youth Club towards new equipment; and £880 to 1st Cranham Girls' and Boys' Brigade's Bugle Band.

Help a London Child will *not* fund:

- individual children or families;
- retrospective funding;
- statutory funding – funding for schools or health projects that would otherwise be covered by designated statutory funding from the local authority;
- salary posts for more than 12 months;
- deficit funding or repayment of loans;
- medical research;
- purchase of a minibus;
- trips abroad;
- distribution to other organisations;

- religious activities;
- general structural changes to buildings.

Applications: Grants are awarded once a year only in November. Application forms (including guidelines) are available from February to May and require an A4 sae. Completed forms must be sent or delivered by hand to the address above. Photocopies or faxes cannot be accepted. The closing date is always the last Friday in May. Applicants will get an acknowledgement in late June along with a reference number. The allocations panel meets during the summer to consider all applications. While additional information may be provided in support of applications, the panel are only given copies of the application form. Applicants will be informed of the panel's decision, in writing, in November.

The HALC office can be contacted on 020 7766 6203/6490 and applicants should quote their reference number. The guidelines add: 'Should you have any questions about filling in the form, please contact the HALC office on 020 7766 6203. Alternatively, you could contact the London Voluntary Service Council, who provide general information about applying for funding (020 7700 8107), or your local CVS office.'

The Horne Foundation

Education, arts, youth, in or near Northampton

Suite 33, Burlington House,
369 Wellingborough Road,
Northampton NN1 4EU
Tel: 01604 629748
Correspondent: Mrs R M Harwood, Secretary

Income: £348,000 (1999/2000)
Grant total: £690,000 (1999/2000)
Grants to youth: £92,000 (1999/2000)

The trust's main priority is to give long-term support to educational facilities primarily in the Northamptonshire area. Grants to youth organisations were £70,000 to Daventry District Council Millennium Gift, towards the construction of playgrounds in Northamptonshire; £12,000 to Northamptonshire Association of Youth Clubs and £10,000 to Northampton Cricket Club.

The foundation 'does not respond to appeals from charities providing local services in communities located outside Northamptonshire'. It prefers organisations without religious affiliation.

Applications: In writing to the correspondent at any time.

The Rita Lila Howard Foundation

Children up to the age of 16

4 Felstead Gardens, Ferry Street,
London E14 3BS
Tel: 020 7537 1118
Correspondent: The Company Secretary

Income: £533,000 (1998/99)
Grant total: £760,000 (1998/99)

The founder of this trust had an interest in children's charities and the trust's grant-making focus is 'to support a few innovative projects that benefit children up to the age of 16 within the British Isles'. Funds are directed to selected projects which 'support the education of young people or to ameliorate their physical and emotional environment'.

Donations are given over a finite period, with the aim that the project can be self-supporting when funding has ended. The trust does not provide a grants list with its accounts.

Grants are not given to individuals, organisations which are not registered charities, or towards operating expenses, budget deficits, (sole) capital projects, annual charitable appeals, general endowment funds, fundraising drives or events, conferences, or student aid.

Applications: The trust states that it does not accept unsolicited applications, since the trustees seek out and support projects they are interested in.

The Hull & East Riding Charitable Trust

General in Hull and the East Riding of Yorkshire

Secretary and Administrator, Greenmeades, Kemp Road, Swanland, East Yorkshire HU14 3LY
Tel: 01482 634664
Fax: 01482 631700
Correspondent: J R Barnes

Income: £268,000 (1999/2000)
Grant total: £223,000 (1999/2000)
Grants to youth: Est. £20,000 (2000/01)

The trust appears to have a preference for organisations working with children/youth, medical/disability and welfare, although other types of organisation are also supported. Many organisations receive regular grants over a number of years. National charities are supported but usually only if they carry out work in the local area. The trust states: 'It is unlikely that the trustees would support

the total cost of a project and applicants should be able to demonstrate that funds have been raised or are in the process of being raised from other sources'.

In 2000/01 grants included those to Hull Boys' Club (£5,000); Active 8 Raleigh International (£4,000); Cottingham Young Peoples Sports (£2,500); Drypool Youth Work Project (£1,000) and Hessle High School Drum Corps and Kingston Crystalettes (£500 each).

Grants are not normally given to individuals. No grants are given to organisations or causes of a political nature, or for religious purposes, although requests for maintenance of significant religious buildings may be considered. If a donation has recently been made the trustees would not expect to receive a further request from the recipient in the immediate future.

Applications: In writing to the correspondent, including the aims of the project and hoped for benefits, the costs involved with budgets/accounts as appropriate, the contribution sought from the trust and details of other funds raised. The trustees meet in May and November and requests for donations will only be considered at those meetings. Applications must be received by 30 April and 31 October.

Irish Youth Foundation (UK) Ltd

Irish young people

The Irish Centre, Blacks Road,
Hammersmith, London W6 9DT
Tel: 020 8748 9640 **Fax:** 020 8748 7386
E-mail: info@iyf.org.uk
Website: www.iyf.org.uk
Correspondent: Linda Tanner,
Administrator

Income: £246,000 (1999/2000)
Grant total: £215,000 (2000/01)
Grants to youth: £38,000 (2000/01)

The foundation works to improve the lives of Irish children and young people in Ireland and the UK, and support is given to organisations working with people up to 25 years of age. Funds raised come from gift aid donations and a series of fundraising events organised throughout the year. A wide range of projects are supported, including cross community initiatives and educational, cultural and social activities. Grants range from £500 to £25,000 and are awarded annually.

Grants fall into the following three categories:
- small grants for up to £2,000
- medium grants for over £2,000 and under £10,000
- large grants for one year or more ranging from £10,000 to £25,000.

In 2000/01 grants to youth clubs in the UK included:
- £15,000 to Cricklewood Homeless Concern in Brent, towards an Irish youth worker's salary;
- £7,000 to Bristol Playbus, towards the salary of a junior youth community development worker;
- £5,000 to London Connection, towards an Irish youth worker;
- £4,000 to Harehills Irish Music Project, towards the salary of a part-time youth worker in Leeds;
- £2,000 to the Corrymeela Community towards a programme for 14 to 18 year olds;
- £2,000 to Foyle Search and Rescue Service towards a cadet scheme for 15 to 17 year olds;
- £2,000 to Tyneside Irish Cultural Society, towards cultural and educational activities for Irish young people;
- £1,000 to St John Bosco Youth Club in Tower Hamlets, towards Irish dance costumes.

Grants are *not* given for:
- projects for people over 25 years
- general appeals
- academic research
- alleviating deficits already incurred
- individuals.

Applications: In writing to the correspondent, requesting an application form. Applications are considered in November and grants are awarded in February of the following year. Applications are assessed on the following requirements: need; continuity; track record/evaluation; disadvantaged young people; innovation; funding sources; and budgetary control.

Kelsick's Educational Foundation

Education in the Old Lakes Urban District, that is Ambleside, Grasmere, Langdale and part of Troutbeck

Kelsick Centre, St Mary's Lane, Ambleside, Cumbria LA22 9DG
Tel: 01539 431289
Fax: 01539 431292
Correspondent: P G Frost, Clerk

Income: £250,000 (2000/01)
Grant total: £150,000 to individuals and organisations (2000/01)
Grants to youth: Est. £30,000 (2000/01)

The trust supports educational establishments and educational community groups in the beneficial area. About a third of the grant total is usually given to the three church schools in the area, especially for special needs; about a third to organisations such as uniformed groups and a third to individuals. The trust sometimes applies the education objects as widely as possible and in the past it has supported toddlers' playgroups, basketball clubs, scout groups and the like. The trust has helped with roof repairs to a scout hut (about £500) and brownies' trips (£130).

Applications: Application forms are available from the correspondent.

The Sir James Knott Trust

General, in Northumberland, Tyne & Wear and Co. Durham

16–18 Hood Street, Newcastle upon Tyne NE1 6JQ
Tel: 0191 230 4016 **Fax:** 0191 230 4016
Correspondent: Brigadier John F F Sharland, Secretary

Income: £1.3 million (2000/01)
Grant total: £1.2 million (2000/01)
Grants to youth: Est. over £120,000 (2000/01)

Grants are normally only made to registered charities, in response to applications from within the beneficial area, and from national charities either operating within, or where the work may be expected to be of benefit to that area. The trust supports a range of causes, including the welfare of young people.

In 2000/01 62 grants were made to young people and children: including: £10,000 to Durham Association of Boys' Clubs; £8,000 to Berwick Youth Project; £5,000 each to Balliol Youth Centre and Southwick & Monkwearmouth Community Transport (Southwick Neighbourhood Youth Project); £3,000 to Army Cadet Force Northumberland and £2,000 to Seaham Youth Initiative, Co. Durham. Four local scouts groups received grants, three of £10,000 and one of £1,000. 14 sea cadet groups were supported, with grants of £750 each.

No applications are considered from individuals or from non-registered charities. Grants are only made to charities from within the north east of England, and from national charities either operating within, or where work may be expected to be of benefit to the north east of England.

Applications: In writing to the correspondent. 'Please be brief. Do not, for example, explain at great length why it is that a blind, starving, bankrupt, one-legged man from Jupiter needs help.'

The trust asks applicants to address all the following questions, although 'not all the questions necessarily apply to you, but they give an idea of the kind of questions that the trustees may ask when your application is being considered':

- Who are you? How are you organised/managed?
- What is your aim? What coordination do you have with other organisations with similar aims?
- What do you do and how does it benefit the community? How many people 'in need' actually use or take advantage of your facilities?
- How have you been funded in the past, how will you be funded in the future? Enclose summary of last year's balance sheet.
- How much do you need, what for and when? Have you thought about depreciation/running costs/replacement? If your project is not funded in full, what do you propose to do with the money you have raised?
- What is the overall cost, what is the deficit and how are you planning to cover the deficit? Is it an open-ended commitment, or when will you become self-supporting?
- If you will never be self-supporting, what is your long-term fundraising strategy? Have you even thought about it?
- Who else have you asked for money, and how have they responded? What are you doing yourselves to raise money?
- Have you applied to the National Lottery? When will you get the result?

If you have not applied, are you eligible and when will you apply?
- What is your registered charity number, or which registered charity is prepared to administer funds on your behalf? How can you be contacted by telephone?

Trustees normally meet in February, June and October. Applications need to be submitted two months (or more) in advance.

Laing's Charitable Trust

General

133 Page Street, London NW7 2ER
Tel: 020 8959 3636
Correspondent: Michael Hamilton, Secretary

Income: £1.9 million (1999)
Grant total: £797,000 to organisations (1999)

This trust is one of a group of Laing Family Foundations and is the most relevant to this guide. However, an application to one Laing Family Foundation counts as an application to all. This trust makes nearly 1,000 grants a year, most of them for amounts of less than £1,000. About half of the funds are disbursed in larger grants, from £1,000 up to £50,000, mostly to regularly supported beneficiaries, typically youth or community development organisations.

The top 50 donations to institutions, listed with the accounts, totalled £585,000. Of these, 17 ranged from £10,000 to £50,000 and these accounted for 54% of the grant total. Nearly all of the recipients of grants of this size had been supported in the previous year, many in the preceding three years or more. Grants included those to Young Enterprise (£30,000) and Raleigh International (£20,000). A number of smaller grants of £100 or £250 were made to scout groups, girl guides and youth clubs.

No grants are given to individuals (other than to Laing employees and/or their dependents).

Applications: In writing to the correspondent. No particular application form is required. Receipt of applications is not acknowledged unless successful, or unless a reply paid envelope is sent with the application.

The Lankelly Foundation

Social welfare, disability

2 The Court, High Street, Harwell,
Oxfordshire OX11 0EY
Tel: 01235 820044
Correspondent: Peter Kilgarriff

Income: £4.6 million (2000/01)
Grant total: £5.3 million (2000/01)
Grants to youth: Est. £350,000 (2000/01)

The trust works in the UK but does not support projects in London. Following a policy review in May 2001 its current priorities are set out below. The trust says it:

- Only supports registered charities.
- Prefers to support community initiatives to meet local needs. It intends to concentrate upon smaller charities, many of which will have only a local or regional remit. The trustees will consider applications from large national charities but support will be rare and limited.
- Looks for user involvement as well as the proper use and support of

volunteers, and applicants will have to provide evidence of sound management and a commitment to equal opportunities.

- Particularly welcomes applications from eligible black voluntary sector and minority ethnic groups.
- Wants its grants to be effective, to achieve something which otherwise would not happen, or to sustain something which otherwise might fail.
- Does not make grants to replace funds that have been withdrawn from statutory sources, or consider applications to replace time expired grants from any national lottery board.
- Makes grants of a minimum of £5,000; grants are always made for specific purposes but they may cover capital or revenue needs. The trust will consider revenue support to a maximum of five years, although three year support will be more common.
- Shall monitor the effectiveness of all grants, but those made over a number of years will involve more detailed evaluation and further visits from staff.

The trust's broad priorities from May 2001 to May 2004 are elderly people, homelessness, neighbourhood work, physical and learning disabilities, families and children, mental health, penal affairs and young people. In addition each year the trustees set aside a sum of money to be distributed in small grants to summer playschemes. The trust says it aims: 'To support work with young people aged 14 to 25 years. Projects that support vulnerable young people through the difficult transition to adulthood, particularly those living in deprived neighbourhoods, at risk of school exclusion or offending, including youngsters leaving local authority care'.

The trust does not make grants to individual youth clubs.

In 2000/01 grants totalling £931,000 were agreed for 25 organisations under the old 'Children and young people' heading. They included:

- £75,000 over three years to Frontier Youth Trust, Bristol, towards appointing a qualified youth worker to work with 125 Project;
- £69,000 to Welsh Association of Youth Clubs, to employ a development worker for West Wales;
- a £60,000 three year grant to Cornerston Church Swansea Trust to underpin the core costs of its community project;
- £30,000 over three years towards the cost of a youth worker post for Kingsway Meadow Community Association in Teignmouth;
- £20,000 to a detached youth work project in York, towards the manager's salary;
- £15,000 to Depaul Trust: Gravelly Hill Community Centre in Birmingham, to help with the capital costs of refurbishing a building to provide local community facilities;
- £10,000 to Perdiswell Young People's Leisure Club in Worcester towards the cost of furnishing the new extension.

Grants totalling £40,000 were made to 125 summer play and holiday schemes throughout the UK.

The trust does *not* contribute to large, widely circulated appeals, nor will it consider retrospective funding for work that has already taken place. It does not make grants in support of:

- adaptations to improve access to buildings
- advancement of religion
- conferences or seminars
- festivals or theatre productions
- individual needs
- large capital projects
- other grant-making bodies
- schools for people with special needs
- travel, expeditions or holidays
- animal welfare
- arts and heritage
- endowment funds
- hospices
- individual youth clubs
- medical research
- publications, films or video
- sport
- vehicles
- formal education including institutes of further and higher education, NHS hospital trusts and those emanating from associated charities concerned with medical projects.

Applications: Your initial letter should describe:

- who you are
- what you do
- why you are seeking the trust's help
- how you will measure success
- how much money you need to raise
- how soon you need it
- who else you have asked to help
- what support you have already attracted.

You should send the above letter with the following:

- brief information about the origins and current company/charitable status of your organisation;
- a copy of your most recent annual report and full audited accounts;
- an itemised income and expenditure budget for your organisation;
- an itemised income and expenditure budget for the work to be funded;
- equal opportunities policy.

The trustees meet quarterly, in January, April, July and October. Applications may be submitted at any time but you should be aware that agendas for meetings are planned well ahead and you should expect a period of six months between an initial application and formal consideration by the trustees.

The Leathersellers' Company Charitable Fund
General

15 St Helen's Place, London EC3A 6DQ
Tel: 020 7330 1444
Correspondent: Capt. J Cooke, Clerk

Income: £1.2 million (1999/2000)
Grant total: £2.2 million to institutions (1999/2000)

Most funds are disbursed by this trust in ongoing annual donations or recurrent grants, normally for between £10,000 and £50,000, to a largely fixed list of beneficiaries. However out of 170 or so grants a year, typically half are one-off payments under £5,000.

Grants are made under eight main category headings, including the category 'Children and youth'. Under this heading £204,000 in total was distributed in 1999/2000. Grants of over £5,000 were listed in the accounts for this year, which included £15,000 to Youth at Risk and £5,000 each to Greater London Scout Group and London Sailing Project.

Applications: To the correspondent in writing. 'It should, however, be noted that before an award is made, the charity is thoroughly investigated and visited which, of necessity, limits the number of appeals capable of being processed in any one year.'

The Levy Foundation
Young people, older people, health, medical research

6 Camden High Street, Camden Town, London NW1 0JH
Tel: 020 7874 7200 **Fax:** 020 7874 7206
E-mail: administrator@levyfoundation.org.uk
Correspondent: Ms Sue Nyfield, Grants Manager

Income: £850,000 (2000/01)
Grant total: £950,000 (2000/01)
Grants to youth: £300,000 (2000/01)

Each year about three quarters of the grants by number are small, often repeated, donations for between £100 and £5,000. However about half of the funds are used for a number of substantial long-term commitments, from £10,000 to £250,000 a year, mainly to organisations involved with medical care and research, Jewish causes, or youth welfare.

In 2000/01 grants to youth causes included: £210,000 to London Youth; £51,000 to Bolton Lads' and Girls' Club; £2,000 to Romford Drum and Trumpet Corps; £1,000 each to Brunswick Club for Young People and Caring for More Kids; and £500 each to Bromley & Downham Boys' Club and Chelsea Youth Club. The trust stated that it will continue to support London Youth in future years.

No grants are given to individuals.

Applications: In writing to the grants manager at any time. No application form or details of the application procedure are available. However, charities considering applying for funds are welcome to telephone and have an initial discussion with the grants manager regarding availability of funds.

London Law Trust

Children and young people

Messrs Alexanders, 203 Temple Chambers, Temple Avenue, London EC4Y 0DB
Tel: 020 7353 6221
Correspondent: G D Ogilvie, Secretary

Income: £145,000 (1998/99)
Grant total: £173,000 (1998/99)

The trust's policy is to focus on charities which support and develop children and young people in the three main areas.
1 Preventing and curing illness and disability (6 grants totalling £25,000 in 1998/99).
2 Alleviating illness and disability (31 grants totalling £85,000).
3 Encouraging and developing the qualities of leadership and service to the community (25 grants totalling £63,000).

Within these categories the trustees tend to favour smaller research projects and new ventures. Grants included those to Outward Bound (£10,000); GAP (£5,000) and Youth in Action (£2,500).

Applications: In writing to the correspondent. The trustees employ a grant adviser whose job it is to evaluate applications. Grant applicants are requested to supply detailed information in support of their applications. The grant adviser makes on-site visits to almost all applicants. The trustees meet twice a year to consider the grant adviser's reports. Most grants are awarded in the autumn.

The London Youth Trust (W H Smith Memorial)

Disadvantaged young people in Greater London

10 Warrior Court, 16 Warrior Square, St Leonards-on-Sea, East Sussex TN37 6BS
Tel: 01424 720061
Correspondent: Revd Brian Walshe

Income: £77,000 (1999/2000)
Grant total: £52,000 (1999/2000)

The trust provides grants 'to serve youngsters of the working class in London'. In practice the trust funds local community groups working on initiatives at street level, in particular making grants to support holiday or training projects. Past beneficiaries have included the Arbour Youth Centre and Streatham Youth Club. No grants are given to individuals or for overseas activities.

Applications: In writing to the correspondent.

John Lyon's Charity

Children and young people in north and west London

45 Pont Street, London SW1X 0BX
Tel: 020 7589 1114 **Fax:** 020 7589 0807
E-mail: jlc@pglaw.co.uk
Correspondent: The Grants Officer

Income: £2.2 million (1999/2000)
Grant total: £2,082,000 (1999/2000)
Grants to youth: £280,000 (2000/01)

The trust makes grants to organisations, generally in the range of £5,000 to £20,000, 'to enhance the conditions of life and improve the life chances of children and young adults' in the London boroughs of Barnet, Brent, Camden,

Ealing, Kensington and Chelsea, Hammersmith and Fulham, Harrow and the Cities of London and Westminster. Grants rarely cover a period of more than three years.

The trust states: 'We give grants:
- to help young people achieve their full potential;
- to support education and training, particularly for young adults, and in conjunction with projects for the homeless, the unemployed and other disadvantaged groups;
- to provide childcare, support for parents, and help where parental support is lacking;
- to broaden cultural horizons, through activities such as dance, drama, music and the visual arts;
- to enhance recreation and leisure, through sports and youth clubs;
- to promote the needs of children and young adults.'

'Certain types of scheme are supported, including youth and sports clubs, and youth arts organisations.'Support has not been limited to the disadvantaged. There has been an equal concern to encourage talent and enable the enabled'.

Grants included:
- £50,000 to be made over three years to Harrow Club W10, towards a salary for an administrator
- £30,000 to Somers Town Youth Club towards a computer room;
- £22,000 a year for three years, to Pinner Parish Church towards youth worker costs;
- £12,000 a year for two years, to Marylebone Bangladesh Society, towards a youth project;
- £10,000 to Brunswick Club for Youth People, towards refurbishment costs;

- £10,000 to Camden Youth Service towards a mentoring scheme;
- £800 to Castlehaven Community Association, towards a summer scheme.

The charity *cannot* give grants:
- to individuals;
- for research, unless it is action research designed to lead directly to the advancement of practical activities in the community;
- for feasibility studies;
- for medical care and resources;
- in response to general charitable appeals, unless they can be shown to be of specific benefit to children and young people in one or more of the geographical areas listed;
- as direct replacements for the withdrawals of funds by statutory authorities for activities which are primarily the responsibility of central or local government;
- to umbrella organisations to distribute to projects which are already in receipt of funds from the charity;
- for the promotion of religion or politics;
- for telephone helplines.

Applications: In writing.You should include the following information:
- a summary of the main purpose of the project;
- details of the overall amount requested;
- over what timescale;
- some indication of how funds from the charity would be allocated.

Where an applicant's first proposal is assessed positively, they will be sent an application form.This must be completed and returned by the deadline date for the project to be considered for funding.

Sir George Martin Trust

General, especially in Yorkshire

Netherwood House, Ilkley, West
Yorkshire LS29 9RP
Tel: 01943 831019 **Fax:** 01943 831570
E-mail: sirgeorgemartintrust@
care4free.net
Correspondent: Peter Marshall,
Secretary

Income: £225,000 (2000/01)
Grant total: £331,000 (2000/01)
Grants to youth: £44,000 (2000/01)

The trust makes grants of between £50
and £15,000 to several specified causes,
including youth projects. Only registered
charities are supported. Grants are made
largely in Yorkshire with particular
emphasis on Leeds and Bradford. Some
grants are made in other parts of the
North of England, and occasionally
major national appeals are considered.
Ongoing grants are not usually made to
new beneficiaries. The trust has a
preference for helping with capital costs
rather than revenue projects, and grants
are not made for running costs or to
areas previously supported by statutory
funds.

In 2000/01 13% of the grant total was
given to youth projects (compared to
46% in 1997/98), and included scouting
organisations and outward bound
organisations. Beneficiaries included:
Hunslet Club for Boys and Girls
(£2,500); Yorkshire Schools Exploring
Society (£2,000); Sea Cadet Corps,
Keighley (£1,500); and Boys' Brigade –
Leeds Battalion and Scout Council –
Humberside (£1,000 each).

Applications: The trust meets in March,
July and December each year to consider
applications. These should be made in
writing to the secretary in good time for
the meetings which take place in the
middle of the month. Applications which
are not within the guidelines cannot be
answered due to a substantial increase in
costs. Applications that are relevant will
be acknowledged and, following
meetings, successful applicants will be
told of the grants they are to receive.
Unsuccessful applicants will not be
informed. The trust is unable to consider
applications from organisations without
charitable status. Telephone calls are not
encouraged as the office is not always
staffed; it is better to write or send a fax.

The Peter Minet Trust

*General in the UK, but mainly in the
boroughs of Lambeth and Southwark*

54–56 Knatchbull Road, London
SE5 9QY
Tel: 020 7274 2266 **Fax:** 020 7274 5222
Correspondent: Angela Freestone,
Administrator

Income: £158,000 (1998/99)
Grant total: £99,000 (1998/99)
Grants to youth: £37,000 to children
and youth (1998/99)

The trust gives priority to registered
charities working with people in the
boroughs of Lambeth and Southwark,
with a preference for certain causes,
including young people's
organisations. The accounts for 1998/99
detailed 83 grants, including 22 to the
Playschemes Committee. About 90% of
grants were for £2,000 or less. Grants
were made to 39 children and youth
organisations, including, playschemes,
holidays, youth clubs, adoption agencies
and sports programmes.

Grants included: £2,000 to London
Association of Youth Clubs, £1,500 each

to Westminster House Youth Club and Young Vic, £1,000 each to Pembroke House Youth Centre and Salman Youth Centre and £500 to Longfield Youth Club.

Grants are only given to registered charities and no grants are made to individuals. The trust will not give to: repetitive nationwide appeals by large charities for large sums of money; overseas appeals; parochial organisations outside Lambeth and Southwark; grant-making charities; or within 12 months of a previous grant.

Applications: A form is available from the correspondent with a leaflet giving guidelines for applicants. The form should be submitted including audited accounts, details of the project (no more than two sides of A4), a budget breakdown, money raised so far, and a list of other bodies where funding has been applied for. Meetings are usually held in January, June and October. Unsuccessful applicants will not be acknowledged unless an sae is enclosed.

The J P Morgan Fleming Educational Trust

Education

Finsbury Dials, 20 Finsbury Street, London EC2Y 9AY
Tel: 020 7417 2332
Fax: 020 7417 2300
Correspondent: Duncan Grant, Director

Income: £918,000 (1999/2000)
Grant total: £759,000 (1999/2000)
Grants to youth: Est. £40,000 (1999/2000)

This trust was previously known as the Save and Prosper Trust. The foundation makes grants towards the furtherance of education in the UK. Its principal areas of interest are:

- educational establishments
- education and training in community projects
- arts education
- education for people who are disadvantaged
- scholarships and bursaries.

Its current policy is particularly to focus on:

- drugs and education
- homelessness and education
- literacy and numeracy.

Grants are either one-off with an annual review or one to three year commitments.

Grants to youth organisations included: £15,000 to Maidstone YMCA to fund a playgroup and detached youth worker; £5,000 to Acorn Centre Youth Project to support youth worker costs; £3,000 to Rural & Urban Training scheme to fund young people at risk to take part at a motor cycle project; and £2,000 to Streatham Youth Centre to fund a photographic club.

Projects *not* usually supported by the foundation include:

- open appeals from national charities
- building appeals
- charity gala nights and similar events
- anniversary appeals
- appeals by individuals for study grants, travel scholarships or charity sponsorships.

Applications: To apply for funding applicants should write a brief letter of not more than two sides of A4 to the correspondent. The trust asks: 'Please avoid bulky items such as cassettes and videos. Set out your reasons for applying along with an indication of the amount of funding required. We do not have an application form and there are no specific closing dates for initial enquiries. Receipt of your request for funding will be initially reviewed within six weeks. If we can take your application forward you will be contacted. Final approval for funding must come from our trustee committee which meets four times a year. You will be informed of the committee's decision as soon as possible. If your application is unsuccessful we suggest you wait at least a year before re-applying.'

Morgan Stanley International Foundation

Education and training

25 Cabot Square, Canary Wharf, London E14 4QA
Tel: 020 7425 6221 Fax: 020 7425 4949
Correspondent: Mrs Heather Bird, Secretary

Income: £937,000 (2000)
Grant total: £548,000 (2000)
Grants to youth: £83,000 (2000)

This foundation is funded by the company Morgan Stanley, and makes grants 'towards non-profit social service, educational, cultural and healthcare organisations, which provide a benefit to the local (i.e. East End) Morgan Stanley community', as outlined in its guidelines for applicants. The East End is defined as the London boroughs of Tower Hamlets and Newham. Grants are focused on organisations operating in three main areas, education/training/employment, hospitals/health and social welfare. Under the latter heading grants can be given for, amongst other things, services for youth organisations of which the primary

mission is providing educational and leadership activities for young people.

Past beneficiaries have included East-Side Educational Trust, Fulcrum Challenge and Newham Docklands Motorcycle Project. Grants ranged up to £56,000 in 2000, however, most grants listed in the accounts were for less than £10,000.

'As a rule, grants will not be made to either international or UK charitable organisations unless they have a project in this local area. In addition, grants will not be made to either political or evangelistic organisations, 'pressure groups', or individuals who are seeking sponsorship either for themselves (e.g. to help pay for education) or for onward transmission to a charitable organisation.'

Applications: In writing to the correspondent. However, please note that the trust has a 'proactive approach to its funding programme and thus rarely will a grant be made in response to an unsolicited application or proposal'.

The P F Charitable Trust

General, with an interest in Oxfordshire and Scotland

Ely House, 37 Dover Street, London W1S 4NJ
Tel: 020 7409 5600
Correspondent: Geoff Fincham

Income: £2.3 million (1999/2000)
Grant total: £1.6 million (1999/2000)
Grants to youth: £98,000 (1998/99)

The trust makes several hundred one-off and recurrent awards to registered charities across the UK each year. Grants average around £2,000, although awards of £500 or less are frequent. The few large grants go as high as around

£30,000. The trust can provide both core and revenue funding, although it is not keen to support salaries. It may renew its commitments after the first three years are completed.

In 1999/2000 grants included £10,000 to Scout Association and £5,000 to Ro-Ro Sailing Project. The remaining grants listed in the trust's accounts for that year were not obviously to youth organisations, however, other grants not listed in the accounts totalled £766,000. In previous years the trust has provided information on categories for its grant-making, which have included the headings 'youth' and 'youth clubs and associations'.

Grants are not made to individuals or non-registered charities. Individual churches and hospices are now excluded.

Applications: In writing with full information to the correspondent at any time. Replies will be sent to unsuccessful applications if an sae is enclosed. The trustees meet monthly.

The Peacock Charitable Trust

Medical research, disability, general

PO Box 902, London SW19 5WE
Correspondent: Mrs Janet Gilbert

Income: £2.3 million (1999/2000)
Grant total: £1.9 million (1999/2000)
Grants to youth: Est. £35,000 (1999/2000)

The trust gives over 100 grants a year, concentrated largely on medical and health charities, but also makes some towards youth work. Grants are made in the UK with a local interest in the Wimbledon/Merton area of London,

where it is based, and to a lesser extent in the area around Chichester, including West Sussex and south east Hampshire.

Two thirds of the grants given out in 1999/2000 were to organisations also supported in the previous year. Although grants can be for more than £100,000, most are for amounts of between £2,000 and £10,000. In 1999/2000 grants included: £12,000 to Youth Clubs UK; £10,000 to SABC Clubs for Young People; £7,000 to Surrey Association of Youth Clubs & Surrey PHAB; £5,400 to Endeavour Boys' Club; and £1,000 to 11th Kingston & Merton Boys' Brigade.

Applications: Registered charities only should apply in writing, preferably early in the year and accompanied by full accounts. Applications should include clear details of the need the intended project is designed to meet, plus any outline budget. No donations are made to individuals and only in rare cases are additions made to charities already being supported. To maximise the use of funds beneficially, only applications being considered will receive replies.

The Jack Petchey Foundation

Young people (11–25 years) in East London and West Essex

Exchange House, 13–14 Clements Court, Ilford, Essex IG1 2QY
Tel: 020 8252 8000 **Fax:** 020 8252 7892
E-mail: information@jackpetchey foundation.org.uk
Website: www.jackpetchey foundation.org.uk
Correspondent: Andrew Billington, Director

Income: £1.6 million (2000)
Grant total: About £1.5 million (2001)
Grants to youth: £240,000 (2000)

The information in this entry is taken from the trust's guidelines and website. 'The foundation's aim is to help develop the potential within young people aged 11–25, especially those struggling with 21st Century problems. In addition the foundation is eager to help young people take advantage of opportunities and play their part in society. The catchment area is ... the boroughs/districts of Barking & Dagenham, Brentwood, Epping Forest, Hackney, Harlow, Havering, Newham, Redbridge, Tower Hamlets, Thurrock, Uttlesford and Waltham Forest.'

Examples of how this trust might support organisations include:

- youth worker's salary;
- community projects run by youth groups/youth organisations;
- youth leadership courses;
- projects that involve young people in constructive activities: sport, after school clubs, volunteering.

The foundation's four main methods of grant support are:

i) Achievement awards (£1 million allocation in 2001)
These are given to young people 'who make a wholehearted contribution to their club, school, group or community'. Over 98% of secondary schools and colleges in East London/West Essex take part in this scheme, as well as a further 200 youth groups, clubs.

ii) Project grants (£1.5 million allocation in 2001)
Projects must benefit young people. The grants can be for capital schemes, training projects, youth development and occasionally charity running costs. The trustees require applicants to raise at least 50% of costs of a project from other sources and evidence of this is normally requested with applications.

iii) Leader awards (£50,000 allocation in 2001)
Awards are given to adults who have demonstrated, in an outstanding way, an ability to encourage and motivate young people aged 11–25 in East London or West Essex.

iv) Sponsorship (£50,000 allocation in 2001)
Young people can be sponsored for undertaking projects, or participating in events, that will benefit other people or specific charities.

'Across all our grantmaking we aim to bring the following approaches:

- we look for maximum value from our grants in bringing about practical and lasting improvements in people's lives and the communities in which they live;
- we look to support excellence and quality wherever possible;
- we prefer to focus on prevention by addressing the root causes of problems rather than coping with the consequences of them;
- as an independent grantmaker we can be creative, flexible and sometimes unorthodox in the use of our funds, we are prepared to take risk;s
- we welcome applications from all sections of the community including people of any race, colour, gender, sexual orientation, religious affiliation, national origin or disability.

'What the foundation is likely to support:
i) organisations and charities that promote community involvement and personal responsibility within society;

ii) clubs and youth groups that demonstrate that they are enabling individuals to achieve their potential, take control of their lives and contribute to society as a whole;

iii) the training of youth leaders;

iv) projects that assist young people to overcome problems that prevent them reaching their potential. These may include addiction, (alcohol, drugs etc.), homelessness, ill health (medical, hospice, hospital);

v) projects that help develop self esteem through involving young people in sport and other worthwhile activities;

vi) youth organisations, scouts, sea cadets, police cadets, guides, army cadets;

vii) schools and other training establishments with grants so that they can provide a better service to young people (care is taken not to give grants where statutory funding is available);

viii) volunteer projects;

ix) schemes that tackle the problems faced by young people from ethnic minority groups.

'There is no upper or lower limit for a grant application and the amount you request should be the amount you need. Grants may be for one year or for a longer period, although this would not normally exceed three years. In 2000 the average grant was for between £1,000 and £10,000.'

Grants in 2000 were categorised in the trust's accounts as follows:

Grants to institutions

Advice/support/
  mentoring/counselling £74,000
Community Links/Essex
  Association of Boys'
  Clubs/London Youth £415,000
Housing £15,000
Medical/hospice/hospital £67,000

Schools £232,000
Sports clubs £129,000
Training/training courses £113,000
Uniformed organisations £53,000
Youth clubs/youth projects £186,000
General £254,000

Grants included: £12,000 to Dalston Youth Project; £5,600 to Tower Hamlets District Scouts; £5,400 to Army Cadet Corps; £5,000 to Belchamps Scouts Centre; £2,400 to South Canning Town Youth Project; £2,000 to Bangladesh Youth Movement and £1,000 to Crown & Manor Youth Club.

The foundation does *not* support:
- organisations which have applied within the last 12 months
- the replacement of statutory funding
- individuals
- work that has already taken place
- work that does not directly benefit people in the UK
- medical research
- animal welfare
- endowment funds
- general appeals or circulars.

The foundation is unlikely to support: building or major refurbishment projects; conferences and seminars; projects whose main purpose is to promote religious beliefs.

Applications: 'You can apply for one of our grants if you are a registered charity, or a group with charitable purposes. If you are not a registered charity or school, you will need to give us some extra information [e.g. a copy of your constitution or set of rules] … The grant must benefit young people in the 11–25 age group and they must be based in our catchment area of East London or West Essex.'

You will need to send, to the correspondent, your annual report/ budget with the appropriate Jack Petchey application form, available on our website. You may also send other documents that you think are relevant to your application. After you have sent the application you will receive an acknowledgement letter. If at this point your application is ineligible and doesn't meet the eligibility criteria, the trust will inform you of this. If your application conforms to our criteria your application will be assessed at the next monthly management meeting. In the meantime the trust may request further information or suggest a meeting to clarify any queries they may have.

'There are no application deadlines, but you should apply in good time before you will need the money. As there is a monthly management meeting the trust normally hopes to reply to applicants with a decision within six weeks. Organisations can apply again if they have already received a grant, but the foundation does not usually make more than one grant to the same organisation at a time. If you have an application refused, you can apply again 12 months after your last application was submitted.

The Prince's Trust

Individual young people aged 14 to 30

18 Park Square East, London NW1 4LH
Tel: 020 7543 7469 **Fax:** 020 7543 7423
Minicom: 020 7543 1374
E-mail: info@princes-trust.org.uk
Website: www.princes-trust.org.uk

Income: £36.8 million (1999/2000)
Grant total: £5 million (1999/2000)

The major part of The Prince's Trust's work is the support of individuals. It helps 14 to 30 year olds develop self confidence, learn new skills, move into work and start new businesses. The Prince's Trust message – *Yes You Can* – encourages young people to believe in themselves, whatever obstacles they face.

In 1999/2000 total charitable expenditure was £37.2 million. Business start-up grants given to young people totalled £1.3 million and £3.7 million was given in individual and group awards, to help disadvantaged young people to gain access to education, training and employment. (Further details about the awards to individuals can be found in the DSC publication *The Educational Grants Directory*.)

A relatively small part of the Trust's work is in supporting organisations. The Prince's Trust Millennium Awards takes over from the previous M-Power awards. Awards of between £3,000 and £15,000 are given to groups wanting to develop projects to help their local community or environment; guide others; use new technology to improve lives or make a positive use of leisure time.

The emphasis is on disadvantaged young people applying for group awards. Applicants should be:
- aged 14–25;
- a member of a group of 3–12 young people;
- unemployed, underemployed, underskilled, within or leaving the criminal justice system, leaving care, disabled, parenting alone or facing discrimination.

Beneficiaries have included:
Another Angle – A group of four young people from Hackney produced a short film to help dispel the myths and misconceptions that young people have

about receiving counselling. Mental health is a significant issue in the London Borough of Hackney, in particular, youth suicide, and there is a greater need for young people to be encouraged to seek counselling for issues that affect their lives. This project has raised awareness of the issues surrounding counselling and informed young people in the community how to find help when in need.

Play Back – A group of ten young people applied for a Millennium Award to develop a project aimed at linking young people with and without disabilities with older people in the Moray area. The team interviewed senior people about their lives and reproduced these memories in a book, on audio tape and a drama production.

Applications: There is a network of local boards which consider applications for grants and loans, and the relevant contact names can be obtained by calling the Freephone number 0800 842 842. The committees meet every month. No applications can be considered by the central office.

The Privy Purse Charitable Trust

General

Buckingham Palace, London
SW1A 1AA
Tel: 020 7930 4832
E-mail: privypurse@royal.gov.uk
Correspondent: John Parsons, Trustee

Income: £338,000 (2000/01)
Grant total: £293,000 (2000/01)

The trust classifies its grants into over 20 groups, including 'Children and youth'

and 'Education'. Grants in these two categories totalled £13,000 and £83,000 respectively in 2000/01. A grants list was not included with the accounts at the Charity Commission and there are no further details as to how many grants were given to youth clubs.

Applications: The trust makes donations to a wide variety of charities, but does not respond to appeals nor to grant applications.

The Joseph Rank Benevolent Trust

Methodist church, Christian-based social work

11a Station Road West, Oxted, Surrey
RH8 9EE
Tel: 01883 717919 **Fax:** 01883 717411
E-mail: rankchar@dircon.co.uk
Correspondent: John Wheeler

Income: £3.1 million (2000)
Grant total: £3.2 million (2000)
Grants to youth: £563,000 (2000)

This is a Christian-based trust interested in initiatives established by Christians to meet social needs. More than half of the trust's funds are given for the maintenance and improvement of Methodist churches. Around £1 million a year is given for a variety of social causes, in grants of up to £100,000. Many are recurrent for up to five years.

Perhaps fewer than 25 new grants are made every year, and even then rarely to beneficiaries new to the trust. Preference is given to Christian organisations. Grants were made to 30 youth causes in 2000, including seven made to projects monitored by the youth department of the Methodist church. No additional youth projects have been taken on as those being supported were in the fourth year of a five year programme. Awards ranged ranged from £2,500 to £43,000, and were generally over £25,000.

Beneficiaries included Chrysalis Youth Project, Castleford (£31,000); Regeneration Trust (£12,000 towards the salary of an IT tutor to develop education/training work with young people); Wakefield Methodist Circuit (£12,000 towards the salaries of outreach workers in night clubs in Wakefield) and Aberfeldy Parish Church (£5,000 towards the costs of a youth worker/ parish assistant).

No grants are given to individuals.

Applications: Unsolicited appeals are considered although the chance of a grant being given is small. This is because the trustees, through established contacts, are active in identifying projects for support and have normally researched a number of projects which the trust will fund as resources become available on completion of existing commitments. General appeals should be addressed to the correspondent and include full details of the appeal and a copy of the most recent audited accounts. Appeals from within Methodism should only be put forward after consultation with the relevant division of the church.

The Rank Foundation

Christian communication, youth, education, general

4/5 North Bar, Banbury, Oxfordshire
OX16 0TB
Tel: 01295 272337 **Fax:** 01295 272336
E-mail: rankchar@dircon.co.uk
Correspondent: Mrs Sheila Gent, Assistant Grants Administrator

Income: £8.3 million (2000)
Grant total: £7.4 million (2000)
Grants to youth: Est. over £2 million (2000)

The directors of the trust take an active part in all areas of its work, including the identification of appropriate initiatives for support and the monitoring of their progress. They have decided that the funds available to them would be best used in firstly identifying projects and then funding them on a significant basis over a number of years.

Large grants are typically part of a three or five year commitment. If small grants (less than £5,000) are given for two or three years consecutively, this is usually to national organisations. Local charities are unlikely to be awarded recurrent funding or multi-year awards.

Under its 'Youth' heading, the foundation runs four main programmes, which account for about 80% of funding. The amounts distributed in 2000 were as follows:

- Youth or Adult? programme – £1 million to 30 projects;
- Investing in Success programme – £805,000 to 15 projects;
- Key Workers programme – £344,000 for 17 posts;
- Rank Volunteer (Gap) Awards – £254,000.

Youth or Adult?

The foundation supports projects over five years to train local youth leaders who are experienced but unqualified. Trainees study for a professional qualification validated by Canterbury Christ Church University College through the YMCA George Williams College. (George Williams College received Rank Foundation grants totalling £151,000 during the year, mostly for students' fees.)

Over £850,000 was given to another 29 ongoing projects, many in Scotland, Wales and Northern Ireland, with an average of £28,000 a year to each organisation. Beneficiaries included Prince's Youth Business Trust (£44,000; £212,000 to date); Northern Ireland Deaf Youth Association (£5,500; £150,000 to date); Linlithgow Young People's Project (£12,000; £74,000 to date) and the Diocese of Swansea and Brecon (£24,000; £118,000 to date).

Investing in Success

This programme builds upon partnerships which have been developed over the years with a number of established organisations. Grants averaged £54,000 in the year, with the largest being as follows: People and Work Unit – £117,000 (£550,000 in total); Mobex North East, a provider of mobile training resources for young people – £78,000 (£294,000) and YouthLink Scotland – £77,000 (£239,000).

Key Workers

A number of strategic posts are supported within organisations with which the foundation has worked for some time and where qualified workers with specialist skills are often needed. This is particularly so in training up young apprentice leaders in areas such as the outdoors, enterprise and employment and in formal and informal education initiatives. Grants ranged from £5,000 to £40,000, averaging £20,000. The largest three grants were: Cumbria Youth Alliance, £40,000 (£116,000 in total); YMCA Scotland, £38,000 (£193,000 in total); and Royston Youth Action, £33,000 (£78,000 in total).

The Rank Volunteer (Gap) Award

This programme encourages full-time volunteering in organisations with which the foundation is already working, either during the period between school and further education or during a period of unemployment. The directors, through the careful monitoring of the projects, continue to be encouraged by the results which are being achieved by the young people who are participating in the various schemes.

The foundation makes further grants under a 'Youth – general' heading. These grants included 20 awards to boys' clubs, scouts and sea cadets/sea scouts. Many of the grants in this list were between £500 and £2,000. Larger grants included £30,000 to Sail Training Association; £4,000 to Army Cadet Force Association; £3,200 to Ocean Youth Association; £2,000 to York Scout Activity Centre and £1,500 to Zebedees (Youth Action for Truro).

Grants are only given to registered charities. Appeals from individuals or appeals from registered charities on behalf of named individuals will *not* be considered; neither will appeals from overseas or from UK-based organisations where the object of the appeal is overseas.

Grants are *not* generally given to projects involved with:

- agriculture and farming
- cathedrals and churches (except where community facilities are involved)
- culture
- university and school building and bursary funds
- medical research.

Applications: The trust states that in considering unsolicited applications, the trust is inclined towards supporting appeals where there are relatively small, attainable targets and they place great importance on clear evidence of local support. The trust also takes into account whether it is likely that any grant that they make will be put to immediate use.

Applications should be addressed to the general appeals office at the address above in Banbury. There is no formal application form, but for administrative purposes it is helpful if the actual appeal letter can be kept to one or two sides of A4, which can be supported by reports and the like.

General appeals, including unsolicited appeals relating to youth projects, should include: charity registration number, brief details about the project and the amount to be raised, details of the amount already raised, and the most recent audited set of accounts.

Preliminary enquiries are welcomed. Unsolicited appeals are considered quarterly in March, June, September and December. All appeals are acknowledged and applicants advised as to when a decision can be expected.

The Ravensdale Trust

General in Merseyside, especially St Helens

Messrs Brabners, 1 Dale Street, Liverpool L2 2ET
Tel: 0151 236 5821
Correspondent: Mrs J L Fagan, Secretary

Income: £100,000 (2000/01)
Grant total: £66,000 (2000/01)
Grants to youth: £13,000 (2000/01)

In 2000/01 the trust gave 74 grants, over 80% of which were recurrent. Over half of the grants are given to Merseyside, especially St Helens. Charities benefiting young people received 37% of the grant total, although many of these were not

youth clubs. 14 grants were made to youth clubs, nearly all of which were girl guide and scouts organisations. Some organisations received more than one grant in the year. Grants were either of £500, £1,000 or £2,000. Beneficiaries included: Christ Church Eccleston (Boys' Brigade); The Guide Association Woodbank Activity Centre; St James' Church youth project and St Helens Girl Guide Association.

No grants are given to individuals.

Applications: In writing to the correspondent. Grants are paid in May and October.

The Sir James Reckitt Charity

Society of Friends, general mainly in Hull and the East Riding of Yorkshire

7 Derrymore Road, Willerby, East Yorkshire HU10 6ES
Tel: 01482 655861
E-mail: jim@derrymore.karoo.co.uk
Website: www.sirjamesreckitt.co.uk
Correspondent: J McGlashan, Administrator

Income: £645,000 (1999/2000)
Grant total: £616,000 (2000/01)
Grants to youth: £48,000 to organisations (1999/2000)

The trust gives priority to causes connected to the Society of Friends, and organisations in the beneficial area. Other national and international charities can be supported, particularly those that are concerned with current social issues. The trust lists one of its eight priorities as youth.

Grants are normally only made to registered charities. Support for new projects without charitable status is usually channelled through an existing registered charity. Grants totalling almost £15,000 were made to 45 individuals, most of which were for individuals taking part in overseas expeditions for Raleigh International, Voluntary Service Overseas and sail-training ventures. Applicants must live in Hull or East Yorkshire.

Larger grants in 1999/2000 to youth organisations were: £6,800 to Hull Boys' Club; £5,700 to Guide Association East Yorkshire; £3,900 to Warren Resource Centre; £3,300 to Pedro Club; £2,900 to Humberside Police Youth & Community Centre; £2,400 to Humberside Scout Association and £2,000 to Ocean Youth Trust. Other grants included £1,200 to Outward Bound Trust and £1,000 each to Sutton Park (Marsdale) Scout Group, Drypool Youth Work Project and Prince's Trust in Hull.

Local organisations outside the Hull area are not supported, unless their work has regional implications. Support is not given to causes of a political or warlike nature and trustees will not normally consider a further appeal if a grant has been paid in the previous two years. Grants are not normally made to individuals other than Quakers and residents of Hull and the East Riding of Yorkshire.

Applications: In writing to the correspondent at any time. Urgent applications that are clearly within the charity's guidelines and require only limited funding can be dealt with rapidly. Standard applications need to arrive a month before the trustees' meetings, which are usually held in May and November.

The Francis C Scott Charitable Trust

Disadvantaged people in Cumbria

3 Lambrigg Terrace, Kendal, Cumbria LA9 4BB
Tel: 01539 741610 **Fax:** 01539 741611
Website: www.fcsct.org.uk
Correspondent: Donald Harding, Director

Income: £1.2 million (1999/2000)
Grant total: £1.3 million (1999/2000)
Grants to youth: £324,000 (1998/99)

The trust prefers to support socially and economically disadvantaged people and communities. Beneficiaries include youth clubs and other organisations working with young people. Grants may be towards capital costs or revenue, and range from under £500 to £15,000. The trust sometimes makes annual grants for up to three years for particularly worthwhile projects, but usually only to charities based in Cumbria.

The trust welcomes and actively seeks funding partnerships with other grant givers and service providers to enable the development of projects particularly within Cumbria. The trust says: 'We aim not to provide substantial funding for services which are statutory responsibilities of local authorities, but we may look favourably on partnership funding with the public sector to provide additional services to the disadvantaged'. It has engaged in a substantial funding commitment to develop Voluntary Action Cumbria with £250,000 given each year over five years. Cumbria Youth Alliance as a network of voluntary organisations working with young people in Cumbria has directly benefited and disburse funds through a bursary scheme.

Beneficiaries in 2000/01 included:

- Cumbria Association of Clubs for Young People which received three grants totalling £67,000.
- Cumbria Youth Alliance which received four grants totalling £52,000 and £25,000 further towards a bursary scheme. It works to coordinate a cooperative approach to the planning of youth service provision in Cumbria.
- Youth Outreach received £12,500 in two grants.
- Whitehaven received £8,000.
- St John Scouts Group Coppull received £2,000.
- Wyndham Youth Centre received £1,500.

Normally only registered charities receive grants. While occasionally grants are given to national charities, these are usually only to fund a local service or appeal. The trust does not fund appeals from individuals. The trustees are reluctant to substitute for expired or withdrawn statutory funding, although they may occasionally do so. Church restoration, medical appeals, expeditions, scholarships and applications from schools are all excluded.

Applications: An application form is available from the correspondent and should be returned with the latest set of audited accounts. Applicants are welcome to telephone the director or his assistant for an informal discussion prior to submitting an application. The trustees meet three times a year, usually in March, July and November. Applications need to arrive one month before each meeting. The whole process from application to receipt of a grant may take up to four months.

Leslie Sell Charitable Trust
Scout and guide groups

Ground Floor Offices, 52–58 London Road, St Albans, Hertfordshire AL1 1NG
Tel: 01727 843603 **Fax:** 01727 843663
Correspondent: J Byrnes

Income: £179,000 (2000/01)
Grant total: £129,000 (2000/01)
Grants to youth: £106,000 to organisations (2000/01)

190 grants totalling £106,000 went to scout and guide groups (including Rangers, Brownies and Sea Scouts groups) throughout the UK from the Orkney Islands to Falmouth. Grants ranged between £500 and £4,000 .

Grants to individual guides or scouts were also made; mostly of around £150.

Applications: In writing to the correspondent.

The Sheldon Trust
General in the West Midlands

Box S, White Horse Court, 25c North Street, Bishop's Stortford, Hertfordshire CM23 2LD
Tel: 01279 657626
E-mail: charities@pothecary.co.uk
Correspondent: The Trust Administrator

Income: £162,000 (2000/01)
Grant total: £208,000 (2000/01)
Grants to youth: Est. £35,000 (2000/01)

The geographical area of giving is the West Midlands, with particular emphasis on: Birmingham City, Coventry City, Dudley, Sandwell, Solihull, Wolverhampton and the County of

Warwickshire. The main purpose of the charity is to relieve poverty and distress, especially in deprived ares, concentrating grants on community projects, as well as those directed to special needs groups.

The trust helps with equipment, furnishings and running costs, but not with the cost of buildings. The trust puts aside a portion of its income for grants by way of Special Projects of which the trustees have personal knowledge or, an organisation which they have supported in the past. The trustees also set aside a designated sum for holidays, and applicants are considered in April each year.

In 2000/01 grants to youth organisations included: £7,500 to Amelia Methodist Trust; £5,000 each to Allens Croft towards a youth participation worker and Cascade and Community Action Centre; £3,000 to St John's Community Project; £2,000 to Shaw Trust; and £500 each to BYV Adventure Camp, Oasis Community Departments and the 3H Fund.

The trustees will not normally support the cost of buildings, or national organisations.

Applications: On a form available from the correspondent. The trustees meet three times a year, in March, July and November, considering 10 to 15 applicants depending on income.

The Skelton Bounty

Social welfare in Lancashire

Messrs Cockshott Peck Lewis, 24 Hoghton Street, Southport, Merseyside PR9 0PA
Tel: 01704 534034

Income: £79,000 (2000/01)
Grant total: £79,000 (2000/01)
Grants to youth: £24,000 (2000/01)

The trust only gives grants to legally constituted charities in Lancashire (as it existed in 1934), which stretches as far south as the River Mersey. The trustees generally prefer to support capital projects but have recently given grants towards the cost of holidays for disadvantaged children and the salaries of wardens or other staff. Local branches of UK charities are only supported if the organisations is based in the beneficial area.

Grants in 2000/01 included: £8,500 to Ocean Youth Trust North West in Birkenhead, as a contribution towards buying new sails for a boat; £3,800 to Newton Boys' and Girls' Club, Newton-le-Willows, for emergency repairs to club premises' roof, and rewiring; and £2,500 to Pearson's Holiday Fund, Surrey, for holidays for disadvantaged children. Grants of £2,000 each were made to: Lancashire Youth Clubs Association, Preston, towards training and awareness for voluntary youth workers; Sea Cadets Watersports Centre, Littleborough, towards the provision of fuel for a safety craft; and 16th Burnley Scout and Guide Group in Clitheroe towards the replacement of its roof. The remaining grants to youth organisations ranged from £100 to £1,000.

No grants are given to individuals, religious charities, medical or scientific research or minibus appeals.

Applications: On a form available from the correspondent, and requests for application forms should be made as soon as possible after 1 January each year. The completed form should be returned before 31 March immediately following.

Applications received after this date will not be considered. The trustees meet annually in July, after which applicants are notified in writing of the trustees' decision. Applications should include the charitable registration number of the organisation, or, where appropriate, a letter confirming charitable status, or a letter from the Chief Inspector of Taxes confirming the organisation's income is tax exempt. Successful applicants receive their grant cheques in late July/early August.

The Henry Smith Charity

Social welfare, older people, disability, health, medical research

5 Chancery Lane, Clifford's Inn, London EC4A 1BU
Tel: 020 7320 6216/6277
Fax: 020 7320 3842
Website: www.henrysmithcharity. org.uk
Correspondent: Miss Judith Portrait, Treasurer

Income: £24.57 million (2000)
Grant total: £23.78 million (2000)
Grants to youth: £2.29 million (2000)

This is one of the largest general purpose national grant-making trusts and gave a total of £23,779,000 in grants in 2000. Grants cover health, medical research, disability and social welfare. The trust covers the UK, with specific small local programmes in East and West Sussex, Hampshire, Kent, Gloucestershire, Leicestershire, Suffolk and Surrey. The trustees are keen, however, to encourage good applications from all parts of the country.

The trust makes grants principally within the three main headings:

- medical
- disabled
- social services and moral welfare.

Grantmaking in the latter category includes young people as well as the elderly, drugs and alcohol, community service, counselling and family advice, homelessness, general, and clergy widows and children. Grants to young people's organisations was the second largest area of grantmaking for the trust. Grants to this group totalled £2,291,800 in 2000, compared to grants to community service organisations which totalled £3,228,000.

The trust has four different programmes:
- The Special List – one-off grants in response to appeals, generally over £10,000 each.
- The General List – three-year grants in response to appeals, mostly over £10,000 each. These are generally made towards to a specific item in the applicant's budget or to a particular project, although in many cases they are towards the core costs and general work of the charity.
- The Major Grants – the trustees select a special area of interest each year. The aim is to make a significant impact in the chosen field.
- Small Grants – supporting grass-roots organisations. Applicants must be local organisations with an annual income of less than £250,000. Grants are of up to £10,000, although most are for £1,000 to £3,000. There is a speedy response to applications which are considered fortnightly.

Special and General grants to youth organisations in 2000 included:
- £75,000 to Merseyside Youth Association, towards fitting out The

Starting Point, an advice/information point and café;

- £40,000 to Newbiggin Hall Detached Youth Work Project (Tyne & Wear) as the final year of a three year grant towards the core costs and general work of the charity;
- £25,000 to the Longbenton Youth Project, Tyne and Wear as the second year of a three year grant for a detached youth worker;
- £20,000 to the Lancashire Association of Clubs for Young People as the first year of a three year grant for a rural development project and mobile facility;
- £20,000 to the OK Club (London) as the first of a three year grant towards the salary and ongoing costs of a Senior Youth Worker;
- £19,300 to the Crewe and District YMCA as the second year of a three year grant towards the salary of a housing support worker for young people with mental health problems;
- £15,000 to the Powerpoint Youth Project, Hampshire as the final instalment of a two year grant to develop and expand youth work on Portsmouth housing estates;
- £12,000 to St Aidan's Care Team (West Midlands); the second of a three year grant towards the salary of a youth and community worker.

Small grants

Over 200 small grants were given to youth organisations, the lion's share being awarded to groups and clubs in the areas of special interest: East and West Sussex, Hampshire, Kent, Gloucestershire, Leicestershire, Suffolk and Surrey, where the charity has established a local grant programme. Beneficiaries included: £10,000 to West Sussex County Scout Council; £2,300 to Leicestershire Clubs

for Young People; £1,000 to Princetown and District Youth Club, Devon; £1,500 to Chaverim South Tottenham Jewish Boys Club; £5,000 to Basingstoke Scouts Group; £4,000 to Coleford Youth Project; £1,000 to Claygate Village Youth Club Association; £500 to Brighton and Hove Jewish Youth Club; and £300 to 26th Brighton Boys Brigade.

The trust *cannot* support education or art, except where they are exclusively for the benefit of people who are disabled, or exclusively for the benefit of the deprived and disadvantaged. Grants are not made for the care or restoration of buildings, or for individuals.

Applications: In writing to the correspondent. The charity does not use application forms but offers the following guidelines to applicants

Main grants programmes:
1 Applications should be no longer than four A4 sides (plus budget and accounts) and should incorporate a short (half page) summary.

2 Applications should:
a) State clearly who the applicant is, what it does and whom it seeks to help.
b) Give the applicant's status (e.g. registered charity).
c) Describe the project for which a grant is sought clearly and succinctly; explain the need for it; say what practical results it is expected to produce; state the number of people who will benefit from it; show how it will be cost effective and say what stage the project has so far reached.
d) Enclose a detailed budget for the project together with a copy of the applicant's most recent audited accounts. (If those accounts show a significant surplus or deficit of income,

please explain how this has arisen and explain the charity's reserves policy.)

e) Name the applicant's trustees/patrons and describe the people who will actually be in charge of the project, giving details of their qualifications for the job.

f) Describe the applicant's track record and, where possible, give the names and addresses of two independent referees to whom The Henry Smith Charity may apply for a recommendation.

g) State what funds have already been raised for the project and name any other sources of funding to whom the applicant has applied.

h) Explain where the ongoing funding (if required) will be obtained when the charity's grant has been used.

i) State what plans have been made to monitor the project and wherever possible to evaluate it and, where appropriate, to make its results known to others.

j) Ask, where possible, for a specific amount.

3 Please keep the application as simple as possible and avoid the use of technical terms and jargon.

Trustees meet in March, June, September and December, and applications must be received at least two months before the relevant meeting.

Summaries of all applications received, which are within the charity's objects and policy, are sent to the members of one of the two Distribution Committees of the Trustees each week.

If there is sufficient support for a particular application, one of the Charity's team of Visitors is instructed to prepare a report on the application, which may include a site visit.

Applicants whose appeals have been considered at a Distribution Committee meeting will be informed in writing of the Trustees' decision within two weeks of the date of the meeting.

Small grants programme

- The programme is available to organisations with an annual income of under £250,000. Applications may be made for grants under £10,000.

- The organisations must be based within the UK but outside the charity's traditional counties, which have their own Small Grants Programme. These are Gloucestershire, Hampshire, Kent, Leicestershire, Suffolk, Surrey, East and West Sussex. *[Applicants within these counties who are unaware of their local programme should be able to get information from a local umbrella body such as the Council for Voluntary Service or Rural Community Council. Ed.]*

- Grants can be for capital or for one-off revenue purposes, but not for running costs. For example, the programme may be ideal for organisations needing equipment or help with the costs of transport, training, information packs, or for volunteer expenses. However, ongoing running costs will not be supported, as grants need to be spent within a six-month period.

- Applications are considered at any time throughout the year and will be processed fortnightly. When applying, please enclose your most recent annual report/audited accounts.

- Applications should be to the Treasurer. The Trustees do not require applicants to use a special application form, but suggest that the following guidelines be used:

1 Applications should be no longer than two A4 sides.

Case study

The difference a grant makes

Two recent beneficiaries of Henry Smith's Charity grants have been the Exmoor Rural Skills project and Walsall Street Teams.

Exmoor Rural Skills

The Exmoor Rural Skills Project was started in 1998 with Rural Challenge funding from the Rural Development Commission. As part of the Somerset Youth Project it received support from Henry Smith 's Charity for three years starting in 2000. This has helped with the salary costs of the project manager and the general work of the charity.

The rural skills project provides training to young people aged 14 to 25. Young people develop skills in hedge laying, drystone walling, footpath maintenance, coppicing and woodland management. As well as specific job skills, the project also enables young people to develop life skills such as self-esteem, communication, literacy and numeracy and team-work. The project links with other organisations such as schools and colleges, the connexions service, the youth offending team and voluntary groups. Between 50 and 60 young people attend the project each week.

One of the main partners of the project is the Exmoor National Park, and the woodland and moorland provide an ideal setting for young people's development. The project manager emphasises that the strength of the application to the Henry Smith Charity lay in its linking the environment of the Exmoor National Park with the opportunities for training. 'It's not just about the charity funding work with young people. Our bid was based on the great opportunities for young people to learn life skills through being in the countryside. We presented this very clearly in our application to Henry Smith's.'

Exmoor Rural Skills website: www.sryp.org.uk

Walsall Street Teams

The relationship between this street based youth project and Henry Smith's Charity started in 1997. At that point there were two part-time workers and around 30 volunteers working with vulnerable young people involved in prostitution and drugs. The teams had grown in response to gaps in service provision, particularly for young people who had survived rape and sexual abuse, or who were involved in the sex industry.

There are now seven projects, staffed by a full-time manager, admin support worker and youth workers attached to different teams. Much of this development was initiated by the investment made by Henry Smith's Charity over four years. Grants of around £61,000 have been made to the work each year and there is now a tapering arrangement as Walsall Street Teams have successfully fundraised for project costs and central core costs.

The project manager has no doubts about the substantial contribution that Henry Smith's Charity has made to the project. 'They have catapulted Walsall Street Teams into having a far more professional standing and enabled the projects to develop from being reactive to being proactive. The Walsall Street Teams projects are also those that people are now able to draw on for good practice guidelines and resources. There is no question that Henry Smith's helped the organisation at a key moment. Without the charity's support Walsall Street Teams would still have been muddling along trying to fulfil growing expectations and demands without the proper resourcing to do it.'

Walsall Street Teams were part of the charity's major grant Black Country initiative which was started in 1998. The organisation was approached by the charity after being suggested by a local voluntary sector contact.

The support of Henry Smith's Charity has made a crucial difference to the development of a small organisation.

For further information on the work of Walsall Street Teams, contact Paul Lapsely, Bradford Street Centre, 51 Bradford Street, Walsall WS1 3QD Tel: 01922 621208; Fax: 01922 629980

2 Applications should also include a detailed budget for the project and the applicant's most recent annual report/audited accounts. If those accounts show a significant surplus or deficit of income, please explain how this has arisen.

3 Applications should:

a) State clearly who the applicant is, what it does and whom it seeks to help.

b) Give the applicant's status, i.e., registered charity.

c) Describe the project for which the grant is sought briefly and clearly. This description should answer the following questions: Why is the project needed? What practical results will it produce? How many people will benefit from it?

d) State what funds have already been raised for the project, and name any other sources of funding applied for.

e) Ask, whenever possible, for a specific amount.

Please keep the application as simple as possible and avoid the use of technical terms and jargon.

The Spitalfields Market Community Trust

Education, employment, welfare in Tower Hamlets

Attlee House, 28 Commercial Street, London E1 6LR
Tel: 020 7247 6689 **Fax:** 020 7247 8748
E-mail: smct.org@virgin.net
Correspondent: Elaine Crush, Grants and Monitoring Officer

Income: £230,000 (1999/2000)
Grant total: £1.1 million (1999/2000)
Grants to youth: £80,000 (1999/2000)

The trust was established with the aim of benefiting the inhabitants of the London borough of Tower Hamlets with particular emphasis on Bethnal Green. Its objects cover a broad charitable base including the relief of poverty, the advancement of education and other purposes of benefit to the community. The directors of the trust are willing to consider applications for funding from organisations whose work might fall within the trust's general objects or any of the following specific areas:

- research into job opportunities

- job training centres and schemes
- workshops and light industrial facilities
- environment improvement
- gardens and open spaces
- sheltered housing facilities.

Criteria

Priority will be given to projects which tackle disadvantage and improve the quality of life of people in Tower Hamlets, particularly in the west of the borough. Applicants should show that:
- there is a need for the project
- local people and project users have been consulted and are involved
- equal opportunities issues have been addressed
- match funding or in kind support has been secured
- partnership working has been explored.

Grants included: £7,300 to Shadwell Basin Outdoor Activity Centre towards outdoor youth activities and the purchase of sailing dinghies; £6,500 to Golden Moon Youth Project towards a young women's programme and study support classes; £5,500 to Urban Youth Association to enable the youth club to open on Saturday evenings and towards the summer youth programme; £5,300 to Bangladeshi Youth Movement to employ a part-time female development worker; and £3,600 to Brick Lane Youth Development Project towards a community safety project, working with youth gangs to combat street violence.

The trust does not fund:
- individuals
- political parties and political activities
- religious activities
- grants which do not benefit people living in Tower Hamlets
- activities or expenditure that has already taken place.

Applications: Organisations requesting £5,000 or more should request an application form. This can be made available on computer disc.

For all applications under £5,000, organisations should send an outline funding request which must include the following details:
- your legal status and aims;
- a statement about your organisation: brief history, current activities and services and references to any previous grants made by the trust;
- a clear account of why the grant is needed, what you would achieve with it, who would benefit and in what way;
- how your project meets the trust's funding criteria;
- where your project will take place;
- a project budget with details of all income;
- precise details of other funding sources and/or in-kind support.

The outline funding request should be accompanied by:
- a job description, if the application concerns a post;
- a list of the names and address of the office holders of your management body;
- you organisation's latest accounts;
- your organisation's bank account and account signatory details.

The application must not exceed three sides of A4 plus necessary appendices.

Applications can be submitted at any time, the grants administrator will be happy to discuss bids before an initial application is made. The trust's directors meet every two months to consider applications. All applications will be acknowledged and applicants will be given the date when their funding request will be considered.

W W Spooner Charitable Trust

General in the UK, with a preference for Yorkshire especially West Yorkshire

Addleshaw Booth & Co., PO Box 8, Sovereign House, Sovereign Street, Leeds LS1 1HQ
Tel: 0113 209 2000
Correspondent: The Trustees

Income: £75,000 (1999/2000)
Grant total: £73,000 (1999/2000)
Grants to youth: Est. £15,000 (1999/2000)

The trust supports charities working in five main areas, including charities working with young people, such as groups focusing on young people's welfare, sport and education including school appeals, youth organisations, uniformed groups and adventure training organisations, and individuals preparing for voluntary work overseas or expeditions.

In 1999/2000 grants were listed under six headings. These included:

- youth outreach – £2,500 in one grant to parish of Tong and Holmewood;
- 'close links status' – 16 grants totalling £8,600 were made, including £3,000 to Yorkshire Association of Boys' Clubs, £600 to 1st Ben Rhydding (de Mohicanen) Scout Group, and £300 each; to Calvert Trust Adventure Centre, 1224 Wharfedale Air Training Corps and 3rd Wharfedale Air Training Corps;
- general – 80 grants totalling £29,000, including £500 to Hunslet Centre for Boys and Girls, £350 to Guide Association Leeds and £300 to 1st Ilkley Sea Scouts.

No grants are given for 'high profile appeals seeking large sums.'

Applications: In writing to the correspondent.

The Stoller Charitable Trust

Medical, children, general, with an interest in Greater Manchester

c/o SSL International plc, Tubiton House, Oldham OL1 3HS
Tel: 0161 621 2003 **Fax:** 0161 627 0932
Correspondent: Alison Ford

Income: £288,000 (1999/2000)
Grant total: £390,000 (2000/01)

The trust supports a wide variety of charitable causes, but with particular emphasis on those which are local, medically-related or supportive of children. There is a preference for charities in Greater Manchester where the trust is based. It also seeks to balance regular and occasional donations and a few large awards and many smaller ones.

In 1999/2000 most grants were for under £1,000, but donations of £10,000 included one to Bolton Lads' and Girls' Club. A full grants list was not available with the accounts at the Charity Commission, or from the trust. The trust informed us that it supports Bolton Lads' and Girls' Club regularly as well as other youth organisations.

The Bernard Sunley Charitable Foundation

General, with some preference for London and the South East

20 Berkeley Square, London W1J 6LH
Tel: 020 7408 2198
E-mail: asstdirbsunleycharfund@ ukgateway.net
Correspondent: Dr B W Martin, Director

Income: £3.3 million (1999/2000)
Grant total: £3.6 million (1999/2000)
Grants to youth: £173,000 (1999/2000)

This foundation makes about 300 grants a year, which are mostly one-off, and almost all for capital purposes, ranging from a few hundred pounds to several hundred thousand. Most large grants are for buildings or their refurbishment, or for medical or research equipment.

Grants in the 'Youth' category were made to 45 organisations. The largest grant was £11,000 to Honeypot Home, in Hampshire, followed by six of £10,000 each to: National Star Centre College for Disabled Youth; Cheltenham, Ocean Youth Trust – North East Area; St James's Montefiore Cricket Club in Brighton; Sea Cadets – TS Royalist Refit Appeal in Weymouth; Youth Sport Trust and YWCA – HQ. Many of the remaining grants were to youth clubs, scout groups and sea cadet associations, from throughout the UK.

No grants are given to individuals. 'We would reiterate that we do not make grants to individuals; we still receive several such applications each week. This bar on individuals applies equally to those people taking part in a project sponsored by a charity such as VSO,

Duke of Edinburgh Award Scheme, Trekforce, Scouts and Girl Guides, etc., or in the case of the latter two to specific units of these youth movements.'

Applications: The trust provided the following information. 'Appeals are considered regularly, but we would emphasise that we are only able to make grants to registered charities and not to individuals. There is no application form, but the covering letter to the Director should give details as to the following points and should be accompanied by the latest approved reports and accounts.

1 What the charity does and what are its objectives.
2 Explain the need and purpose of the project, for which the grant is required. Who will it benefit and how?
3 How much will the project cost? The costings should be itemised and supported with quotations etc. as necessary.
4 What size of grant is required.
5 How much has already been raised and from whom. How is it planned to raise the shortfall.
6 If applicable, how the running costs of the project will be met, once the project is established.
7 Any other documentation that the applicant feels will help to support or explain the appeal.

Trustees normally meet in January, May and October.

The Charles and Elsie Sykes Trust

General in Yorkshire

6 North Park Road, Harrogate, Yorkshire HG1 5PA
Correspondent: David J Reah, Secretary

Income: £403,000 (2000)
Grant total: £432,000 (2000)
Grants to children and youth: Est. £56,000 (2000)

Grants are made to a broad variety of causes and in 2000, children and youth causes received 13% of the grant total.

The trust gave 193 grants in two categories, annual and special donations.

Annual donations – 113 grants totalling £137,000
About half the grants are repeated annually, many to well known, UK organisations. In 2000 only one youth group appeared to receive an annual donation: £1,000 was given to Harold Styan Youth Club.

Special 'one-off' donations – 80 grants totalling £295,000
Grants included: £2,500 each to York Scout Activity Centre and Youth Clubs North Yorkshire; £1,500 each to 1st Barnard Castle Scout Group, Sea Cadets Newcastle and Youth Action in Hull, £1,000 to Filey Sea Cadets and £200 to Yorkshire Youth Orchestra.

The following applicants are unlikely to be successful: individuals; local organisations not in Yorkshire; and recently established charities. Non-registered charities are not considered.

Applications: Applications from registered charities may be made with full details and an sae to the above address. Applications without up-to-date audited or examined accounts will not be considered. The trust regrets that it cannot conduct correspondence with applicants.

The Talbot Village Trust

General in the boroughs of Bournemouth, Christchurch and Poole; the districts of East Dorset and Purbeck

Dickinson Manser, 5 Parkstone Road, Poole, Dorset BH15 2NL
Tel: 01202 673071
Correspondent: G Cox, Clerk

Income: £1.2 million (2000)
Grant total: £410,000 (2000)

A total of 45 grants were authorised in 2000, many to organisations such as schools, churches, youth clubs and playgroups, with grants being given for equipment and capital costs. Grants ranged from £500 to £52,000.

Grants included the following youth organisations: £8,000 to East Hove Youth Centre 'Focus on Youth'; £6,000 to West Moors Youth Club towards refurbishment work to club premises; £5,000 to Linwood Youth Centre towards buying sound equipment; £3,000 to Oakmead Youth Centre towards providing drama/music workshops; and £2,000 to Christian Association for Youth, towards equipping the office and a DJ project.

No grants are given to individuals.

Applications: In writing to the correspondent.

The Joanna Trollope Charitable Trust

Young people

Godwin Bremridge & Clifton,
12 St Thomas Street, Winchester,
Hampshire SO23 9HF
Tel: 01962 841484 Fax: 01962 841554
Correspondent: A Cowgill, Solicitor

Income: Varies, from £5,000 to
£75,000 a year
Grant total: £5,000 to £75,000 a year
Grants to youth: £5,000 to £75,000
a year

The trust was established in 1995, and no
accounts are yet on file at the Charity
Commission. The trust was set up to
support general charitable purposes for
the benefit of people in need, principally
young people and mainly in
Gloucestershire and South West England.
Recent beneficiaries have included:
Cirencester Housing for Young People,
Starlight Children's Foundation,
Rainbow Centre, The Countryside
Foundation for Education, AssistU and
Bournville Junior Activities Club.

Applications: In writing to the
correspondent.

The Tudor Trust

Social welfare, general

7 Ladbroke Grove, London W11 3BD
Tel: 020 7727 8522 Fax: 020 7221 8522
Website: www.tudortrust.org.uk
Correspondent: Christopher Graves,
Director

Income: £14 million (2000/01)
Grant total: £26 million (approved
2000/01)
Grants to youth: £841,000 (approved
2000/01)

The trust's funding policies are reviewed
every three years. During 2000–2003 the
trust aimed to support organisations and
groups which help people fulfil their
potential and make a positive
contribution to the communities in
which they live. The trust focuses its
funding where there is a significant need
in both rural and urban communities.
Schemes addressing rural isolation receive
special consideration. Projects which
offer accessible, integrated and sustained
support to people who are vulnerable or
only just managing are of particular
interest. Groups working with 9–18 year
olds are one of the trust's priorities.

Areas of support include the following,
extracted from the trust's longer list of
priority areas:
- housing for young people (including
  self-build);
- detached youth work;
- IT schemes involving the family;
- recreation projects including those
  which help people and their
  communities to flourish, offer new
  experiences and fun learning
  opportunities, encourage social
  interaction, and provide green spaces
  in urban settings;
- counselling and confidence building
  for young people; and advice for
  young people.

The 'Grants to youth' figure above
reflects grant approvals to youth centres.
Grants made in response to applications
are typically for amounts between
£3,000 and £100,000, although there
are exceptions at both extremes. Grants
can be one-off, or spread over a period of
up to three years. Much larger grants can
be made, but these are more likely to be
the result of proactive work by the trust,
for example through one of its three
'Targeted Funding Committees'

Raising money from grant-making trusts   183

composed of both trustees and members
of staff. These, which accounted for 10%
of the value of grants in 1999/2000,
cover addiction, community development
and 'retracking' for young people at risk.

Unless specifically mentioned (in the
guidelines above) the following
organisations and areas of work are
outside the current guidelines and *cannot*
be considered for funding (Eligibility for
funding is generally assessed by the main
purpose/function of the organisation
applying. The trust does *not* fund
individuals).

**Areas of work which cannot be
considered for funding**
Activity centres
Advice
Advocacy
After-school clubs
Animal charities
Arts
Breakfast clubs
Bursaries and scholarships
Capacity building and technical support
Church and hall fabric appeals
Colleges
Commercial organisations
Community foundations
Community transport
Conferences/seminars
Conservation of buildings, flora & fauna
Councils of Voluntary Service
Counselling
Disabilities (mental and physical)
Endowment appeals
Expeditions/overseas travel
Fabric
Fundraising events/salaries of fundraisers
Halls & church centres
Healthy living centres
Helplines
Holidays/holiday centres
Homework clubs
Hospitals & hospices

Illness (physical)
Large national charities enjoying
   widespread support
Leisure clubs
Medical care
Medical research
Minibuses
Mother tongue classes/cultural
   activities
Museums/places of entertainment
Neighbourhood mediation
Nurseries, creches, pre-school childcare
Playschemes and groups, parent &
   toddler
Playgrounds
Research
Religion
Schools
Scouts, guides and other uniformed
   youth groups
Sponsorship and marketing appeals
Sports
Training and employment schemes
Universities
Victims (of crime, domestic and sexual
   abuse, trauma, war)
Volunteer centres
Women's centres

Applications: Applications can only be
made in writing and cannot be accepted
by fax or e-mail. The trust does not use
an application form. Information
required includes:
- A summary of the current work of the
  organisation, with the latest annual
  report.
- A description of the project/proposals/
  area of work for which funding is
  requested.
- An indication of the numbers of
  people involved/likely to be involved
  and how they will benefit.
- A breakdown of costs (for capital
  works, these might be building costs,
  VAT, fees, furniture and equipment; for

revenue they might be salaries, premises, training, publicity, expenses, etc). Retrospective grants are not available.

- Details of funding raised or committed to date and steps being taken to raise the balance other than the approach to the Tudor Trust.
- Any other relevant information such as catchment area served, numbers attending existing activities per month or per annum, how revenue implications of capital proposals will be met. For new buildings or major refurbishment schemes, drawings/plans and possibly a photo are helpful.
- The latest annual accounts (or a copy of a recent financial/bank statement if the organisation is too new to have annual accounts).

Grants are given for amounts from £500 upwards. Loans are offered occasionally.

Applications may be sent at any time to the correspondent. Each application will be assessed taking account of how the main purpose/function of the organisation fits with current priorities and the funding available. Some applicants will be told almost immediately that the trust cannot help. For the remainder, there is a continuous process of assessment, and applicants will usually be told the outcome eight weeks after all the information has been received by the trust. A visit may be made to the project; but this will be initiated by the trust and will not necessarily result in a grant being approved. Applicants are asked not to telephone for news of progress during this period. A letter will be sent giving the trustees' decision. If a grant has been approved, conditions relating to the release of the grant will be included in the letter. Organisations are asked not to

approach the trust again for at least 12 months after a grant has been paid or notification of an unsuccessful application has been given.

The Variety Club Children's Charity

Children's charities, 'Sunshine Coaches'

Variety Club House, 93 Bayham Street, London NW1 0AG
Tel: 020 7428 8100 **Fax:** 020 7428 8111
E-mail: info@varietyclub.org.uk
Website: www.varietyclub.org.uk
Correspondent: Martin Shaw, Company Secretary

Income: £11 million (1999/2000)
Grant total: £1 million to institutions (15 months 1998/99)

This is an international children's charity originally established in the 1920s in the USA. In 1999 the Variety Club of Great Britain celebrated its 50th anniversary. Its members, who come from entertainment, sport and business sectors, help to raise income each year through fundraising events.

It helps sick, disabled or disadvantaged children, mainly through the provision of Sunshine Coaches and grants to schools, hospitals, children's homes and young people's charities.

Of the several hundred grants awarded each year, over 90% are for under £5,000, averaging about £1,000. These are nearly all one-off donations, though a very few major beneficiaries attract commitments to be paid over a number of years. The 50 largest grants to institutions listed with the accounts, starting at £3,000, totalled £640,000. Nine organisations in receipt of grants for £20,000 or more accounted for a third of the total. For four beneficiaries the grants were apparently part of long-term commitments, all having been supported in previous years; they included London Federation of Clubs for Young People (£42,000); and Outward Bound Trust (£35,000). Other grants included those to: London Youth (£46,000); Browning House (£37,000); The Mulberry Bush (£25,000); and Wyken Adventure Centre and SeeAbility (£8,000 each).

No grants are made towards administration costs.

Applications: In writing at any time to the head of appeals.

The Vec Acorn Trust

Underprivileged and disadvantaged young people in Hampshire

Pennington Chase, Lower Pennington Lane, Lymington, Hampshire
SO41 8AN
Tel: 01590 672088
Correspondent: Mrs S Leary, Secretary

Income: £27,000 (2000/01)
Grant total: £102,000 (2000/01)

The trustees are all involved with community work in the Hampshire area. The trust's interest lies in the south west Hampshire area, in particular to help young people (16 to 25 years old) who are disadvantaged (either medically or as a result of the environment in which they live). To assist in developing their potential which otherwise they may not be able to achieve. The trust aims to support projects which reach a number of people but with the emphasis being on self-help. The trust is willing to enter into joint funding arrangements with

other grant-making or public bodies, after consultation, to help bring this about.

Grants to 53 organisations included: £2,000 each to Friends of the Hampshire County Youth Orchestra and Havant Youth Sail Training Scheme; £1,000 to Hants and Isle of Wight Outward Bound Association; £600 each to 1st West Parley Scout Group, Hampshire County Youth Band and £500 to Bournemouth Youth Walking Association.

Applications: In writing to the correspondent. Trustees meet quarterly. If the application is of interest to the trustees, arrangements would be made for further discussion to take place, possibly followed by a visit. The trustees think it important that any grant should be followed through and evaluated.

The Charity of Thomas Wade & Others

General, community groups, youth in Leeds

Wrigleys, 19 Cookridge Street, Leeds
LS2 3AG
Tel: 0113 244 6100 **Fax:** 0113 244 6101
Correspondent: W M Wrigley

Income: £150,000 (2000)
Grant total: £101,000 (2000)
Grants to youth: Est. £50,000 (2000)

The objects of the charity are to provide 'open spaces' within the pre-1974 city boundary of Leeds and to provide recreation and entertainment facilities for people of all ages in Leeds but in particular youth clubs. In practice it supports a range of charities in Leeds covering largely community/youth organisations. The beneficial area is restricted; organisations must lie within the postal codes LS1–LS17 or benefit people in that area.

The charity is keen to support new organisations and stated that it particularly wishes to receive more applications from east Leeds. It prefers to give one-off grants and recurrent grants are not encouraged, however they are considered. Three major beneficiaries have received recurrent grants for the last few years.

In 2000 the charity made 55 grants, with the average sized grant to youth centres or clubs being £5,800. The largest grant to youth organisations was £16,000 to Hunslet Club for Boys' and Girls'. Other grants included: £5,000 to Leeds Childrens' Holiday Camp Association; £2,500 to Central Yorkshire Scout Council; £2,000 each to South Leeds Youth Theatre and St Luke's Youth Project; and £1,000 to Girls' Brigade and Youth Fellowship.

Grants are not given to individuals or to schools (unless special needs schools). The trustees tend not to support medical/health orientated bodies

Applications: In writing to the correspondent. Applicants must submit accounts, evidence of charitable status and a contact telephone number with the application. They should be submitted not later than one month before the trustees' meeting.

Trustees consider applications in April, July and November. A charity advisor visits most of the applicants and gives them advice, a detailed report is then made on each application for consideration at the trustees' meetings. The charity hopes that this will enable them to identify where there is the greatest need and distribute the grants accordingly. The charity advisor also reports on how

grants have been used and successful applicants are also encouraged to provide follow up reports to help the trust with its future grant-making.

The Wates Foundation

Social welfare especially in Greater London

1260 London Road, Norbury, London SW16 4EG
Tel: 020 8764 5000 **Fax:** 020 8679 1541
E-mail: director@watesfoundation.org.uk
Website: www.watesfoundation.org.uk
Correspondent: The Director

Income: £1.6 million (2000/01)
Grant total: £1.6 million (2000/01)
Grants to youth: Est. £80,000 (2000/01)

The trust's aim is '… to improve the quality of life of the deprived, disadvantaged and excluded in the community in which we live'. The trust has specific priorities which reflect the interests of particular trustees. One of the broadest priority areas is 'Community projects and the disadvantaged' and grants can be made to youth clubs under this heading although it is not a mainstream activity.

Grants are concentrated on the Greater London area with a preference for South London. Preference is given to projects that seek to comply with recognised quality assurance and accreditation schemes.'

Many foundation funded projects share these features:
- the work is about providing solutions to problems rather than making them more bearable;

- there is a clear sense of objectives, and of how to achieve them;
- the work may be innovative, pioneering or risky;
- any grant has a good chance of making a difference.'

Grants are up to £25,000 in any single year. Maximum length of support is three years frequently with instalments tapering in the second and third years. Beneficiaries included:
- £11,000 to Middle Park Playscheme towards funding for three activity schemes for young people in Eltham;
- £10,000 to Accra Centre for the Advancement of Young People, Brixton, towards a football programme;
- £7,500 to St John the Divine Youth Project Kennington, towards the salary of the youth worker to help at the community centre;
- £7,000 to Croydon Youth Development Trust, for a new youth development initiative in the north of the borough;
- £3,000 to St John's Centre (Woolwich) towards part-funding for a youth development project to provide activities to meet the needs of disadvantaged local young people;
- £1,000 to Townmead Youth Club, Fulham, towards its core running costs;
- £250 to 15th Bromley (Bixley and Wigmore) Scout Group, to help provide new toilet facilities in the extension the scout hall.

The trust does *not* generally support:
- any work that is not legally charitable;
- sponsorship of individuals for any purpose;
- large well-established or UK charities;
- umbrella organisations or support to other grant making bodies;

- building projects including the repair of churches and church appeals;
- medical or disaster relief appeals;
- sporting, social or other events;
- foreign travel including expeditions;
- conferences;
- overseas projects and projects outside Greater London.

Applications: Initial applications should be in the form of a letter on no more than four A4 pages addressing the following questions:
- 'who you are and what you do;
- an outline of the project saying what it is, where it will be delivered, over what timescale and how;
- why you are the right organisations to do it and how it fits the foundation's priorities;
- who will do the work and what training or accreditation they will have;
- whether the work will involve those you seek to benefit;
- what difference you hope to achieve and how to intend to measure it;
- how you will monitor and ensure the quality of the work undertaken;
- how the work will promote equal opportunities;
- what funding you are seeking, including any budgetary breakdown, and to whom else you have applied.'

A budgetary breakdown may be attached additional to the four-page limit. Budgets covering more than one year should include elements for inflation. Salary costs should identify NI costs. Letters should be accompanied by signed copies of the most recent annual report and accounts. All requests for support are rigorously filtered and application forms will only be sent to those applicants completing this process. The completed application form must be accompanied by a business plan/work plan where appropriate and include the following additional information:

- staffing details
- composition of the management committee
- the name, address and telephone number of a suitable referee.

The trust is happy for potential applicants to telephone to check if they fall within their guidelines. No new application will be considered within twenty-four months of a completed grant.

The Westminster Foundation

General

70 Grosvenor Street, London W1K 3JP
Tel: 020 7408 0988
Correspondent: J E Hok, Secretary

Income: £2.7 million (2000)
Grant total: £3.8 million (2000)
Grants to youth: £114,000 (2000)

The trust gives nearly 200 grants a year, most for £2,000 or less but the largest for £60,000. Trustees invariably have knowledge of, or a connection with, those charities which are successful applicants. The trustees tend to support welfare causes and not research. In 2000 grants were made to 22 organisations in the Youth category, although some of these may not have been for conventional youth work. The largest grants were £44,000 to NSPCC Trading and £16,000 to Chester Youth Club, followed by £11,000 to Youth Sport Trust; £5,500 to The Country Trust, £5,000 each to Farms for City Children, Lache Adventure Playground Association and London Federation of Boys' Clubs;

and £4,200 to Kidscape. Other beneficiaries included Ocean Youth Trust; 1st Upton Rangers; Chester & District Scout Association and Blacon Project.

Only registered charities will be considered; charitable status applied for, or pending, is not sufficient. No grants are given to individuals, 'holiday' charities, student expeditions, or research projects. The arts and education budgets are fully committed until at least 2004, and homeless and related support until 2005.

Applications: In writing to the secretary, enclosing an up-to-date set of accounts, together with a brief history of the project to date, and the current need.

The Garfield Weston Foundation

Arts, education, health, general

Weston Centre, Bowater House, 68 Knightsbridge, London SW1X 7LQ
Tel: 020 7589 6363
Fax: 020 7584 5921
Correspondent: Fiona M Foster, Administrator

Income: £16 million (1999/2000)
Grant total: £30 million (1999/2000)
Grants to youth: Est. £350,000 (1999/2000)

In 1999/2000 grants totalling £785,000 were made to 183 organisations in the youth category. This covers grants towards disadvantaged youth, organised youth clubs, activity centres, playgrounds, opportunities for volunteering and community work, provision of information, and creative and sporting projects aimed at young people.

Grants of £20,000 and above included: £25,000 each to Bolton Lads' and Girls' Club, London Youth and Raleigh

International, and £20,000 each to Crew YMCA and Youth Clubs UK. Grants of £10,000 each were made to Berwick Youth Project, Downside Clubs for Young People in South East London, New Horizon Youth Centre in North West London and Ocean Youth Club in Gosport. Smaller grants included £5,000 each to Dalston Youth Project and Middlesex Young People's Clubs, £3,000 to Church Lads' and Church Girls' Brigade in Rotherham, £2,000 to Children's Cabin in Manchester, and £1,000 to Beulah Chapel Youth Project. A number of uniformed groups were also supported.

The foundation's grant-making policy states: 'Support cannot be considered for organisations or groups which are not UK-registered charities. Applications from individuals or for individual research or study or from organisations outside the UK cannot be considered. Animal welfare charities are also excluded.

Applications: To the correspondent, including the following information:

- the charity's registration number;
- a copy of the most recent report and audited accounts;
- an outline description of the charity's activities;
- a synopsis of the project requiring funding, with details of who will benefit;
- a financial plan;
- details of current and proposed fundraising.

All applications are considered on an individual basis by a committee of trustees. From time to time, more information about a charity or a visit to the project might be requested. There is no deadline for applications, which are normally processed within three months of receipt. All applicants will be notified of the outcome by letter. 'Charities are asked not to apply within a 12-month period of an appeal to the foundation, whether or not they have received a grant.'

The Matthews Wrightson Charity Trust

Caring and Christian charities in the UK and some overseas

The Farm, Northington, Alresford, Hants SO24 9TH
Correspondent: Adam Lee, Secretary & Administrator

Income: £71,000 (2000)
Grant total: £117,000 to organisations (2000)
Grants to youth: £22,000 (2000)

The trustees favour smaller charities or projects e.g. those seeking to raise less than £25,000. They do not usually support large UK charities and those seeking to raise in excess of £250,000, however support may be given to charities with a turnover greater than £250,000 if they are a previous recipient. There is a bias towards innovation, Christian work and organisations helping disadvantaged people reintegrate into the community. The average award in 2001 was £400. About a quarter of beneficiaries had received grants in the previous year.

Grants were categorised under 10 headings including a 'Youth' heading. Grants in this category in 1999 totalled £22,000 and included those to: 3–2–6 Afterschool Club, Ardnavally Scout Activity Centre, Country Bound, Yetev Youth Club, Dorset Fire Cadets Fire

Services Youth Training Association, Frontier Youth Trust, Lower Wick Community & Youth Project, Netley Marsh Scouts and Guides, Wateringbury Guide and Scout Group, Stelling and Upper Hardres Scout Trip, Walton Youth Project and The Youth Project for Alton.

No support is given to individuals (other than visitors from abroad) seeking education or adventure for personal character improvement. No support is given to local churches, village halls, schools and animal charities.

Applications: In writing to the correspondent. No special forms are used, although the latest financial accounts are desirable. One or two sheets (usually the covering letter) are circulated monthly to the trustees, who meet every six months for policy and administrative decisions. Replies are only sent to successful applicants; allow up to three months for an answer. Please include an sae if an answer is required if unsuccessful. The trust receives over 1,000 applications a year and the trust advises than successful applicants 'have to make the covering letter more attractive than the 90 others received each month'.

The Yapp Charitable Trust

Social welfare

47a Paris Road, Scholes, Holmfirth
HD9 1SY
Tel and fax: 01484 683403
E-mail: yapp.trust@care4free.net
Correspondent: Mrs Margaret Thompson, Administrator

Income: £430,000 (1999/2000)
Grant total: £299,000 (2000/01)
Grants to youth: £45,000 (2000/01)

The trust focuses on small charities, usually local rather than national charities. It accepts applications only from organisations with a turnover of under £100,000 in the year of application. The objects are restricted to registered charities in the UK and cover five categories including the welfare of children and young people (which includes youth clubs, youth hostels and students' hostels and similar institutions). The trust uses the CVS network to make contact with small charities and monitors applications and grants geographically.

Grants are available for capital or revenue costs. Applications for revenue funding can be for up to three years. Although more than half of the applications are for these grants, in practice priority is given to projects in 'less popular' fields where raising funds from the general public is difficult. Preference is also given to very small projects run mainly by volunteers. Grants are usually of up to £3,000 each year for both one-off and recurrent grants.

In 2000/01 grants to youth organisations included:

- £6,700 to Youth-Link, towards introducing a programme of monthly group activities for young people in Dundee who are receiving one-to-one befriending support from volunteers. (The grant is made over three years);
- £2,400 to Westray United Free Church of Scotland, towards buying a large TV screen to show films for young people who are geographically isolated;
- £1,000 to Woolfadisworthy Sports and Community Hall, toward equipping a village hall with stage lighting and curtains to enable young people to take part in stage productions;

- £1,000 to Young Inskip People, towards building a new youth centre in a Lancashire village.

Grants are not made to:
- groups without charitable status applying under the umbrella of a third party which is a charity;
- fundraising groups (e.g. 'Friends' groups);
- individuals, including overseas expeditions, gap year projects, charities raising funds to give grants to individuals or to buy equipment for individuals.

Applications: On a form available from the administrator. Applicants may request a form by e-mail in Word 97 format if preferred, although all applications must be sent by post. All sections of the form must be completed, the correspondent is happy to advise applicants on how to complete the form. Applicants are advised to contact the correspondent to see if the proposal is eligible for consideration.

Applications must include most recent accounts, and annual reports and newsletters are also appreciated, although the trust does not like bulky reports or specialist or technical documents. The trust wishes to make grants in a situation where a small amount will make a significant difference. Applicants needing to raise more than £10,000 should only apply when they are within £10,000 of the target for the first year of the application.

Closing dates for applications are 31 January, 31 May and 30 September for consideration about six weeks later, and notification around two weeks after this. Applications are acknowledged on receipt and all applicants hear the outcome after the trustees' meeting. Late applications will be considered at the following meeting.

8 WINNING COMPANY SUPPORT

WHY APPLY TO COMPANIES?

Giving to good causes by companies has been seen as a source of great untapped income for the voluntary sector. Many groups looking for support assume that because some companies make large profits they must have similarly large pots of money just waiting to be dipped into by deserving organisations. Some fundraisers assume that companies have an unwritten obligation to give to voluntary activity in the community. They do not.

Before applying to companies you must understand why and how they give. Their support will be different from that of other funders. They will not be motivated primarily by philanthropy or by a desire to see new and pioneering voluntary activity. Rather, they will be looking to improve their employee relations and their economic position in relation to their competitors, whether at a local, regional or national level. Any charitable support that they give will be in the light of their profitability and how this decision will be seen vis-a-vis other companies. They have to answer to their share-holders as to how they spend any surplus.

> The top corporate supporters give around £520 million each year to charity. Over half (59%) is in cash donations, the reminder is through gifts in kind, sponsorships, goodwill advertising, employee involvement and secondment and joint promotions. Increasingly, cash grants are used for matching employees' fundraising efforts.
>
> Company giving accounts for around 3.6% of voluntary sector income so you should look at company support as a bonus rather than core income to be relied on year in, year out.

What charities say about company support

'It takes too much time. The support you get does not measure up to the time you put in.' *Maybe.*

'I don't play golf or know anyone in the Rotary Club. How can I get a foot in the company giving door?' *There are other ways to build contacts.*

'Companies? They're only interested in what's in it for them. Photo opportunities, celebrity gala nights, press coverage. We're too small time for them.' *No you're not!*

'You never get to speak to the person who makes the decisions. It's a wild goose chase around departments, until they find someone who can say no.' *If this is the case, you've gone about it the wrong way.*

'You have to start small and then go back for more later. Local shops often help with prizes for raffles, but aren't interested in giving large cash gifts.' *But they can be used as levers to get at people who are.*

---

10 good reasons to apply to companies

- Their employees are connected with your organisation
- They are local and looking for good publicity
- They're interested in young people
- Your event will be good for staff to take part in
- You know the chief executive or personnel officer, or someone in the marketing department helps out in your club
- Young people buy their product
- You're asking for something that's easy for them to give
- They've given to you before
- Your activities help their business
- They like you

10 good reasons to think again about applying

- You know nothing about the company
- It's about to go bust
- They are not located in your area
- Their business is not connected in any way with young people
- They have a stated policy of never giving to unsolicited appeals
- You have received well-publicised sponsorship from a rival firm
- You are asking for £10,000; their total budget is £500
- Their policies, product, image etc. is not compatible with your work with young people
- Your supporters would be against having their support
- Their charitable giving is already fully committed for the next two years

---

Applying for support from companies is time-consuming and can be frustrating. More groups than ever before are chasing very limited company resources. Well-known high street companies receive over 100 applications a day. Many companies end up supporting, at best, one in ten of the applications they receive and most grants are for £250 or less, often tied in with employees' charitable interests. It follows then, that the large majority of charitable applications for company support are unsuccessful, and the large majority of successful applications are for small amounts of money. Company giving can seem small in relation to the amount you are looking to raise.

On the upside, when you are successful, you can have a new source of support that has lots of spin-offs: important contacts; work experience opportunities; management committee members; use of company facilities; in-house expertise provided free or at low cost; staff time and so on.

IT'S NOT JUST ABOUT MONEY

A common mistake when thinking about company giving is to see it as only about raising money. Whilst some companies can and do give large sums of money to voluntary organisations, the majority will not. You have to think clearly about why you are approaching them, what benefits they will receive from being linked with your group, and whether you can ask for something other than financial help.

Case study:

Fitzrovia Youth In Action

A group of 18 year old friends got together to organise a local five-a-side tournament in the West End of London in a residential area near Tottenham Court Road. The area where they played regularly was run down, neglected and many wanted it to be put to another use, especially given the scarcity of land in central London. If the football pitch was to be saved it would mean getting the local community and business onside.

The residential area surrounding the pitch is small compared to the businesses that occupy many of the properties. The football pitch became a focal point for those wanting something more for the residents than a vandalised, unsafe and potentially violent communal space. The young people, who became Fitzrovia Youth Action organised meetings to lobby the Council for change. Building community support was crucial for success, as was arriving at a shared vision of what was wanted for the area - not easy, when local residents initially resisted young people's access to the space. Winning people over was a time consuming process but worth it.

Shell Better Britain Campaign (SBBC) gave a grant towards safe walling and mural design. They wrote about the project: 'The time had now arrived when the young people needed to show that they could indeed rescue the Warren from its disastrous state. Direct action was called for. Begging or borrowing brooms and the shovels, they swept up the glass and dumped the wrecked benches in a skip. They put up their own litter bins. They politely told people not to drop litter and asked dog-owners to clean up after their dogs. Each week they did it again. After a while they realised they they didn't need to do as much clearing up. The message had gone home and people respected the place. It looked as if it belonged to people who cared about its appearance.' SBBC Project Profile, website: www.sbbc.co.uk/resources

The young people kept to their original idea of staging a football tournament and sought local company support to resource it. The group removed business cards from telephone boxes used for advertising by local prostitutes, and the young people recycled the blue-tack to market their tournament with posters. Not only did they gain a supply of blue-tack, but British Telecom in recognition of their clean up service thanked them with a meal in Telecom Tower, overlooking the football pitch.

The group started by asking local businesses for free photocopying. They were sometimes successful, but Andre Schott, one of the founders and currently a coordinator with Fitzrovia Youth in Action, says that it is more than just getting something for free, important though that is. 'It's also a way of developing individual contacts, and keeping local businesses aware of what we're doing. We started off small asking for photocopies, and when we were successful we went back for a bit more each time. It's not easy. You often get turned down, but one success makes the 20 or so times you're knocked back worth it.'

Fitzrovia Youth in Action has been successful with a range of supporters including grant-giving bodies and the local authority. It has nurtured support from the local business community and supporters have included London Electricity, a local hotel, Easynet, McDonalds and Puma. The Embassy of Venezuela offers Fitzrovia Youth in Action the use of meeting rooms.

Andre stresses the importance of building relationships and making business supporters feel involved. McDonalds for instance offered a relatively small grant of £100 to help with the costs of a local event. FYA has developed the link and the local manager sits on the trustee board, and the junior manager gives around six hours a week to the project. There have also been grants and sponsorship for the project from McDonalds' head office.

FYA acknowledges that football works well for bringing in business and community interest. Companies have been happy to be involved in one-day tournaments and leagues. Individual contacts have been maintained and nurtured wherever possible. and interest in the project is high. Invariably company support started small and was built up as trust developed.

Contact: Andre Schott, Fitzrovia Youth In Action, 52 Maple Street, London W1P 5GE Tel and Fax: 020 7636 5886

WHY COMPANIES GIVE

Companies give because it is in their interests to do so. The more they see the donation as a business opportunity, the more likely they are to work with you. The onus is on you to give them good reasons to support your organisation. Some companies give because they see the benefit that will come to the company from being seen to be a good corporate citizen. This enlightened self-interest can be motivated by the following:

- To **create goodwill** within their community. Companies may want to be seen as good citizens and good neighbours, so they support local charities. A quick look through DSC's *Guide to UK Company Giving* will show that most company donations are to local organisations.
- To **be associated with certain causes**. This can help a company's image and provide public relations opportunities. This is one reason why there is strong company support for children and youth charities.
- To **create good relations with employees**. This can be through supporting charities where a member of staff is raising money, or where staff volunteer in their spare time. Some companies have schemes where they match any money raised by an employee; others may give some preference (though not necessarily an automatic donation) to charitable appeals proposed by them.

There can be other reasons why companies give support and these can be broadly categorised as follows:

- **They are expected to**. Companies receive appeals and know that other companies give their support, so they aim roughly to match others' giving.
- They have been asked by an **informal network and peer group**. A large part of company giving can be through donations that have been solicited by company directors on behalf of their favourite charities (or those of their partners). They will pass the hat to directors in other firms through informal networks (i.e. by telephone or over dinner), and if their charity receives support they will be obliged to return the favour when they receive similar requests for those charities favoured by other directors.
- Giving is **decided by the chairman or managing director**. Those causes that they are personally interested in stand more chance of support than others. Even with some large companies that have well-established policies and criteria for their giving, you are more likely to be successful if you can persuade a friend of the managing director to ask on your behalf, even if it does not exactly fit into the company's criteria. Often, you do not need to do the asking yourself; the trick is to find the right person to do it on your behalf. Recruiting an eminent local businessperson onto your fundraising committee and persuading them to approach their colleagues on your behalf saves you time and raises more support. Peer to peer asking is often the most effective way to win support.

- The **director's special interest** where the managing director, chairman or any director uses the company's charitable budget as an extension of a personal account to support their own charitable commitments.
- Because they have **always given**. Some companies will never review their policies. If you are on their list, all well and good; if you are not, it may be almost impossible to join the favoured few.
- Because the **charity persists** in their approach to the company, and the company does not want to keep refusing a worthwhile cause. Persistence can pay, although if you are turned down you should consider whether you can improve your application, or ask for something else.

How much do companies give?

Company giving is not easy to quantify. Companies can help in a number of ways, including products and services for free, staff time, secondments, advertising, low-cost or free use of facilities, expertise, free equipment, as well as money. In its research for the *Guide to UK Company Giving*, DSC assessed the total community contributions of the 550 companies featured to be £520 million, of which £308 million was in cash support (2000/01 figures).

In 2000/01, the top 400 corporate donors gave around £514 million in total community contributions, £300 million of which was cash support. This total support represents 0.27% of these companies' pre-tax profits and accounts for nearly 99% of company giving in the UK. Indeed, the top 25 companies give around 38% of the total corporate support available (or £300 million in community contributions).

BUILDING YOUR CONFIDENCE

A large part of raising support from companies is about confidence. Those who are successful at company fundraising will probably tell you that they started small and worked upwards. Most local groups will have some experience of trawling the local high street for gifts for their annual raffle. To a small organisation, a £20 meat voucher from the youth leader's local butcher or the offer of car valeting from a garage can make a big difference to the amount of money raised from a raffle. Even at this level, use the contacts you have locally to improve your chances of success. Ask the garage or butcher that you use to help out. The local branch where you bank regularly may be prepared to match any money you raise in a sponsored event. Local businesses may think twice about jeopardising your regular custom. Make sure that you give them plenty of notice of the date. Do not leave asking for gifts and contributions until the eve of the event.

Do not ask too often. A good fundraising plan, even for modest amounts, will ensure that you ask people once in a year rather than every three months.

Think carefully about what they can afford, and even here, sell your event as something that will give their enterprise good coverage locally. Word-of-mouth custom is the lifeblood of local shops and businesses. If you live in a very local community such as a village where everyone knows each other, a skill auction with local people and local businesses donating lessons, services or time can be very effective.

Where you have been successful with a small contribution form a local company, you can use this as a foundation for further support. Depending on the size and scale of the company you may want to go back for a larger contribution next time. An estate agent, for instance, may initially give something towards a raffle, and in the future may be persuaded to support a team strip for a local sports competition, or help with a music performance.

Small donations from local businesses can also give fundraisers more confidence to approach large companies for more substantial support, whether in cash or through help in kind. Whilst you may have a regular conversation in your corner shop, you will not necessarily know people in the larger stores and factories in town. This will be a case of building relationships over time and getting to know the business of business.

Start by asking around your organisation – parents, helpers, staff, committee members, the young people themselves, to see if anyone knows any local business people. Build on any links that already exist. A good way to build a relationship may be to have a presentation evening where the manager of a local business is invited to attend and perhaps present an appropriate award. You may have asked them to donate the award, or it may be just a simple way to introduce them to your organisation. If there is coverage in the local press (including the free press) so much the better.

The most common mistake when applying to companies

Most organisations write to companies for support in the same way that they write to grant-making trusts. That is, they write along the lines: 'This is what we do; this is why we are important; and this is what we want.' This is fine for a trust, but will not work well with a company. You must say: 'This is what we do; this is why we are important; this is what we want and these are the benefits the company will see from supporting us.' If you cannot find anything to say about the last part, if you cannot give the company some obvious benefit from its contribution, do not bother writing to the company at all.

Read companies' policies – if they exist – and find out about the company's interests and charitable priorities. Where you know these, abide by them. Dealing with a mass of clearly inappropriate applications is the single biggest headache in corporate giving and has even led some to consider winding up their charitable support programmes altogether.

The local business perspective

Small and medium sized businesses will react quickly to economic conditions. When business is creaking, their concerns will be for their staff, and not giving money to charities. Staff time is also at a premium as numbers are small and people are usually stretched with their workload. Staff volunteering schemes are therefore unlikely to be entered into.

Charitable giving is far more likely to be led by the enthusiasms of the partners or directors, but is also likely to be responsive to causes where staff are involved. Feedback is vital if the often fragile link is to be strengthened. There will be no one with a designated responsibility for deciding on speculative letters asking for support. Decisions are made immediately, and one local businessman gives the following advice:

- Match your request to what the business can afford. If a project is too large and the business can only give a small donation, 'we would see our contribution as being swallowed up and not making any difference at all. It's not worth us bothering'.
- Lengthy letters 'drive us mad. It's much better if they're simple, succinct and concise'.
- Letters should be typed rather than hand-written.
- A professionally written introduction to a letter would be looked at straight away. A good track record gives the appeal credence.
- Corporate giving is not just about money. 'As partners, we tend to give of our time and skills through involvement, more so than cash.'

Once you have contacted and met the local manager or departmental head, you now have a real link with a company. Use your contact to increase the profile of your organisation in the business. They may be able to advertise your activities on the staff notice-board. You could invite a staff team to take part in a fun-day, sponsored event, or a sports contest. There may eventually be an opportunity to have a collecting tin in the staff canteen, or sell charity Christmas cards. You may have opportunities for staff to volunteer and work with your organisation. You need to work out imaginative ways of linking your organisation to the business and keeping them informed of what you are doing. Do not just keep to selling raffle tickets to the staff, or asking them for cash donations. It will become harder to engage the firm's support if you allow news to go stale, or if the contact you have fades through lack of interest on your part. You do need to put time into nurturing the link you have made, and keep the company updated on what you are doing.

Remember that businesses thrive on personal contacts, and also that telephone conversations are a key part of how business works. You cannot avoid using the telephone to make things happen. If this is daunting, either delegate the contact work to someone else (perhaps someone on your management committee who already has links with business people) or try to increase your confidence in some way.

THE KIND OF HELP COMPANIES GIVE

Companies only rarely pay for salaries and almost never for core costs. You should aim to give the company a particular item or project to support. Giving cash is usually the most expensive way for companies to give to charity. There are plenty of other options which are just as valuable to you but cost the company a lot less to give. Here are some of them:

- people
- gifts in kind
- advertising
- sponsorship.

People

The people working in a company are a vital resource for both a voluntary organisation and a business. The best way into company giving is knowing someone in the company and asking them to put the case for the organisation within their business. They are well placed to be an advocate for the cause. So ask around your leaders, parents, and management committee to see who works where.

You can also try to get companies to encourage their staff to volunteer with your organisation. Employee volunteering is a growing area and one which many companies are keen to develop. In some cases, large companies have linked staff volunteering activities with their appraisals, recognising that volunteering brings new skills and experiences which can be valuable in the workplace. You may well be able to find a use for new volunteers, preferably where they have a good time. The greatest advantage in fundraising terms, however, is that these volunteers can then approach the company for money when you need it. Through them you have a really strong link.

You may need some expertise that otherwise you would have to pay for. For example, do you need help with management training, project management, marketing, finance, strategic planning or design? If so, why not ask a company if you can 'borrow' someone for two hours a fortnight to help with this. It gives you the help you need while the person giving the help gains a fresh impetus and challenge in their career. If this is done formally, it is called a 'secondment' and would need clear agreements on both sides. However, you may well be able to get the help you need without the formality of a secondment agreement. If the company is large there may be a volunteer programme manager and this would be the best person to contact. Think clearly about the benefits that volunteering in your organisation can offer. They are likely to be many; team building, cost-effective training, project management, specific skilling and the like. In every case, whether there is a formalised agreement or not, both parties must be realistic about the time, expectations and commitment involved.

Business in the Community (BitC) offers professional help to charities through local businesses offering their services. See the ProHelp contact details at the end of the chapter.

Gifts in kind

If you need general equipment or goods, a company may be able to provide these free. This can be in the form of outdated stock that would otherwise be destroyed (for example, carpeting, scrap paper such as letterheads that have recently been changed, old lines of fabric, wallpaper, paint); or equipment and furnishings that have recently been updated (such as computers, furniture, filing cabinets). When companies have a regular refurbishment, replaced furniture may be kept in store for a while. Banks or building societies, for example, may

What kind of gift is a gift in kind?

Gifts in kind are donations of items or services, rather than the money to buy them. The only limit to gifts in kind that can be given by companies is your imagination. One community investment director with widespread experience of companies and voluntary organisations suggested the following list:

- Donation of coach/airline/ferry tickets
- Advertising on company websites
- Use of surplus storage/sports facilities
- Donation of hotel accommodation
- Use of telephones for helplines
- Design and printing of leaflet/poster
- Donation of surplus food/drinks
- Access to information on customer demography/attitudes/preferences
- Vacant sites for recreation projects
- Free loan of plant, equipment, scaffolding, marquees, portaloos
- Donation of rubble, tarmac, topsoil
- Free advertising space on temporarily unused sites
- Charity leaflet/appeal in a regular business or customer mailshot
- Free servicing of vehicles
- Getting message on franking machine

Reported in *Corporate Citizen*, DSC's journal of company involvement in the community.

have a regional headquarters where discarded equipment is stored. You will have to arrange transport to collect the furniture. Some companies have supplies of waste paper which may be useful for a play scheme or art project.

It's not all about cast offs. Companies can give you their existing products (for example, soft drinks for your fun run) or you may be able to help them launch new ones. Alternatively, some may be able to give limited printing or photocopying facilities. You may be able to borrow a room for a function, seminar or training course.

Companies can give expertise, services or time. This can be worth more than a cash grant if the help is given free or at cost. Some architects and solicitors for example may be able to offer a reduced fee for legal or building consultation. (Others may not as they will not want to muddy the waters at the beginning of a business relationship. You will not find this out unless you ask.) Designers may be able to give you an hour for free, or may be able to give a small project to a junior member of staff as a training exercise. You should not have to compromise on the standard of the work and advice that you need. It does mean however that you have to stick to your guns, and that you are well prepared to take advantage of the limited time that will be available. Make sure you have your outlines and questions well thought out before any meeting to make the most of the time and to ensure that you get what you want from the donation.

Advertising

Voluntary organisations sometimes ask companies to take up advertising space in their publications such as yearbooks, calendars, diaries or, increasingly, websites. This is still a way of generating income but more and more companies, especially national ones, explicitly state that they are not interested in this form of help (see *Guide to UK Company Giving*).

There are two kinds of charity advertising:
- a glorified donation which is a goodwill gesture;
- a commercial exercise where returns are expected for the investment.

With the former, the process is very similar to securing donations from companies where you use personal persuasion, either face to face or over the telephone with a follow-up letter. With the latter, it is a case of selling your charity and using your publication as an advertising opportunity for the company. You will have to calculate the reach and audience for the publicity you are producing. Will this increase the company profile in a way that other advertising does not? Will the company's image be sharpened by the coverage? Will your members, supporters, parents, staff and helpers be translated into customers? Where you are talking about your charity's website, how much internet traffic can you generate, and how will you measure it?

When the advertising is a genuinely commercial exercise you should make sure your rates are realistic. If you expect good coverage with your publication then make sure your advertising rates reflect this and sell the idea to the company accordingly. You will also have to approach marketing and publicity departments rather than those that deal with charities. However, companies are increasingly sceptical about the value of charity advertising and see it as little more than a glorified donation. So you will need to show them that this is a genuinely commercial proposition. The fact that you are a voluntary organisation is irrelevant – you are offering a genuine advertising opportunity.

Sponsorship

Sponsorship arrangements between a charity and a company are where the largest sums of corporate money are to be found. Some companies will be keen on a commercial partnership with a voluntary organisation which goes beyond the advertising opportunities outlined above. Sponsorship can work at a national, regional or local level. A company may be prepared to underwrite the costs of an event, provide money for catering for a presentation, pay for a brochure or sponsor an individual on a training course for example. You will have to be very clear about what you are asking for, and what the company can expect to see as their return. Obviously, the more they sponsor an activity, the higher their investment, and the more benefits they will expect to see.

Firstly, you need to decide what connection you have with the company. Do they already know you and your work? If they do not, you are probably approaching them too soon. Build the relationship between your organisation and their business first. The next question is, are they interested in young people? Do they have a product or service which readily links into the audience of young people? Do they have a record of sponsorship or will this come as a new idea? What sort of budget are they likely to have? (Remember, your proposal must be commercial in its appeal. Again, this is not about you being a charity – it is about you providing a commercial opportunity.)

There are two basic rules in the sponsorship equation:

Sponsor: What will I get from this sponsorship that I cannot get in any other way for the same or less money?

> **A successful sponsorship has three essential elements:**
>
> 1 It matches the *image* of the company and the *work* of the charity.
>
> 2 It has the *correct target audience* for the company.
>
> 3 It *sells the benefits* of sponsorship to the company (including how the sponsorship would meet the company's commercial objectives).

> Remember, sponsorship is a business expenditure, not a donation. You have to go about it in a business-like way.

Organisation/sponsee: What can I offer that cannot be achieved in any other way for the same or less money?

Secondly, you need to tie your proposal into reaching the company's target audience. Sponsorship is about the company selling a product, enhancing its image, gaining access to opinion formers, persuading new audiences and consolidating old ones. You need to show how your sponsorship proposal will help the company to achieve this. If all you can offer are some vague promises or an introduction to the wrong audience, you should forget sponsorship; the company will not be interested.

Sponsorship negotiation can take up a lot of time. Bear in mind the following:

- You should allow plenty of lead-in time (at least nine months before the event, preferably more) to prepare the ground and to make sure that your proposal is sound.
- Precise costings are vital; they should take into account both what the sponsorship will cost, and what the return is likely to be.
- How many people will come to the event, see the product or read the brochure?
- What is their age, sex, income profile, etc?
- Will there be any press coverage and what will this mean?
- Will celebrities be involved?
- How prominent will the company's name be?
- Are there any other companies involved and could these be potential or actual commercial rivals?
- Are there long-term benefits from the arrangement?

You will need to draw up a sponsorship agreement. This is essential if the sponsorship involves large amounts of money. Even if it is a relatively small amount you should draw up a list (or sponsorship audit) of the benefits the sponsorship will bring to your organisation and what return the company can expect to see from their involvement. (See Your Sponsorship Package.)

The key to successful corporate sponsorship is to start small and build up. Make sure that the person responsible for negotiating on your behalf with the company is well briefed and gives regular feedback to others in the organisation. Guidelines on which companies are acceptable to work with, and which are not need to be agreed within the organisation beforehand. This differs from group to group and over time. Recently, some youth organisations steered clear of Shell and their environment initiatives for example.

Never promise more than you can deliver. In fact, try to deliver more than you promise, which will lead to an even more satisfied company. Remember too, that sponsorships have their own shelf-life. After two or three years, the company may wish to pull out of the arrangement, not because the sponsorship is not working, but simply that they have got as much from it as they are going to. Prepare yourself in advance and plan how you will continue the activity. You will need to give yourself time to find another sponsor or to prepare an alternative sponsorship package.

Getting sponsorship – 10 practical tips

1 **Identify the right person** in the company to contact. You need the name of the marketing manager.
2 **Stress the benefits** of the sponsorship to the sponsor. This should be done as often and clearly as possible and backed up with statistics or other supporting information.
3 **The size of the payment will be dependent upon the value of the sponsorship to the sponsor**, not the cost of the work for you. The payment may be more or less than the cost of the project.
4 **Help companies use their own resources to make the sponsorship work**. Suggest, for instance, that they might like a picture story in their house magazine or in the trade press. Most are very keen to impress their colleagues and their rivals, but few think of this without prompting.
5 Sponsorship, especially long-term deals, is all about **working together**. Promise only what you **know** you can deliver, and always try to deliver a little bit more than you promised.
6 Remember that **most sponsorship money comes in sums of under £10,000** and it is a local event you are planning not a balloon circumnavigation of the globe. You do not intend to compete with national events but you have got a lot to offer at the local level.
7 **Get into the habit of reading adverts**. Look particularly at local papers and trade press. Who has got money to spend on promotion? What kind of image are they trying to promote? Who are they trying to reach? How can you help them?
8 **Name drop!** One satisfied sponsor can help you get another.
9 **Before you begin think about an ethical code**. Are there some companies you wouldn't wish to be associated with?
10 **Keep at it!** It is hard work but sponsorships can be really valuable. After every negative letter remind yourself there's another post tomorrow!

From the *Sports Funding Guide* published by DSC

What are companies looking for?

Youth organisations should be able to offer at least some of the following:

- A **respectable partner** (with the right image).
- A real **partnership**. Is there scope for partnership, or is the applicant simply seeking money? What involvement is being looked for from the sponsor, and how well does this meet the needs of the sponsor?
- A **proven track record** (preferably in securing and delivering sponsorships) and a **professional approach**. Has the applicant approached the business of getting sponsorship in a professional way, and can he/she demonstrate a similar professionalism in the running of his/her organisation?
- An **interesting project** (at least to the company management and possibly also company staff) and **initiative**. Does the sponsorship represent a new initiative, something that would not happen without the company's support? Is it interesting and lively? It is much more attractive to back an interesting proposal and an interesting organisation.
- **Continuity**. Is there scope for a continuing relationship (over the next few years), or is the activity/event just a one-off?
- Genuine **value for money**. What are the benefits and how much money is being asked from the sponsor? How does this rate as compared with other possible sponsorships that the company might consider? The relationship of cost to return and the importance of the return to the company are the dominant factors affecting the decision to sponsor or not to sponsor.
- **Visibility**. How 'visible' will the event be, and what specific publicity and PR benefits will accrue to the sponsor? Will the company name be given a high profile?
- **Appropriateness**. Is the activity/event appropriate to the sponsor? Also, are you approaching the right company (e.g. not asking one motor manufacturer to provide a vehicle produced by a rival, an all too common occurrence)?
- **Targeted audience** (possibly leading to direct marketing e.g. providing the company's wine at a reception for young entrepreneurs).
- **Other tangible benefits** (e.g. good publicity; media coverage; link with brand advertising; entertainment opportunities for company directors and staff; access to VIPs; involvement of company employees or retirees; training or experience for employees etc.).

From the *Sports Funding Guide* published by DSC

Cash donations

At the end of the day, money is what most organisations want from companies. Whilst companies are keen to widen the scope of what they give and what charities expect from them, they do give money as well as the forms of help detailed above. In the entries at the end of this chapter we try to give an idea of the range of grants available from the large companies and what they like to support. This varies greatly from company to company. Some will have well-defined policies which work in a similar way to grant-making trusts. They know what they want to give to, and what they do not. Guidelines are publicised regularly and applications may be handled by staff with job titles such as corporate affairs director or head of external affairs.

However, the majority of companies – especially the smaller ones – will have a 'make it up as we go along' approach. Here, any applications will be looked at by anyone from the personnel officer to the chairman, or the chairman's secretary. Unlike their donations management colleagues in other companies, they will not necessarily have any special insight into the voluntary sector. Furthermore, they will be doing the community support task on top of their 'proper' job, and so may have to fit it into the odd Friday afternoon a month. They do not have the time to work through piles of paper or attend lengthy meetings to get to know the issues you are facing and the work you are doing.

Most companies will have some limit on how much they give in a year, and once this is reached the cupboard is bare until next year. A good number of companies will operate on the basis of the chairman's six favourite charities. If you are on the list, all well and good. If you are not, you will have to find a way in, as the company giving policy will already be fixed. Inevitably, if you are successful with this sort of company, you will be successful with others, as part of company giving works on spreading the word and passing the hat on the good cause.

You may stand more chance of success if you can tie your application in with an event or celebration. Anniversaries are useful; your 50th year or your 1,000th member, which you may be able to find a company to tie in your milestone. It will be particularly attractive if you have a time limit to your fundraising – say a year. This gives those working in the supporting company a definite target to work for.

WHO TO APPROACH

The company

You need to decide on a company and then on who you should contact within the company. The choice of company will depend upon what connection you have with them.

- Have they supported you before?

- Are they local to your community?
- Are you consumers of their service or product?
- Do they need better publicity in the community and could you offer that with a link?
- Do your activities contribute to improving the business environment?
- Do they have a stated interest in young people or a project such as the environment that you are organising?
- Is the company a large employer in the area with an interest in the current and future workforce?

The person

Once you have decided on the company, you will need to find out how it is organised and who makes any decisions about charitable giving. Where a company has a number of branches or operating units throughout the country these may have some autonomy in grant decisions. There is usually a maximum amount that they can decide, over which the application will be passed to the next level, regional or national. If you can find this out beforehand it will save time in the long run. You need to tailor your request to the level you are asking at.

Once you have established the level, you will then need to find the right person to talk and write to. Many organisations find this the frustrating part. There is no short cut if you have no inside knowledge of the company. Be prepared to spend time on the telephone, particularly if the company has no decided policy on giving. If there is no policy, there is not likely to be a name at the switchboard either. You may have to go through a number of different departments and repeat your request a number of times before you find someone who knows what the company can help with. At this point, do not give up. You should eventually get through to someone who knows and can give you a name to write to. With all 'cold' applications you must have a name to write to if your letter is to avoid the bin. Make sure it's correctly spelt with the right job title.

You must be clear which budget the money is coming from. Think creatively and laterally. For example, a youth orchestra in the North East secured a sponsorship agreement with a major oil manufacturer located in the area. The orchestra's selling point to the company was: 'You want to recruit your future workforce from the cream of the local population. We have the cream of the local population in our orchestra. Therefore, publicise your company here first with these young people by supporting our orchestra and giving us some money.' Crucially, the payment came not from the company's charitable donations budget, nor from its marketing budget. It came from the personnel budget. It was also much more cost-effective than running adverts in local papers and saved the company time visiting lots of local schools and giving careers talks.

Your sponsorship package

It is not enough to offer 1,000 contacts to a company if they sponsor your event. Most of them may be irrelevant to the company. You need to say which 1,000 people will be involved and how.

Think of each group that you reach in one way or another. Estimate an annual number for each. The following are general groups of people to get the process started but there may be more specialised areas that you are in contact with. Some groups will overlap. The more you can define your different groups of contacts, and the more information you can give about them, the more help it will be to you and potential sponsors.

Group	Number	Group	Number
Adults	————	Clubs	————
Men	————	Employed	————
Women	————	Unemployed	————
Young adults	————	Trainees	————
Teenagers	————	Agencies	————
Children	————	Local authority	————
Consumers	————	Central government	
(what, how and where people		departments	————
buy – drinks, clothes, transport,		Quangos	————
which shops, areas etc.)		Health authority	————
Businesses	————	LSC	————
(who do you use for		Other	————
products, services etc.)			
Schools	————		

Advertising

Advertising space

Look at all the spaces and places where there is room for advertising signs and sponsors' names to be placed and estimate how many people will see it:

	Number
At the entrance to your site or project	_____
Over the door of your building	_____
On a major wall or roof of a building	_____
Inside your building	_____
On the sides of organisational transport	_____
On staff overalls or uniforms	_____
Your own media advertising	_____
Team strips	_____
Achievement awards/badges	_____
Other	_____

Your sponsorship package

Publicity material

This covers all the items that you have printed, and perhaps some that you may like to have printed but are unable to do so without funds. Estimate the number to be printed/produced.

Number

Letter heading _____
Envelopes _____
Press releases _____
Information leaflets _____
Website _____
Email communications _____
Letter franking _____
Catalogues _____
Annual reports _____
Project reports & brochures _____
Programmes _____
Newsletters _____
Event materials _____
Mailings _____
Educational materials _____
(manuals, work packs, games etc.)
Posters _____
Directories _____
Books _____
Guides/maps _____
Tickets _____
Project video/film _____
Slide _____
Exhibitions _____
Other _____

Sponsorship benefits that you might offer

Tick all that apply and try to note numbers where you can.

	Yes	No	how much/how many
Goodwill in the local community	☐	☐	_____
Contact with local authority	☐	☐	_____
Contact with health authority	☐	☐	_____
Contact with government departments	☐	☐	_____
Training	☐	☐	_____
Specifically targeted groups *(which ones?)*	☐	☐	_____
Visits to projects	☐	☐	_____
Contact with celebrities	☐	☐	_____
Events	☐	☐	_____
Opportunities for staff volunteering	☐	☐	_____
Work experience	☐	☐	_____
Other	☐	☐	_____

Your sponsorship package

Media

Say how much coverage you already receive:

	Frequent	Occasional	Possible
National television	☐	☐	☐
Regional television	☐	☐	☐
National radio	☐	☐	☐
Local radio	☐	☐	☐
National press	☐	☐	☐
Local press	☐	☐	☐
Free press	☐	☐	☐
Specialist press	☐	☐	☐
Magazines/journals etc *(circulation?)*	☐	☐	☐
Your national organisation's publications *(circulation?)*	☐	☐	☐
Your own publications *(circulation?)*	☐	☐	☐
Web-site links *(how many visit?)*	☐	☐	☐
Other	☐	☐	☐

The name

When you have tracked your man or woman to their corporate lair have your questions prepared. Even with an initial enquiry, you will need to be concise and to the point in your explanation. You may be asking for general information about how you should apply, but you should also use the opportunity to talk briefly but enthusiastically about your organisation, your proposed project and the way in which the company stands to benefit.

If your letter outlining your proposal follows swiftly on from your telephone call you may stand more chance of being remembered and rise – if only slightly – above the pile of competing applications. Always check on the name and spelling of the individual and the company you are applying to (even to the point of whether they spell it PLC, Plc, plc or whatever). Individuals move on and you may have out of date information. Companies like to see that their name is recognisable rather than prone to misspelling.

The letter

The content of your letter will reflect any relationship that already exists between your organisation and the company. You may need to remind them of past support and how this has helped you achieve some-thing definite. Start with a brief outline of your project and activity. You need to be brief and snappy; the letter may not be read beyond this point if you do not get the reader's attention.

Five dos when asking for money

1 Ask for a small amount first (say £250 or less depending on their budget). You can build up the amount with each subsequent approach, having successfully spent the previous money well.
2 Ask for something specific (a piece of equipment or whatever). Do not imply that the company contribution will just be one of a number and will therefore be almost anonymous.
3 Explain what the PR benefits to the company will be and show how its support will be acknowledged.
4 Use the personal contacts you have to ask for the money (or at least create a link between you and the company).
5 Say thank you for any money you receive, spend it well, achieve publicity for the company, tell them you have done all of this and go back for more.

Make the link between the company and what you are doing as early as you can. The reader will ask themselves at the outset: 'Why should we support this? What's it to do with us?'

Point to results and successes, and name drop. Companies will want to be linked with positive images and will want to see what their support will achieve.

Stress what you have in common, locality; commitment to the community, staff volunteers, historical link with founders, shared anniversary – anything that suggests you know the company and have thought about the mutual benefit that would follow their support.

Make sure you have factual information that is accurate. Do not for instance ask for a Nissan mini-bus if you are writing to Toyota.

Making your case

- Think in terms of a project or specific items to ask for.
- Find the right name in the company to approach.
- Research the company's budget and ask for a realistic amount.
- Make a connection between your activities and those of the company: geography, people, director's interest, customer relations, employee concerns, community profile.
- Find out if they have a defined giving policy – and keep to it.
- Keep your letter short. Aim for one side of A4 at the most – less if possible.
- Don't send circular letters – make sure you have addressed it properly.
- Do persist – unless it is clear that you should not.
- Keep records of companies you have approached, when and what for.

At the end, invite a company representative to an event or to visit, and sign the letter appropriately. Your patron or committee chair may have more clout than a fundraising officer, although the fundraiser may be the best person for the company to contact for further information.

What you should avoid at all costs is the assumption that the company will know your organisation and the importance of the work that you do. They probably will not. It is largely up to you to do the persuading. Do not overload your letter with jargon, technical explanations and long paragraphs. They will probably not be read, and if they are, would they be understood by an outsider? Do not include too much supporting material; it will probably not be read, and you should assume that all the relevant information is in the letter. (For further tips, see Chapter 4 on Preparing and writing a good fundraising application.)

FURTHER INFORMATION

You may find it useful to refer to the *Guide to UK Company Giving* and the *CD ROM Company Giving Guide* for more information. Both published by the Directory of Social Change.

Business Community Connections has details of corporate responsibility programmes and case studies, as well as a community and business partner search facility.

Business in the Community (BitC) has ten regional offices in the UK and a membership of 650 companies. Information is available on the ProHelp scheme.

Charities Aid Foundation has websites on corporate community investment: www.ccinet.org and on tax effective giving: www.allaboutgiving.org

In Kind Direct runs a matching service for charities and companies to provide goods at low cost. Not-for-profit organisations need to register for the service.

The contact details of all these organisations can be found in the section: Useful addresses and sources of information.

COMPANIES THAT SUPPORT YOUTH ORGANISATIONS?

Rather like grant-making trusts the good news is that there are a large number of potential supporters of work with children and youth in the corporate sector. Potentially any company can give to your organisation so long as you:
- make a connection between you and them;
- show them the good commercial reasons why they should support you;
- the company does not have a stated exclusion on support for youth organisations.

Following are the details of those companies that from the research for DSC's *Guide to UK Company Giving* expressed a preference for supporting children and youth. There are over 80 companies below who expressed their enthusiasm for youth organisations and causes, although there may be many more local opportunities for support from companies that are based near you.

In each entry the figure for total community contributions is given which includes in-kind support such as gifts in kind and secondments, as well as monetary donations.

AEA Technology plc

329 Harwell, Didcot, Oxfordshire OX11 0QJ
Tel: 01235 432790 **Fax:** 01235 436656
E-mail: cathy.wright@aeat.co.uk
Website: www.aeat.co.uk
Contact: Mrs Cathy Wright, Corporate Community Involvement Manager

Main company business: A broadly-based science and engineering business focused on five areas: technology-based products, specialised science, environmental management, improving the efficiency of industrial plant and risk assessment and safety management.

Total community contributions: £164,265 (2000/01)

Community support policy: The company supports the environment, the arts, creating awareness and understanding in education of the value of science, engineering and technology. Emphasis is given in these areas to activities which are close to company locations or involve company employees. There is a preference for appeals concerned with the arts, children/youth, education, enterprise/training, environment/heritage and science/technology.

Grants to local/national organisations range from £250 to £4,000. Major grant

beneficiaries during the year included Young Foresight.

Exclusions: No support for advertising in charity brochures, appeals from individuals, religious appeals, sickness/disability, social welfare, or sport.

Applications: In writing to the correspondent.

Aggregate Industries plc

Bardon Hall, Copt Oak Road, Markfield, Leicestershire LE67 9PJ
Tel: 01530 816600 **Fax:** 01530 816666
Website: www.aggregate.com
Contact: Mrs Mary Ford, Assistant Company Secretary

Main company business: The company's main activities are the exploitation of land and mineral reserves principally for the supply of heavy building materials for construction activities. Operations are carried out in the United Kingdom and the United States.

Total community contributions: £70,000 (2000/01)

Community support policy: The company's policy is to provide financial support to national charities which benefit the local areas and communities of Leicestershire and within the aggregates/construction industry.

The company also has sites all over the UK, particularly in the East and West Midlands, London, the South West, Scotland and northern England. It supports charities local to those sites, especially those involved with children/youth, education, elderly people, enterprise/training, environment/heritage or allied to the construction industry, medical research, science/technology, sickness/disability and social welfare.

In 2000, the company made charitable donations amounting to £70,000.

Exclusions: No support for advertising in charity brochures, appeals from individuals, the arts, fundraising events, overseas appeals, or religious appeals.

Applications: In writing to the correspondent.

Alliance & Leicester plc

Carlton Park, Narborough, Leicester LE9 5XX
Tel: 0116 201 1000
Website: www.alliance-leicester.co.uk
Contact: Stuart Dawkins, Director of Corporate Communications

Main company business: Principal activity: supplier of financial services.

Total community contributions: £202,500 (2000/01)

Community support policy: Alliance & Leicester's policy is to direct support into the communities in which it operates. A large element of their support is focused on the Leicestershire area and Merseyside (through ownership of Girobank). A significant proportion of

the charitable and community budget is directed towards matching funds raised by staff.

Exclusions: No support for circular appeals, advertising in charity brochures, appeals from individuals, the arts, education, environment/heritage, fundraising events, overseas projects, religious appeals, science/technology, sickness/disability, sport or local appeals not in areas of company presence.

Applications: In writing to the correspondent, who has stated that the charities committee selects charities to support and, as such, is unable to encourage other appeals. Unsolicited applications will not be acknowledged.

Amersham plc

Amersham Place, Little Chalfont, Buckinghamshire HP7 9NA
Tel: 01494 544000 **Fax:** 01494 542266
Website: www.nycomed-amersham.com
Contact: Director of Corporate Affairs

Main company business: This company was formed through the 1997 merger of Amersham International plc with the Norwegian company Nycomed ASA. In 2001, it changed its name to Amersham plc. Its principal activities are the development, manufacture and sale of specialised products for research-based biotechnology supply and for the diagnosis and treatment of disease. Major UK locations are Amersham, Cardiff, and Gloucester.

Total community contributions: £236,625 (2000/01)

Community support policy: The company supports the community through cash and in kind donations at local (south Buckinghamshire, Cardiff and Gloucester), national and international level. This is primarily directed towards healthcare, education and the environment. However, in addition to these main areas of support, other causes occasionally receiving help at a local level include children/youth.

Exclusions: No support for advertising in charity brochures, appeals from individuals, the arts, fundraising events, overseas projects, political or religious appeals, sport or umbrella organisations raising funds for any such causes.

Applications: In writing only, to the correspondent.

ASDA Group plc

ASDA House, Southbank, Great Wilson Street, Leeds LS11 5AD
Tel: 0113 241 8700 **Fax:** 0113 241 8015
E-mail: cwatts@asda.co.uk
Website: www.asda.co.uk
Contact: Christine Watts, Corporate Affairs

Main company business: Retailing of fresh food and clothing through 241 ASDA stores.

Total community contributions: £3,000,000 (2000/01)

Community support policy: The company stated that it does not make 'head office' donations, but that donations are given through the ASDA Foundation which operates primarily in support of causes recommended and supported by its staff and customers. It is intended to provide support for causes that create involvement and participation by colleagues.

'ASDA's 241 stores and 80,000 colleagues are committed to serving the communities in which they operate. Colleagues (staff) participate in a wide range of community activities both in a fundraising capacity for charities and through supporting local groups and schools with practical help and in-kind support.'

Between May 1999 and December 2000, Asda's cash donations to the community increased over ten-fold from £240,000 to £2.45 million, but this higher figure may include donations from Asda colleagues (staff), customers and suppliers, plus support from the ASDA Foundation.

The ASDA Foundation is now funded primarily by profit made by ASDA Stores Ltd on its midweek lottery. In addition, funds are raised at charitable events organised by staff. It focuses on: children and education, women's health issues, people with disabilities and victims of crime. The 1997/98 report for the foundation stated that it has made donations to a range of hospitals, schools, community groups, and health projects often organised by small volunteer groups who are important locally but who lack a large national presence.

Exclusions: No response to circular appeals. No support for advertising in charity brochures, appeals from individuals, overseas projects, political appeals, religious appeals, or local appeals not in areas of company presence.

Applications: Very few donations are made centrally. The first contact should be made with the local store.

Associated British Foods plc

Weston Centre, Bowater House, 68 Knightsbridge, London SW1X 7LQ
Tel: 020 7589 6363 **Fax:** 020 7584 8560

Main company business: The activities of the group primarily concern the processing and manufacture of food. The ultimate holding company is Wittington Investments Ltd.

Total community contributions: £300,000 (1999/2000)

Community support policy: This company states that it does not itself make charitable donations. All charitable requests sent to them are passed on to the Garfield Weston Foundation (see entry in the Grant-making trusts section of the book).

Exclusions: No sponsorship is undertaken.

Applications: There is no one at head office who deals with charitable donations made directly by the company, rather than by the Garfield Weston Foundation. Applications can therefore be made directly to the subsidiary companies.

AXA UK plc

107 Cheapside, London EC2V 6DU
Tel: 020 7645 1771 **Fax:** 020 7645 1641
E-mail: trevor.short@axa-uk.co.uk
Website: www.axa.co.uk
Contact: Trevor Short, Charitable Appeals Executive

Main company business: The group engages in ordinary long-term insurance business, namely, life assurance, annuities, pension and permanent health insurance

and general insurance business through subsidiary companies.

Total community contributions: £660,000 (2000/01)

Community support policy: As the charity policy of the group was still under review at the time of publication (early 2002), the company were unable to provide detailed information. Major donations (apart from existing commitments) are suspended, although employee led activities continue. The group's charitable budget for 2001 was £660,000. No further details were available.

Exclusions: Specific exclusions were not known at the time of publication, but the policy until now has been no support for appeals from non-charities, campaigning work by charities, small purely local appeals not in an area of company presence, circular appeals, advertising in charity brochures, appeals from individuals, the arts, environment/heritage, fundraising events, political appeals, religious appeals, or sport.

Applications: In writing to the Charitable Appeals Executive.

Bank of England

Threadneedle Street, London EC2R 8AH
Tel: 020 7601 4239 **Fax:** 020 7601 4553
E-mail: linda.barnard@bankofengland.co.uk
Website: www.bankofengland.co.uk
Contact: Mrs Linda Barnard, Community Relations Manager

Main company business: The Bank of England is the central bank of the United Kingdom and aims to maintain a stable and efficient monetary and financial framework in pursuance of a healthy economy.

The bank is based in London and has agencies in Belfast, Birmingham, Bristol, Cambridge, Glasgow, Leeds, Liverpool, Manchester, Newcastle, Nottingham, Southampton, and Greater London. It operates a printing works in Loughton, Essex, in addition to its Registrar's Department in Gloucester. Subsidiaries include companies purchased in the course of its function of regulating the financial markets including Minories Finance (formerly Johnson Matthey Bankers following the sale of that company's principal business).

Total community contributions: £634,000 (2000/01)

Community support policy: The following information is taken from the 2001 Annual Report. 'The Bank's policy on charitable giving generally focuses on initiatives which enable disadvantaged people to access worthwhile employment through training and on supporting the staff's community involvement'.

In addition to financial support, the bank encourages a range of Education Business Partnership activities, particularly in areas close to the bank such as Tower Hamlets and Hackney. The bank were also instrumental in the launch of the Heart of the City initiative which aims 'to research, inform and promote community involvement and charitable giving by companies and individuals in the City of London'.

Exclusions: No response to circular appeals. No support for local appeals not in areas of company presence, personal appeals, sponsorship requests, fundraising events, the arts, advertising in charity brochures, overseas projects, political

appeals, religious appeals, science/technology, or sport.

Applications: Donations can be made locally at the discretion of the branch agent and subject to a limited budget. Otherwise, appeals should be addressed to the correspondent.

Bank of Scotland

Group Community Relations Department, PO Box No.5, The Mound, Edinburgh EH1 1YZ
Tel: 0131 243 7193 **Fax:** 0131 243 7081
Website: www.bankofscotland.co.uk
Contact: Bruce Lowe, Charities Manager

Main company business: Banking, financial and related services in the UK and abroad, provided through branches, offices subsidiaries, joint ventures and associated undertakings.

Total community contributions: £7,961,503 (2000/01)

Community support policy: Although the bank supports charities across the UK, preference is given to those which operate in Scotland. Areas considered for support include homelessness in the community, medical research and care, youth and education, and the environment. The bank's support policy on youth and education is:

- national initiatives developed to increase financial or social awareness within the community;
- development of care and support programmes whose primary objective are to help young people in need and/or those families affected by disability, drug or alcohol abuse;
- the provision of national training and learning opportunities to enable young

people to develop their skills and talents for the benefit of the community.

In addition to charitable donations, the bank supports over 300 events throughout the UK through its sponsorship programme.

During 2000/01, the group contributed nearly £8 million to the community, including donations of £2.3 million to charitable organisations. Grants to national and local organisations range in size upwards from £250.

Exclusions: The following are not generally supported: advertising in charity brochures, appeals from individuals, circular appeals, fundraising events, local appeals not in areas of company presence, overseas projects, or political appeals, organisations which discriminate based on colour, sex or religious beliefs, refurbishment/building projects, conferences or bursary award schemes. Please note that the bank does not sponsor charities or fundraising events in aid of charities.

Applications: Donations are decided upon by an appeal response committee which meets once every month. Applications should be made in writing, providing a brief description of the charity's activities as well as details of any current projects. Appeals should be addressed to the Charities Manager.

Note: Although the bank welcomes appeals, it is receiving too many 'mailshots' where insufficient thought has been given as to why the bank might wish to support the particular cause.

Barclays PLC

Community and Social Affairs,
8th Floor, 54 Lombard Street, London
EC3P 3AH
Tel: 020 7699 2969 **Fax:** 020 7699 2685
E-mail: angie.tymkow@barclays.co.uk
Website: www.barclays.co.uk
Contact: Angela Tymkow or Alice Wilcock, Community Affairs Manager/ Head of Community Affairs

Main company business: Barclays PLC is a UK-based financial services group engaged primarily in the banking and investment banking businesses. In terms of assets employed, Barclays is one of the biggest financial service groups in the UK. The group also operates in many other countries around the world.

Total community contributions: £24,558,000 (1999/2000)

Community support policy: A much greater proportion of Barclays support is now channelled through the group's offices around the country, rather than through its central Community Affairs Department. Supporting staff in their own community activities is also a priority. Support is only given to registered charities or for clearly charitable purposes. The five main categories supported are:

- local communities;
- social needs (including young people, people with disabilities and disadvantaged people);
- education and training;
- economic regeneration;
- the environment.

Besides cash donations, the bank's other main areas of support are arts and good-cause sponsorship, and secondments. In the past main beneficiaries have included Scout Association and YMCA. Local appeals are assessed by Barclays' network of regional offices and major sites, each of which has its own donations budget. Overseas support is given through the group's operations in the countries concerned.

Exclusions: No support for individuals, circular appeals, fundraising events, overseas projects, political or religious appeals, science/technology, sport or intermediate fundraising bodies.

Applications: Appeals to head office should be sent to the correspondent above. Local appeals should be sent to regional offices which have their own budgets.

Advice to applicants: Barclays has made the following comments about the appeals it receives.

1 No specific application forms are required. However, it will be necessary to send a copy of the latest annual report and audited accounts (the last two years in the case of an initial approach).

2 The group sometimes receives appeals from several different sources within the same charity, or the same appeal is sent to several different employees within the group. This should be avoided.

3 It dislikes the use of advertising agencies to sell space in magazines, brochures or programmes for charity benefits.

4 It receives too many appeals from the same charities during a 12-month period.

Barloworld PLC

3rd Floor, Medici Court, 67–69 New Bond Street, London W1S 1DF
Tel: 020 7629 6243 **Fax:** 020 7409 0556
Contact: Carolyn Munro, Joint Secretary to the Charities Committee

Main company business: Barlow International PLC is a wholly owned subsidiary of Barlow Ltd of South Africa. The company is an international group of manufacturing and distribution companies. Activities comprise the distribution and servicing of materials handling equipment, earth-moving equipment and other capital equipment; paper making and converting; and the manufacture of laboratory, optical and scientific equipment.

Total community contributions: £87,600 (1999/2000)

Community support policy: Support is given to 'traditional charities', particularly those concerned with elderly, young, sick and disabled people, education, the arts, enterprise and training, environment and heritage, medical research, science and technology and social welfare on both a national and local basis. Preference is given to projects in areas where the company has a presence and to appeals where a member of staff is involved. In 1999/2000, local projects received 28% of the total, the young 25%. Grants normally range from £250 to £1,000, with most being for £250 or £500.

Exclusions: The company does not support appeals from non-charities, and rarely advertises in charity brochures for fundraising events. No support for appeals from individuals, fundraising events, overseas projects, political appeals, religious appeals or sport.

Applications: Written applications should be sent to Carolyn Munro or Ruth Pollard, Joint Secretaries to the Charities Committee which meets three times a year to consider appeals.

BG Group plc

100 Thames Valley Park Drive,
Reading, Berkshire RG6 1PT
Tel: 0118 929 3274 **Fax:** 0118 935 3343
E-mail: carey.francis@bg-group.com
Website: www.bg-group.com/
foundation/bgfoundation.htm
Contact: Carey Francis, Director, BG Foundation

Main company business: A leading international energy company, managing the development and operation of long-term capital assets across the gas chain from exploration and production of gas and oil, to liquefied natural gas manufacture and transportation, transmission and distribution, power generation and gas storage.

Total community contributions: £3,000,000 (1999/2000)

Community support policy: The company concentrates community support in three main areas of activity. It places strong emphasis on being forward-looking so as to anticipate society's issues, and thus pilot innovative practical solutions, and aims to ensure help is given to local community projects at a grassroots level. The three areas of activity are:

- Developing community well-being – 'We seek to minimise social deprivation and to regenerate local communities. We support projects that help people turn their community into a safer, more prosperous and better place.'

- Improving local environments – 'We want to make run down and economically deprived areas more enjoyable places to live. We will fund projects that make a contribution to improving living surroundings – both urban and rural.'
- Life-long learning – 'We believe people should be equipped with the right skills for a better future. That means, we look for projects that develop abilities, unlock potential and build confidence in people of all ages.'

Support is given in three different ways:
- Flagship and major projects – A number of projects are selected each year, to which significant levels of funding, employee skills and time are donated. These projects receive board level involvement. One initiative is support for Green Futures, which the foundation funds in partnership with Groundwork. The programme runs in the government's priority areas: Merseyside, East Midlands, South Yorkshire and the North West, and aims to bridge the gap between long-term unemployment and mainstream jobs. It will enable young people to receive paid work and training through delivering environmental services and help them find permanent employment or further training.
- Regional involvement – To benefit the community at a grassroots level support is given to a programme of local projects, which also provides employees with opportunities to get involved. An additional Innovation Fund rewards and encourages innovative ideas from the regions.
- International assistance – The company operates in 17 countries, and each international office is actively involved

in helping the differing needs of their local communities.

Exclusions: No support is given to circular appeals, appeals from individuals, purely denominational (religious) appeals, large national appeals, political appeals, bricks and mortar appeals or animal organisations.

Applications: In writing to the correspondent. British Gas Regions deal with requests for assistance to local projects. The unit at headquarters handles all requests which have national implications.

Birmingham Midshires

PO Box 81, Pendeford Business Park, Wobaston Road, Wolverhampton WV9 5HZ
Tel: 01902 302247 **Fax:** 01902 325602
E-mail: debbie_dance@birmingham midshires.co.uk
Website: www.askbm.co.uk
Contact: Debbie Dance, Community Relations Coordinator

Main company business: Financial services division of Halifax plc

Total community contributions: £180,000 (1999/2000)

Community support policy: The following is taken from the society's 1997 Annual Report: 'We continue to focus our community involvement on areas that relate to our business, particularly on helping people overcome financial difficulty and assisting with the plight of the homeless.'

Exclusions: No response to circular appeals. No support for advertising in charity brochures, appeals from individuals, purely denominational

(religious) appeals, local appeals not in areas of company presence, large national appeals, overseas projects, building restoration or political purposes.

Applications: In writing to the correspondent, from whom policy guidelines are available.

Bombardier Aerospace – Short Brothers plc

Airport Road, Belfast BT3 9DZ
Tel: 028 9073 3564 **Fax:** 028 9073 3399
E-mail: morrisons@shorts.co.uk
Website: www.bombardier.com
Contact: Sylvia Morrison, Corporate Community Involvement Manager

Main company business: The principal activities of the company are the design, development and manufacture of aircraft components and related products and services.

Total community contributions: £551,670 (2000/01)

Community support policy: The company has a charity committee that decides which applications are supported. Preference is given to appeals relevant to company business, service charities, local charities and community organisations in areas of company presence. Charitable donations are made by the Shorts Foundation, a charitable trust, which receives 1% of the company's income before tax. The foundation supports local Northern Ireland charities which are educational, cross–community, social/welfare, or provide economic regeneration.

The company's activities include charitable donations, assistance with employee volunteering, financial support for employee payroll giving and employee charitable fundraising, sponsored community projects often with Shorts apprentices undertaking them in work time as part of their training, involvement with key Northern Ireland social and economic organisations such as the Northern Ireland Growth Challenge, as well as education and industry programmes for schools and universities.

Recently the company, either through the foundation or through supporting the activities of employees, has provided donations or practical help to youth groups, community support bodies, schools and agencies for disabled children and adults, cross-community groups, community regeneration projects, and education and industry programmes for schools, colleges and universities.

Applications: In writing to the correspondent.

British Energy plc

3 Redwood Crescent, Peel Park, East Kilbride G74 5PR
Tel: 013552 62809
Website: www.british-energy.com
Contact: Chrystall Rutherford, Communications Manager

Main company business: The group's principal activity is the generation and sale of electricity.

Total community contributions: £350,000 (2000/01)

Community support policy: The company states in its 1998/99 annual report that it supports a wide range of activities with the emphasis on safety, the environment, teamwork and the next generation. Individual power stations

operate local community programmes with particular emphasis on education.

Exclusions: No support for circular appeals, fundraising events, appeals from individuals, purely denominational (religious) appeals, local appeals not in areas of company presence or overseas projects.

Applications: In writing to the correspondent.

British Nuclear Fuels plc

Risley, H380, Warrington, Cheshire WA3 6AS
Tel: 01925 832000 **Fax:** 01925 835619
Website: www.bnfl.com
Contact: Robert Jarvis, Head of Corporate Community Involvement

Main company business: The principal activity is the expertise across the whole range of the nuclear fuel business. The group acquired Magnox Electric plc on 30 January 1998. The recent acquisition of Westinghouse in March 1999 has broadened the group's range of nuclear businesses and geographical spread. Locations are: Capenhurst (Cheshire), Chapelcross (Annan), Risley (Warrington), Sellafield (Cumbria) and Springfields (Preston), Bradwell Power Station (Essex), Hinkley Point A Power Station (Somerset), Sizewell A Power Station (Suffolk), Berkeley Power Station (Gloucester), Trawsfynydd Power Station (Gwynedd), Dunganess A Power Station (Kent), Oldbury Power Station (Gloucestershire), Wylfa Power Station (Gwynedd), Hunterston A Power Station (Ayrshire).

Total community contributions: £4,100,000 (2000/01)

Community support policy: The company's policy is to establish long-term relationships with the local communities around sites, with support covering economic regeneration, education, charitable help and sponsorship particularly within the communities where its sites are based. Outside of this preference is given to organisations concerned with community and economic welfare, health issues, sports and renewal activities, enterprise and training, science and technology, environment and heritage, fundraising events, cultural activities and education, especially when targeted at under-privileged people, particularly children/youth and elderly people. Fundraising events may also be supported.

Typical national grants range from £100 to £15,000. Local grants range from £25 to £1,000.

The company is currently focusing support on youth related issues, especially those tackling social problems such as drugs, youth crime and homelessness. Recent examples include: Cumbria Community Foundation, which aims to improve the quality of community life of people in Cumbria; Merseyside Police – Police and Youth Encouragement Scheme; support of the Prince's Youth Business Trust through staff secondments and financial support; the CADAS (Cumbria Alcohol & Drug Advisory Service) Peer Counselling project.

Exclusions: No support for circular appeals, large national appeals (except North West based), small purely local appeals not in areas of company presence, advertising in charity brochures, overseas projects, political appeals, or religious appeals.

Applications: In writing either to the correspondent above or to the General Manager of the nearest factory. A donations committee meets monthly.

British Sky Broadcasting Group plc

6 Centaurs Business Park, Grant Way, Isleworth, Middlesex TW7 5QD
Tel: 020 7705 3013 **Fax:** 020 7805 7600
E-mail: ben.stimson@bskyb.com
Website: www.sky.com
Contact: Ben Stimson, Head of Corporate Affairs

Main company business: The leading satellite pay television operator, BSkyB launched its digital television services in the UK on 1 October 1998 offering 200 channels including sport, news, first run films and general entertainment.

Total community contributions: £1,500,000 (2000/01)

Community support policy: The company supports both national charities and charities in areas local to main offices in Isleworth, Livingston and Dunfermline. The company also supports a variety of causes, particularly those aiming to encourage young people in pursuing education, the performing arts, television and sports.

Main beneficiaries in the past have included Youth Culture Television and Isleworth & Syon School.

The Arts: Investment in the production of original British programming has resulted in Sky supporting the development of 'home-grown' talent. Organisations to benefit from this include: Young Writer's Festival, The Script Factory, and the Skills Investment Fund.

Education: Sky Television Production Workshops at the Museum of Photography, Film and Television provide people of all ages with the opportunity to participate in the making of television programmes. Funding ensures that children can take part free of charge. Youth Culture Television provides socially excluded young people with the opportunity to learn about all aspects of television production in a professional studio environment.

Sport: Through the Sky Television Soccer Roadshow, in partnership with the Bobby Charlton Soccer School, grassroots participation is made possible. Working with the Education Action Zones in England and local schools elsewhere, thousands of children across Britain are receiving free professional soccer training. The company is also actively involved in supporting sport at school and are looking at ways to encourage more young people to take part.

Exclusions: No support for appeals from individuals, elderly people, environment/ heritage, overseas projects, political or religious appeals, science/technology, sickness/disability charities or social welfare.

Applications: All formal requests for support must be made in writing. Funding decisions are made in two ways: Nationally, the Director of Corporate Affairs and the Community Affairs Manager meet regularly to discuss proposals and requests. Locally, each site has its own committee which decides on funding for local projects. The company endeavours to respond in writing to every written request within 21 days of receipt.

British Vita PLC

Oldham Road, Middleton, Manchester M24 2DB
Tel: 0161 643 1133 **Fax:** 0161 653 5411
Website: www.britishvita.com
Contact: Mrs Alison Vesey, Public Relations Manager

Main company business: The manufacture and processing of polymers, including cellular foams, synthetic fibre fillings, specialised and coated fabrics, polymeric compounds and mouldings, and engineering thermoplastics.

Total community contributions: £61,066 (1999/2000)

Community support policy: The charitable donations figure given is in fact the sum of a large number of normally modest donations by separate Vita companies. There is therefore a preference for local appeals where these companies operate, those relevant to company business and those in which a member of staff is involved. Priority is given to charities concerned with children and youth, education, enterprise/training, and science/ technology.

Exclusions: Unsolicited appeals are not welcome, nor are large national appeals, denominational appeals, political appeals, appeals from individuals, overseas projects or advertising in charity brochures.

Applications: In writing to the correspondent.

Cable and Wireless plc

124 Theobalds Road, London
WC1X 8RX
Tel: 020 7315 4945 **Fax:** 020 7315 5126
E-mail: swati.patel@cw.com
Website: www.cw.com/community
Contact: Ms Swati Patel, Community
Investment Executive

Main company business:
Telecommunications, main focus on
IP and Data.

Total community contributions:
£6,300,000 (2000/01)

Community support policy: The
company states: '[Our] objective is to
encourage international projects and to
establish partnerships with local, regional
and international charitable community
organisations. We aim to support
initiatives which fall into the following
categories:

- those with a specific
  telecommunications requirement;
- those with the goal of improving
  access to, or understanding of,
  communications;
- those linked to the theme of
  'communications' in its broadest sense;
- preference is given to projects which
  have a strong focus on education,
  training and economic development.'

Each of the company's businesses is
responsible for developing programmes
that are best suited to the particular needs of
their local communities. Key projects in
1999/2000 included (with examples):

- helping young people to communicate
  – Working with Atlantic College
  (student sponsorship), Childnet
  International and GAP;
- bringing communications to aid
  agencies in the field – Children's Aid
  Direct and RedR;

- helping people to learn through
  communications – Befrienders
  International, Book Aid International
  and Deafax.

Exclusions: The company only supports
proposals that match its policy and only
advertises in brochures for charities with
which they are already involved. No
support for individuals other than
employees. Proposals must relate to
locations where the company does
business or have potentially global scope.
No support for political or religious
causes.

Applications: In writing to the
correspondent. On its website the
company produces a 'Step-by-step Guide:
Applying for Community Sponsorship'
giving guidance when applying for
community sponsorship. This is
reproduced here.

1 Developing your community project
- Identify the strengths, weaknesses,
  opportunities and threats of your
  organisation and your project idea.
- Measure your available resources and
  decide on needs for funding, cash or
  in-kind.
- Write a project plan.

2 Search for relevant fundraising opportunities
- Match your project and organisation
  with funding bodies relevant to your
  needs
- Assess your project against the criteria
  of the funding body
- Check Cable & Wireless' policy for
  community sponsorship

3 Writing a proposal
- Follow the guidelines for Cable &
  Wireless' community sponsorship
  funding

4 Presentation of your project
- Meetings with your sponsors for developing a successful partnership
- Marketing and external relations with media and other relevant groups in the community.

5 Implementation and evaluation
- Implementation of project in co-operation with sponsors
- Monitoring and flexible assessment of changes throughout the project
- Evaluation and reporting.

CGNU plc

St Helen's, 1 Undershaft, London EC3P 3DQ
Tel: 020 7662 8165 **Fax:** 020 7662 8070
E-mail: ruby-oo@cgnu.net
Website: www.cgnu.net
Contact: Miss Ruby Oo, The Appeals Officer

Main company business: The company transacts life assurance and long-term savings business, fund management, and all classes of general insurance through its subsidiaries, associates and branches in the UK, Continental Europe, North America, Asia, Australia and other countries throughout the world. The Group also invests in securities, properties, mortgages and loans and carries on the business of trading in property.

Total community contributions: £3,000,000 (1999/2000)

Community support policy: This company became known as CGNU following the merger of Commercial Union and General Accident with Norwich Union plc. The company's charitable funds are allocated mainly in the form of long-term support to a carefully selected group of charities in categories ranging from medical research and care to arts and conservation and from welfare of the elderly to education and support for the young. Local charities are dealt with by local branches; many appeals are then referred to head office.

Exclusions: No support for circular appeals, advertising in charity brochures, appeals from individuals, fundraising events, overseas projects, political or religious appeals.

Applications: Due to the company's committed support to a selected group of charities, very few donations are allocated to charities that apply in writing.

Clerical Medical Investment Group Ltd

Narrow Plain, Bristol BS2 0JH
Tel: 01275 554327 **Fax:** 01275 554311
E-mail: communityaffairs@clerical medical.co.uk
Website: clericalmedical.co.uk/whois/community.asp
Contact: Carol Morris, Community Affairs Officer

Main company business: Financial services. Long-term insurance business and other associated investment activities.

Total community contributions: £187,478 (1999/2000)

Community support policy: Clerical Medical is part of the Halifax Group. The company favours causes where staff are involved and those in the Bristol area. Priority is given to community and education causes, although other appeals are considered.

Exclusions: No support is given to individual schools, religious or political appeals, overseas projects, or towards salaries or building projects.

Applications: In writing to the correspondent.

Clydesdale Bank PLC

40 St Vincent Place, Glasgow G1 2HL
Tel: 0141 248 7070 **Fax:** 0141 204 0828
Contact: Myra Grant, Corporate Affairs Department

Main company business: The company is a wholly owned subsidiary of National Australia Bank Ltd. It offers a full range of banking services through 260 branches in Scotland, England and the Isle of Man. In addition to general banking business, these services include investment management, executor and trustee work, insurance broking, debtor finance, corporate finance, corporate trusteeship, registration and global custody.

Total community contributions: £88,000 (1999/2000)

Community support policy: The bank prefers to support Scottish organisations concerned with medicine, sickness and disability, the arts, elderly, enterprise and training, heritage, social welfare, education and youth, environment and local natural disasters (i.e. in Scotland). National grants range from £100 to £10,000. Local grants range from £50 to £500.

Exclusions: No response to circular appeals. No grants for fundraising events, purely denominational (religious appeals), local appeals not in areas of company presence, large national appeals, overseas projects, political activities or individuals.

Non-commercial advertising is not supported. The company does not sponsor individuals or travel.

Applications: In writing to the correspondent. Applications are considered by a charitable donations committee.

Co-operative Bank plc

1 Balloon Street, Manchester M60 4EP
Tel: 0161 829 5478 **Fax:** 0161 839 4220
E-mail: gayle.ramouz@co-operative bank.co.uk
Website: www.co-operativebank.co.uk
Contact: Gayle Ramouz, Community Affairs Manager

Main company business: The provision of banking and financial services in the UK. The Co-operative Bank is the only UK clearing bank to publish an ethical stance whereby it clearly tells its customers where it will, and will not, invest its customers money.

Total community contributions: £1,001,326 (1999/2000)

Community support policy: The bank supports community groups, particularly those involved in ethical, ecological and co-operative ventures. Generally the bank makes only small charitable donations. Support may also be given to other charities in the fields of inner city regeneration, equal opportunities, education, children and youth, animal welfare, overseas projects, sickness/disability and social welfare.

Banking services: The bank offers 'Community Direct', a low-cost interest-bearing current account for small community groups charities. For larger community groups and charities, banking services are negotiated on an individual basis with the bank's Charities Unit. The bank also operates a postal donations processing service, which may include the acknowledgement of the donation and forwarding of, for example, charity literature to the donor.

Exclusions: No support is usually given to appeals from individuals, the arts, political appeals, religious appeals, sport projects or local appeals not in areas of company presence.

Applications: In writing to the correspondent.

Cornhill Insurance plc

32 Cornhill, London EC3V 3LJ
Tel: 020 7626 5410
Fax: 020 7929 3562
Website: www.cornhill.co.uk/group/cominv.htm
Contact: Vicky Flynn/Jamie Lewis

Main company business: The group undertakes all classes of insurance business. It has 13 UK branches.

Total community contributions: £101,541 (1999/2000)

Community support policy: The company makes most of its donations to registered charities through the Charities Aid Foundation. There is a preference for charities where the business is located and in which a member of staff is involved and for charities working in the fields of children and youth, social welfare, education, elderly people, enterprise/training, sickness/disability charities, medical, and environment.

Exclusions: No response to circular appeals. No support for fundraising events, advertising in charity brochures, appeals from individuals, political or

religious appeals, science/technology, sport, the arts, animal welfare charities, local appeals not in areas of company presence or overseas projects.

Applications: To obtain policy guidelines and an application form please contact either, Vicky Flynn (national appeals) or, Jamie Lewis (local appeals).

Degussa UK Holdings Ltd

Nations House, 103 Wigmore Street, London WC1H 9AB
Tel: 020 7399 2400 **Fax:** 020 7399 2401
Contact: Ray Ward, Donations Secretary

Main company business: Degussa is a German-owned international chemicals group engaged in the development, manufacture and marketing of speciality chemicals. It has a London-based holding company to administer its UK-based business.

Total community contributions: £30,000 (2000/2001)

Community support policy: The company prefers to support local charities and projects in the vicinity of its industrial sites which are mainly located in the Midlands and the north of England, or major national charities where central support is more appropriate. Each appeal is considered separately by a donations committee who try to spread donations as widely as possible over many different deserving groups.

The company prefers to support national charities serving people who are disabled or disadvantaged. Grants are also given to medical research, youth vocational training, charities linked to the chemical industry, education, environment/

heritage, social welfare and the arts. Typical grants to national organisations range from £100 to £5,000, and to local organisations from £25 to £500.

Exclusions: It is company policy not to take advertising space in souvenir brochures or programmes in aid of charitable events, nor to purchase tickets for charity performances. No support is given to individuals, circulars, fundraising events, purely denominational (religious) appeals, overseas projects, small purely local appeals not in areas of company presence or in the form of secondment. Continuous support is not generally given to any one organisation within a category. The committee does not give twice to any organisation in a 12 month period, however worthy the cause.

Applications: A donations committee meets quarterly. Appeals must be in writing and should be directed to the correspondent.

Deloitte & Touche

Hill House, 1 Little New Street, London
EC4A 3TR
Tel: 020 7303 7149 **Fax:** 020 7583 8517
E-mail: richard.stone@deloitte.co.uk
Website: www.deloitte.co.uk/
community
Contact: Richard Stone, Director of
Community Investment

Main company business: Audit, tax, corporate finance, corporate recovery and management consultancy services.

Total community contributions:
£1,060,000 (2000/2001)

Community support policy: Deloitte & Touche is committed to supporting the community at a national and local level through its network of 24 offices

throughout the UK. Each region has a small budget for supporting local charities. A number of major donations are made each year to selected charities dedicated to areas such as children and young people, medicine and research and social deprivation. Major beneficiaries included the Youth at Risk.

Exclusions: No support for advertising in charity brochures, appeals from individuals, the arts, enterprise/training, environment/heritage, overseas projects, political/religious appeals, science/technology or sport.

Applications: In writing to the Deloitte & Touche Charity Committee. However, few ad hoc or unsolicited requests for funding are approved by the committee. Further information for applicants is available on the company's website.

Dixons Group plc

Maylands Avenue, Hemel Hempstead,
Hertfordshire HP2 7TG
Tel: 01442 353000 **Fax:** 01442 354517
Website: www.dixons-group-plc.co.uk
Contact: Clare Brine, Community
Relations Manager

Main company business: The company's main activity is the retailing of high technology consumer electronics, personal computers, domestic appliances, photographic equipment, communication products and related financial and after sales services. UK subsidiaries include: Currys; Dixons; PC World; The Link; @Jakarta; and Mastercare Service and Distribution.

Total community contributions:
£804,000 (2000/2001)

Community support policy: The company concentrates its support on charities concerned with education and training, medical research, crime prevention and, to a lesser extent, those falling under the heading of quality of life. All giving for the group is centralised and requests from charities are administered by the Dixons Foundation. Stores do not have a budget for appeals, and local requests are forwarded to head office. Grants tend to range from £100 to £10,000 with donations below £1,000 generally being made in the form of gift vouchers.

Exclusions: No response to circular appeals. No support for appeals for individuals, overseas projects, political activities, single expeditions, secondment, or sport.

Applications: All charity requests are put before a committee on a regular basis and should be made in writing to the Community Relations Manager. Unsuccessful applications are not usually acknowledged.

Dow Chemical Company Ltd

Estuary Road, King's Lynn, Norfolk PE30 JD
Tel: 01553 692100 Fax: 01553 694552
Website: www.dow.com
Contact: Carol Allen, Public Affairs

Main company business: The company is a worldwide manufacturer and supplier of chemicals and performance products, plastics, hydrocarbons and energy, and consumer specialities including agricultural products, and consumer products.

Total community contributions: £70,000 (1999/2000)

Community support policy: Dow donates more than $18 million each year worldwide with most support meeting at least one of the following criteria:
- addresses a demonstrated need in a city/community in which the company has a presence;
- provides an opportunity for a hands-on science experience for students below the college level, thus improving the pool of talented students from which future employees can be chosen;
- supports a university project or programme involving science, engineering, business or other related areas that also improve the pool of talented students from which future employees can be chosen;
- enhances the environment.

In the UK, the company has established criteria for donations. The main focus is charities and organisations Dow employees are involved with and the communities where the company has plants and offices. There is some preference, however, for appeals connected with children/youth, education, enterprise/training, environment/heritage, fundraising events, science/technology, sickness/disability and social welfare.

Exclusions: No response to circular appeals. No support for advertising in charity brochures; appeals from individuals; the arts; medical research; overseas projects; political appeals; religious appeals or sport.

Applications: All donations are identified by the company through its donations guidelines. Unsolicited applications/blanket appeal letters and charity advertising will not be considered.

Dresdner Kleinwort Wasserstein

20 Fenchurch Street, London EC3P 3DB
Tel: 020 7623 8000 **Fax:** 020 7475 9710
E-mail: jennifer.emptage@dresdnerkb.com
Contact: Jennifer Emptage, Administrator, Kleinwort Benson Charitable Trust

Main company business: Investment banking

Total community contributions: £1,096,085 (1999/2000)

Community support policy: Most grants are channelled through the Kleinwort Benson Charitable Trust. Only registered charities are supported and normally charities will receive no more than one donation within a 12-month period. Donations are principally made in the fields of medicine, welfare, youth, conservation, inner cities and the arts. Support is mainly directed to national charities rather than to local charities and sympathetic consideration is given to charities with which staff members of Dresdner Kleinwort Benson have an active involvement.

Exclusions: The company states that appeals from local charities outside the City of London and the boroughs of Hackney, Tower Hamlets and Newham, or from branches of national charities, are unlikely to receive favourable consideration. No support for appeals on behalf of individuals, political/religious groups, sporting activities or for fundraising events. Overseas projects only rarely receive support.

Applications: In writing to the correspondent. Grant decisions are made by a charities committee which meets quarterly. No grant decisions are made by subsidiary companies, but overseas grants are handled individually by overseas offices.

Esso UK plc

Exxon Mobil House, Leatherhead, Surrey KT22 8UX
Tel: 01372 222312 **Fax:** 01372 223222
Website: www.esso.co.uk/caff/essouk/citizen-esso/index.html
Contact: Stella Crossley, Community Affairs Adviser

Main company business: The exploration for, production, transportation and sale of crude oil, natural gas and natural gas liquids; the refining, distribution and marketing of petroleum products within the UK. The company's interests are spread throughout the UK and include a refinery at Fawley on Southampton Water, a research centre at Abingdon, major terminals in Birmingham, Purfleet and West London, and offices at Leatherhead.

Total community contributions: £2,151,633 (1999/2000)

Community support policy: The company gives priority to three main areas: environment, education (particularly in the areas of science, technology and maths) and projects in areas which are near main employing points – New Forest, Abingdon and Leatherhead.

Esso proactively plans its programmes and likes to strike up long-term working partnerships with the organisations it works with in the voluntary sector. Almost all funds are committed at the beginning of the year, therefore unsolicited requests are rarely supported.

Exclusions: No response to circular appeals. No support for appeals from individuals, fundraising events, religious appeals, political appeals or overseas projects.

Applications: The company responds to all appeals received, but in view of the policy outlined above unsolicited appeals are very rarely successful.

Family Assurance Friendly Society Limited

17 West Street, Brighton, East Sussex BN1 2PL
Tel: 01273 725272 **Fax:** 01273 736958
E-mail: t.horton@family.co.uk
Website: www.family.co.uk
Contact: Tony Horton, Community Affairs Manager

Main company business: Provision of financial services (life assurance, savings and protection schemes).

Total community contributions: £197,000 (1999/2000)

Community support policy: The company's support of charitable organisations is predominantly through non-cash assistance i.e. arts sponsorship and gifts in kind. There is a preference for charities local to Brighton & Hove and the East Sussex area, and for those in which a member of staff is involved.

Support is generally considered for organisations concerned with the arts, children/youth, education, elderly people, environment/heritage, fundraising events, medical research, and sport (where young people are involved).

Applications: In writing to the correspondent. Further information and advice are available to applicants from the society.

Fiat Auto (UK) Ltd

Fiat House, 266 Bath Road, Slough, Berkshire SL1 4HJ
Tel: 01753 786400 **Fax:** 01753 577710
Contact: Karl Gravenor, Chief Accountant

Main company business: Fiat car distributors.

Total community contributions: £150,749 (1999/2000)

Community support policy: The company's donations are made through the Fiat Auto (UK) Charity. There is a preference for organisations working with children and youth. In 1998, the main beneficiary was the Children's Society which received £100,000. Three other organisations each received £6,000, Sick Kids Friends Foundation, Macmillan Cancer Research and York Hill Royal Hospital for Sick Children.

Exclusions: Generally no support for circular appeals, appeals from individuals, purely denominational appeals, local appeals not in areas of company presence or overseas projects.

Applications: In writing to the correspondent.

Findel plc

Burley House, Bradford Road,
Burley-in-Wharfedale, West Yorkshire
LS29 7DZ
Tel: 01943 864686 **Fax:** 01943 864986
Website: www.findel.co.uk
Contact: Dr I Bolton, Company
Secretary

Main company business: The sale of
greeting cards, paper products, gifts and
educational supplies through mail order
catalogues and the provision of e-
commerce and mail order services to
third parties.

Total community contributions:
£75,000 (2000/2001)

Community support policy: The
company has seen a decrease in its level
of giving since the demerger of Creative
Publishing plc (now acquired by
Hallmark Cards). Donations are spread by
the company among more than 200
organisations with particular emphasis on
those working with children and disabled
people, including many less well-known
charities. Donations are generally in the
range of £100 to £500, though in
special circumstances they can be larger.

Applications: In writing to the
correspondent.

Foster Wheeler Ltd

Shinfield Park, Reading RG2 9FW
Tel: 0118 913 1234 **Fax:** 0118 913 2333
Contact: G J Rimer, Company
Secretary

Main company business: Industrial
services and equipment

Total community contributions:
£73,558 (1999/2000)

Community support policy: The
company has divided its charitable giving
into three sections:
1 National charities with strong
   representation in areas where the
   company operates in the UK
   (Reading, Glasgow and Teesside). Two
   charities are chosen each year in
   January.
2 Support for the arts centred mainly on
   Berkshire.
3 Support for the local community – by
   means of a five-year commitment to
   the Berkshire Community Trust – by
   direct grants to local organisations.

Support is only given to local charities in
areas where the company operates (ie.
Reading area, Teesside, and Glasgow),
with a charity committee deciding who
benefits. There is a preference for appeals
relevant to company business and
charities in which a member of company
staff is involved. Preferred areas of
support are the arts; children/youth;
education; elderly people; enterprise/
training; environment/heritage; medical
research; science/technology; sickness/
disability; social welfare and sport.

Exclusions: No response to circular
appeals. No grants for advertising in
charity brochures; appeals from
individuals; fundraising events; overseas
projects; religious or political appeals;
local appeals not in areas of company
presence; or large national appeals.

Applications: In writing to the
correspondent.

GKN plc

PO Box 237, West Malling, Kent
ME19 4DR
Tel: 01732 520168 **Fax:** 01732 520001
Contact: Michael Theodorou,
Corporate Appeals Administrator

Main company business: An
international company involved in
automotive, aerospace and industrial
services.

Total community contributions:
£1,152,319 (1999/2000)

Community support policy: The
main emphasis of GKN's community
involvement continues to be on
education. In the UK, it continued its
core support of both the Technology Tree
and Young Enterprise schemes for
primary and secondary schools
respectively.

The company lists its main areas of
charitable support as education, the
community, health and welfare. This
includes children/youth, education,
enterprise/training, medical research,
science/technology, sickness/disability
charities and social welfare. Preference is
given to appeals from local and
community organisations in areas where
the company has a branch (particularly
local to the GHQ in Redditch,
Worcestershire). Donations are made
through the Charities Aid Foundation.

Exclusions: No response to circular
appeals. No support for advertising in
charity brochures; political appeals;
religious appeals; sport or local appeals
not in areas of company presence.

Applications: Appeals, in writing,
should be addressed to the Company
Secretary at the address shown above.
Local appeals should be sent to local
branches. Subsidiary companies make
small grants independently of head office.

Advice to applicants: As a substantial
proportion of the company's charitable
budget is already committed to
community projects/charities, only a
small proportion remains for donations
to individual appeals. Applicants should
therefore ensure that they send only
appropriate appeals.

The Go Ahead Group PLC

Cale Cross House, Pilgrim Street,
Newcastle-Upon-Tyne NE1 6SU
Tel: 0191 232 3123 **Fax:** 0191 221 0315
Website: www.go-ahead.com
Contact: Martin Ballinger, Managing
Director

Main company business: The principal
activities of the group are the provision
of passenger transport services in the
United Kingdom and the operation of
aviation ground handling services.

Total community contributions:
£231,000 (2000/2001)

Community support policy: The
company's annual report states 'The
group supports local communities' events
in which its employees participate. The
group commits a proportion of its pre-
tax profits to community activities
principally in the North East and in the
fields of education and training.

Exclusions: No support for appeals from
individuals, the arts, environment/
heritage, overseas projects, political
appeals, religious appeals, social welfare
or sport.

Applications: In writing to the
correspondent. Charities should contact
their local branch/subsidiary. The contact

for the North East is Paul Matthews at 117 Queen Street, Gateshead, Tyne and Wear NE8 2UA.

Guardian Media Group plc

164 Deansgate, Manchester M60 2RR
Tel: 0161 832 7200 **Fax:** 0161 832 0155
Website: www.gmgplc.co.uk
Contact: P E Boardman, Company Secretary

Main company business: Newspaper and magazine publishing. The group has national newspapers as well as regional evening and weekly papers in the North West, Berkshire and Surrey.

Total community contributions: £157,100 (2000/2001)

Community support policy: The company gives donations to a number of charities and trade associations. There is a preference for charities local to Manchester and London, then the North West and South East. Smaller appeals are considered every three months, when around 200 appeals are considered and about 10 receive a donation. For smaller appeals, donations range between £50 and £200.

Exclusions: No support for environment/heritage, political or religious appeals.

Applications: In writing to the correspondent. Appeals sent directly to individual papers are dealt with separately.

Hammerson plc

100 Park Lane, London W1K 7AR
Tel: 020 7887 1000 **Fax:** 020 7887 1137
E-mail: sjhaydon@hammerson.co.uk
Website: www.hammerson.co.uk
Contact: Stuart Haydon, Company Secretary

Main company business: Property investment and development. 70% of the company's property assets are in the UK, with the remainder in France and Germany. Within the UK, the office property portfolio is mainly in London, with retail interests in Birmingham, Brent Cross, Grimsby, Reading, Romford, Slough, and Stockport.

Total community contributions: £59,755 (1999/2000)

Community support policy: A brief comment in the company's 1998 annual report states: 'donations are made to a variety of social, medical and arts charities and to charities in localities where the group owns property. In addition to these charitable donations, the company provides financial assistance to other projects of benefit to the community'. There is a preference for supporting causes connected with the arts, children/youth, education, elderly people, enterprise/training, environment/heritage, medical research, science/technology, sickness/disability and social welfare.

Exclusions: No support for political appeals.

Applications: In writing to the correspondent. Each application is considered on its merits, but about 95% of applications will be unsuccessful.

Henderson Global Investors Ltd

4 Broadgate, London EC2M 2DA
Website: www.henderson.com

Main company business: Investment advisory and management services.

Total community contributions: £100,000 (2000/2001)

Community support policy: Support is given to charities in which a member of company staff is involved, local to the City of London. There is a Preference for causes concerned with the arts; children/youth; education; elderly people; enterprise/training; environment/heritage; fundraising events; medical research; sickness/disability charities and social welfare.

Exclusions: No support for appeals from individuals; overseas projects; political appeals; religious appeals or sport.

Applications: The company no longer invites external applications for funding. All money is given in support of staff initiatives.

HSBC Holdings plc

10 Lower Thames Street, London EC3R 6AE
Tel: 020 7260 0715 **Fax: 020 7260 0501**
E-mail: communityaffairs@hsbc.com
Website: www.hsbc.com
Contact: Peter Bull, HSBC in the Community Executive

Main company business: The group provides banking and related financial services.

Total community contributions: $6,698,000 (1999/2000)

Community support policy: HSBC states that it operates according to certain key business values, one of which is: 'the promotion of good environmental practice and sustainable development and commitment to the welfare and development of each local community'. The two principal causes supported are education, particularly for those less fortunate in society, and the environment. Members of HSBC are expected to allocate 75% of their donations and non-commercial sponsorship budgets to these activities, with the greater emphasis on educational initiatives which include:

- primary and secondary schooling for under-privileged children or support for schools in economically deprived areas;
- programmes to promote international understanding among young people;
- activites that promote interest in and sensitivity to other cultures;
- language programmes, particularly the learning of Asian languages;
- programmes which encourage youth to have a greater understanding of business and finance.

These activities are supplemented by direct support for other good causes.

Applications: In writing to the correspondent.

IMI plc

PO Box 216, Witton, Birmingham B6 7BA
Tel: 0121-332 2214 **Fax:** 0121 331 1736
E-mail: elaine.morgan@imi.plc.uk
Website: www.imi.plc.uk
Contact: Elaine Morgan, Secretary, Charitable Appeals Committee

Main company business: IMI is a diversified engineering group operating in the areas of hydronics, drinks dispense, fluid power and energy controls. It manufactures and sells internationally and has major plants in the UK, North and South America, and Continental Europe.

Total community contributions: £594,000 (1999/2000)

Community support policy: Most donations are distributed by head office through the Charities Aid Foundation. The balance is distributed by the main subsidiaries which have their own separate budgets for charitable donations. There is a preference for charities of direct or indirect benefit to the business, those which benefit or are likely to benefit employees (present, past and potential) and charities located and working in areas where the company has its major interests. (The company has plants in Birmingham, Liverpool, Manchester and Yorkshire.)

IMI prefers to support organisations working in the following areas: the arts, education, health and medical care, religion, social welfare, and sport. Support may also be given to animal welfare, children/youth, elderly people, enterprise/training, environment/ heritage appeals, and science/ technology.

Exclusions: Company policy is to give direct to charities and not to organisations which are themselves collecting for charity. No support for circular appeals, advertising in charity brochures, small purely local appeals not in an area of company presence, appeals from individuals, fundraising events, circular appeals, political appeals, large national appeals or overseas projects.

Applications: In writing to the correspondent. Grant decisions are made

by an appeals committee which meets on an ad hoc basis. Local appeals should be sent to the relevant local plant or branch.

Advice to applicants: The company welcomes appeals from charities but its appeal mail is getting too large to handle. Applicants should therefore ensure that they can establish some link with the company. Appeals should, where applicable, give details of the total amount to be raised and a description of how the money is to be spent. If possible, the latest statement of accounts should accompany the appeal. The company correspondent complains that many appeals are poorly presented and some not even signed.

Jaguar Cars Ltd

Browns Lane, Allesley, Coventry
CV5 9DR
Tel: 024 7620 2040 **Fax:** 024 7640 5581
E-mail: lratclif@jaguar.com
Website: www.jaguarcars.com
Contact: Les Ratcliffe, Manager, Community Relations

Main company business: The design, development, manufacture and marketing of luxury cars and specialist sports cars.

Total community contributions: £300,000 (1999/2000)

Community support policy: The company gives support through its charitable trust exclusively for local charities in areas of company presence and charities in which a member of staff is involved. Within these geographical constraints, which are strictly adhered to, the company prefers to support organisations concerned with children and youth, social welfare and medical. The company will support national charities if they have a local branch, or can in some way, benefit the groups' employees and their families. (There are company plants in Birmingham, Coventry and Halewood.)

Exclusions: No support is given to fundraising events, advertising in charity brochures, appeals from individuals, purely denominational (religious) appeals, large national appeals or overseas projects.

Applications: In writing to the correspondent. Decisions are made by a donations committee which meets quarterly.

The Kelda Group

Western House, Halifax Road, Bradford BD6 2LZ
Tel: 01274 692586 **Fax**: 01274 692621
E-mail: cheryl.wright@yorkshirewater.co.uk
Website: www.yorkshirewater.com
Contact: Cheryl Wright, Community Affairs Manager

Main company business: Water and sewerage services.

Total community contributions: £900,000 (2000/2001)

Community support policy: The company has for several years focused support on young people, economic regeneration and the environment. It is now developing a programme with greatly strengthened focus on employee volunteering and the response to the community interests of its own staff.

Programmes recently run, some of which are continuing, include skills development for young people on the estates of Hull, consultancy and other

support for deprived young people in Leeds, working with the Hull Daily Mail on its Reading Passport Scheme, working with the Sheffield Lifestyles Project and People United Against Crime as routes to creating partnerships with the local police and other organisations actively supporting them. In Bradford and Leeds, two major Barnardo's projects have received financial support from a fund established with the charity in 1996 and 1997.

Exclusions: No grants for purely denominational appeals, local appeals not in areas of company presence, appeals from individuals, political appeals, medical research, overseas projects, religious appeals, science/technology, social welfare or animal welfare.

Applications: In writing to the correspondent.

Kellogg's

The Kellogg Building, Talbot Road, Manchester M16 0PU
Tel: 0161 869 2601 **Fax**: 0161 869 2246
E-mail: communityaffairs@kellogg.com
Website: www.thekellogcompany.co.uk
Contact: Chris Woodcock, Community & Public Affairs Director

Main company business: The company is a manufacturer of breakfast and convenience foods.

Total community contributions: £822,794 (1999/2000)

Community support policy: The company concentrates its community involvement programme in the areas around its manufacturing sites in Trafford Park and Wrexham, and its European headquarters in Old Trafford, Manchester. The communities of Old Trafford, Moss Side and Hulme, Wythenshawe and Wrexham are the principle beneficiaries of its local commitment. The company also offers significant support to a small number of national and regional charities.

The Kellogg Community Affairs Programme has three overlapping themes: Community Development; Young People (see below); and Well-being. Kellogg's is keen to focus resources on organisations working to help those at greatest disadvantage.

Although most of the larger sums of money are 'locked up' in relationships with long-term partner organisations, the company will consider new applications for support. For smaller amounts of money (average donation £250), the company's Community Donations Fund is open to local charities and voluntary organisations all year round.

'Young people – We believe that it is vital that young people are offered the best opportunities possible to contribute positively to their communities. We will support those organisations and initiatives that complement and enhance statutory learning provision and offer young people real chances in life. Examples of the types of organisation that we currently work with include:

Young Enterprise: For over thirty years Kellogg's has been actively involved in this Programme which enables 14 to 18 year olds to learn about business by setting up and running their own companies. Kellogg's currently chairs the Trafford Area Board and is involved in regional and national developments.

Rathbone: A national charity providing training and support for over 10,000 young adults each year, particularly for those with learning difficulties, to enable them to achieve jobs and a brighter future. We have been on the Board for three years, and have supported the costs of Rathbone's Special Education Advice Line for several years.

The Weston Spirit: An expanding national youth charity providing tailor made development packages for young people so that they can realise their full potential. Kelloggs has provided cash to contribute towards the strategic development of the organisation as well as the actual delivery of programmes of activities for young people.'

Exclusions: Donations will not normally be given to circular appeals, advertising in charity brochures, appeals from individuals, the arts, fundraising events, overseas projects, political appeals, religious appeals, science/technology, or able-bodied sport.

Applications: All applications for support should be addressed to the Kellogg Community Affairs Team at the Talbot Road offices. Applications received by the manufacturing sites in Wrexham and Old Trafford will be passed on to the Community Affairs Team. All applicants should read the information on the Community Affairs page of the website before they apply for help.

The application process for the Community Affairs Fund is designed to be quick, simple and applicant friendly. Kelloggs have reduced the need for supporting information to an absolute minimum, and endeavour to reply to all applicants within weeks. Please refer to the website for further details.

Kingfisher plc

North West House, 119 Marylebone Road, London NW1 5PX
Tel: 020 7725 4891 **Fax:** 020 7706 4485
E-mail: alan.knight@kingfisher.co.uk
Website: www.kingfisher.co.uk
Contact: Alan Knight, Head of Social Responsibility

Main company business: The Group trades principally as home improvement, electrical and furniture and general merchandise retailers with stores in the UK, Continental Europe and the rest of the world. In addition, the Group has extensive interests in property, which are actively managed in the UK through Chartwell Land. The company has a significant presence in Croydon, Eastleigh, Harrow, Hayes, Hull, Leeds, London Middlesex.

Total community contributions: £2,000,000 (2000/2001)

Community support policy: The company focuses its activities on supporting opportunities which:

- are pioneering and innovative;
- fit well with and contribute directly to Kingfisher's mainstream business activities, customers and products;
- allow the company to add real value;
- give scope for company employees to become involved, develop their full potential or gain new skills and experiences;
- involve developing longer term relationships.

Efforts are concentrated on issues affecting the home and family and in particular education/youth and child development, older people, community safety and crime prevention, environment and equal opportunities.

In all these areas the company works with government and national voluntary organisations to pinpoint areas where group expertise and resources can help most. The company and its subsidiaries are contributors to a number of community projects, either in cash, in kind or by donation of human resources.

In June 1999, Woolworth's launched an independent registered charity, Woolworth's Kids First (Charity Commission no. 1073947). Woolworth Kids First was formed after extensive consultation with both customers and employees. It enables Woolworth's' 25,000 employees to get involved in their local communities in ways which directly benefit children. Teams in stores, offices and distribution centres choose local initiatives that they wish to support, either through fundraising, or the giving of time/expertise.
Contact: Trevor Dahl, Woolworth's Kids First, Woolworth House, 242–246 Marylebone Road, London NW1 6JL.

Exclusions: No response to circular appeals. No grants for advertising in charity brochures; appeals from individuals; the arts; environment/heritage; fundraising events; overseas projects; political appeals; religious appeals; science/technology; sport or local appeals not in areas of company presence.

Applications: Applications to operating subsidiaries should be addressed to the contacts given above and local appeals to the appropriate branch or retail outlet.

Lloyds TSB Group plc

71 Lombard Street, London EC3P 3BS
Tel: 020 7356 2462 **Fax:** 020 7356 2403
Website: www.lloydstsb.com
Contact: Jo Lewis, Head of Public
Affairs

Main company business: The Lloyds
TSB Group is one of the largest financial
services company in the UK, covering
retail banking, commercial and corporate
banking, mortgages, life assurance and
pensions, general insurance, asset
management, leasing, treasury and
foreign exchange dealing.

Total community contributions:
£43,000,000 (2000/2001)

Community support policy: Lloyds
TSB Group is rooted in local
communities throughout the UK and
believes it has a responsibility to support
those communities that it serves as a
business. The group's charitable donations
are channelled through four independent
charitable trusts, the Lloyds TSB
Foundations.

Lloyds TSB Group's Corporate
Community Investment programme
focuses on education, regeneration and
staff support for community causes. The
Lloyds TSB Foundations are four
independent grant-making trusts,
covering England and Wales, Scotland,
Northern Ireland and the Channel
Islands. They are shareholders in Lloyds
TSB Group and together receive one per
cent of the group's pre-tax profits,
averaged over three years, instead of the
dividend on their shareholding. The
broad objectives are to fund UK
registered charities which:

- meet social and community needs;
- promote education and training.

Full details of each of the foundation's
grant-making criteria and areas of special
interest can be obtained from the
relevant address for your area listed
below. Potential applicants should
carefully check the list of 'Exclusions'
(below) before considering to request an
application form.

Exclusions: For Lloyds TSB
Foundations: The foundations will not
support individuals, including students, or
organisations which are not registered
charities. There is no support for:
environment (including geographic/
scenic, conservation and protection of
flora and fauna), activities which are
primarily the responsibility of local or
national government or some other
responsible body, mainstream schools,
universities and colleges (except when
benefiting disabled students), hospitals
and medical centres (except for projects
which are clearly additional to statutory
responsibilities), sponsorship or
marketing appeals, restoration of
buildings, fabric appeals for places of
worship, promotion of religion, activities
which collect funds for subsequent
redistribution to other charities or
individuals, endowment funds, general
appeals, fundraising events, corporate
affiliation or founder membership of a
charity, loans or business finance,
expeditions or overseas travel.

Applications: For Lloyds TSB
Foundations only: Further details of
grant-giving policies and an application
form can be obtained by contacting the
appropriate Lloyds TSB Foundation for
your locality.

Lloyds TSB Foundation for England and Wales
PO Box 140, St Mary's Court,
20 St Mary at Hill, London EC3R 8NA;
Tel:020 7204 5276; Website: www.lloyds tsbfoundations.org.uk

Lloyds TSB Foundation for Scotland
Henry Duncan House, 120 George Street, Edinburgh EH2 4LH;
Tel: 0131 225 4555

Lloyds TSB Foundation for Northern Ireland
4 Queens Square, Belfast BT1 3DJ;
Tel:028 9032 5599

Lloyds TSB Foundation for the Channel Islands
25 New Street, St Helier, Jersey, Channel Islands JE4 8RG; Tel: 01534 503052.

For Lloyds TSB Group plc only:
Contact: Jo Lewis, Head of Public Affairs, Lloyds TSB Group plc, 71 Lombard Street, London EC3P 3BS.

The M & G Group

M & G House, Victoria Road,
Chelmsford, Essex CM1 1FB
Tel: 01245 266266 **Fax:** 01245 390735
Website: www.mandg.co.uk
Contact: Vicki Chapman, Charity & Community Relations Manager

Main company business: Unit and investment trust management.

Total community contributions: £80,000 (2000/2001)

Community support policy:
Preference for local charities in areas of main operation (i.e. City of London and Essex), appeals relevant to company business and charities in which a member of staff is involved. Preferred areas of support are: advertising in charity brochures; the arts; children/youth;

education; elderly people; enterprise/training; environment/heritage; fundraising events; sickness/disability charities and social welfare. Grants generally range from £250 to £2,500.

Exclusions: Generally no support for circular appeals, appeals from individuals, overseas appeals, political or religious appeals.

Applications: In writing to the correspondent. The address for the Charities Secretary is M & G Group plc, M & G House, Victoria Road, Chelmsford CM1 1FB.

Marconi plc

One Bruton Street, London W1J 6AQ
Tel: 020 7493 8484 **Fax:** 020 7493 1974
Website: www.marconi.com/html/news/community/htm
Contact: N C Porter, Secretary

Main company business: The company acts as holding company; its subsidiaries and associated companies are principally engaged in the provision of communications equipment and services together with associated support applications. The company has plants in Camberley, Chelmsford, Colchester, Coventry, Edinburgh, Hatfield, Leeds, Liverpool, Peterborough, Portsmouth, Rochester, Stafford, Stanmore and Stevenage.

Total community contributions: £827,000 (2000/2001)

Community support policy: Marconi plc formerly operated under the name of the General Electric Company plc. The following refers to that company's policy in 2000 when its policy for sponsorship and donations was to:

- support the advancement of science,

engineering, technology and business education;

- encourage young people to take up science and engineering carers;
- support community activities that involve GEC personnel.

Preference is given to local charities in areas of company presence, appeals relevant to company business and charities in which a member of staff is involved. Direct support is preferred. Grants to national organisations ranged from £1,000 to £5,000 and to local organisations from £500 to £2,000.

Exclusions: No support for circular appeals, advertising in charity brochures, appeals from individuals, fundraising events, purely denominational (religious) appeals, building appeals or local appeals not in areas of company presence.

Applications: Appeals (other than local appeals) should be made in writing to the correspondent and are considered by a donations committee which meets as required. Applications for local support should be made in writing to your local GEC operating unit in the UK. These subsidiaries and operating units have their own budgets.

Marsh Ltd

Aldgate House, 33 Aldgate High Street, London EC3N 1AQ
Tel: 020 7357 1454 **Fax:** 020 7357 1484
Website: www.marsh.com
Contact: Augustin de La Brosse, Community Programmes Administrator

Main company business: Management and insurance services company.

Total community contributions: £513,000 (1999/2000)

Community support policy: Recipient organisations must be registered charities. The company prefers to give to national or local charities in areas where there is employee involvement, and to appeals relevant to company business. There is also a preference for charities in the areas of youth, enterprise and training, social welfare, medicine and the arts.

Exclusions: Donations are not made to individuals, schools, churches, or for expeditions. The company does not support circular appeals, advertising in charity brochures, purely denominational appeals or local appeals not in areas of company presence.

Applications: In writing to the correspondent. The company does not welcome unsolicited appeals from charities as the charitable budget is too limited.

McDonald's UK

11–59 High Road, East Finchley, London N2 8AW
Tel: 0870 241 3300 **Fax: 020 8700 7068**
E-mail: shall@uk.mcd.com
Website: www.mcdonalds.co.uk
Contact: Stephen Hall, Corporate Community Affairs Manager

Main company business: The activity of the company is quick service restaurants.

Total community contributions: £918,000 (1999/2000)

Community support policy: 'McDonald's community involvement programme encompasses child welfare, the environment, education and youth related social issues. The principal recipient of donations and funds raised is

Ronald McDonald Children's Charities (RMCC).'

In 1999, McDonald's made total community contributions of £877,000. This included £678,000 in cash donations. 'A registered charity, Ronald McDonald Children's Charities (RMCC) has raised over £10 million since its inception in 1989, to support projects which benefit children. These include the Ronald McDonald Houses at Guy's, Alder Hey Children's Hospital, Liverpool and The Royal Hospital for Sick Children, Yorkhill, Glasgow, which provide home-away-from-home accommodation for families of children with serious, often long-term illnesses requiring extended hospital care.'

Since 1994, RMCC's Big Smile Appeals have raised over £2 million for hundreds of local children's causes.

Exclusions: No grants for appeals from individuals, purely denominational (religious) appeals or overseas projects.

Applications: In writing to the correspondent. Regional and local appeals should be directed to the appropriate communications departments in London, Manchester (Salford) or Birmingham (Sutton Coldfield). The contact for RMCC is Melvyn Lynch, Head of RMCC. Specific education-related requests should be made to James Graham, Head of McDonald's Education Service.

John Menzies plc

108 Princes Street, Edinburgh EH2 3AA
Tel: 0131 459 8159 **Fax:** 0131 459 8111
E-mail: margaret.scott@menziesgroup.com
Website: www.menziesgroup.com
Contact: Miss M Scott, Secretary to the Charities Committee

Main company business: Logistics support services group.

Total community contributions: £134,000 (2000/2001)

Community support policy: In 1997/98, the company donated £158,000 to various charitable, community and arts organisations. It prefers to support charities in the fields of job creation, health/welfare, youth/sport, the services and environmental charities. Particular support is given to Scottish charities and charities in areas of company presence. The group prefers to give support on a long-term covenanted basis. Products may also be donated to local fundraising events. Community contributions are also made through secondment of managers to voluntary organisations.

In addition to the above group donations figure, Early Learning Centre (a subsidiary company) supported Save the Children Fund with a donation of £53,000 raised through product sales.

Exclusions: No support for advertising in charity brochures, or overseas projects.

Applications: In writing to the correspondent.

The Mersey Docks & Harbour Company

Maritime Centre, Port of Liverpool, Liverpool L21 1LA
Tel: 0151 949 6000 **Fax:** 0151 949 6300
Website: www.merseydocks.co.uk
Contact: W J Bowley, Secretary to the Dock Charitable Fund

Main company business: The principal activities of the group are the operation and maintenance of port facilities on the Rivers Mersey and Medway, provision of cargo handling and associated services, and the conservancy and pilotage of the Ports of Liverpool and Medway and their approaches and the development of their respective dock estates.

Total community contributions: £89,065 (1999/2000)

Community support policy: The company has a preference for local charities in the areas of company presence and appeals relevant to company business. Preferred areas of support are children and youth, social welfare and medical. The £63,000 given in charitable donations included £50,000 to the Dock Charitable Fund (Charity Commission number 206913), which gives grants annually to certain local charities. The trustees of this charitable trust are the board of directors of the company. The trust was set up with three objectives:
- reward of people assisting in the preservation of the life of the crew of any ship wrecked in the port of Liverpool or in the preservation of the ship or cargo or in the preserving or endeavouring to preserve people from drowning;
- relief of sick, disabled or superannuated men in the dock service or the families

of such men who were killed in service;
- benefit of charities in the town or port of Liverpool.

Exclusions: No support for circular appeals, fundraising events, advertising in charity brochures, appeals from individuals, purely denominational (religious) appeals, local appeals not in areas of company presence, large national appeals or overseas projects.

Applications: In writing to the correspondent.

MFI Furniture Group plc

Southon House, 333 The Hyde, Edgware Road, Colindale, London NW9 6TD
Tel: 020 8913 5244 **Fax:** 020 8913 5171
Website: www.mfi.co.uk
Contact: Justine Jewell, Public Relations

Main company business: Manufacture and retail sale of furniture.

Total community contributions: £120,484 (1999/2000)

Community support policy: There is a preference for children and youth charities, with the NCH Action for Children being the main beneficiary. The small remaining budget is given to a wide range of other appeals, but generally in areas of company presence. Grants tend to range from £50 to £250. The company operates the Give As You Earn payroll giving scheme.

Exclusions: No grants for purely denominational (religious) appeals, local appeals not in areas of company presence or overseas projects.

Applications: In writing to the correspondent.

Michelin Tyre plc

Campbell Road, Stoke-on-Trent
ST4 4EY
Tel: 01782 402081 **Fax:** 01782 403372
E-mail: paul.niblett@uk.michelin.com
Website: www.michelin.co.uk
Contact: P Niblett, Head of Communications

Main company business: Manufacture and sale of tyres, tubes, wheels and accessories.

Total community contributions: £57,731 (1999/2000)

Community support policy: The company has a strong preference for local charities (i.e. Stoke-on-Trent, Burnley, Ballymena, and Dundee), especially those in which a member of staff is involved and appeals relevant to the company's business. These three stipulations form the basis of the company's donating philosophy, but the company considers all appeals presented. In particular it supports charities concerned with children and youth, social welfare, enterprise and education and training.

Exclusions: No support for circular appeals, appeals from individuals, the arts, fundraising events, overseas projects, political appeals, religious appeals, social welfare, sport or local appeals not in areas of company presence.

Applications: In writing to the correspondent.

National Express Group PLC

75 Davies Street, London W1K 5HT
Tel: 020 7529 2000 **Fax:** 020 7529 2135
E-mail: nmarsden@natex.co.uk
Website: www.nationalexpressgroup.com
Contact: Nicola Marsden, Group Communications Manager

Main company business: Provision of passenger transport services in four areas: coaches, buses, airports and trains.

Total community contributions: £212,614 (1999/2000)

Community support policy: 'The group operates a devolved management system which means that its subsidiary businesses have day to day responsibilities for their operations. This includes their involvement with the communities they serve. The group does not consider that it is appropriate to control this activity as we have a high number of businesses spread throughout the UK. Local community groups should contact their nearest local National Express Group business.

'National Express Group's Head Office selects certain charities or sponsorships at the time of setting its budget, usually during the autumn. In view of the group's geographic coverage, it prefers to select a national rather than local initiative, although we welcome contact with local groups in the Hampshire area and will assess each on their merits.'

In general, organisations supported:
- Will be well-run and publish annual reports of their spending and success.
- Should be a registered charity.
- Should offer a well-balanced programme of activities which reflect the current needs and trends in society.

The group is also keen to encourage staff in any contributions, voluntary or otherwise, which they make to their own communities.

Exclusions: No support for political or religious appeals.

Applications: In writing to the correspondent.

Nationwide Building Society

Nationwide House, Pipers Way, Swindon SN38 1NW
Tel: 01793 655143 **Fax:** 01793 657569
Website: www.nationwide.co.uk
Contact: Michelle Leighton, Community Affairs Manager

Main company business: The group provides a comprehensive range of personal financial and housing services.

Total community contributions: £7,928,904 (2000/2001)

Community support policy: The Nationwide Foundation was established during 1998. There are four broad themes within Nationwide's Community Affairs strategy and any activities should normally embrace at least one of these themes:
- homes – housing initiatives;
- initiative – training, youth projects, education/schools/preparation for life;
- caring – counselling and advice, disabled support/access, health, discrimination (various);
- heritage/environment – saving things (as well as money), conservation.

There is a preference for projects with the potential for staff involvement. Support is given to national and local charities. The company will also normally consider supporting causes concerned with the arts, children/youth, elderly people, fundraising events, and sport.

Exclusions: No response to circular appeals. No support for advertising in charity brochures, appeals from individuals, medical research, overseas projects, political appeals, religious appeals, science/technology, or for commercial (as opposed to community related) sponsorship.

Applications: Applications to the company for donations or sponsorship should be sent to the correspondent named above. For applications to the Nationwide Foundation, further information can be obtained from Glynis Johnson at the foundation's office (Tel: 01793 457182). On a local basis, giving depends on the local area managers, who have small budgets for local community projects.

Nestlé UK Ltd

York YO91 1XY
Fax: 01904 603461
Website: www.nestle.co.uk
Contact: Peter J Anderson, Community Relations Manager

Main company business: Manufacture and sale of food products and associated activities.

Total community contributions: £1,038,000 (1999/2000)

Community support policy: The company makes its donations to registered charities through the Nestlé Charitable Trust (Charity Commission no. 281792) and also supports non-registered good causes locally. There is a preference for charities that have company staff involvement.

The company considers donations in various fields which relate to arts and culture, community development, education, enterprise, environment, health (medical), or young people's sport. Support is given to properly managed activities of high quality in their particular field.

Company charitable donations are considered at a national level by a representative group of managers at the head office in Croydon. There are also local management groups at the main factories, which consider applications from local charities and good causes. However, a relevant link or connection with the company's business is usually looked for. This may be geographic (within the catchment area of company factories, located throughout the UK, see below), related to the food industry or through connections with university departments or employee activities.

Company sites are in Aintree, Ashbourne, Aylesbury, Bardon, Barrhead, Bromborough, Buxton, Castleford, Croydon, Dalston, Fawdon, Girvan, Hadfield, Halifax, Hayes, Leicester, Middleton, New Malden, Northwich, Omagh, Rickmansworth, Scunthorpe, Southall, Spalding, Staverton, Telford, Tetbury, Watford, Welwyn Garden City, Wisbech, Worksop, York.

Exclusions: No support for advertising in charity brochures, appeals from individuals (including students), local appeals not in areas of company presence, political organisations, religious appeals or overseas projects. Overseas aid is controlled by the head office in Vevey, Switzerland.

Applications: Applications for support of local good causes should be made to the manager of the nearest Nestle location, but for large scale donations or national charities the request should be sent to the Community Relations Department, Nestle UK Ltd, Haxby Road, York YO91 1XY. The company supports about 3,000 of the 15,000 requests received each year.

Northern Foods plc

Beverley House, St Stephen's Square, Hull HU1 3XG
Tel: 01482 325432 **Fax:** 01482 226136
Website: www.northern-foods.co.uk
Contact: Mrs Helen Bray, Social Responsibility Committee

Main company business:
Manufacturer and distributor of chilled foods, meat and convenience foods, biscuits and savoury pastry products.

Total community contributions:
£458,000 (2000/2001)

Community support policy:
Recipient organisations should normally be registered charities. Resources are concentrated on three areas: relief of deprivation in inner cities (including enterprise and training); sustainable aid to the third world; and selective education projects. There is a preference for youth and social welfare, especially for local charities in areas of company presence, for example, Sheffield, Manchester, Nottingham and Batley. Grants to national organisations range from £5,000 to £10,000 and to local organisations from £25 to £5,000.

Exclusions: The company does not generally support the larger national charities, religious or political bodies.

Support given to health charities and the arts is extremely limited. No grants for circular appeals, advertising in charity brochures, appeals from individuals, environment/heritage, fundraising events, medical appeals, science/technology, sickness charities or sport.

Applications: In writing to the committee, including supporting information. Applications are considered by a committee comprising Directors and Executives which meets on a quarterly basis.

Northumbrian Water

Abbey Road, Pity Me, Durham DH1 5FJ
Tel: 0191 383 2222
Website: www.nwl.co.uk
Contact: John Mowbray, Head of Corporate Affairs

Main company business: Water supply and sewage services.

Total community contributions: £70,048 (1999/2000)

Community support policy: The company supports local charities in its area of operation and appeals relevant to company business. Preferred areas of support are children and youth, education, enterprise, environment and heritage. Grants range from £50 to £10,000, although most are for less than £1,000, averaging around £200 to £300. The three community foundations in the area all receive support i.e. the Tyne & Wear Foundation, Cleveland Foundation and County Durham Foundation.

Exclusions: No support for circular appeals, advertising in charity brochures, local appeals not in areas of company presence, large national appeals or overseas projects (other than support for WaterAid).

Applications: In writing to the correspondent.

Oxford, Swindon & Gloucester Co-operative Society Ltd

New Barclay House, 234 Botley Road, Oxford OX2 0HP
Tel: 01865 249 241
E-mail: members@osg-co-op.co.uk
Website: www.osg-co-op.co.uk
Contact: Peter Couchman, Membership & Corporate Marketing Manager

Main company business: The society has a number of diverse trading activities covering: food, motor, finance, property, travel and funeral services.

Total community contributions: £116,000 (2000/2001)

Community support policy: The Oxford, Swindon & Gloucester Co-op has established a policy unique amongst UK consumer co-ops of returning at least one per cent of its profits to the communities it serves. To facilitate this policy, two major new schemes were launched in 1998.

The first of these involved the launch of its own Community Dividend Scheme which resulted in grants of up to £1,000 each being given to charities and organisations across the society's trading area who are involved in projects that have a real benefit for local communities and people.

The second phase of the scheme (Community Partners Scheme) offers more substantial grants to a small number of organisations for a fixed period of three years. The society will enter into a partnership with each organisation to support work that will be of lasting benefit to the community.

Finally, the board also announced its new policy of allocating a minimum of one per cent of the society's profits to the creation, development and promotion of other co-operatives in its area.

Exclusions: Applications from outside the operating area of the OSG Co-operative Society.

Applications: Further details regarding the method of application can be had by writing in the first instance to the correspondent.

The Rank Group Plc

6 Connaught Place, London W2 2EZ
Tel: 020 7706 1111 **Fax:** 020 7402 4164
Website: www.rank.com
Contact: Charles B A Cormick, Company Secretary

Main company business: The Rank Group supplies products and services to the film and television industries, owns holidays and hotel businesses and operates organised recreation and leisure facilities in the UK and overseas. Rank has a joint investment with MCA in the Universal Studios motion picture theme park at Orlando, Florida.

Total community contributions: £82,000 (1999/2000)

Community support policy: Support is given to a broad range of charities in the categories of: children and youth, social welfare, medical, education, environment/heritage and the arts. Grants to national organisations range from £500 to £15,000 and to local

organisations from £100 to £500. Some support is on-going for up to five years. The company has moved away from sponsorship towards direct giving to charities.

Exclusions: No response to circular appeals. No support for individuals – students, expeditions etc. No grants for fundraising events, advertising in charity brochures, appeals from individuals, local appeals not in areas of company presence or overseas projects. Support is not usually given to church roof or similar appeals.

Applications: In writing to the correspondent, who receives 50 to 70 applications each week, most of which cannot be supported.

N M Rothschild & Sons Ltd

New Court, St Swithin's Lane, London EC4P 4DU
Tel: 020 7280 5000 **Fax:** 020 7929 1643
Website: www.nmrothschild.com
Contact: Secretary to the Charities Committee

Main company business: The company and its subsidiaries carry on the business of merchants and bankers. The parent company is Rothschild Continuation Ltd and the ultimate holding company is Rothschild Concordia A G, incorporated in Switzerland.

Total community contributions: £977,000 (2000/2001)

Community support policy: The main area of charitable support is social welfare, although support is also given in the fields of health and medical care, education, scientific research, and the arts. About 300 grants to national charities are made each year, ranging from £250 to £1,000. Local grants are not normally given. The company operates a payroll giving scheme. Financial support is given to employee volunteering. The company's subsidiaries around the world support causes in their areas of operation.

Exclusions: Donations are not normally made to local groups. No response to circular appeals. No grants for advertising in charity brochures; appeals from individuals; environment/heritage; fund-raising events; overseas projects; political appeals; religious appeals or sport.

Applications: In writing to the Secretary to the Charities Committee, which meets quarterly to make grant decisions. Sponsorship proposals should be addressed to the Group Corporate Affairs Department.

The Royal London Mutual Insurance Society Ltd

Royal London House, Middleborough, Colchester, Essex CO1 1RA
Tel: 01206 773400 **Fax:** 01206 773511
E-mail: stephen.humphreys@royal-london.co.uk
Website: www.royal-london.co.uk
Contact: Stephen Humphreys, Head of Corporate Communications

Main company business: The transaction of main classes of insurance business and, through subsidiaries, unit trust and investment management.

Total community contributions: £70,398 (1999/2000)

Community support policy: Having completed a review of all corporate community involvement activities in 1999, a new policy was implemented

called the Helping Hand. The policy has three main elements:
1 A national charity partner – for 1999/2000, this was the National Deaf Children's Society.
2 The Royal London Community Fund – a four year covenanted fund of £50,000 administered in conjunction with the Essex Community Foundation to local voluntary and charitable organisations in and around Colchester. Grants are made twice a year.
3 Employee matched donation scheme – matching employees' fundraising for individual charities up to £250 per person.

Organisations benefiting from grants in 1998 included St Edmunds Child Contact Centre and Highwoods Kids Clubs.

Exclusions: No support for advertising in charity brochures, appeals from individuals, environment/heritage, overseas projects, political appeals, religious appeals, science/technology, or sport.

Applications: In writing to the correspondent to whom sponsorship proposals should also be addressed. The company produce a brochure on their community partnership entitled Helping Hand.

J Sainsbury plc

Stamford House, Stamford Street, London SE1 9LL
Tel: 020 7695 6000 **Fax:** 020 7695 7050
Website: www.-sainsburys.co.uk/partnerships
Contact: Mrs S L Mercer, Sainsbury's Community Affairs Department

Main company business: Principal activity: the retail distribution of food. Other activities include home improvement, garden centres and hypermarkets. Apart from the Sainsbury supermarket chain (400 stores in England, Scotland, Wales and Northern Ireland), activities include Shaws Supermarkets Inc USA, a wholly owned subsidiary, and Sainsbury's Bank.

Total community contributions:
£14,067,290 (2000/2001)

Community support policy:
Sainsbury's community programme has a proactive approach and supports projects in UK trading areas only. It receives the major project-based appeals. Appeals from organisations working with disabled and elderly people, under–fives and families will be considered. Other areas of support include the arts, education, elderly people, fundraising events and sickness/disability charities. Project support ranges from £50 to £10,000. Projects requesting support for up to £2,000 are considered weekly.

All stores have a community budget to support local fundraising efforts with raffle prizes. Write to the store manager.

Exclusions: No response to circulars. No support for individuals, restoration/ fabric of buildings, National Health projects, overseas projects, local appeals not in areas of company presence, political or religious causes, core or pump priming.

Applications: Appeals to head office should be addressed to the correspondent. Applications can be received at any time, and should include details of: aims and objectives, target audience and PR opportunities. Local appeals should be sent to local stores who will then approach the donations committee. This meets quarterly, but a sub-committee meets as and when necessary.

A separate budget exists for small donations to local charities/voluntary groups, administered at store level, in the form of vouchers.

There are also a number of Sainsbury Family Trusts with major grant-making programmes. These are administered separately although close contact is maintained with the company's donations programme.

Advice to applicants: Sainsbury's advises applicants to try to avoid stereotyped circulars. All appeals are responded to, but charities often underestimate the time required for consideration of their appeals. So, applicants should be patient!

Christian Salvesen PLC

500 Pavilion Drive, Brackmills, Northampton NN4 7YJ
Tel: 01604 662600 **Fax:** 01604 622605
Contact: Jayne Davies, PA to the Chief Executive

Main company business: Logistics and food services.

Total community contributions:
£50,000 (2000/2001)

Community support policy: The company supports education and youth activities, industrial training, and community and environmental charities local to where the company has an operational presence as well as projects where a member of staff is involved.

Exclusions: National charities (unless specific to local operational area); circular appeals; advertising in charity brochures; medical research; overseas projects; political appeals; religious appeals.

Applications: Apply in writing to the Community Affairs Department. The Group Charities Committee meets quarterly.

Securicor plc

Sutton Park House, 15 Carshalton Road, Sutton, Surrey SM1 4LD
Tel: 020 8770 7000 **Fax:** 020 8661 0204
Website: www.securicor.com
Contact: Mrs A P Munson, Chair of the Charitable Trust

Main company business: Securicor plc is the holding company for the Securicor group of companies. Principal activities of the group include the transportation and care of cash and valuables; cash processing; security guards and patrols; custodial services; container transport, contract distribution and warehouse management, express parcels, freight haulage, document delivery; vehicle fleet services; and the development, supply and operation of information systems.

Total community contributions: £58,000 (1999/2000)

Community support policy: The company has a preference for supporting community development, job creation/training, arts, music and sport. Donations are in cash and in kind, helping with cash collection/delivery and parcel services. The company also makes donations to the Securicor Charitable Trust, which deals with smaller appeals from registered charities, favouring those in the areas of children/youth, social welfare, health, elderly people, sickness/disability, and medical research. The maximum grant is

usually £250, although occasionally larger grants are made.

In kind support: includes occasional provision of cash collections and guards for fundraising events, and occasional delivery services for charities.

Exclusions: Securicor Charitable Trust will offer no support for advertising in charity brochures; fundraising events; personal appeals from individuals; requests for educational grants; the arts; enterprise/training; science/technology; overseas projects; political appeals; religious appeals; sport or expeditions.

Applications: In writing to the correspondent. The trustees meet every two months. Only written applications for specific projects will be considered. No telephone calls. Sponsorship proposals should be addressed to the Group Marketing Manager.

Advice to applicants: Personal applicants should note the excluded areas, in particular educational and expedition grants. Agencies should note that telephone applications will not be considered and the trust does not support charity advertising.

SEEBOARD plc

PO Box 639, 329 Portland Road, Hove, East Sussex BN3 5SY
Tel: 01273 428612 **Fax:** 01273 428645
Website: www.seeboard.co.uk
Contact: Zara Watkins, Community Sponsorship Executive

Main company business: The distribution and supply of electricity to domestic, commercial and industrial customers, gas supply, electricity generation and electrical contracting.

Seeboard is a subsidiary of the US company CSW.

Total community contributions: £281,522 (1999/2000)

Community support policy: Support is concentrated in the company's operating area. This includes most of Kent, all of East Sussex, large parts of West Sussex and Surrey and the London boroughs of Croydon, Kingston and Richmond. It is coordinated under its Community Links programme. There is a preference for charities in which a member of company staff is involved.

Support is given in five categories:
- community projects
- education
- environment and countryside projects
- sport
- the arts.

The value of SEEBOARD's support varies from donations of small items, to fundraising raffles and large sponsorships worth between £5,000 and £20,000 each. Most grants, however, fall into the £100–£1,000 range, although they can be for as much as £10,000.

Community projects: Support is given to local charities or local branches of national charities based in the SEEBOARD area. National charities connected with the electricity industry may also be helped. Activities supported range from care for the elderly to support for the young, from hospital donations to fundraising for youth activities. Charities with staff involvement will usually receive financial support.

Exclusions: No support for circular appeals, local appeals not in areas of company presence, advertising in charity brochures, appeals from individuals participating in expeditions or sponsored

events, overseas projects, political appeals, or religious appeals.

Applications: To apply please write to the correspondent, giving brief details of your organisation, the amount sought, and what the money will be used for. The correspondent stated: 'Seeboard makes every effort to reply to all appeals. We do, however, receive a large number of applications and can support only a small proportion of them.' Telephone and faxed applications cannot be considered.

Shell International Limited

Shell Centre, York Road, London
SE1 7NA
Tel: 020 7934 3199 **Fax:** 020 7934 7039
E-mail: susan.s.saloom@si.shell.com
Website: www.shell.com
Contact: Ms Susan Saloom, Manager
UK Social Investment

Main company business: The business of the company is the exploration for and production of oil and natural gas, oil refining and chemicals manufacturing, and the marketing of the resulting products.

Total community contributions: £1,033,583 (1999/2000)

Community support policy: The company supports a cross section of charitable organisations with a UK remit, which would generally be situated near a major Shell location. Support is also given to organisations across the UK where a member of staff/retired staff is actively involved with the work of the organisation.

Exclusions: No support is given to circular appeals, fundraising events, appeals from individuals, organisations of a sectarian nature, sport, building appeals, local appeals not in areas of major company presence, 'bricks and mortar' appeals, overseas projects, expeditions, or for advertising in charity brochures.

Applications: Enquiries should be addressed to UK Social Investment Manager, Shell International Limited, Shell Centre, York Road, London SE1 7NA for the attention of the relevant manager.

Contacts: Susan Saloom, UK Social Investment Manager; Steve Smyth, Manager Shell Education Service

Six Continents plc

20 North Audley Street, London
W1K 6WN
Tel: 020 7409 1919 **Fax:** 020 7409 8512
E-mail: community@sixcontinents.
com
Website: www.sixcontinents.com
Contact: Walter J Barratt/Nicola
Latham, Charities Administrator/Public
Affairs Executive

Main company business: Six Continents is a global hospitality group operating in hotels, bars, restaurants and pubs

Total community contributions: £2,000,000 (1999/2000)

Community support policy: The Policy Guidelines (which are available from the Charitable Donations Committee) state:

1 Bass supports a wide range of charities and in particular seeks to work with charities for mutual benefit. Charities where Bass employees are actively involved are given especially favourable consideration.

2 The main impetus of funding effort is directed to four broad areas –

community, youth and education, environment and the arts.

The company tries to give significant donations to selected national charities as well as supporting local charitable organisations at a more modest level.

Community: Community care is an important part of the company's charitable giving, embracing such areas as help for the sick, terminally-ill, disabled, homeless, young offenders and numerous other aspects of real need within the community.

Youth and education: Bass continues to identify itself as a company committed to the development of young people. The company also supports the development of skills of citizenship and social awareness in young people outside places of education. In supporting youth-oriented charities the company looks with special interest at the development of adult youth leaders. Bass supports the furtherance of interest in careers within industry.

Exclusions: Because resources are limited, the following will not be considered:

- charities not registered nor of legal charitable status;
- political parties or organisations with political affiliations;
- charities or organisations with religious affiliations;
- expeditions and adventure travel groups;
- individuals seeking personal sponsorship;
- intermediaries acting between charity and donor;
- applications from organisations from areas where the company has no involvement;

- advertising space in souvenir programmes, brochures, lotteries, sponsored events and so on.

Applications: In writing to the correspondent. Local appeals should be addressed to the public relations manager at the appropriate regional office. Established charities should always send up-to-date audited accounts with any appeal. Policy guidelines are available from the correspondent.

Slough Estates plc

234 Bath Road, Slough, Berkshire
SL1 4EE
Tel: 01753 537171 **Fax:** 01753 820585
E-mail: nickh@sloughestates.com
Website: www.sloughestates.com
Contact: Air Commodore N Hamilton
(Retired), Manager External Affairs

Main company business: Industrial and commercial property development, construction and investment, supply of utility services and the provision of services associated with such activities.

Total community contributions: £287,000 (1999/2000)

Community support policy: The company gives support to a wide range of causes in the fields of art, music and culture; health research and care; youth; old age; education; relief of unemployment; the environment and conservation; welfare and the relief of poverty; fundraising events; animal welfare charities; advertising in charity brochures and sport. There is a preference for local appeals in areas of company presence, principally the Slough area. All cases are considered on their merits. Typical grants range from £25 to £5,000.

Exclusions: No grants for non-charities; circular appeals; local appeals not in areas of company presence; appeals from individuals; political appeals; religious appeals or overseas projects.

Applications: Decisions are made by a committee which meets quarterly. Air Commodore Nick Hamilton should be contacted for donations. Sir Nigel Mobbs, D R Wilson and D E F Simons are the directors responsible for charitable affairs.

St James's Place Capital plc

27 St James's Place, London
SW1A 1NR
Tel: 01285 640302
E-mail: gail.mitchell-briggs@sjpc.co.uk
Website: www.sjps.co.uk
Contact: Mrs Gail Mitchell-Briggs, Secretary, St James's Place Foundation

Main company business: St James's Place Capital plc is a financial services group involved in the provision of wealth management services.

Total community contributions: £374,800 (1999/2000)

Community support policy: The company makes its charitable donations through the J Rothschild Assurance Foundation. All administrative and management costs are met by J Rothschild Assurance plc, from whom the members of the management committee are drawn. The objective of the foundation is to raise money for distribution to organisations that meet its current theme. The theme for the years 1996 to 1998, 'Cherishing the Children' has been the provision of support aimed at pre-teen children who are either physically or mentally handicapped or both, or suffering from a life-threatening or degenerative illness. For 1999, the theme was extended to include all children aged 17 and below who satisfy the same criteria. The foundation will only consider applications from established charities or special needs schools that meet the selection criteria.

There is a further corporate donation which is distributed differently from the other funds raised. It was agreed between the management committee and the trustees, the corporate donation should be used to fund larger projects not necessarily in keeping with the foundation's theme. The first of these projects is Hope & Homes for Children. The foundation has made a commitment of £250,000 over two years. The first £125,0000 was given in January 2000, and will be used to support the charity's work in the Ukraine.

In 1999, the Foundation made almost 80 grants. The largest grant was £10,000 to Cerebral Palsy Children's Charity to equip a multi-sensory room. Three other grants were for £9,000 or more, to Lineham Farm Children's Centre (£9,500 to provide a climbing 'starter wall' and heat a play barn), Greater London Fund for the Blind (£9,563 for computers, bursaries and an electronic trailor in relation to a project providing tutoring for 16/17 year olds in computer usage), Children's Hospital Trust Fund (£9,000 towards the Newborn Baby Support Project at Westminster Children's Hospital. Five grants were for £8,000 or more to Children's Hospital Appeal Trust (£8,500 to upgrade the equipment in one of 100 accident and emergency ambulances), Mental Health Foundation (£8,337 towards their Young People's Peer Support Programme, a

support system provided by young people for young people.

Exclusions: No response to circular appeals, advertising in charity brochures or individuals. Due to charitable funding being reduced some policy changes have been made: 'Local and disaster fund categories can no longer be supported; charities applying to the trust for funding may be asked to provide evidence that they can obtain the same amount of money from a third party to equal the sum our trust is considering donating; the trust does not undertake sponsorships, corporate advertising or take tickets for charitable and other events.'

Applications: Appeals should be in writing to the correspondent enclosing appropriate financial or other supporting documentation.

Advice to applicants: This company has established a procedure for giving which puts it among the leaders in the field of corporate charitable giving. By concentrating on specific issues, local action and general appeals of interest to staff and shareholders, the company is able to make a very positive contribution with the funds at its disposal. Any potential applicant should be aware of the company's current policy and appeals falling outside this very clear policy are unlikely to be supported. It should also be noted that, in general, no undertaking of continued support is given when a donation is made.

Stagecoach Holdings plc

10 Dunkeld Road, Perth PH1 5TW
Tel: 01738 442111 **Fax:** 01738 643648
E-mail: dscott@stagecoachholdings.com
Website: www.stagecoachgroup.com
Contact: D Scott, Company Secretary

Main company business: Public
transport services. Subsidiary companies
are spread throughout England, Wales and
Scotland, as well as overseas, but are too
numerous to mention. Full details are
available on: www.geocities.com/
motorcity/downs/8661.

Total community contributions:
£700,000 (2000/2001)

Community support policy: Preferred
areas of support are: appeals from groups,
children/youth, education, elderly
people, sickness/disability charities,
enterprise/training, medical research, and
social welfare. There is a preference for
supporting charities local to subsidiary
operations.

The group continues with its
commitment to Save the Children to
provide £250,000 over a five year
period. The company also supports
employees' volunteering/charitable
activities by considering, where
appropriate, financial help, allowing
company time off to volunteer, matching
employee fundraising, and loaning
equipment/facilities.

Exclusions: No support for advertising
in charity brochures; appeals from
individuals, the arts; fundraising events;
political appeals; religious appeals;
science/technology or sport.

Applications: In writing to the
correspondent.

Telegraph Group Ltd

1 Canada Square, Canary Wharf,
London E14 5DT
Tel: 020 7538 6257 **Fax:** 020 7538 6242
Website: www.telegraph.co.uk
Contact: Charlotte Ibarra, Corporate
Affairs Department

Main company business: Publication
of national newspapers. Within the UK
the company publishes the Daily
Telegraph, Sunday Telegraph, Weekly
Telegraph, Electronic Telegraph and the
Spectator. Most staff engaged in the
publication of the company's titles are
employees of the subsidiary Telegraph
Publishing Ltd and are not included in
the total above.

Total community contributions:
£289,000 (1999/2000)

Community support policy: The
company supports UK charities working
in the fields of medical research, hospice
care, the disabled, education, the elderly,
ex-servicemen appeals, children and
youth targeted projects and newspaper
printing and publishing charities. As the
company is a member of the PerCent
Club, its community contributions
should have totalled over £200,000. The
trust makes its grants through the Daily
Telegraph Charitable Trust, originally set
up in 1944 (Charity Commission no.
205296). Appeals from charitable causes
located in East London are given special
consideration.

Exclusions: Generally no support for
circulars with stamped or imprinted
signatures, fundraising events, brochure
advertising, individuals, political causes or
purely denominational (religious)
appeals.

Applications: In writing to the
correspondent. The appeal committee

usually meets quarterly to decide on donations, and these will generally only be made to organisations with recognised charitable status.

Toyota Motor Manufacturing (UK) Ltd

Burnaston, Derbyshire DE1 9TA
Tel: 01332 282121
E-mail: sue.shakespeare@toyotauk.com
Contact: Directors Office, Planning & Communications Department

Main company business: Car and engine manufacture.

Total community contributions: £134,000 (1999/2000)

Community support policy: Priority is given to projects which add to the welfare of local communities and support or enhance community life. Projects must have some long-term tangible benefit for the wider community.

Employee involvement in the community is encouraged, and where suitable, the company will offer financial support to member fundraising activities or to local community organisations in which members play an active role. For example, a major fundraising initiative on behalf of the NSPCC in Derbyshire and Deeside raised more than £25,000 in a month.

Exclusions: No support for political or religious organisations, overseas aid or local appeals not in areas of company presence. No response to circular appeals.

Applications: In writing to the correspondent. Contributions are determined by an internal committee which meets quarterly to consider more

substantial requests and to discuss strategy. Smaller requests are processed monthly against an agreed set of criteria.

Vauxhall Motors Ltd

Public Affairs–B5, Griffin House, Osborne Road, Luton LU1 3YT
Tel: 020 8658 1819 **Fax:** 020 8658 3292
Website: www.vauxhall.co.uk
Contact: Paul Patten, Charities Coordinator

Main company business: The company manufactures, markets and services passenger cars, recreational vehicles and light vans. Vehicle and component manufacturing activities are located at Ellesmere Port, Cheshire and Luton, Bedfordshire. The V6 engine plant located at Ellesmere Port produces engines for GM's European and worldwide operations. Parts and accessories for the UK market are supplied from the Aftersales warehouse situated at Luton Road, Chalton, Bedfordshire.

Total community contributions: £597,120 (1999/2000)

Community support policy: The company states that each request for support, be it an appeal for a financial contribution, sponsorship, a product, personnel, secondment or promotional support, receives appropriate consideration. Every request received is replied to. The company concentrates its support on activities directly associated with the industry and its employees' interests, and in areas covered by its plants (ie. Luton and Ellesmere Port).

A wide range of organisations are supported including sickness/disability, education, elderly people, family support, social welfare, sport and children/youth. It takes a proactive role in supporting a small number of national organisations such as BEN (The Motor Allied Trades Benevolent Fund) and Crime Concern. Other major beneficiaries have included NSPCC and Scout Association.

Exclusions: No grants for circular appeals, appeals from individuals, local appeals not in areas of company presence, overseas projects, political, religious or sectarian organisations. The company does not give raffle prizes or company products.

Applications: Enquiries regarding charitable sponsorships and donations should be addressed to the correspondent. Enquiries about educational matters and secondment should be sent to R B Lindop, Manager, Educational Affairs, Personnel Department. Commercial sponsorship to Alan Denton, Manager, Promotions/Sponsorship.

Whitbread Group PLC

Whitbread House, Park Street West, Luton LU1 3BG
Tel: 01582 424200 **Fax:** 01582 396068
Website: www.whitbread.co.uk
Contact: Jerry Marston, Community Investment Director

Main company business: The company is a major food, drinks and leisure company.

Total community contributions: £4,264,000 (2000/2001)

Community support policy: The company supports a wide range of charities, through its charitable trust, under six broad headings: medical and health, welfare, education, humanities, environmental resources, and the arts.

Each year the company highlights a number of priority areas to support, which may vary slightly from year to year.

A priority is also given to local appeals in areas where the company has a strong trading and employment presence. The typical level of support for local appeals is £50 to £500. Appeals should be initially directed to the Company's Charity Co-ordinator who will consult with a Regional Community Affairs Director or Regional Education Manager on the merit of each application.

Exclusions: The following are not usually supported: advertising in charity brochures, ticket purchases for charity events, appeals from religious bodies (unless for the benefit of the community as a whole), political organisations, medical research, charitable organisations operating overseas and individuals.

Applications: All appeals must be made in writing accompanied by a copy of the organisations current annual report and accounts and should be sent to: Paul Patten, Charities Co-ordinator at the above address. The Board Director responsible for community affairs is D M Thomas (Group Chief Executive). The Community Investment Director is I S Anderson.

WPP Group plc

27 Farm Street, London W1J 5RJ
Tel: 020 7408 2204 **Fax:** 020 7493 6819
E-mail: fmcewan@wpp.com
Website: www.wpp.com
Contact: Elena Hayter, Executive PA

Main company business: Principal activity: the provision of communications services worldwide.

Total community contributions:
£191,000 (1999/2000)

Community support policy: The following policy relates to donations and support provided by the UK parent company. Support is also provided by the operating companies, particularly from the UK advertising agencies, J Walter Thompson and Ogilvy & Mather (see the addresses below).

WPP Group has a preference for appeals relevant to company business and charities in the areas of children and youth, medical, enterprise, sickness/disability and education. Other areas of support are advertising in charity brochures, appeals from individuals, the arts, elderly people, overseas projects, social welfare and sport. Grants to national organisations range from £100 to £40,000, and to local organisations from £100 to £5,000. No geographical area is given preference; each application will be considered on merit.

Main areas of non-cash support include gifts in kind (eg. donations of office equipment/office supplies to charities and children's hospitals), arts sponsorship and training schemes. Further details of the companies charitable support can be found in the Corporate Citizenship section of the annual report.

Applications: In writing to the correspondent above or to Amanda Fisher, Charity Co-ordinator, J Walter Thompson: 40 Berkeley Square, London W1X 6RD or Steve Lepley, Charity Co-ordinator, Ogilvy & Mather: 10 Cabot Square, Canary Wharf, London E14 4QB.

Yorkshire Bank plc

20 Merrion Way, Leeds LS2 8NZ
Tel: 0113 247 2000 **Fax:** 0113 242 0733
Contact: Nicola Ashcroft, Secretary to the Yorkshire Bank Charitable Trust

Main company business: The group provides a comprehensive banking system in the North and Midlands. The bank is a member of the National Australia Bank Group.

Total community contributions:
£74,000 (1999/2000)

Community support policy:
Donations are made directly by the bank to the Yorkshire Bank Charitable Trust. Recipients must be registered charities and within the area covered by branches of the bank ie. in England from north of the Thames Valley to Newcastle upon Tyne. The trust's guidelines state that it supports:
- charities engaged in youth work;
- facilities for less able-bodied and mentally disabled people;
- counselling and community work in depressed areas;
- the arts and education, occasionally.

The trustees are unlikely to make more than one donation to a charity within any 12 month period. Grants are usually one-off for a specific project or part of a project, ranging from £100 to £1,000.

Exclusions: Applications from individuals, including students, are ineligible, as are appeals for advertising in charity brochures, environment/heritage, medical research, overseas projects, political appeals, religious appeals and science/technology. No grants for general appeals from national organisations.

Applications: In writing to the correspondent, including relevant details of the need the intended project is designed to meet. Grants decisions are made by a donations committee which meets twice a month; responses may take three or four weeks to process. Requests for community involvement should be addressed to the Secretary to the Yorkshire Bank Charitable Trust and for arts sponsorship to the Corporate Communications Manager.

Yorkshire Building Society

Yorkshire House, Yorkshire Drive, Bradford BD5 8LJ
Tel: 01274 472015 **Fax:** 01274 735571
E-mail: jmhowarth@ybs.co.uk
Website: www.ybs.co.uk
Contact: Joanne Howarth, Community Liaison Officer

Main company business: Building society.

Total community contributions: £60,000 (1999/2000)

Community support policy: The Yorkshire Building Society Charitable Foundation was set up in April 1998. All requests made to the society will be referred to the foundation. The foundation's priorities are to support registered charities or good causes operating in local communities and involving the elderly, anyone who is vulnerable (particularly children or people with special needs) and people suffering hardship. Other local charities and organisations that the society's staff wish to support will be considered. The foundation's geographical area of operation is limited to the UK, principally to areas where the society's members live and work and where the

branches or subsidiaries are located. It prefers to assist with specific items rather than a general fund.

The following (non–exhaustive) list provides examples of projects or activities which the foundation would consider as likely to fall within its main areas of focus:

- Anything specifically to help priority cases of vulnerable people, people who are in need such as children, the elderly, or anyone with special needs, or people who are suffering hardship.
- People who are in genuine financial need – to be genuine a person does not have to be classed as destitute.
- Activities relating to the relief of hardship. 'Hardship' does not have to be permanent or long-term. It may be possible to consider grants where temporary hardship has been caused by job loss or long-term sickness.
- Help to be given to those who are sick, or with special needs, or learning difficulties and/or who are physically disabled.
- The provision of land, buildings or machinery for public use, e.g. community centres, specially adapted buses, other vehicles or equipment. This may extend to provision of equipment for youth clubs.
- The resettlement and rehabilitation of offenders and drug abusers.
- The provision of relief for victims of natural and civil disasters.
- Help to be given to an individual beneficiary e.g. special equipment for a disabled person or for a child in need.
- Help given to particular geographic or social areas of benefit, or groups of people where it can be shown that such areas or groups are in need. Examples would be groups of people suffering hardship, pupils at a special

school, residents of a particular community or an individual within a community.

The maximum amount given is £500, as the foundation wants 'to help as many people in as many areas as possible'.

Exclusions: The following fall outside the foundation's priority areas:

- Fundraising for the purposes of pursuing political or propagandist activities.
- The support of religious activities or the advancement of religion (although this would not prevent consideration for support to members of a group or community that was otherwise in need).
- Any fundraising or activity under which those organising the fundraising activity would or could have a personal benefit.
- Provision of support for a person or people who do not come within the priority of the foundation or are not in genuine need.
- Provision of support for an activity where assistance is otherwise available from national or local organisations or authorities, i.e. from local social services, local housing authorities, Department of Social Services, or other authorities.
- Any organisation considered to be illegal or which may act illegally, or where funds are raised from, or for immoral purposes.
- Provision of sport generally or seeking to achieve excellence or professionalism in sport. For example this would exclude any sponsorship activities, or the provision of equipment for sports teams. The only exception to this would be, for example, some sporting activity for

children who are in need, or disabled people, or other people suffering hardship.

- Support for individuals or groups engaged in expeditions or projects requiring them to raise funds to enable them to participate.
- Proposals which are purely concerned with raising funds for other organisations or charities and/or where such funds are likely to go to the administration expenses of such organisations e.g. provision of sponsorship to an individual or individuals participating in another charitable event.
- Carnivals or shows which are concerned with mainly entertaining the public and where there is no control over the eventual destination of funds raised.
- Any purposes concerned with the promotion of friendship or international friendship e.g. town twining associations.
- Projects or activities outside the foundations geographic area.

Applications: In writing to the correspondent. Initially applications will be assessed by the branches or head office departments then forwarded to the foundation. Decisions are made continuously by the trustees.

9 RAISING SUPPORT FROM LOCAL AUTHORITIES

At some point during their lifetime, most groups that work with young people will look to their local town hall for help. You may need equipment, help with understanding the law, buildings, sessional support, running costs, training, contacts or advice. In many cases the local authority may have someone who can answer your question or know of resources you can apply for.

Local authorities are allocated funds from central government to provide services for young people in their area. Spending varies from authority to authority. A DfEE report *Transforming Youth Work* included figures from the National Youth Agency database which estimated that in 1999/2000 the average (median) amount spent per 13-19 year old in their area by local authorities was £59. The minimum amount spent was £30 and the maximum was £261.

Although the bulk of local authority support for young people is through its youth service, support from other areas has been introduced to increase the amount of funding available, or at least to maintain a level of provision. Employment and training agencies, youth justice support, health monies and expanding education funds have contributed significantly to the range of funding sources local authorities have used to resource their work with young people.

Local authority support for voluntary organisations comes in a number of forms:

- capital, for buildings, refurbishment, play areas, equipment and the like;
- revenue, for what it costs to run your activity, from salaries and telephone calls to sessional youth workers and courses.
- rate relief.

The climate of local authority support has changed. Voluntary organisations and community groups need to recognise that local authorities have many different functions and in the light of the Local Government Act 2000, will have a key new role in leading their community. The development of local strategic partnerships and joining up service delivery plans places new responsibilities on local authorities to make connections between community needs and services.

Competition for all resources is becoming fiercer. Areas such as youth services and community development have to compete against other local authority responsibilities such as education, housing and mainstream social services. Unlike grant-making charitable trusts, local authorities do not exist just to give money away. Neither are they solely interested in the development of young people. As never before, questions are being asked about effectiveness and the value for money that grants budgets bring to the local authority. The introduction of best value brings a new drive to evaluate the benefit of funding one thing rather than another. All local voluntary groups have to bear in mind that they must offer 'added value' or something extra to increase their chances of success in securing local authority support.

Lots of people and organisations are competing for local authority support. Your relationship with the local authority will be made up of many parts: lobbying, profile-raising, partnership-building as well as applying for support. You will need to be clear about what you do and what you need. You must then make sure that the people who matter in the local authority become equally clear. You will need to be clued up on the local authority's priorities and what they are looking for from the relationship. This will take time and effort, but it usually pays dividends.

THE RELATIONSHIP FACTOR

Local authorities are similar to other funders in this Guide in that personal relationships count. You need to build your relationship with your local authority as you would any other potential supporter. The days of widespread grant aid for anything and everything are over, and few local authorities now want to be cheque-writing machines. Particularly if you are a new project, you should not start by asking the local authority for money. You need to work with them, ideally in that much overused word, partnership, to develop a project and win

---

How local authorities can help

These are some examples of what local authorities support. Each area and authority will be different, and yours may support work with young people in other ways as well.

- Advice
- Equipment – to buy or loan
- Salaries
- Running costs – heating, lighting etc.
- Project start-up costs
- Training
- Bursaries
- Buildings
- Transport

- Refurbishment
- Sessional hours
- Sports and arts activities
- Help with programme development
- Access to other funders and programmes
- Publicity
- Endorsement
- Rate relief

support for the idea. All too often voluntary organisations begin their relationship with the local authority on the wrong foot, by asking for money rather than winning support for their proposal.

Rate relief

Local authorities can also give valuable indirect support to local charitable organisations through rate relief. The level of relief varies greatly from area to area, but the mandatory rate is 80%, and the discretionary allowance can be up to 100%. The amount will be governed by the authority's policy and may depend upon the type of organisation.

Rate relief is only given if you apply, and cannot be given retrospectively. Contact the local authority for further details of their policy and how to apply. Claim any rate relief you are entitled to while you can as there is an ongoing review of local authority discretionary rate relief.

WHICH LOCAL AUTHORITY?

Local government in England has been transformed in recent years and the structure of local government will be different in each part of the country. In England you may have several levels to take into account: your county council, a district council, a borough or city council. There may be a further level still if you have a parish or town council. Or you may have just one, say a London borough, a metropolitan district such as South Yorkshire or one of the unitary authorities such as Bristol.

Where you are not sure how your local authority is structured, ask around. Someone on your committee, a member, a volunteer or a parent may know. You can also ring your local councillor and ask about the local authority and how it works. (You will need get to know him or her sooner or later, so this will be a useful introduction.) If you do not already have their number, the town hall will. Ask for the chief executive's department and they will inform and direct you from there. Local authorities have websites to publicise their initiatives and to increase accountability. A directory of sites is at: www.tagish.co.uk

Contacting the appropriate office in your local authority can be time-consuming and frustrating. How your local authority is set up will directly affect who you apply to, and what you ask for. So it is worth spending some time getting to know the system. Once you are inside the gates, understanding how the authority works and making progress should become easier.

If you work within a unitary authority (these include London boroughs and metropolitan districts, as well as many towns and cities), you have one authority to think about. In each of these cases, it will be a matter of making contact with the appropriate offices to talk about your proposal. Depending on how your local authority works, you may be liaising with departments, directorates, units, or some other variation.

District or county?

Where you are working with a county council which also includes district, borough and possibly city councils, you need to take account of the two-tiered structure. Here, the responsibilities and functions of the local authorities are divided between the two levels. For example:

The county council will have responsibility for the large services and facilities which benefit the whole county. These include education and social services.

District and borough councils on the other hand are responsible for services and resources that benefit their local areas. These include housing, environmental services and local planning.

There will be some cross-over in the responsibilities of county and district councils.

Whether you apply at the county or district level will depend upon what you are applying for. You should consider how wide the geographical area is that you cover. Does your project have a county-wide interest with large numbers of participants or is it more local? A regional youth association for example may organise activities that take in more than one town or district, such as a young people's counselling and information service. A local youth club is more likely to focus on its local area. One will have a county-wide appeal, the other will link more easily with the district council.

If you are looking for county support you may have to lobby strongly. At this level it can help to have councillors, key officials and local politicians arguing the merits of your case and persuading others of the county-wide benefits of your scheme. Council committees, where decision-making powers lie, are not just made up by councillors. There may also be representatives of voluntary organisations, trade unions and similar local interests, all of whom can usefully be lobbied.

Once you have decided how your local authority is organised, you need to approach the appropriate officials. The named office which has responsibility for youth varies from authority to authority. Youth services may come under Education; some include youth provision under Leisure Services; others will have a wide-ranging function called Community Services, or Cultural and Community Services where youth services will be found. Where there is one, a key contact will be the Principal Youth Officer.

However your local authority is organised, find out:

- Who takes the lead in developing and supporting young people? Which council, county, district etc. and then, which departments?
- Who makes the policies which affect young people? (Councillors, committees)
- Who makes these policies happen? (Officers and offices)

And then get to know the key people and policies.

Parish and town councils

In some villages and county towns in England and Wales there can be a further tier of local government. Parish or community councils work at a very local, parochial level. Called parish or town councils in England, and neighbourhood or community councils in some urban areas, these bodies are responsible for maintaining and providing leisure and recreation facilities. In practice they look after village halls and playing fields as well as car parking, street lighting and such like. They must also be consulted in any local planning applications.

This local council will decide on local priorities for spending and fix its own rate which will be collected by the district council. The parish council will not have vast sums of money available, but it will direct the money to very local concerns. If you are a very local club needing or using a very local facility, and your activities contribute directly to the life of the community, you may find support from the parish council. Often in villages there will be a Village Plan which may include details of young people's resources, both actual and planned. Make contact with your parish council, either by attending the open meetings or by meeting parish councillors.

Council officers will be able to tell you how much is available, if anything, and how it is spent. Councillors may also be able to lobby on your behalf. Some parish council meetings are attended by local authority councillors. They may use meetings as a sounding board to find out what the local priorities are. If your name is mentioned here and wins support, there may be more note taken at a district level. Lists of local parish councillors will be posted in town and county halls, in your village hall (if you have one), or your local post office, parish church or library. The local citizen's advice bureau may also have information.

Youth Councils

In many areas Youth Councils have been formed, largely made up of representatives of youth organisations in the area, including young people themselves. These councils may exist alongside any of the local government tiers (county, district, borough, city, parish etc.). They may have grant-giving powers or have a consultative role with other local authority committees, and their primary focus is to give young people a voice in local decisions and policies. Here again, you need to find out who is on the council and get to know them. There may be opportunities for a representative from your own organisation to be appointed or elected onto the council. With low rates of participation by young people in national and local elections increasing young people's involvement in decision-making structures is of increasing interest to those shaping policy.

The British Youth Council has details of youth councils. Contact: 2 Plough Yard, Shoreditch High Street, London EC2A 3LP Tel: 020 7422 8640; Fax: 020 7422 8646; e-mail: mail@byc.org.uk; Website: www.byc.org.uk

WHO DOES WHAT IN THE LOCAL AUTHORITY?

Fundraising at any level is most effective when you connect with key people who are enthusiastic about your cause and can support you. You may need to enthuse them first and then get them to enthuse others. Writing endless letters is often the least effective way of raising funds. It is more helpful to your cause to meet with people face to face. In local authorities the main players to contact are:

- local authority officers
- local councillors.

You should not leave making these contacts until it is too late. Too often groups leave meeting the people who can influence and help until the eleventh hour when their funding is about to run out, or even after their application has failed. It is far better to involve local authority staff, councillors, MPs and other local people at an early stage to help the process along. If you do not yet know of any local people that have influence in the community, ask around your members, parents, volunteers and staff to find someone who does. If you have someone connected with your organisation who has particular experience or knowledge of making things happen locally, use them to make introductions for you and to promote the project themselves.

Local authority officers

Your first point of contact with the authority will usually be an officer within one of the departments or directorates. These are very important to your cause and can help your project in many ways. They are paid members of staff employed to implement council policies. In some local authorities a principal youth officer heads up the statutory youth service in the area. In some areas there will be only one youth officer; in others there will be several with their own projects and expertise (maybe in funding or training), or with responsibility for particular youth areas. You should also bear in mind that administrative officers often have detailed knowledge of what is happening, and may have the most information.

You need to think more widely than just those officers connected with youth provision. There may be other staff working in other departments that can also advise and help. For instance, if you are running a counselling service there may be officers in social services that you should speak to. An after-school club or work with those at risk of exclusion from school should be of interest to the education department. Where your work involves young people with disabilities, young women and girls, or young people from a particular ethnic group, there may be an officer with specific responsibilities for services under these headings. If you are using sport, a sports development officer may be able to help.

In all cases you will need to keep officers informed about your organisation and ensure that your activities are promoted within their department. If you are unsure which officer you should speak to, contact the chief executive's office which will be able to give you a name as a starting point. More and more local authorities are now establishing External Funding Units to help with liaison and signposting to appropriate offices and personnel.

Officers make recommendations to councillors to act upon and you should brief them well and update them regularly. They will want to know how your proposal is to work; what resources (not just money) will be required; whether there is community support; whether there is opposition, and any possible repercussions from supporting your activity. Like other funders, they may want clear acknowledgement of, and publicity for, the support given by the council. You should have an idea of how you will do this. Increasingly, your briefing should include an awareness of the strategic plans of your local authority and how they are implementing best value measures within the authority.

Try to make sure that officers are well-informed and enthusiastic about your proposal. If your activity is modest, support may be directly authorised by officers, although this is less the case now than it used to be. Councillors more than ever are keen to control spending decisions and to make sure that the council's support for projects is politically and financially transparent. Where the proposal needs further endorsement, officers can recommend it for councillors' support at the committee level. It may be, however, that you need to persuade councillors personally to give their backing when it reaches their committee(s).

> When contacting councillors and local authority officers, follow up telephone calls and meetings with a letter, summarising the key points you wish to make. Copies are often passed on to other local authority colleagues with notes written on.

Councillors

Councillors are representatives of a ward or a county division. They are also politicians with an agenda. They serve on committees and decide policy following briefings given by local authority officers. The fact that they are local representatives gives you the greatest point of leverage as their first duty is to represent the people in their ward. If you are working with young people you are contributing to local communities and councillors should be interested in what you are doing.

Where you need help from a number of different departments within the local authority, councillors can sponsor your application, oil the local government wheels, and generally help the progress of a proposal. They may help to broker a deal between departments that can give larger funding to a project than could be given by a single department. Where you are looking for county funding (as opposed to district), councillors can also help to cross district council lines. You may need to promote the regional benefits of your proposal. Local councillors on your side will help to identify which county officers to speak to and the channels to go through. They can also make a difference on the committees they participate in.

Local councillors are listed in the local press, your town hall, the citizen's advice bureau which will also give details of their surgery hours, or the *Municipal Yearbook* available in your local library. Some local authorities list councillors and committee members on their websites. You can contact your local ward councillor at their home address (they expect this) or through the local authority.

You should write care of the local authority when contacting other councillors. Letters are always helpful. Busy councillors can attach a quick note and pass it on to the relevant officer.

Be realistic in your approach and consider the scale of your activity and what you are asking help for. Remember that whilst the chair and vice-chair of any committee are obviously central to any decision-making, they are also the busiest people. They will be key contacts, but you will have to work around committed schedules. Many committee meetings are open to the public and publicised daily in the town hall.

Bear in mind that the balance of political power can be very different between the various tiers of local government. It is important to be able to present your case in different ways to attract the support of politicians in different parties. Keeping informed and aware of political and structural change will help your approach. One local authority officer observes: 'Local authorities are, at the end of the day, political organisations, and political priorities and considerations will often come into play. However, there is a move in many authorities towards having clear policy and funding priorities for grants and resisting pressure to support projects outside these priorities (thus reducing the scope for political patronage).'

Promoting your cause may seem daunting at first. However, if you are clear about why they should support you, your enthusiasm and a well-argued case will at least guarantee a hearing. Local authorities are like other funders, and will want to know why they should support you and what they are getting for their support. Briefing councillors and officers is part of this process. It may be useful to refer to *Promoting Your Cause*, published by DSC (see Useful addresses and sources of information).

> When briefing councillors, ensure that what you say is based on facts, and argue your case on its merits. Do not assume they have background knowledge of your organisation, the issue or approach you are taking, or where young people contribute to the community. Councillors may not have the papers or information to hand and will need filling in. Relationships built up with councillors over time will prove the most valuable, so try and involve them in your work: invite them to address a meeting of your supporters for example. As politicians, councillors like being loved, and few will resist the temptation to say positive things about you that they know will please the audience – and that you can hold them to in the future. Early evening appointments are often best.

WHICH DEPARTMENTS SHOULD YOU APPROACH?

Local authorities organise their departments in different ways. They have various functions; for example, housing, community services, social services, education and so on. Each of these functions includes a number of different responsibilities. For example, cultural services (which may be a separate department or be part of community services) will be responsible for parks, gardens, cemeteries, arts and libraries, sports development and recreation, and sometimes the youth service.

Depending upon your project there may also be a number of other departments that may be supportive of your project. Some are obvious, the others less so. In each case you should research their current priorities. You also need to think who benefits from your project and how it fits in with current local authority concerns.

Each local authority is different and will reflect local issues and priorities. The following is therefore a brief outline of the departments that may support work with young people.

The youth service

Although in some authorities grant aid to the voluntary youth sector has been reduced from previous levels, the youth service will still be the first main point of contact for those applying to the local authority for support for their work with young people. Support will not just be about funds, but may include some sessional hours, help with equipment and project development.

Organisations will have to make their case clearly and link their work to the objectives of the statutory youth service to improve their chances of sustained funding and support. Ofsted inspects and reports on the youth service. Where the inspection has taken place in your area, look at the report and research the current priorities and local concerns. The pattern of funding and any gaps in provision will be recorded. Copies of completed reports are available on the website: www.ofsted.gov.uk

Where the youth service has an application form, ask for advice from officers as to how to complete it. Equal opportunities and inclusiveness as well as up to date policies on health and safety, employment and child protection are essential for local authority funding. Furthermore, you will need to show, even for relatively modest grants how you will measure the outcomes of your work. Can you do what you say you can and how will you show this to the local authority?

There may be additional support under the Standards Fund, and at the time of writing the Transforming Youth Work Development Fund was in development, although this is likely to be concerned with the statutory youth service and its relationship with Connexions. Youth officers who are helping you with the form should have up to date details of any additional funding that your project may attract, but again, it will be closely tied to local authority targets and priorities.

Other departments

Depending upon what your project is there may be further departments in the local authority that you could approach. Some are obvious, others less so. In each case you will need to look into their current services, priorities and timetables for applications. Research their budgets, usually available through committee minutes, as it is useful to know how much they have to spend.

You also need to look closely at who benefits from your activities, and whether there are other parts of the local authority that may be interested in your proposal. There may be help for those working with young people under the following:

- education
- social services
- sports development
- the arts
- opportunities for those with disabilities
- ethnic minorities
- women

- health promotion
- increasing awareness of the local authority
- urban development and regeneration
- rural isolation
- environmental improvement
- voluntary sector liaison
- community safety.

Where your project fits in with a department's current priorities and concerns they may welcome your approach. The Social Services department for example, may be interested in projects such as:
- after school clubs
- work with young mothers and young men
- work with young people who are asylum seekers or refugees
- work with young people who are travellers
- counselling and information services
- work with young gays and lesbians
- work with young people leaving care
- work with young carers
- reducing youth crime.

The education department may consider projects such as:
- playground activities in schools
- work with those at risk of exclusion from school or non–attenders
- training
- literacy and numeracy support
- playschemes
- work with unemployed young people
- work with young people with special needs
- health education.

Education

Since the first edition of this book there has been a marked increase in the number of opportunities for organisations working with young people to connect their activities with services needed by local schools. Local Management for Schools (LMS) has changed how money is spent on education by the local authority. Individual schools hold the purse strings and have more flexibility and autonomy over how they form partnerships with voluntary organisations.

However, schools are not grant-givers; their interest will be in buying in a service which you are providing. You may, for example, be offering self-esteem activities to link with personal and social education elements of the curriculum; team-building for those already excluded from mainstream education or at risk of becoming excluded; literacy support; counselling services; playground games;

sports and arts activities, and breakfast and after-school clubs. There are a number of opportunities to link into education initiatives such as Excellence in Cities, Education Action Zones or the Standards Fund for example.

The New Opportunities Fund, among others, has opened up new possibilities for partnerships between schools and voluntary organisations. The benefits can and should be mutual, but both sides need to build the relationship so that both school and voluntary organisation see the rewards of a combined approach. Some local authorities have school liaison officers who can give you the overall picture of which schools are doing what and where they might welcome an approach. It remains the case, however, that these partnerships often work best where good relationships already exist and any formalised partnership builds upon a foundation that has been laid well in advance.

Making the case for your project

What features of your project make it attractive to your local authority?

How do any of the following apply to your organisation or project?

- Fits in with local authority priorities (essential)
- Local benefits
- Regional benefits
- Large number of different groups benefit (which ones?)
- Community run; participation of young people
- Innovative approach
- Addressing special needs
- Matching funds raised
- Established track record
- Excellence
- Sound finances
- Includes 'hard to reach' groups
- Fills a gap or augments local authority service provision
- Number of different bodies/organisations involved (which ones?)
- Established and enthusiastic membership
- Large number of benefits from a small grant (what benefits?)
- Local support
- Good publicity for the local authority
- Value for money
- Other (list)

GENERAL GRANT-GIVING

As well as the specific departments, most councils will have a general grant-giving committee. Bear in mind that all local authority grants are discretionary, but this particular source has wider discretionary powers and can give to a range of organisations for events and activities which are not necessarily covered by other departments. The fund is sometimes called the Community Chest (although different to those described on page 314 as part of the Neighbourhood Renewal Fund) and can be applied for by any organisation within the authority's area. Grants may well be small (up to £500) and for items such as equipment or training fees.

The scheme is often operated from the chief executive's office, which may also be responsible for events and activities that are not covered by other functions, including the marketing of the local authority. Events such as youth conferences, festivals or tournaments may have authority-wide benefits and may be supported more on the lines of a sponsorship, particularly if there are publicity and increased profile opportunities or links with other countries, through town-twinning and the like.

There may be restrictions on how many times a year you can apply. This need not alter your application for equipment at a certain point in the year, but if you have volunteers looking to attend training courses at different times in the year, you will need to plan accordingly. All departmental budgets have allocations to be spent by the end of each financial year. If you apply towards the end of a budgetary period there may be too little money in the coffers, or too much. Where there is a surplus, officers will be keen to see it spent before the next financial year; your application may be received particularly warmly. However, if the cupboard is bare you will have to wait until the next financial year. If you get to know your council officers they may be able to tell you how much money is left within a particular budget.

LOCAL AUTHORITIES AND OTHER BODIES

Local authorities often work in partnership with other organisations and often apply for funding themselves (e.g. for SRB funding or European grants programmes). They generally work with other organisations such as Learning and Skills Councils, the police, businesses, health authorities and youth justice services to achieve a variety of aims and to draw up and implement locally defined strategies on a wide range of issues. This has never been more clearly the case than with the advent of Local Strategic Partnerships (LSPs). In many of the larger funding programmes small groups going it alone will not stand much chance of winning bids on their own. Where they are known and trusted by large bodies however, their chances of being included in plans for the area increase greatly.

Increasingly, local authorities are gatekeepers to other forms of funding and influence. Where local authorities are working closely with other bodies on funding bids or service provision, there may be opportunities for voluntary organisations to become involved, including organisations working with young people. However, to be involved at any meaningful level you will have to be at the right meetings and in the right networks to get an invitation to the bidding table.

Local authorities have regular meetings, or representatives sit on partnership boards, with a host of other public agencies such as the the Youth Employment Service, the local Youth Offending Team, police authorities and the local health authority. These meetings propose and advise on approaches to local issues and concerns and how services will be delivered. Where your activities reach groups targeted by these bodies or you have an approach that is innovative and professional, you can make a strong case for being included in any consultation, and then being considered as part of any service delivery.

The significance of local authorities

- May give core-funding
- Can publicise activities and events
- Access to networks
- Lead bodies e.g. in SRB, European bids
- Relationships with health authorities, police authorities, Learning and Skills Councils etc.
- Expertise on form filling
- Policy and legislation issues e.g. health and safety

In some cases the absence of a local authority from a partnership bid can cause suspicion. Some of the larger funding programmes will want to see the authority's involvement if they are to take the application seriously.

Again, each area is different, but health authority initiatives may include health promotion, fitness campaigns and the like which contribute to the local health strategy which details health priorities for the area. These may link with local authority environmental and education programmes and priorities. Similarly, a multi-agency initiative combining with the Youth Offending Team and police force may include diversionary activities for young people which include sports and activities, and playschemes.

Key questions

The following questions will help to develop your relationship with the local authority:

- Who is the first point of contact for organisations working with young people?
- Have we contacted them for advice or other support? When?
- Are there officers who specialise in young people who are already involved in our project, or groups of young people who we would like to involve?
- Do they produce guidelines for those applying for grants?
- Do we know what their overall budget is?
- Have we got up to date information?
- What is the maximum and minimum grant available?
- Is there help with equipment costs; revenue or running costs such as salary and administration; or with capital such as buildings or site development?
- Do we know of any organisations similar to ours who have had help, and what was it for?
- Is in kind support available such as sessional support or the loan of equipment?

APPLICATIONS

By the time you fill in any application form you will know how your local authority works. You should be able to enlist the support of officers and local councillors. The application procedure will differ from authority to authority, although in almost every case there will be an application form to fill in. This may be specific to a particular named department or be a general form for the whole of the authority.

In general you need to know:
- the maximum and minimum grants available;
- current priorities and criteria, either for the council as a whole or the funding programme in particular;
- how you should fill in the application form;
- what information is needed and how it should be presented;
- the application timetable and deadlines for submission.

Where you are applying for a large project with other funders involved you need to allow for time lags and delays in submission and approval. Lead-in times differ according to which partners are involved, how many, and how good the relationships are. If a proposal is to go before a committee for a decision, you need to find out the timetable and to lobby for your cause well in advance.

Be clear and concise. Take advice from officers as to how the form should be filled in. Once submitted, a regular (although not too frequent) telephone call will keep you in touch with how the application is progressing. If by this time you are on good terms with the relevant officers this can be a friendly, informal chat that can help to keep the application 'live'.

Basically, there are three ways of getting a project supported by the local authority:

- Applying for a grant, but amounts are limited and available money is generally used up on commitments made in previous years. There is now more emphasis on 'priority-driven' support rather than historic funding.
- Through service level agreements or contracts, where you are competing with a whole range of organisations – including commercial ones.
- Getting the local authority to include your project in an SRB, ESF or other bids. Many local authorities now act as gatekeepers for external funding. But all this takes time and forward planning.

Remember, local authorities are like other funders in what they want to know from you:
- What do you want to do?
- Why do you want to do it?
- How will you make it happen?
- Who will be accountable?
- What difference will the work make to the local area?
- What do you want from the local authority?

In other words, they will look to see if you:
- have identified a clear need;
- have produced a good and workable plan;
- have costed your work;
- will be able to measure the value and outcomes of your work.

Think differently

The key thing is that when you meet with your local authority, don't talk about funding; talk about collaboration. Local authorities are not cheque-writing machines. They do not see themselves as there to underwrite your core costs year in, year out. They have their own views on what service provision they want to see happen in the area. Show how you fit into and understand their priorities and concerns, rather than expect them just to support you to do whatever you like.

Like other funders, local authorities should be thanked for their support and acknowledged appropriately. Local authorities appreciate credit and recognition for their contribution to a project. Show how you will publicise their grant and generally help people to view their local authority more positively.

Do

- Find out how your local authority works
- Find and contact key local officers
- Build good relationships with local councillors across the party divides
- Find out about and understand authority/department priorities
- Think creatively about your project
- Use local media to raise your profile
- Attend meetings regularly
- Be clear and to the point
- Keep well informed about changes in criteria/priorities
- Be persistent
- Budget realistically
- Find out about application procedures and deadlines
- Plan ahead
- Research fully

Don't

- Give up
- Leave talking to councillors and officers until you need money
- Limit your project to one narrow departmental interest
- Forget in kind support from your local authority
- Be bashful about what you can offer
- Let information become out of date
- Plan in the short-term – look to the future
- Waffle
- Take local authority support for granted

Other information

The Local Government Association produces information on policy and updated local government news. Contact: Local Government Association, 26 Chapter Street, London SW1P 4ND. Info line: 020 7664 3131; Fax: 020 7664 3030; e-mail: info@lga.gov.uk; Website: www.lga.gov.uk

10 RAISING MONEY FROM GOVERNMENT

Grants from central and regional government sources are likely to be a smaller part of a voluntary organisation's income than funds raised through trusts, public fundraising, or fees from contracts with the local authority. However, many voluntary organisations apply for support from central and regional government, and as this chapter shows, there are numerous and increasing possibilities. Voluntary organisations are being welcomed into partnerships with government bodies as never before as they are seen as vital in delivering government policy. This is particularly the case with organisations working with young people.

Where organisations are prepared to look closely at the possibilities offered by government, research policy objectives and then customise their approach, there are a number of opportunities for funding.

There has been a movement away from centralised control towards giving more say to regional offices. Voluntary organisations now have a variety of funders to get to know and a number of tiers to work with.

The government department with central responsibility for funding youth work is the Department for Education and Skills (DfES). A small part of their overall budget supports the statutory youth service and there is a small dedicated grant programme for national voluntary organisations working with young people. A further central government allocation is made to the National Youth Agency which supports youth work development (see below).

In addition to dedicated youth programmes, there are a number of other government departments, agencies and public bodies which may also be interested in working with your organisation, not because you work with young people but because you fulfil one of their policy objectives. Each department and government body has its own set of priorities which will not necessarily include

What this chapter covers

- Grants to national youth organisations
- International exchanges
- Youth music
- Sport
- Health
- Combating disadvantage
- Community safety and youth justice
- Learning and training
- Regeneration
- Rural communities
- Environment
- Voluntary and community involvement

young people. You will have to be working on issues that are familiar to them and fit in with their existing policies. Where your work with young people involves main government focus areas such as crime prevention, job creation or training, more funding opportunities may open up to you. However, it will be on the strength of your ability to deliver training, regeneration, new enterprise or environmental improvement that you will secure funding, rather than your commitment to the social development of young people.

One head of a government grants unit stated: 'Government grants are primarily designed to meet departmental policies and programme outcomes. These should of course be reflected in the published criteria for grants. Applications are, therefore, expected to demonstrate clearly how they will help departments achieve their objectives. Too many applicants seem to assume that the core work of their organisation is reason enough to secure a government grant. I am afraid that no matter how effective or important the work of your organisation, you need to show how it meets the objectives of the funder.'

Many government schemes are now regionally administered and are part of locally defined strategies and priorities. A general principle applies: find out as much as possible about what is happening locally and regionally, and try to find ways to influence economic planning and local development, so that you are not just better informed, but that policy makers know about the local needs of young people and how organisations like yours can be part of the delivery of local solutions.

The current tiers of government that voluntary organisations should consider are:

- government departments (such as Education and Skills, Environment, Home Office, Transport and the Regions);
- regional bodies (such as Government Offices for the Regions and Regional Development Agencies);
- non-departmental public bodies and organisations (such as the Countryside Agency);
- local bodies (such as Connexions partnership boards, Learning and Skills Councils, Youth Offending Teams, and health authorities administering funds and contracts for employment and training, youth justice and health);
- area based initiatives (such as health action zones, education action zones, sports action zones, Children's Fund Local Network).

Some of these bodies will give money centrally, others through regional offices, others through local networks. Partnership with other bodies is now a feature common to a number of the programmes. You may also find that government money can be used to match funds from other sources such as Europe or the National Lottery.

Government funds can provide new opportunities to finance your work;

they can also bring constraints and new challenges to an organisation. Some money will only be available if there is a problem attached, such as drugs, crime or social exclusion. If you cast your funding net wide to take in some of the different statutory schemes, your organisation needs to be clear about what it is doing and why. Consider the following:

- *'We applied because it was there' dilemma.* Is the project you are applying for something you have planned to do in response to needs that you see, or have you conjured up a project to fit with the latest government funding programme?
- *Sustainability syndrome.* How will you continue the work once statutory funding has finished? Will you have had to take on extra resources to do the work, and how will these be used when the one, two or three-year funding has ceased?
- *The compatibility conundrum.* How do the large streams of government money fit in with the young people you work with and how they see themselves? Are there difficulties in linking these young people with social inclusion initiatives and so on?
- *The cuckoo in the nest.* If you are successful in gaining support from a particular programme, will it alter the way your organisation works? How will the organisation adapt to meet any new demands that the funding will bring?

Research and local planning

There are all kinds of regional and local economic planning initiatives which will differ throughout the country but have an impact upon how resources are used. Some of the more generally applicable plans and bodies to take account of will be:

- Local Strategic Partnerships (LSPs)
- Single Programming Documents (SPDs) which give a framework for how European Funds are used in an area
- strategies prepared by local authorities and Learning Skills Councils
- programmes and policies drawn up by Regional Development Agencies
- childcare and education strategies
- housing plans
- health strategies, such as regional health investment plans and health improvement programmes, and those of Drug Action Teams
- crime reduction strategies and crime and disorder partnerships
- local Compact arrangements between the voluntary sector and local authorities

GRANTS TO NATIONAL YOUTH ORGANISATIONS

National Youth Voluntary Organisations Grants

Youth Service Unit, DfES, Room E4A, Moorfoot, Sheffield S1 4PQ
Tel: 0114 259 1214
Contact: Kevin Brady, Team Leader

Under its National Voluntary Youth Organisation (NVYO) Grant Scheme, the Department for Education and Skills (DfES) gives grants to organisations to further the personal and social education of young people. The scheme gave grants totalling £3,986,970 for 2000/2001 and around £12 million from 1999 to 2002. Following a review priorities have been set for the next three year period, 2002–2005. One of DfES' aims is to develop ways in which voluntary organisations can participate in Connexions, the careers, training and employment guidance service for young people.

The priorities for funding under the scheme for 1999/2002 are:

- the combating of social exclusion and inequality through work with disadvantaged priority groups such as those in the inner cities, rural areas or deprived housing estates; work with disaffected young people and those at risk of becoming involved in crime; minority ethnic communities and young people with disabilities;
- the raising of the standard and quality of youth work by, for instance, increasing young people's participation in decision-making and training for youth workers and volunteers.

Most grants are between £10,000 and £100,000 a year and are for up to 50% of the total programme cost. Funding is given to support core costs, but this cannot constitute more than 30% of the total amount applied for. As a general rule, the majority of the grants are awarded to cover the specific costs of project administration and only small amounts are available for capital expenditure or running costs. Organisations are usually funded for up to three years, although the second and third year's funding may be conditional on satisfactory outcomes achieved in the first year. Partnerships between organisations are encouraged and resources are dedicated to promote collaborative working.

The awards process
There are two stages to the awards process. The Youth Service Unit at the DfES holds a central register of youth organisations eligible for a grant and organisations must first join the register. (There are currently 91 organisations listed on the register.) The register was revised in 1999 when ten new organisations were added and the list was closed with funding committed up to 2001. The same process of advertising the register and inviting organisations to apply to join will follow the review setting priorities for the next period, 2002–2005.

To be included in the NVYO register, organisations must be both national and voluntary in nature; with large numbers of members in the 13–19 target age group; and have the planned personal and social education of young people as one of their primary aims. Their activities must also cover a significant part of England. Organisations should contact the Youth Service Unit for further details of the registration process.

The second stage of the process involves organisations on the register being invited to submit project proposals for funding. 84 organisations were supported in the 1999/2002 round, some with single projects and some with ongoing support over a three year period. (See below.) Nine were joint programmes involving more than one organisation.

Examples of organisations receiving grants

- African Caribbean Evangelical Alliance – for work with young black people and training for those working with young people in black majority churches: £10,000 per year
- Army Cadet Force – £20,000
- Boys Brigade – to raise the standard of youth work: £19,000 in year 1; £18,000 each in year 2 and year 3
- Catholic Youth Services – £15,000
- Divert Trust – £80,000
- Duke of Edinburgh's Award – for Youth Access, a programme to improve the quality of youth work: £130,000 in year 1; £110,000 in year 2 and £100,000 in year 3
- Endeavour Training – for work with schools addressing non-participation and underachievement in the final two years: of school: £175,000 each year
- Fairbridge – £145,000 in year 1; £159,000 in year 2
- Friends for Young Deaf People £85,000 in year 1; £70,000 in year 2
- Inner Cities Young Peoples Project – £20,000
- International Voluntary Service – to establish a mentoring scheme and to encourage volunteers from disadvantaged and ethnic minority communities to participate in IVS camps: £8,000 per year
- Leap Confronting Conflict Programme – for education work in conflict-related issues: £65,000 in

year 1; £63,000 in year 2 and £62,000 in year 3
- Lubavitch Youth – £35,000
- National Association of Youth Theatres – for a regional development programme: £37,000 per year
- National Federation of Young Farmers' Clubs – £120,000
- National Federation of Youth Action Agencies – £30,000
- Oasis – £40,000 in year 1; £60,000 in year 2
- The Quakers/Leaveners – for work to counter bullying, to raise the standard of youth work and for the Quaker Youth Theatre: £24,000 in year 1; £20,000 each in years 2 and 3
- Scout Association – £135,000 in year 1; £130,000 in year 2
- Woodcraft Folk – £38,000
- Young Muslim Organisation – £20,000
- Youth at Risk – £70,000 in year 1; £80,000 in year 2
- Youth Clubs UK – to encourage the social inclusion of young people through a range of activities: £238,000 in each year

Examples of joint projects

- Boys Brigade/Girls Brigade – £5,000
- Council for Environmental Education/ Guide Association/Federation of City Farms/Watch Trust Environmental Education/Youth Clubs UK – £40,000
- Outward Bound Trust/Trident Trust – to develop a social and personal education programme for disaffected young people in South Yorkshire: £35,000 in year 1; £50,000 each in year 2 and year 3
- Youth Hostels Association/RSPB/ Youth Clubs UK – for further development of the peer education environment programme: £17,000 in

year 1; £23,000 in year 2 and £26,000 in year 3

Umbrella bodies
- British Youth Council – £60,000
- National Council for Voluntary Youth Services – £125,000 in year 1; £90,000 in year 2
- Youth Access – £80,000 in year 1; £100,000 in year 2

Applications: During 2001 the DfES reviewed its arrangements for giving awards. Organisations which are interested in joining the register to apply for a grant in the next cycle can contact the department throughout the three year period. They will then be notified nearer the time with details of any new arrangements. To approach the department about joining the register, or if you need any information about the scheme, you should contact the Youth Service Unit.

Other resources
The National Youth Agency

The National Youth Agency is the national agency with responsibility for supporting youth work. It commissions development work through its Partners-In-Innovation programme. Ten projects were contracted in the most recent round, including a rural information café and young trustee programme; a mentoring programme, a project to tackle racism, a young black men's project and a programme of help for young black people moving from care to independent living. The aim is to establish good practice and inform youth work generally through the experience of the commissioned projects.

Further information on Partners-In-Innovation is available on the NYA website: www.nya.org.uk, and by telephone: 0116 285 3737.

The Philip Lawrence Awards

The NYA also plays an important role in administering the Philip Lawrence Awards which promote active citizenship in young people aged 11–20. 'The awards focus on exceptionally praiseworthy activities rather than on the individuals involved. We are looking in particular for achievements in combating lawlessness and violence, in promoting community safety and racial harmony and in encouraging others to do likewise.' The Philip Lawrence Awards emblem is awarded, and small cash awards of up to £1,000 can also be given to support the winning activity. Awards are decided following a simple nomination and judging process. In 2001, recipients included: DIY Collective, Scarborough for their arts activities; Sahara Video Group, Brighton; Anything but STR8 for their support to young gay and lesbian people; and the Holsworthy Seriously Senior Youth Group, Devon.

For further details of the awards and how to nominate, contact: Information Services, The National Youth Agency, 17–23 Albion Street, Leicester LE1 6GD Tel: 0116 285 3792; Fax: 0116 285 3775

The Neighbourhood Support Fund

The NYA also administered the DfES' Neighbourhood Support Fund and its strand concerned with voluntary and community based youth work organisations. Funding was distributed to over 80 youth projects. The fund used existing networks including organisations working directly with young people such as the Gateshead Borough Youth Organisations Council, Merseyside Youth Association and Cleveland Youth Association.

The fund supported work with disaffected 13–19 year olds living in the most deprived local authority areas in England to help them to participate in learning and employment. It linked with the Connexions Service start-up (see page 307).

Projects that have been supported are based on established youth work practice with activities such as: drama, music and video; internet and ICT; volunteering and voluntary action; developing job-related skills; peer education; motor projects; residential and outdoor events; sports; counselling, advice and information.

Projects were funded over the three years and further details of these are available from the NYA. Contact: 0116 285 3700

INTERNATIONAL EXCHANGES

Commonwealth Youth Exchange Counvil (CYEC)

Commonwealth House, 7 Lion Yard, Tremadoc Road, Clapham, London SW4 7NF
Tel: 020 7498 6151 **Fax:** 020 7720 5403
E-mail: Mail@cyec.demon.co.uk
Contact: Máire Ní Threasaigh, Exchanges Officer

The Commonwealth Youth Exchange Council is an independent charity funded by the government to promote two-way exchanges through giving advice, information, training and grants. Around £167,000 is given annually in grants.

It supports two-way international exchanges for groups of young people aged 16 to 25 in the UK – and their peers in the Commonwealth – which focus on the personal social development of the young people involved.

Although there is a total of 54 Commonwealth countries most exchanges take place in the Caribbean, Africa and Asia. The minimum length of the whole project is two years and the young people should be involved in all stages of the planning and preparation. There should be clear benefits to the young people in terms of new attitudes, skills, knowledge and understanding. Groups of 5 to 13 young people (excluding youth leaders) are supported. There must be both a hosting and a visiting element to the exchange, and return visits must take place within two years. Visits must last at least 21 days for exchanges with countries outside Europe and at least 14 days for Cyprus, Gibraltar and Malta.

Priority is given to:
- new or particularly innovative programmes;
- organisations new to exchanges;
- exchanges with Africa, Asia and the Caribbean;
- exchanges involving young people who would not normally have the opportunity to take part in an international exchange;
- local British groups (rather than national groups);
- exchanges involving young people with disabilities;
- exchanges with an environmental theme.

Grants are given on a per head basis and are usually for up to 40% of international travel and not more than 40% of the total costs of hosting the partner group.

The group needs to decide which country they would like to find a partner group in, and look at their community and within their group for possible connections. CYEC provides support and telephone advice throughout the exchange process.

Courses and seminars are also provided for young people, youth workers, teachers and youth and community managers. Residential training can be provided for leaders and young people. Guidelines and examples of good practice are available.

Examples of recently funded exchanges

- The Cary–Mufulira Community Partnership Trust is a Somerset–Zambia exchange project. The exchange has developed over a number of years, and the most recent focus area was 'Safer Lifestyles' which looked particularly at HIV and Aids. The theme was developed through a variety of arts activities including drama, music, dance and art.
- The Pestalozzi Children's Village Trust, East Sussex is involved in an exchange with India. The theme is development action and includes looking at alternative technology.
- The Volunteer Centre in Hackney has been supported in its exchange with Ghana. Its most recent theme was IT with peer education workshops, and a dance and drumming workshops leading to a performance.

Applications: Contact the above address for an information pack.

Connect Youth International (CYI)

The Information Unit, The British Council, 10 Spring Gardens, London SW1A 2BN
Tel: 020 7389 4030 **Fax:** 020 7389 4033
E-mail: connectyouth.enquiries@ britishcouncil.org
Website: www.connectyouth international.com
Contact: Sujata Saikia, Information Officer

Connect Youth International (formerly the Youth Exchange Centre) is a department of the British Council which provides advice, information, training and grant support to UK youth groups taking part in international exchanges. These can take place in any country, although the majority involve European countries. In 1999/2000 CYI gave a total of £4.73 million in grants.

It currently administers youth exchanges, arrangements for the European Voluntary Service, Group Initiatives and Future Capital as part of the YOUTH programme of the European Commission (see page 337 for further information).

CYI administers the Causeway British–Irish Exchange programme to strengthen and improve relationships between young people in Ireland and Britain.

Non-European exchanges can also be supported. Funds are available for bilateral exchanges with the former Soviet Republics (mainly Belarus, Russia, Ukraine), USA, Israel, Palestine, Japan and China.

Commonwealth exchanges are supported through the Commonwealth Exchange Council (see above).

Exchanges

Grants are available for British young people aged 15 to 25 in groups of between eight to 30 participants (including youth workers) to take part in cultural exchanges. Grants can be given towards outward travel costs and the costs of hosting the partner group. The average grant is around £100 per person.

Projects should be planned around a programme of joint activities. This programme can focus on a particular theme, be about the local community or be broadly based on youth issues. The exchange should be a minimum of seven days. Organisers looking for support in preparing exchanges can apply for grants for Advance Planning Visits.

There is a preference for projects involving those who would not normally have the opportunity to take part in an international exchange, or who face particular barriers.

CYI does *not* support: tours to several countries, or several cities in one country; competitions; purely tourist visits; exchanges that are part of an educational curriculum; youth wings of political parties; individual young people proposing to live, work or study in another country.

Applications: Activities are supported through a regional network of twelve local committees which give advice and support and select projects and award grants. Details of local committees are available from the contact above. Contact addresses and telephone numbers for the committees are available from the main office. As well as deciding the majority of the grants, the regional committees provide information on how to raise the funds, plan a programme and find a partner for the exchange. Application forms are also available from the website.

YOUTH MUSIC

National Foundation for Youth Music

1 America Street, London SE1 0NE
Tel: 020 7902 1060 **Fax:** 020 7902 1061
E-mail: info@youthmusic.org.uk
Website: www.youthmusic.org.uk
Contact: Claire Dolling

Youth Music supports a range of music activities and forms for children and young people including 'country to concertos, folk to funk, garage to gamelan, jazz to jungle, rap to raga, songs to symphonies'. It aims to increase music-making opportunities for young people under 18 and particularly to make a difference in areas where young people have few opportunities to make music. The foundation supports music groups and non-music organisations wishing to develop music in their work, and priority is given to groups based in areas of social and economic need and to help those new to music. As well as financial support, help is given by providing information and encouragement.

The foundation runs different programmes. Past initiatives include the Music Maker Programme which supported groups led by an experienced musician to develop music skills in young people. Another programme, Singing Challenge, supported a wide range of singing groups and projects.

Plug into Music

Plug into Music is the foundation's funding programme to encourage the use of technology in music-making. 'From DJ decks to midi didgeridoos, Plug into Music is about helping children and young people to make creative musical use of the tools that technology offers.'

The programme is open to not-for-profit groups such as:

- community music groups
- education authorities
- groups of schools (individual schools are not eligible)
- partnerships of organisations
- professional arts organisations
- youth clubs.

The programme aims to support projects which take place outside school hours such as lunchtime activities, after-school clubs, evenings, weekends and holidays. Activities that may be supported include:

- DJ workshops and performances
- sequencing and sampling projects
- workshops and jams by web-cam
- internet collaborations and re-mixes
- compositions for digital and acoustic instruments.

Grants range from £7,500 to £30,000. 10% of the total grant amount can cover equipment costs, but projects are encouraged to make use of existing facilities. This may mean working with other local organisations including recording studios or enhancing resources and equipment already owned by the project.

Applications will be accepted until 1st March 2002 and successful projects are to be completed by September 2002.

Get Sorted in Rotherham received £30,000 Plug into Music funding. This will help to set up a computer suite with six work stations and help young people aged between eight and 18 to develop studio skills, sequencing and sampling. The project is also working towards the accreditation of courses.

Other programmes

The foundation is currently developing future programmes and those interested should contact the above address or visit the website for up to date information. Singing Challenge 4 starts from January 2002, as does Music Maker and First Steps which follow the lines of previous programmes. Awards will be announced in April 2002.

The Instrument Swap Scheme follows on from the Instrument Amnesty previously run by the foundation. The latest scheme aims to get unused and broken instruments out of school and music service cupboards and back into use. Youth Music is offering repair grants of up to £10,000 per music service as well as an online bidding system to swap instruments between services.

Youth Music Action Zones

The foundation has committed £10 million to establishing and resourcing 20 Youth Music Action Zones by December 2001. Zones established so far are: Birmingham, Cornwall, Greater Manchester, the Humber region, Lancashire, Liverpool and Merseyside, London, Norfolk, North of England, North Yorkshire, Shropshire and Herefordshire, South East England, South Yorkshire, Staffordshire, and Thanet.

The foundation can give financial support to music projects, community centres, consortia of schools, and youth clubs which are working together to increase the opportunities for young people to make music. Details of individual zones' activities and contact details are available from the website and by contacting the above address.

Applications: Information on current and future funding programmes is available from the website or by contacting the above address.

Application forms can be requested from the website, or by contacting the

National Foundation for Youth Music,
c/o PO Box 214, 35 Winckley Square,
Preston PR1 3GJ; Tel: 08450 560560;
Fax: 01772 836199

SPORT

Sportsmatch

**The Institute of Sports Sponsorship,
Warwick House, 25/27 Buckingham
Palace Road, London SW1W 0PP
Tel: 020 7233 7747 Fax: 020 7828 7099
E-mail: info@sportsmatch.co.uk
Website: www.sportsmatch.co.uk
Contact: Nicola Ratcliffe, Scheme
Manager, Development**

Sportsmatch aims to attract business
sponsorship to grass-roots sport in
England. It is funded by the Department
for Culture, Media and Sport (DCMS)
through Sport England and around £3
million is available in match funds every
year. In Scotland and Wales it is funded
by the Scottish and Welsh Sports
Councils respectively.

The business partner must be a first-
time sponsor of a grass-roots organisation
or be increasing its amount of
sponsorship, and must be contributing at
least £1,000. For every £1 the sponsor
contributes in the first year, Sportsmatch
will match with £1, up to £50,000 for
any one event or activity.

Events or activities should be
competitive or challenging and involve
physical effort and skill. They should also
involve increased participation and/or
improved performance at grass-roots
level where participation is not unduly
restricted. When there is a high demand
for funds, priority is given to projects
benefiting young people, disabled people,
schools and school-related projects,

ethnic minorities and, in particular,
events or activities in urban or rural
recreationally-deprived areas with
community involvement.

Awards can be given for revenue
activities or capital equipment directly
related to sporting activities. Capital
projects can be supported if the total
budget is less than £5,000.

Around 96% of Sportsmatch awards go
to schemes that involve youth. Recent
examples include:
- Charlton Athletic Football and
Community Scheme, sponsored by
Railtrack and awarded £50,000 for
football coaching sessions for young
people to reduce trespassing and
vandalism on the railway. The
programme used roadshows and visits
to estates and youth clubs to
communicate a safety message.
- Panathlon Foundation, sponsored by
Royal & Sun Alliance Insurance Group
and awarded £25,000 for a multi-
sport programme offered to schools
with limited sports provision. Each
school received 100 hours of coaching
and £1,000 worth of equipment and
kit.
- Colchester Phoenix Swimming Club,
sponsored by Royal London Insurance
and awarded £1,000 for a competitive
swimming programme which included
training and coaching for young
people with a disability. The 50-week
programme culminated in a swimming
gala with teams invited from clubs in
the eastern region.

Applications: Booklets covering
commercial sponsorship of disability
sport, women and girls, and ethnic
minorities are available from the address
above. They includes details of how
Sportsmatch works, case studies and
budgets, and advice on planning and

costings. An application pack and details of closing dates are also available from the above address. Applications should be received at least 12 weeks before a proposed activity or event is to start. The scheme manager or deputy reviews each application with a coordinator before the application goes forward to the award panel.

Other resources

There are currently 12 *Sport Action Zones* in England with a further 18 planned. Each zone responds to local community needs and aims to improve sporting provision where there is high social, economic and sporting deprivation. Some zones may include support to organisations working with young people. Contact: www.sportengland.org for further information.

HEALTH

HEALTH ACTION ZONES

Department of Health, Quarry House, Quarry Hill, Leeds LSU 7UE
Tel: 0113 254 5002 **Fax:** 0113 254 6343
E-mail: Michael.Swaffield@doh.gov.uk
Website: www.haznet.org.uk
Contact: Michael Swaffield, Policy and Communications Manager

There are 26 Health Action Zones (HAZ) covering areas which are part of 34 health authorities and 73 local authorities. These areas are:
- first wave HAZs established in 1998 – Bradford, East London and the City, Lambeth, Southwark & Lewisham, Luton, Manchester, Salford & Trafford, North Cumbria, Northumberland, Plymouth, Sandwell, South Yorkshire Coalfields, Tyne & Wear;

- second wave HAZs established in 1999 – Brent, Bury & Rochdale, Camden & Islington, Cornwall & the Isles of Scilly, Hull & East Riding, Leeds, Leicester City, Merseyside, North Staffordshire, Nottingham, Sheffield, Tees; Wakefield, Walsall, Wolverhampton.

The 26 areas have been decided using indicators of deprivation and poor health, and through a variety of projects aim to reduce inequalities in health and develop local solutions to health problems. The zones represent a 'joined up' approach and recognise the need to tackle public health concerns by looking at housing, regeneration, employment, education and disadvantage. There are initiatives for example which aim to raise awareness of sexual health concerns; projects to reduce teenage pregnancies; and programmes to break down social exclusion by training and sports activities

An example of HAZ activity is in Lambeth, Southwark and Lewisham and their focus 'Children First'. The aim is to improve the future for children and young people in South East London through: building healthier environments and communities; improving opportunities for disabled children and young people to bring them back into the mainstream; reducing unwanted teenage pregnancies and improving sexual health; reducing youth crime; reducing substance misuse; increasing employment opportunities and health through work; and stopping smoking.

Hull and East Riding HAZ is developing a schools mental health programme to build self-esteem and tackle bullying and behavioural problems. Leeds HAZ has a drop-in teenage health service involving education, primary and community healthcare youth workers.

HAZ guidelines

Merseyside HAZ produces guidelines for its small grants scheme. It advises:

'HAZ is *not* about:
- A pot of money to be bid against
- Short term peripheral 'projects'
- Doing things the way they have always been done
- Replacing funding for mainstream activities
- Providing a time-limited exit strategy for existing projects
- Isolating the HAZ programme from the local Health Improvement Programme
- A "stand alone" initiative working in isolation

HAZ is about:
- Changing the way our partner organisations work
- Experimenting with new ways of working
- Learning from experience and sharing the learning across Merseyside and beyond
- Involving local communities and front-line staff
- Ensuring better access to services/facilities for marginalised groups
- Doing things which make a difference to the lives of disadvantaged people
- Value for money'

The HAZ Innovations Fund is supporting the 'Let's Get Serious' project to help 160 boys aged 8–16 who are in danger of being marginalised from society through educational underachievement and high drug use. 30 previously unemployed adult mentors are used by the project with support from other staff.

HAZ partnerships include a combination of local bodies including the NHS, local authorities, voluntary and private sector organisations and community groups. Initiatives are determined by the partnership, but focus on two strategic objectives:
- to identify and address the public health needs of the local area, and in particular developing new ways to tackle health inequalities;

- to modernise services by increasing their effectiveness, efficiency and responsiveness.

HAZs also contribute to the development of local strategic partnerships (LSPs), and in some areas HAZs are playing a leading role in LSP formation.

HAZ initiatives and funding arrangements differ greatly from area to area. Some have small dedicated community funding schemes. These include:
- Lambeth, Southwark and Lewisham has a Healthy Living Fund totalling £1.5 million which will be allocated by March 2002.
- Merseyside HAZ can give a small number of grants up to £1,000 to community groups working in

particular fields. The Disabled Children's Participation Group was supported with training to enable disabled young children to run consultation exercises and the YMCA was helped with exercise equipment costs to expand their work in schools.

- Tyne & Wear HAZ established a communities fund totalling £150,000 for a nominated area of North Tyneside.
- Wolverhampton HAZ makes grants of between £100 and £500 to community groups to increase participation in health concerns.

In some areas, HAZs will target a particular age group and develop specific projects. South Yorkshire Coalfields HAZ has developed an allotment project through a Community Food programme. A committee of young people manages the project.

The HAZ website includes information on both the Children and Young People network and the Community Involvement network which are two areas of activity that are likely to be of interest to those working with young people and looking to work in partnership with HAZs.

Applications: For information on local priorities and arrangements, contact the HAZ directly.

Bradford HAZ, Tel: 01274 366132
Brent HAZ, Tel: 020 8966 1060
Bury and Rochdale HAZ,
   Tel: 0161 762 3125
Camden & Islington HAZ,
   Tel: 020 7853 5536
Cornwall & Isles of Scilly HAZ,
   Tel: 01726 627888
East London and City HAZ,
   Tel: 020 7655 6623

Hull & East Riding HAZ,
   Tel: 01482 672070
Lambeth, Southwark & Lewisham HAZ,
   Tel: 020 7716 7000
Leeds HAZ, Tel: 0113 295 2001
Leicester HAZ, Tel: 0116 258 8693
Luton HAZ, Tel: 01582 657591
Manchester, Salford & Trafford HAZ,
   Tel: 0161 912 1271
Merseyside HAZ, Tel: 0151 285 2340
North Cumbria HAZ, Tel: 01900 324134
North Staffordshire HAZ,
   Tel: 01782 298084
Northumberland HAZ,
   Tel: 01670 394455
Nottingham HAZ, Tel: 0115 912 3324
Plymouth HAZ, Tel: 01752 515470
Sandwell HAZ, Tel: 0121 500 1669
Sheffield HAZ, Tel: 0114 271 1311
South Yorkshire Coalfields HAZ,
   Tel: 01302 320111 ext 3203/4
Tees HAZ, Tel: 01642 304132
Tyne & Wear HAZ, Tel: 0191 461 9200
Wakefield HAZ, Tel: 0192 421 3154
Walsall HAZ, Tel: 01922 720255
Wolverhampton HAZ,
   Tel: 01902 444968

Other resources

Two other area based initiatives that may include support to organisations working with young people are Education Action Zones and Sport Action Zones. Both initiatives respond to local needs and have local policies. Contact: www.standards.dfes.gov.uk/eaz for information on education action zones, and www.sportengland.org for information on Sports Action Zones.

COMBATING DISADVANTAGE

The Children's Fund

Children and Young People's Unit, AE,
Caxton House, 6–12 Tothill Street,
London SW1H 9NA
Fax: 020 7273 5657
E-mail: CYPU.MAILBOX@dfee.gov.uk
Website: www.dfee.gov.uk/cypu

This programme focuses on children and
young people in the most deprived areas
of England. It is administered by the
Children and Young People's Unit which
is located within the DfES and 'carries a
cross-departmental brief for children and
young people'. The fund is worth £450
million in total over three years and is
split into two parts:

- the Children's Fund: preventative
  services (totalling £380 million) will
  be distributed through local
  partnerships;
- the Children's Fund Local Network
  (£70 million available) will be
  distributed in small grants to voluntary
  groups working with young people
  and children living with disadvantage
  and in poverty.

The Children's Fund (prevention)

The Children's Fund (prevention) will
initially cover 40 of the most deprived
areas of England over a three year period.
The coverage of the Fund increased with
a further two waves covering another
109 areas. Funds will be received in 2002
and will run until 2004. Confirmation of
funding beyond this period will be given
in the light of the next government
spending round. 'However, planning for
the partnerships and the subsequent

service delivery represents an ideal
opportunity for interested organisations
to make contact and get involved.' The
government regional offices will be the
first point of contact for interested
organisations. (Contact details below.)

Partnership plans from the first wave
areas were submitted and assessed in
summer 2001 and contained proposals
which included:

- mentoring programmes
- out of school activities
- behaviour support for children
- support for children of asylum seeking
  and travelling families
- parenting support
- community development initiatives,
  including the use of volunteering and
  community groups in service delivery
- multi-agency working within and
  between statutory agencies and the
  voluntary and community sectors.

The Children's Fund is aimed at children
and young people aged 5–13 at risk of
social exclusion. (The Local Fund
Network can support voluntary groups
working with children and young people
up to the age of 19.) The over-arching
objective of the Children's Fund between
2001 and 2004 is to 'provide additional
resources over and above those provided
through mainstream, statutory, specific
programmes and through the specific
earmarked funding streams. It should
engage and support voluntary and
community organisations in playing an
active part and should enable the full
range of services to work together to
help children overcome poverty and
disadvantage.'

Two further objectives are outlined:

- to ensure that in each area there is an
  agreed programme of effective
  interventions that pick up on early

signs of difficulties, identify needs and introduce children and young people and their families to appropriate services;

- to ensure that children and young people who have experienced early signs of difficulties receive appropriate services in order to gain maximum life-chance benefits from education opportunities, health care and social care.

There are seven sub-objectives outlined in the Part 2 Guidance notes to the Children's Fund. These are:

- to promote attendance in schools attended by the majority of the 5–13 year olds in the area;
- to achieve overall improved educational performance among children and young people aged 5–13;
- to ensure that fewer young people aged between 10 and 13 commit crime and fewer children between 5 and 13 are victims of crime;
- to reduce child health inequalities among those children and young people aged 5–13 who live within the area;
- to ensure that children, young people, their families and local people feel that the preventative services being developed through the partnerships are accessible;
- to develop services which are experienced as effective by individual and clusters of children, young people and families commonly excluded from gaining the benefits of public services that are intended to support children and young people at risk of social exclusion from achieving their potential;
- to involve families in building the community's capacity to sustain the programme and thereby create pathways out of poverty.

This last sub-objective acknowledges the importance of building community capacity and supporting local networks to enable them to carry out the objectives of the Children's Fund. Part 2 of the Guidance states: 'Consideration needs to be given to the effect on community groups and small local voluntary bodies of participation. They are often very stretched with single staff members having multiple roles. To add on contributing to a partnership or planning service developments would be impossible without compensatory investment in cash or kind. Partnerships may wish to consider building this into their proposals.'

Details are available in Part One Guidance and Part Two Guidance (available from the address above, or can be downloaded from the website). These documents detail how partnerships should be constituted (with the usual conditions on local representation) and examples of types of services they might develop. They should also indicate the extent of collaborative working with other local initiatives such as: Sure Start; Connexions; Quality Protects; Early Years Partnerships and Childcare Partnerships; Youth Offending Teams; Excellence in Cities; Education Action Zones and Health Action Zones.

Plans will also need to refer to Local Strategic Partnerships; Neighbourhood Renewal Strategies and Children's Services Plans.

The Children and Young People's Unit have released indicative planning figures as guidance for how much is available overall in each area from 2001 to 2004 per wave. The precise level of funding will not be known until partnership proposals have been submitted and assessed.

Regional allocations: wave 1

East (Total £6.3 million)
Norfolk £6.3 million

East Midlands (Total £15 million)
Leicester £4.8 million
Lincolnshire £5.1 million
Nottingham £5.1 million

London (Total £32.55 million)
Camden £2.4 million
Greenwich £3.87 million
Hackney £4.2 million
Haringey £4.23 million
Islington £2.7 million
Newham £5.7 million
Southwark £4.35 million
Tower Hamlets £5.1 million

North East (Total £16.59 million)
Gateshead £2.4 million
Hartlepool £1.5 million
Middlesbrough £2.4 million
Newcastle upon Tyne £3.6 million
Stockton-on-Tees £2.1 million
Sunderland £4.59 million

North West (Total £53.4 million)
Blackburn with Darwen £2.7 million
Blackpool £1.8 million
Bolton £3.6 million
Halton £1.8 million
Knowsley £3 million
Lancashire £12 million
Liverpool £8.4 million
Manchester £8.7 million
Oldham £4.11 million
Rochdale £3.99 million
Salford £3.3 million

South East (Total £14.13 million)
Kent £11.1 million
Portsmouth £3.03 million

South West (Total £10.14 million)
Bristol £4.83 million
Cornwall £5.31 million

West Midlands (Total £22.83 million)
Birmingham £18 million
Sandwell £4.83 million

Yorkshire and the Humber
(Total £30.48 million)
Bradford £8.25 million
Doncaster £3.9 million
Kingston upon Hull £4.5 million
Leeds £7.8 million
Sheffield £6.03 million

Regional allocations: wave 2

East (Total £5.64 million)
Luton £2.2 million
Suffolk £3.46 million

East Midlands (Total 15.22 million)
Derby £2 million
Derbyshire £3.8 million
Northamptonshire £3.62 million
Nottinghamshire £4.4 million
Peterborough £1.4 million

London (Total £14.5 million)
Barking and Dagenham £1.6 million
Brent £2.5 million
Hammersmith and Fulham £1.2 million
Lambeth £2.6 million
Lewisham £2.2 million
Waltham Forest £1.4 million
Wandsworth £1.4 million
Westminster £1 million

North East (Total £10.38 million)
County Durham £3.8 million
Darlington £0.8 million
North Tyneside £1.4 million
Northumberland £1.8 million
Redcar and Cleveland £1.2 million
South Tyneside £1.4 million

North West (Total £15.34 million)
Sefton £2 million
Cheshire £3.2 million
Cumbria £2.6 million
St Helens £1.4 million
Tameside £1.8 million

Trafford £1.2 million
Wirral £3.14 million

South East (Total £8.63 million)
Brighton and Hove £2.02 million
East Sussex £2.6 million
Isle of Wight £0.8 million
Medway £1.6 million
Southampton £1.6 million

South West (Total £11.83 million)
Bournemouth £0.8 million
Bristol £4.83 million
Devon £3.6 million
Plymouth £1.8 million
Torbay £0.8 million

West Midlands (Total £12.1 million)
Coventry £2.4 million
Solihull £1.7 million
Stoke-on-Trent £2.2 million
Telford and Wrekin £1.2 million
Walsall £2.4 million
Wolverhampton £2.2 million

*Yorkshire and the Humber
(Total £13.82 million)*
Barnsley £1.8 million
Calderdale £1.4 million
Kirklees £3.2 million
North East Lincolnshire £1.4 million
North Lincolnshire £1 million
North Yorkshire £2.82 million

Regional Allocations: wave 3
East (Total £7 million)
Cambridgeshire £1 million
Essex £3.1 million
Hertfordshire £2 million
Southend-on-Sea £0.5 million
Thurrock £0.4 million

East Midlands (Total £1.14 million)
Leicestershire £1.1 million
Rutland £40,000

London (Total £9.2 million)
Barnet £0.7 million
Bexley £0.5 million

Bromley £0.6 million
Croydon £1.1 million
Ealing £1 million
Enfield £1 million
Harrow £0.4 million
Havering £0.5 million
Hillingdon £0.6 million
Hounslow £0.7 million
Kensington and Chelsea £0.3 million
Kingston upon Thames £0.2 million
Merton £0.4 million
Redbridge £0.7 million
Richmond upon Thames £0.2 million
Sutton £0.3 million

South East (Total £9.3 million)
Bedfordshire £0.8 million
Bracknell Forest £0.1 million
Buckinghamshire £0.8 million
Hampshire £2.4 million
Milton Keynes £0.6 million
Oxfordshire £1.1 million
Slough £0.4 million
Surrey £1.3 million
West Berkshire £1.4 million
West Sussex £1.4 million
Windsor and Maidenhead £0.1 million
Wokingham £0.1 million

South West (Total £5.7 million)
Bath and East Somerset £0.3 million
Dorset £0.8 million
Gloucestershire £1.2 million
North Somerset £0.3 million
Poole £0.3 million
Somerset £1.2 million
South Gloucestershire £0.4 million
Swindon £0.4 million
Wiltshire 0.8 million
Yorkshire and the Humber (Total
£2.3 million)

East Riding of Yorkshire £0.7 million
York £0.4 million
Wakefield £1.2 million

Applications: There is a Children's
Fund (prevention) coordinator in each of

the Government Offices, and these should be the first local contact for voluntary groups looking for further information.

Government Office – East:
Philip White, Victory House, Vision Park, Histon, Cambs CB4 9ZR
Tel: 01223 202001
E-mail: pwhite.go-east@go-regions.gsi.gov.uk

Government Office – East Midlands:
Russell Coughtrey, The Belgrave Centre, Stanley Place, Talbot Street Nottingham NG1 5GG
Tel: 0115 971 2694
E-mail: rcoughtrey.goem@go-regions.gsi.gov.uk

Government Office – London:
Brenda Pearson, 4th Floor, Riverwalk House, 157–161 Millbank, London SW1P 4RR
Tel: 020 7217 3306
E-mail: bpearson.gol@go-regions.gsi.gov.uk

Government Office – North East:
Tony Batty, Wellbar House, Gallowgate, Newcastle upon Tyne NE1 5TD
Tel: 0191 202 3623
E-mail: tbatty.gone@go-regions.gsi.gov.uk

Government Office – North West:
Pam Flynn, Cunard Building, Pier Head, Water Street, Liverpool L3 1QB
Tel: 0151 224 2928
E-mail: pflynn.gonw@go-regions.gsi.gov.uk

Government Office – South East:
Derek Fisher, Bridge House, 1 Walnut Tree Close, Guildford, Surrey GU1 4GA
Tel: 01483 882264
E-mail: dfisher.gose@go-regions.gsi.gov.uk

Government Office – South West:
Ian Chancellor, 5th Floor, The Pithay, Bristol BS1 2PB
Tel: 0117 900 1844
E-mail: ichancellor.gosw@go-regions.gsi.gov.uk

Government Office – West Midlands:
Sue Naughton, 77 Paradise Circus, Queensway, Birmingham B1 2DT
Tel: 0121 212 5406
E-mail: snaughton.gowm@go-regions.gsi.gov.uk

Government Office – Yorkshire and the Humber:
Roy Porritt, PO Box 213, City House, New Station Street Leeds LS1 4US
Tel: 0113 283 5252
E-mail: rporritt.goyh@go-regions.gsi.gov.uk

The Children's Fund Local Network

17 areas across England have been allocated further funding from 2001 though the Children's Fund Local Network. £70 million is available through this network in small grants to local voluntary and community groups tackling poverty and disadvantage among children and young people aged 0–19.

The Local Network will be established over three years and by 2003/4 some funding will be available in areas of England. The first year's funding will focus on the areas with the highest levels of need and disadvantage amongst children and young people.

Local network projects are funded under four themes:

- *Aspirations and experiences* – projects to give children experiences, or help them achieve goals that more privileged children may take for granted. Examples of early grants include: £2,150 given to buy equipment for a musical workshop for disadvantaged young people; and £5,000 to pay for equipment and activities costs for young people participating in orienteering and canoeing.

- *Economic disadvantage* – projects to help families improve their living standards and cope with the difficulties that come from living on low incomes. An example of an early grant was £900 to support a project running a mobile toy library providing toys for families on low incomes. Several grants of around £5,000–£7,000 have been made to YouthBanks to help young people gain experience of grant-making.
- *Isolation and access* – projects to help children who are isolated or alone, or have trouble connecting with services that can help them. An example of a grant is £3,000 given to buy IT equipment for a rural community outreach project helping young people.
- *Children's voices* – projects to give children and young people a chance to express their opinions and to give advice on matters that concern them. Examples of grants given to projects include: £6,000 given to a group of children living in an area of high poverty to make a film with professional support telling the stories of children in their local area; and £7,000 for a project for children and young people living in refuges to express their views on the support they need.

Grants range between £250 and £7,000 and are distributed locally by local grant makers. By April 2004, the local network will include around 50 funds. The Community Foundation Network has been appointed to work locally with bodies such as rural community councils and grant-making trusts to provide an experienced fund administrator in each area. Grants decisions are made by local assessment panels; the Children and Young People's Unit will not be funding projects directly. Further information, including details of each local network fund administrator, is available on the website.

Local network areas for 2001/2002

- Birmingham and Solihull
- The Black Country (Sandwell, Walsall and Dudley, Wolverhampton)
- Cornwall (Cornwall with Isles of Scilly)
- East Norfolk
- East Sussex (Brighton and Hove, East Sussex)
- Greater Manchester (Bolton, Bury, Manchester, Oldham, Rochdale, Salford, Stockport, Tameside, Trafford, Wigan)
- Humberside (East Riding, Kingston upon Hull, North Lincolnshire, North East Lincolnshire)
- Lancashire (Blackpool and Blackburn, Lancashire)
- Leicestershire (Leicester and Leicestershire)
- London (All boroughs)
- Merseyside/Halton (Halton, Knowsley, Liverpool, St Helens, Sefton, Wirral)
- North East Tees Valley (Darlington, Hartlepool, Middlesbrough, Redcar and Cleveland, Stockton–on–Tees)
- Nottinghamshire (Nottingham and Nottinghamshire)
- Tyne and Wear (Gateshead, Newcastle upon Tyne, North Tyneside, South Tyneside, Sunderland)
- South East Kent (Kent, Medway)
- South Yorkshire (Barnsley, Rotherham, Sheffield)
- West Yorkshire (Bradford, Calderdale, Leeds, Wakefield)

Applications: Details of local fund administrators are available from the DfES, the Community Foundation Network or from local councils of voluntary service. Organisations can contact the Local Network Call Centre on 0845 1130161 for information and an application pack. The Community Foundation Network website: www.communityfoundations.org.uk also has details of the Local Fund Network.

COMMUNITY SAFETY AND YOUTH JUSTICE

Communities Against Drugs Initiative

Action Against Drugs Unit, Home Office, 50 Queen Anne's Gate, London SW1H 9AT
Tel: 020 7273 2346
Website: www.crimereduction.gov.uk

The Communities Against Drugs programme was launched in spring 2001. £220 million over three years has been allocated to local police and community partnerships to counteract the effects of drug-related crime. A further £15 million over three years has been directed towards the 150 Drug Action Teams, and £5 million to a Positive Futures programme to use sport as an alternative to anti-social behaviour, crime and drug use among 10–16 year olds.

Local communities through Crime and Disorder Partnerships will be able to identify ways to tackle drug problems in their areas. Allocations to areas have been made on the basis of the incidence of drug-related crime with regions receiving the following amounts for the first year:

East Midlands	£4,125,400
Eastern	£4,499,500
London	£7,514,600
North East	£2,508,100
North West	£7,012,400
South East	£6,881,600
West Midlands	£5,235,700
Yorkshire and Humberside	£4,930,700

Although only the first year's allocation had been announced at the time of writing, year 2 and year 3 allocations are likely to be at a similar level.

Voluntary organisations working with young people should contact their local Crime and Disorder Partnership for detailed plans of how the programme is to be developed in their area. There may be scope for organisations working with young people to develop personal and social development activities such as sport, art and IT as an alternative to drugs use for those young people most at risk of becoming involved. This could support local plans under Communities Against Drugs programme.

The Positive Futures programme is administered by the UK Anti-Drugs Coordination Unit, The Youth Justice Board and Sport England.

Applications: Organisations should contact their local Crime and Disorder Partnership and the regional Home Office Crime Reduction Teams (for local information and policy). These can be contacted through the regional government offices, .

Positive Futures

Action Against Drugs Unit, Home Office, 50 Queen Anne's Gate, London SW1H 9AT
Tel: 020 7273 4504 **Fax:** 020 7273 3821
Contact: The National Coordinator

Positive Futures is part of the Communities Against Drugs Initiative. The programme is jointly funded by the UK Anti-Drugs Co-ordination Unit, Sport England and the Youth Justice Board. £5 million over two years has been directed towards reducing drugs use, crime and anti-social behaviour among 10–16 year olds. In the first year (2001–2002), almost £1 million has been allocated to the programme.

Positive Futures aims to:
- reduce young offending in the area of the project;
- reduce drug use among the target group of 10–16 year olds;
- increase participation in sport by 10–16 year olds.

It is intended that this will be achieved by projects promoting the use of sport as an alternative activity for those most at risk of drugs misuse; training and mentoring programmes; the development of leadership skills using sport and educational programmes; and the promotion of sports participation and healthy lifestyles.

There are currently 24 projects with a further 80 planned. Projects are administered by local partnerships of youth offending teams, Sport England regional offices, local authorities and sporting and non-sporting organisations. Core elements of any project will be:
- a clear focus on 10–16 year olds who are disaffected;
- a sporting activity programme with links to 'mainstream sport';

- an inclusion programme including drug prevention, social inclusion and social responsibility;
- an education and training programme around long-term lifestyle attitudes and healthy living.

Areas where projects are taking place include: Barking, Bolton, Bristol (Southmead), Derby, Gateshead, Hastings, Hull, North East Lincolnshire, Norwich, Nottingham, Oxford (Blackbird Leys and East Oxford), Plymouth, Portsmouth, Salford, Sheffield, Southampton, Southwark, Teeside (Hartlepool, Middlesbrough, Stockton, Redcar and Cleveland), Walsall, West Midlands (Kings Norton and Sandwell), Wolverhampton.

Applications: In the first instance, contact the National Co-ordinator for details of the programme.

Drugscope Millennium Awards

DrugScope, 32 Loman Street, London SE1 0EE
Tel: 020 7928 1211 **Fax:** 020 7928 1771
E-mail: services@drugscope.org.uk
Website: www.drugscope.org.uk

The DrugScope Millennium Awards Scheme is funded by the Millennium Commission and supported by the Home Office Drugs Prevention Advisory Service and the Mentor Foundation (UK). The scheme is run by the national drugs charity, DrugScope.

Grants of between £1,000 and £3,500 will be given to individual award winners to fund practical activities which tackle any aspect of drug use or misuse. It is intended that around 500 awards will be made over the three years of the scheme.

DrugScope suggests that appropriate projects could include 'developing drug prevention initiatives including diversion schemes, establishing community support groups or training to become a peer educator'.

It is hoped that applications will be submitted by young people, black and minority ethnic groups, ex-offenders, current or ex-drug users and other residents looking for solutions to drug use in their neighbourhood. Local networks working with target groups will be used to encourage applications.

Applications: Contact DrugScope for further information.

Youth Justice Board

11 Carteret Street, London SW1H 9DL
Tel: 020 7271 3033 **Fax:** 020 7271 3020
E-mail: enquiries@yjb.gsi.gov.uk
Website: www.youth-justice-board.
gov.uk
Contact: Tom Ellis, Grants
Administration Manager

The Youth Justice Board aims to prevent children and young people from offending. (The following information relates only to its Community Intervention initiatives, and does not include information on funding opportunities that relate to Secured Facilities.) In 1999/2000 it allocated £85 million for three years under the development fund to a number of measures to support this aim. In subsequent years it has launched several additional funding rounds in a number of areas of youth justice work.

Although some of the YJB's activities such as bail supervision are administered by local authorities, there are

opportunities for voluntary organisations working to fulfil the YJB's aim of intervention to reduce the risk of re-offending.

Intervention measures where voluntary organisations may be able to apply for support are in the following areas:
- alcohol, drug and substance misuse
- cognitive behaviour
- education, training and employment
- mentoring
- parenting
- prevention
- restorative justice
- accommodation
- mental health
- street crime
- and a variety of preventative work.

The YJB also runs a number of early preventative programmes:
- the Youth Inclusion Programme (YIP) which works with around 50 young people who are most at risk in 70 of the most deprived neighbourhoods in England and Wales;
- Splash schemes that focus on 13 to 17 year olds at risk in high crime neighbourhoods, and provide activities in Easter and Summer holidays to help reduce crime;
- Positive Futures (see page 303) which uses sport to reduce anti-social behaviour; crime and drug misuse among 10 to 16 year olds in selected neighbourhoods.

Examples of support for voluntary organisations' intervention projects
The following projects received three years' support from the YJB development fund, and have secured local partnership funding to match the YJB grant.
- £224,300 to Tardis Youth Project and Lifeline, West Yorkshire to contact

young people to work on drug abuse concerns;

- £156,000 to Barnardos North West for their work with young people with abusive sexual behaviour patterns;
- £148,500 to INCLUDE, County Durham for work experience, education and vocational training, and personal and social development for 14 to 16 year olds at risk.

In October 2001 the small bids round under the development fund awarded three year grants to voluntary organisations which included:

- £79,600 to Coram Family for their boys2MEN Phoenix Project for self development;
- £61,200 to the Brandon Centre for Counselling and Psychotherapy for Young People to run a mental health scheme in Haringey and Islington.

Awards under the intensive mentoring for minority ethnic young offenders, and mentoring help with numeracy and literacy rounds, included:

- £165,300 to the Black Partnerships, Advocacy, Learning and Mentoring (Black PALM) to run an intensive mentoring project in Sheffield, Rotherham, Doncaster and Barnsley;
- £90,000 to Crime Concern's Mentoring Plus Manchester project to help with numeracy and literacy.

The Youth Justice Board has had ten grants rounds so far including themes such as mentoring and adult volunteering schemes. The YJB's most recent grants round was completed in September 2001 and was aimed at voluntary organisations to run projects to prevent youth offending in the fields of accommodation; mental health; preventative work; and street crime.

There was a particular focus on less established organisations, and those who had not yet received YJB support.

Funding has often been given for three years, after which continuation funding is to be found locally. The YJB does not give guidance about continuation funding, and will require plans to be in place concerning how the project will continue.

There are no plans for further rounds of funding for voluntary organisations until the publishing of the Government Spending Plan in 2002. Details will be published on the YJB website. In each case, endorsement by the local Youth Offending Team (see below) will be essential in an applicant's approach for funding.

Youth Offending Teams

The YJB works with 154 Youth Offending Teams (YOTs). Each YOT is responsible for an average budget of £500,000, made up of contributions from partner agencies: the police, probation services, social services, education, health, the local authority chief executive and other additional funding such as YJB, and SRB.

As well as working with national priorities, the YOT determines local priorities working with Crime and Disorder Partnerships. Local priorities are usually related to the needs of local young people and linked to offending, such as prevention. The YOTs also have other local targets which are for example related to the Quality Protects initiatives.

Some of the YOT's budget from partner agencies may be earmarked for certain initiatives but the YOTs also have a pooled budget which is made up of contributions form one or more agencies. This budget is under the delegated control of the YOT a manager/ Head of Youth Offending Services.

Applications: The YJB funding initiatives vary according to the conditions of the programme. A typical cycle for funding rounds for voluntary organisations would be:

- a consultancy paper is distributed to selected voluntary organisations for comment;
- application details are provided to YOTs, umbrella voluntary organisations and potential applicants, and details are posted on the YJB website and advertised in the press and journals;
- applications are submitted within three months of the details being posted;
- applicants are notified around six weeks after the application deadline.

The support of the local YOT will be essential for any voluntary organisation applying to the Development Fund. The contact in each case will be the YOT manager. The contact in each case will be the YOT manager. Local team contact details can be found on the website under the Youth Offending Team link, or by telephoning the above number.

LEARNING AND TRAINING

Adult and Community Learning Fund

This fund is now in its sixth round (the deadline for submission of bids was December 2001). The ACLF is a DfES funded programme to increase the participation in learning and improve basic skills. The fund is administered jointly by the National Institute of Adult Continuing Education (NIACE) and the Basic Skills Agency (BSA), and around 400 projects have received grants ranging from a few hundred pounds to over £100,000.

Examples of beneficiaries from Round 5

- £30,000 to the Depaul Trust, Newcastle, towards a basic skills and sport programme for young people aged 16–25;
- £8,800 to Tranmere Community Project, Merseyside to involve young people in personal development, IT and basic skills courses
- £30,800 to Bangladesh Youth and Cultural Shomiti, Leicester, to develop short courses for isolated Bangladeshi adults;
- £10,000 to Derby Changes to provide informal learning opportunities in arts, sports and recreational activities for young people who are leaving care;
- £30,000 to Charnwood Community Council, East Midlands, to use football to motivate young people, support leaders as community champions and encourage individual development;
- £37,500 to Shadwell Youth Action, London £37,500 for a youth based training programme with youth work leading to a national qualification.

Details of any further rounds will be announced on the website: www. lifelonglearning.co.uk/aclf

The two administering agencies will also have information. Contact:

The Basic Skills Agency (BSA)
Commonwealth House, 1–19 New Oxford Street, London WC1A 1NU
Tel: 020 7405 4017 **Fax:** 020 7440 6626;
E-mail: enquiries@basic–skills.co.uk
Website: www.basic–skills.co.uk

National Institute of Adult Continuing Education (NIACE)
21 De Montfort Street, Leicester
LE1 7GE
Tel: 0116 204 4200 **Fax:** 0116 285 4514
E-mail: enquiries@niace.org.uk
Website: www.niace.org.uk

Connexions Service

Connexions Service National Unit,
W4b, Moorfoot, Sheffield S1 4PQ
Tel: 0114 259 3539
E-mail: connexions.funding@dfee.
gov.uk
Website: www.connexions.gov.uk

The government has allocated £420 million by the end of 2002/3 to create a new support service (to replace the careers service) to help young people aged 13–19 years with training and career choices. The resulting Connexions service was launched in 12 areas in April 2001 with a further three partnerships starting in September 2001.

There are now Connexions partnerships in 15 areas: the Black Country; Cheshire and Warrington; Cornwall and Devon; Coventry and Warwickshire; Cumbria; Greater Merseyside; Humberside; Lincolnshire and Rutland; Milton Keynes, Oxfordshire and Buckinghamshire; North London; Shropshire, Telford and the Wrekin; South London; South Yorkshire; Suffolk; and West of England.

Further partnerships are planned to start in April 2002 and the Connexions service will eventually cover the country. When the entire service is in place, 47 Connexions partnerships will be running to offer local services to young people in their areas.

The Connexions Service National Unit will allocate £420 million to Connexions partnerships in 2002/2003, increasing to £455 million in 2003/4. The Unit states: 'This grant funding is not the only funding available to the Connexions service. Partnerships must build on services that are delivered locally and co–ordinate, draw together and build on services that are already delivered locally.'

A further £15.9 million has also been allocated in development funding for 2001/2002 to help Connexions partnerships which have yet to start their local service. This support is for activities such as demonstration projects, implementing structures, consultation events involving young people and engaging voluntary and community organisations. The extent of development funding for each area varied according to local needs and the scale of the task that the partnership faced.

Those areas which have not yet set up a local Connexions partnership board could bid for between £40,000 to £60,000 development funding. As well as development funding to develop the new services, there was also funding to train Personal Advisers who will give advice and guidance to young people on post–16 job, training and careers options. Voluntary and community organisations were invited to be included in the training of personal advisers.

Each Connexions partnership works to address its local priorities, although there are elements common to all, such as:
- the involvement of young people (consultation, mapping, representation etc.);
- the role of Personal Advisers, their recruitment, training and support;

- the profile of Connexions services (high street presence, one–stop shops etc.);
- targeting of 'hard to reach' groups of young people (offenders, young people with disabilities or learning difficulties; young carers; English as a second language etc.);
- plans to involve the youth service and voluntary youth organisations;
- innovative uses of the arts, sport and IT;
- robust financial plans.

The role of voluntary and community organisations

The National Unit states: 'The involvement of the voluntary and community sectors is crucial to the success of Connexions and there are opportunities for them to be actively engaged'. In some partnerships, organisations are members of the partnership or have helped the service to develop locally by being involved in the consultation phase. It is expected that partnerships will research and map local services provided by voluntary and community organisations so that this can be incorporated into the development of Connexions locally.

When partnerships 'go live', there are opportunities for the voluntary and community sector to be involved in delivering the Connexions service locally. This may happen through the sub-contracting of services by the partnership, or by smaller groups who may not be able to be part of a contract, applying for small amounts of funding through the small grants scheme administered locally.

The National Unit states: 'Under this small grants scheme, partnerships can choose to make money available to those community groups they judge would make a valuable contribution to the Connexions services, but where the use of a formal contract would be a barrier to their involvement. They can allocate up to 5% of their grant funding form the Connexions Service National Unit to the scheme in any one year, and up to £30,000 for any one organisation in a year. The actual amount which will be awarded, within these limits, is at partnerships' own discretion. This money will usually be paid in arrears, after the activity to be paid for has taken place. However, there is some flexibility for payments to be made in advance if partnerships consider this appropriate.'

The small grants scheme must be used to fund activities that support the Connexions service and be closely linked to local priorities which are included in partnerships' business and delivery plans. Activities that are not related to delivering the Connexions service will not be funded. These small grants are not available for larger national voluntary and community sector organisations which are in a position to compete for contracts.

Connexions and the Devon Youth Association

An example of a voluntary organisation being included in the establishing of a Connexions partnership is that of Devon Youth Association. Over two years the association was involved in a range of activities alongside the Connexions development in Cornwall and Devon. In the first year during the pilot period the association contributed to a range of 'development and theme' groups including those on data exchange; the voluntary sector; development of the personal adviser; involving young people; care leavers; information; advice and support services; business planning and quality assurance. The association also signed up as a partner agency with their chair becoming a representative on the Connexions board.

As well as developmental work, the association was also commissioned by Connexions, Cornwall and Devon to:

- co-pilot work with care leavers, using mentoring and peer education approaches;
- co-lead young people's involvement in developing Connexions, including the development of the personal adviser role;
- facilitate young people's involvement in the development of information exchange and confidentiality;
- pilot Connexions linked rural one-stop shops;
- participate in developing the 'Sorted' survival guides.

Further work has been commissioned to:

- pilot the development of investors in young people (with young people trained and supported as quality assurance assessors);
- the provision of a mobile one-stop shop for Dartmoor;
- the development of one-stop shops across East Devon;
- the mapping of counselling services across Cornwall and Devon in schools and health and community facilities.

Throughout the pilot stage and the running of the partnership, personal advisers have worked with Devon Youth Association staff in their one–stop shops and have been involved in staff training.

Applications: Local organisations working with young people should contact their nearest partnership for information about local priorities and how voluntary sector activities might contribute to the Connexions service .

Contact details for partnership areas

Barnsley, Rotherham and Doncaster: 0800 169 9338
Black Country: 0800 252 972
Cheshire and Warrington: 0800 980 9877
Coventry and Warwickshire: 02476 607 906
Cumbria: 0800 435 709
Devon and Cornwall: 0800 975 5111
Greater Merseyside: 0151 709 0550
Humber: 0800 371 2623/0808 180 4636
Lincolnshire and Rutland: 0800 163 026
London Bromley: 020 8313 9500
London Croydon: 020 8401 0301
London Finchley: 020 8346 4509
London Edgware: 020 8381 0068
London Edmonton: 020 8807 5561
London Enfield: 020 8366 9586
London New Malden: 020 8410 4105
London Tottenham: 020 8808 0333
London Waltham Forrest: 020 8521 9020
Milton Keynes, Buckinghamshire and Oxfordshire: 01235 535319
Sheffield: 0800 652 9900
Shropshire, Telford & Wrekin: 0800 252 972
Suffolk: 01473 581405
West of England: 0800 923 0323

Learning and Skills Council

Cheylesmore House, Quinton Road, Coventry CV1 2WT
Tel: Helpline: 0870 900 6800; Other enquiries: 0845 019 4170
Fax: 024 7686 3112
E-mail: john.bolt@lsc.gov.uk
Website: www.lsc.gov.uk
Contact: John Bolt, Funding Manager, Eligibility

The Learning and Skills Council assumed responsibility for all post–16 education and training, replacing the Further Education and Funding Council (FEFC) and training and enterprise councils (TECs). £6 billion each year has been allocated to the council to cover around six million learners.

Training initiatives are the responsibility of two steering committees: The Adult Learning Committee and the Young Persons Learning Committee. Local training programmes are delivered by local LSCs which each have a budget of over £100 million. Voluntary organisations may be able to contribute to the implementation of these programmes, and should contact their local LSC officer to discuss proposals.

The Local Initiatives Fund

In addition to learning initiatives originating from local LSCs, there is also the Local Initiatives Fund (LIF). This will be administered by LSCs locally and will be open to agencies including community organisations which can support the LSCs' strategic aims. Each LSC will have a number of locally determined objectives which support the national priorities of:

- raising attainment particularly amongst the target group that lacks basic literacy and numeracy skills;
- increasing participation in post–16 education and training;
- improving the quality of education and training.

There is no timetable for this fund, and each bid is considered on merit. At the time of writing, the LSC was reviewing all of its funding arrangements. Existing arrangements will continue until the results of the review are announced, and further information will be available through the website or by contacting local LSCs.

Applications: Those working with young people should contact the Executive Director of the local LSC in the first instance for details of local priorities and initiatives.

Local LSCs
East Midlands
Derbyshire:
Tel: 0845 019 4183 **Fax:** 01332 292188
E-mail: derbyshireinfo@lsc.gov.uk

Leicestershire:
Tel: 0845 019 4177 **Fax:** 0116 228 1801
E-mail: leicestershireinfo@lsc.gov.uk

Lincolnshire and Rutland:
Tel: 0845 019 4178 **Fax:** 01522 561563
E-mail: lincsrutlandinfo@lsc.gov.uk

Northamptonshire:
Tel: 0845 019 4175 **Fax:** 01604 533046
E-mail: northantsinfo@lsc.gov.uk

Nottinghamshire:
Tel: 0845 019 4187 **Fax:** 0115 872 0002
E-mail: nottsinfo@lsc.gov.uk

East of England
Bedfordshire and Luton:
Tel: 0845 019 4160 **Fax:** 01234 843211
E-mail: bedsandlutoninfo@lsc.gov.uk

Cambridgeshire:
Tel: 0845 019 4196 **Fax:** 01733 890809
E-mail: cambridgeshireinfo@lsc.gov.uk

Essex:
Tel: 0845 019 4179 **Fax:** 01245 451430
E-mail: essexinfo@lsc.gov.uk

Hertfordshire:
Tel: 0845 019 4167 **Fax:** 01727 813443
E-mail: hertsinfo@lsc.gov.uk

Norfolk:
Tel: 0845 019 4173 **Fax:** 01603 218802
E-mail: norfolkinfo@lsc.gov.uk

Suffolk:
Tel: 0845 019 4180 **Fax:** 01473 883090
E-mail: suffolkinfo@lsc.gov.uk

London
London Central:
Tel: 0845 019 4144 **Fax:** 020 7896 8686
E-mail: londoncentralinfo@lsc.gov.uk

London East:
Tel: 0845 019 4151 **Fax:** 020 8929 3802
E-mail: londoneastinfo@lsc.gov.uk

London North:
Tel: 0845 019 4158 **Fax:** 020 8882 5931
E-mail: londonnorthinfo@lsc.gov.uk

London South:
Tel: 0845 019 4172 **Fax:** 020 8929 4706
E-mail: londonsouthinfo@lsc.gov.uk

London West:
Tel: 0845 019 4164 **Fax:** 020 8929 8403
E-mail: londonwestinfo@lsc.gov.uk

North West
Cheshire and Warrington:
Tel: 0845 019 4163 **Fax:** 01606 320082
E-mail: cheshireandwarringtoninfo@
lsc.gov.uk

Cumbria:
Tel: 0845 019 4159 **Fax:** 01900 733302
E-mail: cumbriainfo@lsc.gov.uk

Greater Manchester:
Tel: 0845 019 4142 **Fax:** 0161 261 0370
E-mail: GrManchesterinfo@lsc.gov.uk

Greater Merseyside:
Tel: 0845 019 4150 **Fax:** 0151 672 3533
E-mail: merseysideinfo@lsc.gov.uk

Lancashire:
Tel: 0845 019 4157 **Fax:** 01772 443002
E-mail: lancashireinfo@lsc.gov.uk

North East
County Durham:
Tel: 0845 019 4174 **Fax:** 01325 372302
E-mail: countydurhaminfo@lsc.gov.uk

Northumberland:
Tel: 0845 019 4185 **Fax:** 01670 706212
E-mail: northumberlandinfo@lsc.gov.uk

Tees Valley:
Tel: 0845 019 4166 **Fax:** 01642 232480
E-mail: teesvalleyinfo@lsc.gov.uk

Tyne and Wear:
Tel: 0845 019 4181 **Fax:** 0191 491 6159
E-mail: tyneandwearinfo@lsc.gov.uk

South East
Berkshire:
Tel: 0845 019 4147 **Fax:** 0118 975 3054
E-mail: berkshireinfo@lsc.gov.uk

Hampshire and Isle of Wight:
Tel: 0845 019 4182 **Fax:** 01329 237733
E-mail: hampshire-IOWinfo@lsc.gov.uk

Kent and Medway:
Tel: 0845 019 4152 **Fax:** 01732 841641
E-mail: kentandmedwayinfo@lsc.gov.uk

*Milton Keynes, Oxfordshire and
Buckinghamshire:*
Tel: 0845 019 4154 **Fax:** 01235 468200
E-mail: MKOBinfo@lsc.gov.uk

Surrey:
Tel: 0845 019 4145 **Fax:** 01483 755259
E-mail: surreyinfo@lsc.gov.uk

Sussex:
Tel: 0845 019 4184 **Fax:** 01273 783550
E-mail: sussexinfo@lsc.gov.uk

South West
Bournemouth, Dorset and Poole:
Tel: 0845 019 4148 **Fax:** 01202 299457
E-mail: bdpinfo@lsc.gov.uk

Devon and Cornwall:
Tel: 0845 019 4155 **Fax:** 01752 754040
E-mail: devonandcornwallinfo@
lsc.gov.uk

Gloucestershire:
Tel: 01452 450001 **Fax:** 01452 450002
E-mail: gloucestershireinfo@lsc.gov.uk

Somerset:
Tel: 0845 1019 4161 **Fax:** 01823 226074
E-mail: somersetinfo@lsc.gov.uk

West of England:
Tel: 0845 019 4168 **Fax:** 0117 922 6664
E-mail: WestofEnglandinfo@lsc.gov.uk

Wiltshire and Swindon:
Tel: 0845 019 4176 **Fax:** 01793 608003
E-mail: wiltswindon@lsc.gov.uk

West Midlands
Birmingham and Solihull:
Tel: 0845 019 4143 **Fax:** 0121 345 4503
E-mail: birminghamsolihullinfo@
lsc.gov.uk

The Black Country:
Tel: 0845 019 4186 **Fax:** 0121 345 3777
E-mail: blackcountryinfo@lsc.gov.uk

Coventry and Warwickshire:
Tel: 0845 019 4156 **Fax:** 024 7945 0242
E-mail: CWinfo@lsc.gov.uk

Herefordshire and Worcestershire:
Tel: 0845 019 4188 **Fax:** 01905 721403
E-mail: HWinfo@lsc.gov.uk

Shropshire:
Tel: 0845 019 4190 **Fax:** 01952 235556
E-mail: shropshireinfo@lsc.gov.uk

Staffordshire:
Tel: 0845 019 4149 **Fax:** 01782 463048
E-mail: staffordshireinfo@lsc.gov.uk

Yorkshire and Humberside
Humberside:
Tel: 0845 019 4153 **Fax:** 01482 213206
E-mail: humberinfo@lsc.gov.uk

North Yorkshire:
Tel: 0845 019 4146 **Fax:** 01904 690430
E-mail: northyorkshireinfo@lsc.gov.uk

South Yorkshire:
Tel: 0845 019 4171 **Fax:** 0114 275 2634
E-mail: southyorkshireinfo@lsc.gov.uk

West Yorkshire:
Tel: 0845 019 4169 **Fax:** 01274 444009
E-mail: westyorkshireinfo@lsc.gov.uk

REGENERATION

Coalfields Regeneration Trust

2 Portland Place, Spring Gardens,
Doncaster DN1 3DF
Tel: 01302 304400 **Fax:** 01302 304419
E-mail: info@coalfields-regen.org.uk
Website: www.coalfields-regen.org.uk

The Coalfields Regeneration Trust is an independent grant-making body. It was set up in 1999 as part of the government's response to alleviate problems in former coalfield areas and to promote the social and economic regeneration of the coalfields of England (and Wales and Scotland). It received further government funding of £45 million which becomes available in April 2002 to run until March 2005.

The trust has four offices in England covering the former coalfield areas. These are: Midlands and Kent; North East; North West; and Yorkshire. Each of the regional offices supports projects in deprived areas and will have details of the wards that are covered.

The trust supports voluntary and community organisations which are contributing to the regeneration of the coalfield areas. Grants can be for capital or revenue costs (up to two years) and can be up to 100% of the amount required. Although the trust does not require projects to match awards, there is an expectation that applicants will have gained additional funding wherever possible.

The types of application are:
- Small Grant Applications are for grants of up to £20,000. There is no minimum grant.
- Medium and Large Grant Applications are for voluntary and community organisations where the amount applied for is over £20,000. (Town, parish, community councils and schools can apply.)
- Partnership Applications for existing regional and national charities or agencies looking to develop a programme of projects in several coalfield areas or in several locations within one coalfield area.

The range of activities supported is extensive. Examples of recent awards include sports facilities, education projects, environmental, arts and cultural activities and work with young people. The trust states: 'Within each priority a good project could cost as little as £500 (or even less) or as much as £5 million.' The trust's objectives are set out in six priority areas:
- resourced and empowered communities – improving community facilities, access to welfare and debt services, community transport and community involvement in existing and new initiatives;
- enterprising communities – increasing the range, diversity and accessibility of local community businesses, start-up opportunities and local business compacts;
- lifelong learning communities – supporting and helping communities with access to education, employment, learning facilities and the developing of new skills;
- attractive communities – improving local environments, open spaces and

supporting community involvement in managing and providing housing;
- working communities – improving employment and access to employment opportunities by supporting intermediate labour market initiatives, New Deal and training opportunities;
- promoting good practice – helping to identify excellent projects, good ideas and activities that 'make a difference' and spread that knowledge throughout the coalfields in partnership with other agencies.

These priorities will remain in the next phase of the trust's grantmaking, although there may be a particular emphasis placed on elements within the themes.

The trust will *not* fund:
- projects which are outside the trust's aims and objectives
- retrospective costs
- projects which are exclusively or primarily intended to promote religious beliefs
- projects which are properly the subject of statutory funding
- grants to individuals.

Examples of projects supported by CRT
- Shafton Youth and Community Group – £160,000 to establish a summer camp scheme for 16 year old school leavers
- Young Women's Christian Association –£97,800 for a trainer, women's worker, childcare and IT equipment
- Chrysalis Youth Project – £73,800 to support 10 trainees in work placements, and £69,000 to contribute towards the building of a go-kart track

- 3rd East Kirkby Scout Group – £52,800 to refurbish and extend the scout hut
- Friends of Warsop Youth Club – £41,800 for a youth development worker and office equipment
- Scouts Association (Yorkshire) – £19,600 for a septic tank, roadway and car park
- Focus on Young People in Bassetlaw – £11,700 for two youth street workers
- Fitzwilliam Tigers BMX – £6,700 for fencing around a BMX track
- Biddulph Skater Hockey Club – £6,000 for facility hire and safety equipment
- Normanton Parish Church – £4,500 for a youth worker
- Peterlee Youth Centre –£4,000 for an education trip for young people
- South Elmsall Piscatorial Youth Section – £2,400 for IT equipment

Applications: Application forms are available from the regional offices below. Regional offices can also give information and advice to potential applicants to guide them through the process.

A small grants form should be completed for amounts of less than £20,000. A more detailed application form is required for larger amounts. Applicants should include with the small grants form a constitution, trusts deed or rules; recent accounts; signature of a local independent referee and an organisation and project description. Applications are assessed at the head office.

Regional offices

Midlands/Kent
Ian Campbell, Regional Development Worker, 1st Floor, 42 High Street, Coalville, Leicestershire LE67 3EG
Tel: 01530 510456 **Fax:** 01530 510678

North East
Jen McKevitt, Regional Development Worker, Room 9, The Eco Centre, Windmill Way, Hebburn, Tyne & Wear NE31 1SR
Tel: 0191 428 5550 **Fax:** 0191 428 5005

North West
Kate Williams, Regional Development Worker, Bold Business Centre, Bold Lane, Sutton, St Helens WA9 4TX
Tel: 01925 222066 **Fax:** 01925 229315

Yorkshire
Andy Lock, Regional Development Worker, 3 Portland Place, Spring Gardens, Doncaster, South Yorkshire DN1 3DF
Tel: 01302 304400 **Fax:** 01302 304419

Community Chests

Neighbourhood Renewal Unit, Regeneration Directorate, Eland House, Bressenden Place, London SW1E 5DU
Tel: 020 7944 8383 **Fax:** 020 7944 8319
E-mail: neighbourhoodrenewal@dtlr.gsi.gov.uk
Website: www.dtlr.gsi.gov.uk
Contact: Philip Graham, Community Participation Team

The DTLR has allocated £50 million over three years to the development of Community Chests as part of the government's national strategy for Neighbourhood Renewal. Community Chests are available in the 88 deprived areas where the Neighbourhood Renewal Fund (NRF) operates, and are aimed at involving communities in local regeneration.

Neighbourhood Renewal Fund areas
- East England (Luton, Great Yarmouth)
- East Midlands (Ashfield, Bolsover, Derby, Leicester, Lincoln, Mansfield)

- London (Barking and Dagenham, Brent, Camden, Croydon, Ealing, Enfield, Greenwich, Hackney, Hammersmith and Fulham, Haringey, Islington, Kensington and Chelsea, Lambeth, Lewisham, Newham, Southwark, Tower Hamlets, Waltham Forest, Wandsworth, Westminster)
- North East (Derwentside, Easington, Gateshead, Hartlepool, Middlesbrough, Newcastle-upon-Tyne, North Tyneside Redcar and Cleveland, Sedgefield, South Tyneside, Stockton-on-Tees, Sunderland, Wansbeck, Wear Valley)
- North West (Allerdale, Barrow-in-Furness, Blackburn with Darwen, Blackpool, Bolton, Burnley, Halton Borough, Hyndburn, Knowsley, Liverpool, Manchester, Oldham, Pendle, Preston, Rochdale, St Helens, Salford, Sefton, Tameside, Wigan, Wirral)
- South East (Brighton and Hove, Hastings, Portsmouth, Southampton)
- South West (Bristol, Kerrier, Penwith, Plymouth)
- West Midlands (Birmingham, Coventry, Dudley, Nuneaton and Bedworth, Sandwell, Stoke-on-Trent, Walsall, Wolverhampton)
- Yorkshire and Humber (Barnsley, Bradford, Doncaster, Kingston upon Hull, Kirklees, Leeds, Rotherham, Sheffield, Wakefield)

In each of the 88 areas the local community will determine how Community Chests are spent. Government Offices will, however, oversee the Community Chest programme in their local area and appoint a local voluntary sector organisation to administer the programme.

The criteria for allocating the funds will be flexible to ensure that they respond to a community's needs. Examples of support might include printing a community newsletter, hiring a room to hold a first meeting, buying toys for a creche to enable parents to participate in community meetings and renovating premises for use as a group's headquarters.

In the first year (2001/02) a total of £10 million will be available, with £15 million in 2002/03, rising to £25 million in 2003/04. Around £50,000 was given in the first year to each of the 88 areas, and at least £75,000 will be given each subsequent year. (Government offices will have details of the allocation for their area.) Each community will decide the exact level of grant to be given, but individual grants will generally be between £50 and £5,000.

Applications: Contact the government office for the regions for details of local arrangements.

Government Office for East England
Tel: 01223 202000 Fax: 01223 202020
Website: www.go-east.gov.uk

Government Office for East Midlands
Tel: 0115 971 9971 Fax: 0115 971 2404
Website: www.go-em.gov.uk

Government Office for London
Tel: 020 7217 3456 Fax: 020 7217 3450
Website: www.go-london.gov.uk

Government Office for North East
Tel: 0191 201 3300 Fax: 0191 202 3744
E-mail: general.enquiries.gone@go-regions.gov.uk
Website: www.go–ne.gov.uk

Government Office for North West
Manchester office:
Tel: 0161 952 4000 Fax: 0161 952 4099

Liverpool office:
Tel: 0151 224 6300 **Fax:** 0151 224 6470
Website: www.go-nw.gov.uk

Government Office for South East
Tel: 01483 882255 **Fax:** 01483 8822
Website: www.go-se.gov.uk

Government Office for South West
Bristol:
Tel: 0117 900 1700 **Fax:** 0117 900 1900
Cornwall:
Tel: 01209 312622 **Fax:** 01209 312628
Plymouth:
Tel: 01752 635000 **Fax:** 01752 227647
Website: www.gosw.gov.uk

Government Office for West Midlands
Tel: 0121 212 5050
Website: www.go-wm.gov.uk

Government Office for Yorkshire and the Humber
Tel: 0113 280 0600 **Fax:** 0113 244 4898
Website: www.goyh.gov.uk

Community Empowerment Fund

Neighbourhood Renewal Unit, Regeneration Directorate, Eland House, Bressenden Place, London SW1E 5DU
Tel: 020 7944 8383 **Fax:** 020 7944 8319
E-mail: neighbourhoodrenewal@dtlr. gsi.gov.uk
Website: www.dtlr.gsi.gov.uk
Contact: Philip Graham, Community Participation Team

The Community Empowerment Fund operates in the 88 deprived local authority areas covered by the NRF (see above) as part of the National Strategy for Neighbourhood Renewal. It supports community and voluntary sector involvement in Local Strategic Partnerships (LSPs).

The Community Empowerment Fund (CEF) may be used to support activities such as residents' meetings, outreach to canvas local residents' views and training to help residents take part in their Local Strategic Partnership.

The CEF totals £35 million over the three years 2001 to 2004, and each area received at least £300,000 in the first year. Government Offices for the Regions administer the fund, and appoint a voluntary sector organisation to distribute the funds.

Applications: Contact the government office for the regions for details of local arrangements:

Government Office for East England
Tel: 01223 202000 **Fax:** 01223 202020
Website: www.go-east.gov.uk

Government Office for East Midlands
Tel: 0115 971 9971 **Fax:** 0115 971 2404
Website: www.go-em.gov.uk

Government Office for London
Tel: 020 7217 3456 **Fax:** 020 7217 3450
Website: www.go-london.gov.uk

Government Office for North East
Tel: 0191 201 3300 **Fax:** 0191 202 3744
E-mail: general.enquiries.gone@ go-regions.gov.uk
Website: www.go-ne.gov.uk

Government Office for North West
Manchester office:
Tel: 0161 952 4000 **Fax:** 0161 952 4099
Liverpool office:
Tel: 0151 224 6300 **Fax:** 0151 224 6470
Website: www.go-nw.gov.uk

Government Office for South East
Tel: 01483 882255 **Fax:** 01483 8822
Website: www.go-se.gov.uk

Government Office for South West
Bristol:
Tel: 0117 900 1700 **Fax:** 0117 900 1900
Cornwall:
Tel: 01209 312622 **Fax:** 01209 312628
Plymouth:
Tel: 01752 635000 **Fax:** 01752 227647
Website: www.gosw.gov.uk

Government Office for West Midlands
Tel: 0121 212 5050
Website: www.go-wm.gov.uk

Government Office for Yorkshire and the Humber
Tel: 0113 280 0600 **Fax:** 0113 244 4898
Website: www.goyh.gov.uk

New Deal for Communities

Neighbourhood Renewal Unit, DTLR, Zone 4/A6, Eland House, Bressenden Place, London, SW1E 1DU.
Tel: 020 7944 3783 Fax: 020 7944 3749
E-mail: rachel.dickenson@dtlr.gsi. gov.uk
Website: www.neighbourhood.dtlr. gov.uk
Contact: Rachel Dickenson

The New Deal for Communities aims to help some of the most deprived neighbourhoods in the country. The programme seeks to address five key themes:
- tackling worklessness
- improving health
- tackling crime
- raising educational achievement
- housing and the physical environment.

The NDC programme is delivered in local areas by community based partnerships which represent: local people, community and voluntary organisations, public agencies, local authorities and businesses. Partnerships develop initiatives and projects in neighbourhood areas covering a total of 1,000 to 4,000 households (about 10,000 people).

The 39 NDC Partnerships will receive between £30 million to £56 million each to spend in their neighbourhood over the 10 years of the programme – this amounts to approximately £1.9 billion in total.

There are no plans to create any further NDC Partnerships – the aim of the NDC programme is to learn lessons from the NDC partnerships and generalise them and communicate them to other people across the country.

Details of the other programmes run by the Neighbourhood Renewal Unit – such as the Neighbourhood Renewal Fund, Community Chests and Neighbourhood Management – can be found at the website given above. (Also, see page 314)

NDC areas and neighbourhoods
- East Midlands: Derby (Derwent), Leicester (Braunstone), Nottingham (Radford)
- East of England: Luton (Marsh Farm), Norwich (North Earlham and Marlpit)
- London: Hackney (Shoreditch), Hammersmith and Fulham (North Fulham), Haringey (Seven Sisters), Islington (Finsbury), Lambeth (Clapham Park), Lewisham (New Cross Gate), Newham (West Ham and Plaistow), Southwark (Aylesbury Estate), Tower Hamlets (Ocean Estate), Brent (South Kilburn)
- North East: Hartlepool (West Central), Middlesborough (West), Newcastle-upon-Tyne (West Gate), Sunderland (East End and Hendon)
- North West: Knowsley(Huyton), Liverpool (Kensington), Manchester

Making it work - successful partnerships

Bidding for central government and regional funds is time–consuming and can be frustrating where bids are not approved despite your best efforts. One major factor for success is the creation of successful partnerships. Where voluntary sector bids have been successful there are some common features:

- good partnerships with other bodies were already in place;
- those bidding, including the voluntary organisation, kept in touch with key agencies such as the regional government regional office and worked with the advice that was offered;
- projects were well thought out and offered real benefits that fitted in with local strategic plans;
- an early start had been made on the bid and there was a long preparation period;
- local bodies such as local authorities worked together with voluntary organisations and officers supported voluntary involvement.

The website: www.lgpartnerships.com offers resources to improve partnership working.

(Beswick and Openshaw), Oldham (Hattershaw and Fitton Hill), Rochdale(Old Heywood), Salford (Charlestown and Lower Kersal)
- South East: Brighton (East), Southampton (Thornhill)
- South West: Bristol (Barton Hill), Plymouth (Devonport)
- West Midlands: Birmingham (Kings Norton), Birmingham (Aston), Coventry (Wood End Henley Green, Manor Farm and Deedmore), Sandwell (Greets Green), Walsall (Bloxwich East and Leamore), Wolverhampton (All Saints and Blackenhall)
- Yorkshire and Humberside: Bradford (Little Horton), Doncaster (Doncaster Central), Hull (Preston Road), Sheffield (Burngreave)

NDC and young people

Youth organisations will need to be connected to their neighbourhood partnership to access funding opportunities. Those working with schools may also attract support through local NDC education projects, which aim to improve educational achievement and tackle social exclusion. NDC partnerships may also have access to local community chests, which can provide small grants for community capacity building, to encourage greater participation from residents and organisations.

- Sheffield NDC used a £35,000 grant to involve around 20 voluntary and statutory groups working with young people. Activities included consultation with young people and a young people's conference involving 250 local young people.
- Bradford NDC has a scheme in which sixth form students are paid £750 a year in exchange for spending two weeks helping children with basic skills.
- Brighton NDC's anti-crime strategy includes clubs for young people.

Applications: Youth organisations seeking further information on NDC initiatives in their area should contact their regional Government Office.

Government Office for the East of England
Tel: 01223 202000 **Fax:** 01223 202020
Website: www.go-east.gov.uk

Government Office for the East Midlands
Tel: 0115 971 9971 **Fax:** 0115 971 2404
Website: www.go-em.gov.uk

Government Office for London
Tel: 020 7217 3456 **Fax:** 020 7217 3450
Website: www.open.gov.uk/glondon

Government Office for the North East
Tel: 0191 201 3300 **Fax:** 0191 202 3744:
E-mail: general.enquiries.gone@go-regions.gsi.gov.uk
Website: www.go-ne.gov.uk

Government Office for the North West
Manchester Office:
Tel: 0161 952 4000 **Fax:** 0161 952 4099
Liverpool Office:
Tel: 0151 224 6300 **Fax:** 0151 224 6470
Website: www.go-nw.gov.uk

Government Office for the South East
Tel: 01483 882255
Website: www.go-se.gov.uk

Government Office for the South West
Bristol office:
Tel: 0117 900 1700 **Fax:** 0117 900 1900
Cornwall Office:
Tel: 01209 312622 **Fax:** 01209 312628
Plymouth office:
Tel: 01752 635000 **Fax:** 01752 227647
Website: www.gosw.gov.uk

Government Office for the West Midlands
Tel: 0121 212 5050
Website: www.go-wm.gov.uk

Government Office for Yorkshire and Humberside
Tel: 0113 280 0600 **Fax:** 0113 244 4898
Website: www.goyh.gov.uk

Single Regeneration Budget

Department for Transport, Local Government and the Regions,
1/B2 Eland House, Bressenden Place, London SW1E 5DU
Tel: 020 7944 3792 **Fax:** 020 7944 3809
E-mail: srb@dtlr.gsi.gov.uk
Website: www.regeneration.detr.gov.uk/srb

Since 1994 the Single Regeneration Budget (SRB) has been the major source of urban funding in England. It supports regeneration initiatives carried out by local partnerships in areas of need with the aim of reducing the gap between deprived areas and other areas by supporting projects which make a real and sustainable difference. The SRB is administered regionally by the Regional Development Agencies and, in London, by the London Development Agency. Support will differ from region to region but will mostly cover some, or all of the following objectives, which are to:

- improve the employment prospects, education and skills of local people;
- address social exclusion and improve opportunities for the disadvantaged;
- promote sustainable regeneration, improve and protect the environment and infrastructure, including housing;
- support and promote growth in local economies and businesses;

- reduce crime and drug abuse and improve community safety.

SRB partnerships are expected to involve a diverse range of local organisations. They should use the talent, resources and experience of local businesses, the voluntary sector and the local community.

Under SRB rounds 1–6, over 900 schemes worth over £5.5 billion have been supported. In the current round, SRB funding is expected to attract private sector funding and European funding worth over £10 billion.

SRB 6 is the most recent round of the fund. A number of successful bids have made young people a priority in their regeneration plans. These include:

Forest of Dean Young People's Project
(Scheme total £2,234,000; SRB commitment £1,000,000; £20,000 in the first year)
The scheme aims to increase young people's access to social and personal development opportunities, and in particular focuses on those who are socially excluded, those in rural isolation and those at risk of becoming involved in crime or substance misuse. Outcomes from the scheme include: a youth forum, youth cafés, transport services, a mobile outreach service, night–stop emergency accommodation, employment of a young person's health worker and a drug and alcohol project.

Bridging the Gap – Boston Youth Inclusion Programme *(Scheme total £3,336,000; SRB commitment £1,216,000, £28,000 in the first year)*
This is a five year programme to bridge the gap between 16–25 year olds and current training and employment options. Outcomes from the scheme include a strategy for community

involvement in regeneration; involving one third of the target group of young people through personal and social development projects; and new credit union facilities for young people.

In terms of the future direction of SRB schemes, the DTLR stated: 'There will not be a national bidding round for new schemes in 2002/3. Instead, those regional development agencies with sufficient resources, after commitments form earlier SRB rounds are taken into account, have put forward proposals for using funds from the SRB expenditure line in their corporate plans for 2001/2002. Each RDA will be able to decide on its own approach … From April 2002, RDAs have been given new flexibilities to deliver their regional strategies … A key flexibility is the introduction of a single budget which will subsume all current RDA funding streams.'

Applications: For details of proposals for 2001/2002 and beyond, organisations should contact their Regional Development Agency. SRB proposals are invariably complex and voluntary organisations need to allow plenty of lead–in time to develop initiatives.

RDAs now come under the DTI departmental remit (website: www.dti. gov.uk, although the current DTLR website will carry information until the transfer: www.local-regions.detr. gov.uk/rda).

Regional Development Agencies

East Midlands Development Agency
Tel: 0115 988 8300 **Fax:** 01223 713940
Website: www.emda.org.uk

East of England Development Agency
Tel: 01223 713900 **Fax:** 01223 713940
Website: www.eeda.org.uk

London Development Agency
Tel: 020 7983 4800 **Fax:** 020 7983 4801
Website: www.lda.gov.uk

One NorthEast
Tel: 0191 261 2000 **Fax:** 0191 201 2021
Website: www.onenortheast.co.uk

North West Development Agency
Tel: 01925 400 100 **Fax:** 01925 400400
Website: www.nwda.co.uk

South West of England Regional Development Agency
Tel: 01392 214747 **Fax:** 01392 214848
Website: www.southwestrda.org

South East England Development Agency (SEEDA)
Tel: 01483 484200 **Fax:** 01483 484247
Website: www.seeda.co.uk

Advantage West Midlands
Tel: 0121 380 3500 **Fax:** 0121 380 3501
Website: www.advantagewm.co.uk

Yorkshire Forward
Tel: 0113 243 9222 **Fax:** 0113 243 1088
Website: www.yorkshire-forward.com

(DTLR) Special Grants Programme

Community Participation Branch, Urban Policy Unit, Department for Transport, Local Government and the Regions, Zone 4/H10 Eland House, Bressenden Place, London SW1E 5DU
Tel: 020 7944 3724/3726
Fax: 020 7944 3729
E-mail: mumuna.shallow@dtlr.gsi.gov.uk or priti.varu@dtlr.gsi.gov.uk
Website: www.regeneration.dtlr.gov.uk
Contact: Mumuna Shallow or Priti Varu

£2 million was allocated to this programme for 2002/2003. Grants are available for national projects, development or strategic activities that support the DTLR's housing, urban and regeneration objectives. The programme has previously supported voluntary organisations with grants of around £10,000 to £80,000. The DTLR will consider larger bids submitted through the 2002/2003 round of the programme if the amounts can be justified in proposed work programmes.

Project grants run for three years, and are intended to support an organisation's ongoing costs, including salaries. Match funding of at least 50% will be needed from non–governmental funding sources (which can include in-kind contributions). Organisations that can be funded by other government funding programmes will not be eligible under the Special Grants Programme.

Examples of organisations working with young people funded under the programme are:
- The Foyer Federation – awarded £21,600 for a one year project in 2001/2002 to develop an accredited professional training programme for staff and volunteers working with disadvantaged young people in supported housing schemes.
- The Children's Society – awarded £38,000 in 20001/2002, with a second and final award of £31,000 in the following year. It received support for its demonstration project using local and national networks to show how children and young people can be successfully included in sustainable regeneration.

Applications: One round of the SPG programme closed in October 2001. There will be a further round in 2002, although applicants should note that the programme is under review and there may be some changes to its implementation. Further details are available from the website.

Applicants must show how their project complements the housing, regeneration and urban objectives of the DTLR. Full details of current DTLR policy are available on the website or by contacting the SPG team.

Application forms and guidance notes are available from the website or by contacting the DTLR. Assessment of applications will take around two months.

RURAL COMMUNITIES

ACRE – Action with Communities in Rural England

Somerford Court, Somerford Road, Cirencester, Gloucestershire GL7 1TW
Tel: 01285 653477 **Fax:** 01285 654537
E-mail: acre@acre.org.uk
Website: www.acre.org. uk
Contact: Carole Garfield, Head of Member Services

Action with Communities in Rural England (ACRE) is a national charity which supports sustainable community development. It acts nationally with rural community councils (RCCs), other bodies and individuals to alleviate rural disadvantage in England.

ACRE does not centrally fund projects specifically for young people. However, RCCs may be able to work with young people's organisations which are running or looking to set up projects which support rural community development. RCCs may be able to direct them towards appropriate funding. Organisations supporting rural community development should contact

ACRE for details of the RCC in their area. Each RCC operates differently; they may have attracted support for a youth council development programme for example, or can help with voluntary sector capacity building measures.

Applications: Organisations should contact ACRE for details of their nearest RCC. RCC and project information is also on the ACRE website.

Countryside Agency

John Dower House, Crescent Place, Cheltenham, Gloucestershire GL50 3RA
Tel: 01242 521381 **Fax:** 01242 584270
E-mail: info@countryside.gov.uk
Website: www.countryside.gov.uk
Contact: Dale Langford, Publications Office

The Countryside Agency aims to conserve and enhance the countryside and to promote opportunities for the people who live there. It works with local organisations, such as local authorities, parish councils, rural community councils, businesses, farmers, landowners, voluntary groups and organisations and individuals. It also has a role in tackling social exclusion in the countryside.

There are a number of programmes detailed below, some of which include grant giving.

- Rural Assurance – improving the quality of rural life
- Countryside Capital – enhancing countryside assets
- Wider Welcome – widening access
- Market Towns – improving rural service centres
- Countryside on your Doorstep – creating green spaces close to home

- Finest Countryside – safeguarding landscapes
- Vital Villages – equipping local communities
- Local Heritage Initiative – helping people care for local landmarks and traditions

The Countryside Agency administers regeneration programmes regionally which give priority to areas of deprivation. Programmes include the Community Service Fund to support villages and rural parishes in the planning and funding of services and Rural and Parish Transport Funds. In the latter case, funds for small-scale local transport schemes will be made available through parish councils.

Grants are normally to cover between 20%–50% of the eligible cost of the project. There must be clear, public benefit and a specific target, with measurable outputs.

One example of a youth project receiving support was the Sherborne Youth and Community Centre with a grant of £9,700 in 1999/2000.

Applications: In all cases, preliminary enquiries should be directed to the nearest regional office (see below for contact details).

There are no deadlines for applying for support, although organisations are advised to discuss their plans at the earliest possible date with the regional office. The agency's priorities are determined in September for the following year. Some of the agency's schemes have an application form which can be obtained from the regional offices.

Countryside Agency Regional Offices

East Midlands
18 Market Place, Bingham, Nottinghamshire NG13 8AP
Tel: 01949 876200 **Fax:** 01949 8762224

East of England
Ortona House, 110 Hills Road, Cambridge CB2 1LQ
Tel: 01223 354463 **Fax:** 01223 313850

North East
Cross House, Westgate Road, Newcastle upon Tyne NE1 4XX
Tel: 0191 232 8252 **Fax:** 0191 222 0185

North West
7th Floor, Bridgewater House, Whitworth Street, Manchester M1 6LT
Tel: 0161 237 1061 **Fax:** 0161 237 1062

Haweswater Road, Penrith, Cumbria CA11 7EH
Tel: 01768 865752 **Fax:** 01768 890414

South East & London
Dacre House, 19 Dacre Street, London SW1H 0DH
Tel: 020 7340 2900 **Fax:** 020 7340 2911

Sterling House, 7 Ashford Road, Maidstone ME14 5BJ
Tel: 01622 765222 **Fax:** 01622 662102

South West
Bridge House, Sion Place, Clifton Down, Bristol BS8 4AS
Tel: 0117 973 9966 **Fax:** 0117 923 8086

2nd Floor, 11–15 Dix's Field, Exeter EX1 1QA
Tel: 01392 477150 **Fax:** 01392 477151

West Midlands
1st Floor, Vincent House, Tindal Bridge, 92–93 Edward Street, Birmingham B1 2RA
Tel: 0121 233 9399 **Fax:** 0121 233 9286

Strickland House, The Lawns, Park
Street, Wellington, Telford TF1 3BX
Tel: 01952 247161 **Fax:** 01952 248700

Yorkshire and Humber
2nd Floor, Victoria Wharf, No 4, The
Embankment, Sovereign Street, Leeds
LS1 4BA
Tel: 0113 246 9222 **Fax:** 0113 246 0353

ENVIRONMENT

ENTRUST – Landfill Tax Credit Scheme

6th Floor, Acre House, 2 Town Square,
Sale, Cheshire M33 7WZ
Tel: 0161 972 0044 **Fax:** 0161 972 0055
E-mail: information@entrust.org.uk
Website: www.entrust.org.uk

ENTRUST is the regulator of the
Landfill Tax Credit Scheme. This scheme
enables organisations to receive money
from Landfill Operators (LOs) to carry
out environmental projects. LOs are
often private companies but can be run
by the local authority and are charged
£12 a ton to dispose of waste when it
goes to landfill. Up to 20% of this landfill
tax can be diverted by LOs to be used in
environmental projects.

By June 2001, LO contributions
totalled £390 million and have gone to a
variety of projects involved with:
- reclamation of land, or reducing or
preventing pollution on land where
use has been prevented because of
some previous activity;
- research, development and education,
where the emphasis is on recycling,
waste prevention and the use of energy
from waste;
- providing and maintaining public
amenities and parks (these must be

within a 10 miles radius of a landfill
site);
- restoring and repairing buildings for
religious worship, or of architectural or
historical interest (within 10 miles of a
landfill site);
- funding the cost of administrative,
financial or other similar services
supplied to other enrolled
environmental bodies.

ENTRUST is not a grant-giving body,
but the regulator of Environmental
Bodies (EBs). To apply for money from
Landfill Operators organisations need to
enrol as an EB with ENTRUST at a cost
of £100. The Landfill Operator must be
approached directly by the organisation
applying for funds and it is suggested that
this approach is made first, before
enrolling with ENTRUST. Of any funds
received under the scheme, 2% must be
given to ENTRUST to cover the
administration costs of regulation.
Amounts received by EBs can range from
about £500 up to £46.5 million.

Youth organisations are most likely to
be supported under the scheme for waste
minimisation projects and also under the
providing/maintaining public amenities
or parks category. Recent youth
beneficiaries include two scout and guide
groups in Suffolk and Cheshire. The 1st
Kesgrave Scout Group had £6,000 spent
on its headquarters and store, and the 1st
Sutton (St James) Scout and Guide
Group had £5,000 spent on re-cladding
and essential repairs to the scout hut
which was also used as the village hall.
Birchwood Youth Association,
Warrington had £25,000 to be spent on
a purpose built centre for community
activities and Kingsteignton Youth
Centre, Devon has received £75,000 to
be spent on redeveloping a youth and
community centre. The Surrey

Association of Youth Clubs and Surrey PHAB Ltd have received £255,000 to spend on educational materials to encourage re-cycling, re-use and waste minimisation.

Applications: There are a number of stages to the application process. It is recommended that potential applicants first research their local LO and whether it will be interested in their proposals. The waste department of your local authority should be able to provide details of local LOs, or a list is available from Customs and Excise on 08459 128484. (A list is also available from the Customs and Excise website: www.hmce.gov.uk/bus/excise)

Where there is a positive relationship between the applicant organisation and the LO, the organisation can apply to ENTRUST to enrol as an environmental body. Forms available in the ENTRUST application pack should then be completed to apply for project approval. Organisations need to liaise with the LO and agree arrangements for funding. (Applicants should use up to date forms. The website and local offices have information and can advise.)

Once the project has been implemented, project management and financial returns should be sent to ENTRUST. The LO also needs to be kept informed of progress and sent a copy of ENTRUST returns. A resource pack is available to advise on how to account for the money received from the LO. The website has detailed information on eligibility and how to apply.

Owing to the initial investment required to access the scheme, small organisations should research local partnership approaches to maximise community benefit from the Landfill Tax Credit Scheme. Wiltshire Rural

Community Council for instance was involved in a local partnership that secured a contribution of £100,000 for local community projects under the scheme. Other partnerships have also been successful in attracting support for a range of projects.

VOLUNTARY AND COMMUNITY INVOLVEMENT

The Active Community Unit

Active Community Unit, Room 264, Home Office, Horseferry House, Dean Ryle Street, London SW1P 2AW
Tel: 020 7217 8439
E-mail: ACU.GrantsEnquiries@home office.gsi.gov.uk
Website: www.homeoffice.gov.uk/acu/ acu.htm

The Active Community Unit aims to:
- promote increased voluntary and community involvement;
- support the development of active communities.

Current programmes include the Active Community Grants programme, a voluntary action development fund and mentoring initiatives.

Active Community Grants
This initiative promotes volunteering and develops the capacity of local voluntary and community organisations. Project themes vary from year to year. At the time of writing, the emphases were on:
- diversifying the volunteer base of voluntary organisations;
- supporting black and minority ethnic led organisations;

- promoting community self-help to combat social exclusion;
- improving services that develop the capacity of local voluntary and community organisations.

The programme aims to support a wide range of organisations. Bids for less than £50,000 are more likely to succeed that applications for larger amounts.

Applications: Guidance and information on the different programmes and application forms are available form the contact address above, and through the website. Applicants are strongly advised, particularly if applying to the ACU for the first time, to discuss their proposals with the unit before completing the application form.

Development Fund

At the time of writing a development fund to encourage voluntary activity in the most deprived areas of England was announced. £4.5 million will be available each year over three years from voluntary and community groups to bid for. It is anticipated that around 90 projects will be supported with grants of up to £50,000 to 'recruit and train someone who will inspire local people to get involved in voluntary activity that tackles social exclusion'.

'It may be that there is a project that is already working in the community – which knows the problems and what needs to be done – but does not have staffing or money to provide the service needed. With this money, someone form within the community could be recruited full time to develop the work and encourage others in the community to help.'

Applications: Forms and guidance are available from the website, or by telephoning the Active Community Grants Enquiry Point 020 7217 8565. Bids need to be submitted to the Development Fund Administrator by 1 March 2002.

Mentoring support

Young people are one of the focus areas for the ACU's support of mentoring initiatives. There have been a number of measures, including the most recent to support the establishment of 'Mentor Points' to match volunteer mentors with mentoring opportunities. Details of further initiatives will be published on the website.

11 RAISING MONEY FROM EUROPE

THE GOOD AND THE BAD

The good news for those looking towards Europe for youth funding is that young people are close to the Community's heart. A number of funding programmes include a youth element. The bad news is that, as ever, raising money is not easy. Whilst the European budget is large (the EU spends around £100 billion) much is tied to general priority areas such as agriculture (which takes almost a half of the EU budget) and help for poor countries or regions. (The Structural Funds and Cohesion Fund accounts for about a third of the EU budget.) Even when you are successful, it is very unlikely that the EU grant will pay for all the costs of your activity. You will have to find at least half the money for the project from non-EU sources. Securing co-funding is essential to the success of any EU funding effort.

Raising money from Europe requires expertise and a large investment of time. You will have to learn new rules for playing the game. You should think carefully about what your organisation does, how it does it and who benefits from what you do. You should note the impact your activities have on your local area and region, and also be aware of any Europe-wide dimension there is to your work.

But if European funding seems too daunting, think again. Whilst it may involve a new language, literally, it can also pay dividends. The potential of European money can be one way to unlock co-funding in the UK (including National Lottery support and central and local government funds). Furthermore, transnational partnerships (that is, projects involving people from more than one European country), which are at the heart of a number of funding programmes, can give valuable experience to young people and leaders, as well as bringing resources to your organisation. It would also be a mistake to think about the EU purely in terms of the money that can be secured. When groups and organisations widen their perspective and think in terms of influencing European policy the experience can be a rewarding one.

This chapter is a brief guide to the pots of European money that are most appropriate for those working with young people. These are not the only ones, as those who are prepared to think more widely about their project and its impact will find other opportunities under the 150 or so EU budget lines that cover all areas of EU interest. Competition is fierce. This is more the case than

Europe – the good and the bad

The good

✔ New source of funding

✔ Matching money for other funders

✔ Increased profile for the organisation

✔ Participation of young people

✔ New skills

✔ New ideas

✔ Partnerships

✔ Exchange opportunities

The bad

✘ Greater administration

✘ Red tape to get through

✘ Large investment of time

✘ Commitment of resources to uncertain outcome

✘ Programmes change frequently

✘ Some programmes have large co-funding conditions

✘ Time lags; delays and cash flow concerns

✘ Monitoring requirements are heavy and can shift over the lifetime of the grant

ever following Agenda 2000 which prepares for the enlargement of the Union and the tighter focusing of resources on those countries and regions that need to 'catch up' with a more developed Europe.

PRELIMINARY RESEARCH

There are plenty of European funding sources. You have to decide which ones, if any, are appropriate to you. This may be straightforward and based on advice and expertise within your organisation or that given by a consultant. Increasingly, matching your project to the right budget line and programme needs extensive information gathering and may benefit from some specialised knowledge. You should do some preliminary research first. Take soundings from any groups you know that have been successful or who have failed in their bid. This will be invaluable in giving an insider's view of the process. There are a number of documents and general handbooks that give information on procedure, policies and programmes (see the end of the chapter for two suggestions). Local councils of voluntary service, or local authorities, regional development agencies or regional government offices will all have information and details of local arrangements. Increasingly, internet access is vital for collecting and viewing information as it becomes available. E-mail is also central to the process of forging transnational relationships.

Remember, a large part of European money has already been allocated to particular countries regions and policy areas. This money is then distributed through existing networks based on published policies. You need to explore what is already out there and work within that. You should find out what the local economic strategies are in your area and how any bid you make would fit in, as this will strengthen any application. You should find out from the regional government office what the programming documents contain, as these will outline national and regional plans. If for example, you can show how your work with young people is part of local employment training initiatives and fits with a regional plan, you will increase your chances of success with certain EU programmes.

The local authority (economic development department or European officer), or regional government office (European officers or secretariat) often have experience and knowledge and can give advice. You should also talk to Commission officials, MEPs and technical staff to get as much information as possible. There are a number of consultants working in and out of Brussels who will be able to help put a bid together and iron out some of the wrinkles. Whether you favour the custom built consultant-crafted model, or the Do-It-Yourself flat pack assembly approach, get as much advice as you can.

There are over 150 different budget lines that could apply to the not-for-profit sector. These and their programmes change over time, sometimes to be replaced by similar initiatives, sometimes to finish altogether. The European funding scene is constantly shifting, although the fondness for abbreviations and naming programmes after philosophers is likely to continue. You will have to be determined and commit to keeping in touch with developments at a local, regional, national and European level. There are often long lead-in times to the call for proposals and the chances of success increase where organisations have been able to plan their approach and time the preparation of their bid. The level of detail needed for a successful application is considerable, and the deadline for submission is often close to it being publicised. The more aware you are of the cycle of a programme, the more likely you are to catch the wave at the right time.

> European officials and all Commission switchboard staff speak good English. Commission offices are as approachable as central government departments, and are often easier to get clear information from. They are busier around submission deadlines. Get as much information as you can by fax and e-mail before you telephone.

Budget lines, Directorate Generals and programmes

European funding is divided into two streams. There is money attached to named funding programmes (ESF, ERDF, YOUTH, LEONARDO and so on), but there is also money given under certain budget lines. As with central and local government money in the United Kingdom, European funds are administered by different departments. Each department or Directorate General (DG) has responsibility for an area of European policy and its own budget line. Youth policy for instance, comes under the Directorate General for Education and Culture which covers education as well as youth. It may be the case that you can apply under a budget line rather than a programme. If for example you

The 15 Member States of the European Union

Austria	Germany	The Netherlands
Belgium	Greece	Portugal
Denmark	Ireland	Spain
Finland	Italy	Sweden
France	Luxembourg	United Kingdom

New Member States by 2003

Cyprus	Hungary
Czech Republic	Poland
Estonia	Slovenia

The European Economic Area (EEA) also includes:

Iceland
Liechtenstein
Norway

are working with young refugees, you may contact the Directorate General for Employment and Social Affairs direct which has a responsibility for refugees within the Community. As with central and local government departments, if money has not been allocated under the period of the budget your proposal may receive particular attention.

Developing links with other Member States

Some of the European funding programmes detailed below (for example, LEONARDO) will only give money to projects which involve a number of different Member States. Projects which have more than one country participating give additional benefits or 'added value' to the Community.

Developing partnerships across the Community is not just about unlocking European money. When viewed positively, it can lead to the exchange of information and ideas which is often innovative and pioneering. Participants can learn more about their own organisation as well as others, and see different ways of doing things. There are also opportunities to raise the profile of the organisation both in the home country and within the community, which will help to open up new funding opportunities.

You will only be eligible for some of the schemes outlined above if you have, or are developing, significant links with organisations in other Member States. These are known as transnational relationships. You will need to evaluate your long-term strategy as an organisation and consider the investment of time and resources, particularly of staff, that will be needed if you are to make the most of transnational opportunities.

Transnational project funding will be of particular interest to organisations wishing to promote exchanges of young people and staff; establishing networks throughout the community for like-minded organisations; exchanging information, and raising awareness through activities such as conferences and training events. For example, you may be planning an international youth arts festival or organising a training conference on good practice for youth workers. In each case you will need to connect with similar bodies in other countries.

There is no fail-safe way of matchmaking, and there may be some trial and error involved. You should also be wary of making partnerships too complicated. Too many partners can cause as many problems as too few. Projects can become difficult to manage where there are a number of players involved. Make sure you have answered all the whys, wheres, and hows within your own organisation before you join discussions with other partners. Internet access to research and look for potential partners, as well as e-mail to contact them are essential.

Frequently asked questions

What should we be applying for: building work, running costs or to try an innovative piece of work?

Look at the programme criteria carefully. If it says pilot project, that is what it means, and your work should be genuinely new. If you are looking for capital investment you will need to fit in with existing economic and infrastructure development plans in your area. Running costs, as ever, are not widely funded, although programmes supporting training should allow for some core costs.

Do we need a consultant?

Look at your budget first. This may decide the question anyway. If your expertise is minimal you may need some initial help. Ask other organisations for their experiences and for their recommendations.

Do we have the resources to manage a transnational project?

Look at your existing expertise and what gaps in resources there are. Draw up a resources inventory that shows what you have available within the organisation and what will have to be developed. Be realistic. It can be more costly to develop links with organisations in other Member States than any income you may eventually secure. Is it something you want to do anyway?

Do we need clear objectives and measurable outcomes?

European applications are rigorously scrutinised to make sure they have specific expected results, and that these can be measured. If these are not in place, how can the organisation and the Commission assess whether the project has been successful? You should write and present the intended outcomes clearly and test-drive them for good road-holding first before approaching potential European partners and funders.

How do we know how local and regional European applications are prepared?
Find out. Talk to local authorities, RDAs, learning and skills councils and regional government offices before you prepare your bid. They are likely to have some expertise and can tell you where your activities fit into existing plans.

Can we divide our project into smaller, independent units if necessary?
Look carefully at each element of your project. Where it is possible, break it down into smaller parts. If one part has to go then the whole project need not necessarily be abandoned. This is particularly important when negotiating with partners in other countries so that the aims, methods and expectations are agreed.

Does our project have to have regional, national and international impact?
It helps greatly. Assess your project for any applications it may have beyond your local area. It will strengthen your proposal if the results and good practice arising from your project can be applied in other parts of the Community.

The mating game

Transnational projects stand or fall by the quality of the relationships between organisations. If your organisation is not yet linked with partners across the Channel, you may be able to find organisational buddies through:

- past contacts through individuals, exchanges, conferences, international events;
- European newsletters, journals and periodicals with case studies;
- national bodies and networks such as national youth association and European youth networks;
- local town twinning associations, local authority twinning officers, Chambers of Commerce;
- contacts through colleges, training organisations or local youth associations;
- national 'dating agencies' such as the partner finding service run by the the British Council's LEONARDO and Europass unit or the ESF Unit for example;
- the internet has information posted on funding programmes and organisations, LEONARDO for instance has details of potential partners, and you can also give details of your organisation. (look at: leonardo.cec.eu.int/psd/)

STRUCTURAL FUNDS

The EU has committed significant resources to those parts of its community which are in need of additional support. It has established structural funds, of which the two main ones are:

- The European Regional Development Fund (ERDF) for capital investment in deprived communities
- The European Social Fund (ESF) for training and employment initiatives.

(There are two further structural funds concerned with agricultural and forestry regions, and fisheries.)

Both ERDF and ESF are administered regionally by regional government offices. ESF is the most likely source of support for the voluntary sector and is covered in detail below.

The European Social Fund

The European Social Fund is an important source of funding for activities which develop employability and human resources (in line with the European Employment Strategy). For 2000–2006, the ESF will support five fields of activity:

- active labour market policies;
- equal opportunities for all and promoting social inclusion;
- improving training and education and promoting lifelong learning;
- adaptability and entrepreneurship;
- improving the participation of women in the labour market.

The ESF (unlike other structural funds) covers every part of Great Britain under one or more of three objectives:

- Objective 1 covers areas that are economically disadvantaged: Merseyside, South Yorkshire, Cornwall, West Wales and the Valleys, Highlands and Islands of Scotland;
- Objective 2 covers areas that that are in decline as a result of changes in industrial, urban, rural and fishing sectors;
- Objective 3 operates everywhere except Objective 1 areas.

As well as the general ESF provision, the Community Initiative, EQUAL (outlined below) supports new ways to fight discrimination and inequality in the labour market and differs from other ESF Objectives in its emphasis on new and creative ideas and co-operation between EU Member States.

What the ESF funds

ESF support is normally up to 45% of the costs of a project. The remaining funds have to be found from other sources.

The European Community is largely an economic entity. Many of its activities centre on the economic development of the Community with job creation encouraging economic competitiveness. Europe will be more welcoming if your organisation can help to further these ends.

'Projects can include those for training, employment, education, research and childcare. ESF will pay for any actual eligible costs you spend in carrying out an approved activity. These can include staff and utilities (gas, electricity and water) costs.

Support under ESF is available between 2000 and 2006 under the current EU regulations, and organisations can apply for more than one project during this period. Projects are selected through competitive bidding and are generally supported for up to 24 months.

Any legally constituted organisation i.e. any organisation formed with a legal document such as an agreement or memorandum of association, can apply for ESF ... individuals cannot apply for ESF money. All organisations will need to receive some financial support from a public authority.'

Application forms and guidance are available from the local regional government office. Potential applicants should contact their office well in advance of any submission deadlines to discuss their proposals.

Information on ESF is available at: www.esfnews.org.uk

EUROPEAN SOCIAL FUND COMMUNITY INITIATIVE

EQUAL

GB EQUAL Support Unit, Priestly House, 28–34 Albert Street, Birmingham B4 7UD
Tel: 0121 616 3660
Information line: 0121 616 3661
Fax: 0121 616 3662
E-mail: equal@ecotec.co.uk
Website: www.equal.ecotec.co.uk
Contact: Margaret James

EQUAL is the current community employment initiative funded through the European Social Fund alongside the Objective 1, 2 and 3 programmes. It aims to find new ways of tackling discrimination and inequality experienced by both those who are working as well as those looking for a job, and follows on from previous ESF initiatives, ADAPT and EMPLOYMENT. The initiative will run between 2000 – 2006, with a total allocation to the UK of €388 million (around £240 million).

EQUAL incorporates the four pillars of the European Employment Strategy: employability, entrepreneurship, adaptability and equal opportunities. It is directed at those who are at most disadvantage in the labour market, and target groups include ethnic minorities, older workers, women, people with disabilities, refugees, ex-offenders and those misusing drugs and alcohol.

Within the four themes, funding is allocated as follows:

- *Employability* – i) improving access and return to the labour market for disadvantaged people (30% of the programme funds); and ii) combating racism and xenophobia (10% of the programme funds)
- *Entrepreneurship* – i) opening up business creation opportunities to all (10% of the programme funds); and ii) strengthening the third sector or social economy (10% of programme funds)
- *Adaptability* – i) promotion of lifelong learning and inclusive work practices for those experiencing discrimination and inequality (12.5% of the programme funds); and ii) supporting adaptability of businesses and employees with regard to economic change, the use of IT and new technologies (12.5% of programme funds)
- *Equal opportunities* – 5% of the programme funds towards reducing gender inequalities and supporting job desegregation.

EQUAL also makes a further 10% of the programme funds available to support technical assistance (5%) and initiatives directed towards the social and vocational integration of asylum seekers (5%).

In England the employability element focuses on the 157 local authority areas that contain at least one of the 10% most deprived wards. There is room for Development Partnerships to develop beyond these areas, but priority will be given to areas experiencing deprivation.

Development partnerships

The programme is transnational and will be implemented through Development Partnerships (DPs) and Thematic Networking Groups (TNGs). DPs can be developed according to common geographical, economic sector or industrial sector links. Although partnerships can be formed nationally, regionally and locally, it is expected that the majority will be at a local level.

DPs must include at least one other DP in another Member State. Partnerships can also include partners from within the EU but which are not covered by EQUAL, or partners from outside the EU as long as the potential value to the partnership is clear and the partner can cover their costs. Partnerships should include representatives of the target group of their proposed activities. The ESF Unit has a searchable database for contacts and partners on their website and the Support Unit can help in finding partners. The European Commission website also hosts a transnational partner database. This can be accessed through

A word from an organisation working with young people that successfully raised support from the EU over a period of time:

'The EU programme we applied for was suitable for what we wanted. What was crucial was that we were looking to fund something we were doing anyway, not coming up with something to fit the guidelines. Our information project is innovative; it is about forming international links between young people; it fitted in with social and economic development in a needy area; and it had employment and education training at its heart. It is a truly transnational project and is one of the keys to its success.'

the UK EQUAL website or directly through the EU EQUAL website: http://europa.eu.int/comm/employment_social/equal/index_en.html

Funding

EQUAL has allocated funding to the following four actions:

- Action 1 – setting up DPs and transnational co-operation (5% of the budget);
- Action 2 – implementing the activities of the DPs (75% of the budget);
- Action 3 – thematic networking, dissemination of good practice and contributing to national policy (15% of the budget);
- Action 4 – technical assistance to support actions 1, 2 and 3 (5% of the budget).

77 DPs (67 in England) have been selected under Action 1 to progress to develop activities to be implemented through Actions 2 and 3, following the agreement of plans. The process of submission and selection for development Actions 1 and 2 takes around four months. The first round of funding under all actions will have been implemented and activities started by May 2002. Projects in the first round will run until 2004 and will be funded up to a maximum of £60,000. Funding has to be matched from other sources, and there are detailed guidance notes on what is allowable. Match funding has to be in place at the time of the submission for EQUAL support.

There is no maximum or minimum grant following Action 1, although the need for match funding will limit the scope and extent of bids.

A second application round will include a call for applications in mid 2003, with projects up and running by 2004. Potential applicants should keep in touch with developments in the programme as there are likely to be small changes following the first round. The website will have the most up to date information and briefings are offered by the support unit.

At the time of writing it was too early to discern how EQUAL will support activities which involve young people. However, the programme will cover those leaving school at 16, and is likely to include activities such as mentoring, developing qualifications, e-learning and peer support. Again, the website and the Support Unit's information line will have up to date information as it becomes available.

Applications: Enquiries and information should in the first instance be directed to the Support Unit. As well as hosting the website, there is a 24 hour information line and an opportunity to submit a draft proposal for comment. There will be opportunities for organisations to ask for initial help from the Support Unit in the development of their project under each round of EQUAL.

Application forms and full guidance notes can be downloaded from the website, or by contacting the Support Unit.

EXCHANGES/ VOLUNTEERING

YOUTH

Connect Youth International (CNY), The British Council, The British Council, 10 Spring Gardens, London SW1A 2BN **Tel:** 020 7389 4030 **Fax:** 020 7389 4033 **E-mail:** connectyouth.enquiries@ britishcouncil.org **Website:** www.connectyouth international.com **Contact:** Sujata Saikia, Information Officer

CNY is the national agency with responsibility for administering the European Community YOUTH programme, which prioritises those with special needs, or those from less advantaged backgrounds. Participants should be aged between 15 and 25.

The YOUTH programme has five actions:

- *Action 1* is the youth exchange programme which supports bilateral, trilateral and multilateral exchanges with grants to groups of between 15 and 60 young people from three or more European Union member states. There are also options for exchanges involving the Mediterranean Basin, Latin America and Central and Eastern Europe. Exchanges can run for 6 to 21 days, excluding travel time and should follow a programme of activities.

The programme can support up to 70% of sending group's travel costs; a fixed amount of £300 for the sending and host group towards local transport costs, board and lodging, insurance; and preparation of briefing materials and communication costs. Up to £10 per head, per day can be paid for participants

from both the hosting and visiting groups, together with a lump sum of £600 (or £1,200 for multilateral exchanges). This covers the costs of the programme activities; local accommodation and transport; insurance; administration and evaluation.

- *Action 2* of the YOUTH programme covers the European Voluntary Service. Young people who want to volunteer in Europe for between three weeks and twelve months can be sent by a sending project to work with a host project. All costs of each volunteer place can be funded by the YOUTH programme. Volunteers have to be aged between 18 and 25 years of age. CNY has details of sending projects.
- *Action 3* is Youth Initiatives which helps small groups of young people in activities connected with employability. Projects should be inspired and managed by young people aged between 15 to 25, and should reflect social, cultural and entrepreneurial local community interests. Awards of up to 10,000 euro can be given. Projects are expected to cover an issue such as homelessness, racism, HIV or AIDS that has a Europe wide interest.

Action 3 also includes a Future Capital initiative which follows on from an EVS placement. Returned volunteers can apply for funding of up to ¤5,000 to cover the costs of a project that leads on from the EVS experience. Examples might be a professional activity such as setting up a shop, a one-off project such as a training programme for other young people or personal development (not university or language courses) such as a tourism qualification.

Future Capital projects cannot run for more than one year and must start within two years of the end of the EVS placement, and must not be a continuation of the EVS activity.

- *Action 4* covers joint actions linking education (SOCRATES) and vocational training (LEONARDO DA VINCI) with the YOUTH programme.
- *Action 5* covers support measures to prepare for projects, find partners and develop youth work skills as well as exchanging good practice, developing transnational partnerships and develop youth policy.

Applications: Further details of all the measures, including how to apply, are available from CNY. CNY also has details of grant holders and can help with examples of good practice.

Town Twinning

The European Commission's town twinning grant programme supports twinning activities within the EU., and there is an enthusiasm for involving more young people in twinning activities. Preston Youth Conference in 2000, for example was supported by the EC in bringing together 250 young people

Case study

One successful organisation that has developed both Youth Initiatives projects and the European Volunteer Service locally is South Tyneside Youth Action Volunteers. The organisation has around 200 young people committed to volunteering and has successfully introduced a European dimension to their work. Youth Initiatives have included young people who have been 'left out' of formal education and training and encourage entrepreneurship and management skills as well as creativity and teamwork. Young people design a project, apply for Youth Initiative support and run the project. As it develops, so their skills and training can be assessed with the help of a mentor and they can find appropriate training, which can lead to accredited qualifications.

The European Voluntary Service is also promoted through the group in partnership with South Tyneside MBC. There are a number of volunteering opportunities offered to local young people, including:
- restoration of ancient buildings in Athens
- working on a city farm in Berlin
- working with young cancer patients in France
- helping a youth project in Madrid
- environmental work in Hungary.

South Tyneside Youth Action Volunteers, Stanhope Complex, Gresford Street, South Shields NE33 4SZ

South Tyneside EVS contact: Steve Southern 0191 424 7761; steve.southern@ s-tyneside-mbc.gov.uk

from six EU states to consider nationality, racism and xenophobia. Involvement in a local twining association can also be a route to developing transnational partnerships.

The programme has recently been reviewed with changes to deadline arrangements and a sharper focus. Young people and education are included as one of the named themes for twinning activities.

Further information on the programme and deadlines is available from:
europa.eu.int/comm/dgs/education_culture/towntwin/index/_en.html

International Links Team, Local Government International Bureau, 35 Great Smith Street, London SW1P 9BJ Tel: 020 7664 3115; Fax: 020 7664 3128; E-mail: susan.handley@lgib.gov.uk; Website: www.lgib.gov.uk

VOCATIONAL TRAINING

LEONARDO da vinci (Mobility Measure)

Leonardo and Europass Unit, The British Council, 10 Spring Gardens, London SW1A 2BN
Tel: 020 7389 4389 **Fax:** 020 7389 4426
E-mail: leonardo@britishcouncil.org
Website: www.leonardo.org.uk and www.centralbureau.org.uk

LEONARDO da Vinci is the European Union's vocational training programme which aims to support Member States' policies in promoting employability, lifelong learning and social inclusion. LEONARDO supports a range of measures, including transnational mobility projects which aim to

encourage the development of skills and exchange of good practice between participating countries.

The second phase of the LEONARDO programme was launched at the beginning of 2000 and will run until December 2006. The total budget of €1.15million is for all participating countries and for the entire duration of the programme.

The programme has three main objectives:
- to improve people's skills and competences in initial vocational training;
- to improve the quality of, and access to, continuing vocational training, and lifelong learning;
- to promote innovation through training, to improve competitiveness and entrepreneurship, and to foster co-operation and partnership.

The programme is open to any organisation, including voluntary organisations, which is involved in vocational training or education. Six types of project can be supported:
- mobility – for work placements and trainer exchanges in another European country (managing agency: The British Council);
- pilot projects – for the production of training materials to develop innovation and promote quality in training (managing agency: Ecotec);
- language competences – the production of vocationally specific language materials (managing agency: Ecotec)
- transnational networks – to help the transfer and exchange of good practice (managing agency: Ecotec);
- reference materials – research and statistics (managing agency: Department for Education and Skills);

- Joint Actions – for collaborative projects with programmes such as Socrates and YOUTH (managing agency: Department for Education and Skills).

Mobility projects

The British Council administers the Mobility measure of the LEONARDO programme. Two types of activity are covered: exchanges and placements.

Placement Projects enable people to develop vocational, linguistic and key skills through periods of work-based training in another European country. Placements are open to a range of target groups: people in initial vocational training; students in higher education; and young workers, recent graduates or job seekers. Placements can last between three weeks and one year depending on the target group and the nature of the project.

Placements involve a number of young people from the UK going to another European country covered by LEONARDO, and taking part in activities which directly relate to the vocational training they are engaged on. A strong partnership with at least one other participating country is essential for the application to progress and the project to be successful.

Participants benefit through improved skills and competences, enhanced awareness of another European country, and increased employability. There is no maximum or minimum number of participants included in any one exchange, although applicants should make sure that their proposals are focused and worth the work and time involved.

Trainer exchange projects involve the exchange of experience or skills in a particular area of vocational training. Participants are usually trainers, vocational mentors, careers advisers or language specialists in business or vocational training. Visits can last between one and six weeks.

LEONARDO generally funds up to around 75% of the total project cost. The

---

Case study

The Fawside Foundation is a small charity in Allendale, Northumberland. It gives help and advice within a rural community and is involved in environmental and conservation projects, some of which include transnational partnerships in Europe.

The charity administers a LEONARDO backed project with eight unemployed young people from a rurally isolated area gaining skills in environmental management and conservation. The young people have also participated in the Millennium Volunteers programme run locally with BTCV.

The placements have been for three weeks in Sweden and Spain where participants helped with local community projects concerned with the ecology of landscape. The aim of the LEONARDO project is to improve skills and employability, as well as developing partnerships with similar organisations across Europe.

programme funds actual travel and insurance costs, a basic subsistence allowance, and a contribution to management costs and the costs of a language and cultural preparation (if applicable). The maximum mobility grant which can be paid is ¤5,000 per participant (excluding management and preparation). Where justified, there is additional support for projects which focus on the disadvantaged, or on people with disabilities.

Applications: Guidelines and advice are available from the UK LEONARDO website and individual parts of the UK National Agency. Application packs for mobility projects can be downloaded from the website.

Applicants are advised that:
- LEONARDO is not open to individuals;
- organisations can submit applications under more than one measure such as pilot and mobility projects, although the proposals must be submitted separately;
- proposals must address one programme objective and one priority (that is one of the three main objectives listed

above) under the current call for proposals.

The deadlines for measures are:
- 18 January 2002 for all measures
- 26 April 2002 for mobility projects only
- 26 July 2002 for mobility projects only.

The UK Call document on the UK LEONARDO website has information on the earliest and latest start dates for mobility projects.

Applicants should keep in touch with the relevant part of the National Agency for changes in application deadlines.

There are two services that can help organisations looking for transnational partners. The LEONARDO and Europass Unit runs a Vocational Training Links service; contact: Michael Butterworth 020 7389 4581; e-mail: michael.butterworth@britishcouncil.org

The European Commission has an Partner Search Database on its website: leonardo.cec.eu.int/psd/

Information on other measures (pilot projects, language competences and transnational networks is available from Ecotec Tel: 0121 616 3770; e-mail: leonardo@ecotec.co.uk

OTHER EU BUDGET LINES

In the entries above, the focus has been on the funding programmes most likely to support the activities of small and medium sized organisations working with young people. There are many other European budget lines, although not necessarily with large amounts of accessible money attached, which may have opportunities for those working with young people. For example:

Culture: europa.eu.int/comm/culture/index_en.html

Health: europa.eu.int/comm/health/ph/index_en.html

Combating violence against children, adolescents and women – DAPHNE: europa.eu.int/comm/justice_home/project/daphne/en

Environment: europa.eu.int/comm/life/home.htm

European contact points

UK Offices of the European Commission

These provide information on policy and all things European, although it can take time to get through on the telephone. The website has an overview of funding: www.cec.org.uk

England:
8 Storey's Gate, London SW1P 3AT
Tel: 020 7973 1992 **Fax:** 020 7973 1900/020 7973 1910

Northern Ireland:
9–15 Bedford Street, Belfast BT2 7EG
Tel: 028 9024 0708 **Fax:** 028 9024 8241

Scotland:
9 Alva Street, Edinburgh EH2 4PH
Tel: 0131 225 2058 **Fax:** 0131 226 4105

Wales:
4 Cathedral Road, Cardiff CF1 9SG
Tel: 029 2037 1631 **Fax:** 029 2039 5489

Members of the European Parliament (MEPs)

A full list of MEPs can be obtained from the UK Office of the European Parliament

2 Queens Anne's Gate, London SW1H 9AA
Tel: 020 7227 4300 **Fax:** 020 72274302
E-mail: eplondon@europarl.eu.int
Website: www.europarl.org.uk

Information networks

There are Euro Info Centres, European Documentation Centres (EDCs), Carrefours (for rural information) and European Resource Centres throughout the UK, often in universities and libraries, where European information can be easily accessed. Details of your local centre can be found at:www.europe.org.uk and www.cec.org.uk/info/sources.htm

Euro Info Centres are in Belfast, Birmingham, Bradford, Bristol, Cardiff, Chelmsford, East Anglia, Exeter, Glasgow, Hertfordshire, Hull, Inverness, Kent, Liverpool, London, Manchester, Newcastle, Nottingham, Slough, Southampton, Stoke on Trent, Sussex, and Telford. Further information is available at: www.euro-info.org.uk/centres/centres.html

Useful websites, coming to a screen near you ...

The key to European funding is accessing and managing the information that is available on the EU. A good starting point is the map of European Union grants provided at UKOnline. At the time of writing it could be accessed for free, but is likely to move to a subscription service in the future. web.ukonline.oc.uk/funding.digest/

Current news and policy information can be found at: www.europe.org.uk

When you have separated your Daphne from your LEONARDO and your ERDF from your EQUAL, the EU official website has several warehouses full of information. You have to know what you are looking for. The entry point is: europa.eu.int

Start with the Directorate Generals as a jumping off point, as each DG has responsibility for a part of EU policy. A list can be found at: europa.eu.int/comm/dgs_en.htm

The Directorate-General for Education and Culture for example, has responsibility for Education and Training, which includes EQUAL, LEONARDO and YOUTH. This DG can be found at: europa.eu.int/comm/europa.eu.int/index_en.html

Government Regional Offices have responsibility for administering the structural funds for their area.

Further reading

For further information on raising money from Europe, the following may be useful: *A Guide to European Funding for the Voluntary Sector*, available from DSC and *A Guide to European Union Funding for NGOs*, (has a helpful section on drawing up a budget for an EU application), also available from DSC, published by ECAS, 53 rue de la Concorde, B-1050 Brussels, Belgium Tel: +32 2 548 0490; Fax: +32 2 2 548 0499; e-mail: admin@ecas.org; website: www.ecas.org

12 YOUTH ORGANISATIONS AND CHARITABLE STATUS

Many youth organisations are eligible for charitable status, as long as their objects, structure and activities meet certain requirements. There are many benefits to being a charity, but it can also bring restrictions. This chapter looks at the pros and cons of being a charity, who can register as a charity and how you do this.

What are the benefits of being a charity?

There are a number of advantages to being a charity. Most of them are financial. Here are some of the main ones:

- Charities are exempt from paying most direct taxes (e.g. Income Tax, Corporation Tax, Capital Gains Tax), although there is no general exemption from VAT.
- Investment income is exempt from tax so bank and building society interest can be paid gross.
- Charities receive a mandatory 80% relief from the Uniform Business Rate. This can be increased to 100% relief at the discretion of the local authority.
- Members of the public are generally sympathetic to charities and people are often more prepared to give time and money to a charity.
- Some funders, such as grant-making trusts (see Chapter 7) will only give grants to registered charities.
- Tax-payers, whether they are individuals or companies can make tax effective gifts to the charity using gift aid. In the case of individuals, the charity can recover the basic rate tax (currently 22%) paid by the taxpayer. Companies pay gift aid gross (so there is no further tax to reclaim).
- Gifts to charity are free of Inheritance Tax and Capital Gains Tax.

What are the disadvantages of being a charity?

The disadvantages of being a charity are some bureaucracy and more importantly greater regulation and restrictions on the actions and activities of the organisation. These include the following:

- Charities have to prepare annual reports, accounts and those with an annual income of £10,000 or more have to send them to the Charity Commission. They also have to send them to members of the public on request, although you can charge a reasonable administration fee for this. Charities with an annual income of £10,000 or more must also state the fact that they are a registered charity on most published materials including cheques, receipts and invoices.

- Charities also have to make an annual return to the Charity Commission although this is not very onerous (particularly for smaller charities).
- If charities are also companies they have to report to Companies House each year and fulfil company law requirements as well as those of charity law.
- Charities are run by trustees (these may also be called management committee members or directors). These people cannot usually receive any benefit from their trusteeship.
- Charity trustees have legal responsibilities and potential liabilities.
- Matters such as the disposal of land and buildings are subject to special rules and procedures.
- Charity law imposes restrictions on several types of activity such as political activities, campaigning and trading.
- Some amendments to the constitution will require Charity Commission consent.
- If a charity is wound up, the assets and funds must all be transferred to another similar charity or for some similar charitable objects.

What is a charity?

A charity is a body which is established exclusively for charitable purposes. This means that all its purposes (or objects) must be charitable in law. It is not enough to be partly charitable. Purely social activities for example are not charitable. If an organisation has exclusively charitable objects then it is automatically a charity. It must register with the Charity Commission if it has a gross annual income of over £1,000.

There is no statutory definition of what is a charity. Charity law is based on a statute of 1601 which has been clarified and developed by case law through the centuries. Charities must come under one or more of the following 'heads' of charity.

- the relief of poverty, sickness and distress;
- the advancement of education;
- the advancement of religion;
- other purposes beneficial to the community in a way recognised as charitable.

To be a charity, it is not enough simply to be established for good causes or to be non-profit making. The objects clause of your constitution must contain exclusively charitable purposes and this must reflect the actual activities. Charities must also exist for the public benefit. A youth club limited to a small number of selected members run as a private members' club would not satisfy the public benefit test and would not be charitable.

The education and setting up in life of young people has been charitable since the original 1601 statute. Youth organisations today may come under several different categories or 'heads' of charity.

Educational charities

Many youth organisations have educational objects. These are some of the areas they may cover:

- formal education in schools and colleges;
- scholarship funds;
- vocational training and work experience;
- sports organisations for young people, provided there is open access and training for all members;
- arts organisations for young people such as youth theatre groups or musical bands.

To be an educational charity there must be some element of training and the subject must be of some educational worth. A young people's chess club has been held to be charitable, but a tiddlywinks club would probably not qualify. Many youth clubs have been registered with objects to educate young people to develop their skills so as to develop their full potential as members of society.

Recreational charities

The Recreational Charities Act of 1958 specifically included the provision of facilities for recreation – or any other leisure time occupation in the interest of social welfare – as being charitable if the organisation is established for the public at large or for any disadvantaged group, which includes young people.

Many youth clubs and organisations involved in outdoor activities will come within the Act.

Other heads of charity

Youth organisations may also come within several other heads of charity. Church groups or religious youth organisations for example may be charitable under the advancement of religion. Organisations for young people with some type of disability would come within the relief of sickness and distress. Organisations coming under the head of poverty would include those giving direct financial assistance or legal advice or the provision of housing to financially disadvantaged young people.

Organisations concerned with finding employment for young people may often be charitable and these would also come under the head of the relief of poverty.

Different legal structures

Charity registration depends on the objects of the organisation, not its legal form. Several legal structures are acceptable. The most common are:

a) an unincorporated association which has a constitution;
b) a trust which is governed by a Trust Deed;
c) a company limited by guarantee which has a Memorandum of Association and Articles of Association.

(a) and (b) are less complicated to set up and run than (c). However, they also bring a greater risk of personal liability for their trustees and the property must be held in the names of individuals. The particular circumstances of the organisation will determine the most appropriate legal structure and advice should normally be taken on this point.

How do you register as a charity?

In order to be registered with the Charity Commission they must be satisfied that your objects are charitable in law. they will also want some evidence of how you intend to operate within those stated objects, and they will check that your constitution is appropriate for a charity. The procedure is as follows:

1 Write to or telephone the Charity Commission for a copy of their charity registration pack (see address below). This includes information on setting up a charity and some of their guidance booklets as well as an application form. Tell them if you intend to use an agreed model constitution as a special application form will be available for these cases.
2 Establish your organisation either by executing and stamping the Trust Deed, adopting the constitution at a members' meeting or incorporating the company.
3 Send a certified copy of the governing document to the Charity Commission, together with completed application forms, a copy of the latest accounts (if any) and a declaration by trustees.
4 If all the documentation is acceptable, the charity will be registered and you will receive written confirmation and your charity registration number. If not, the Charity Commission may call for additional information or require amendments to the governing documents. In straightforward cases, particularly those using a model constitution, registration will only take about three weeks. More complex cases may take considerably longer.

Model constitutions

As stated above, it is essential that the constitution and particularly the objects clause complies with charity law. In many cases, it may well be advisable to use a model constitution.

- If you are a branch or a local group of a national organisation you should first approach your national body which will usually have a model constitution that has been agreed with the Charity Commission.
- For a sports charity for young people (up to university age) contact the Central Council for Physical Recreation, Francis House, Francis Street, London SW1P 1DE Tel: 020 7854 8500; Fax: 020 7854 8501; e-mail: info@ccpr.org.uk
- For a youth club, contact: UK Youth, 2nd Floor, Kirby House, 20–24 Kirby Street, London EC1N 8TS Tel: 020 7242 4045; Fax: 020 7242 4125; E-mail: info@ukyouth.org.uk; website: www.ukyouth.org
- For a general charitable trust, constitution or Memorandum and Articles of Association contact the Charity Commission or the Charity Law Association (see addresses below). These models do not include objects clauses.

Sources of advice

The Charity Commission has three offices which charities are entitled to contact for guidance:

London: Harmsworth House, 13–15 Bouverie Street, London EC4Y 8DP
Tel: 0870 333 0123; Fax: 020 7674 2300

Liverpool: 20 Kings Parade, Queens Dock, Liverpool L3 4DQ
Tel: 0870 333 0123; Fax: 0151 703 1555

Taunton: Woodfield House, Tangier, Taunton, Somerset TA1 4BL
Tel: 0870 333 0123; Fax: 01823 345003

A number of guidance documents are available to download from the Charity Commission website: www.charity-commission.gov.uk

You may need to get legal advice, especially if you are not using one of the model constitutions. If you need legal advice, make sure you find a solicitor who specialises in charity law. Information about suitable solicitors is available from the Charity Law Association.

Scotland and Northern Ireland

The Charity Commission only has jurisdiction in England and Wales.

Organisations in Scotland should contact: The Director, The Scottish Charities Office, Crown Office, 25 Chambers Street, Edinburgh EH1 1LA (0131 226 2626).

Organisations in Northern Ireland should contact: The Department of Health and Social Services, Charities Branch, Annexe 2, Castle Buildings, Stormont Estate, Belfast BT4 (01232 522780).

Other addresses

The Charity Law Association c/o Plaza Publishing Ltd, 3 Rectory Grove, London SW4 0DX (020 7819 2000)

The National Council for Voluntary Organisations (NCVO) has a Legal Advice Team for Charities. They can be contacted at: Regent's Wharf, 8 All Saints Street, London N1 9RL (020 7713 6161).

DSC is grateful to Philip Kirkpatrick of Bates, Wells & Braithwaite, Solicitors for his help with this chapter. Contact: Bates, Wells & Braithwaite, Cheapside House, 138 Cheapside, London EC2V 6BB; Tel: 020 7551 7777; Fax: 020 7551 7800; E-mail: mail@bateswells.co.uk; Website: www.bateswells.co.uk

---

Model Constitution for a Youth Club

UK Youth has produced the following constitution for clubs.

Name
1. The name of the club shall be _____

Object
2. The object of the club is to help young people, especially but not exclusively through leisure time activities, so to develop their physical, mental and spiritual capacities that they may grow to full maturity as individuals and members of society.

Membership
3. Membership of the club shall be open to young people between the ages of _____ and _____ residing in _____

Committees

Members' Committee (see Note 1)
4.1 The conduct of the day to day running of the general affairs of the club shall, in conjunction with the leader, be controlled by a members' committee consisting of not less than _____ members elected annually by ballot. The members' committee shall appoint such officers as they deem necessary. Only those members with membership of at least _____ weeks shall be allowed voting rights or to hold any office.

4.2 The members' committee shall in addition to the responsibilities stated in 4.1 be responsible also for such matters of policy and finance as are appropriate, subject to the ultimate oversight and responsibility of the elected Management Committee.

Model Constitution for a Youth Club

Management Committee (see Note 1)
4.3 The club shall be managed by a committee of not less than _____ persons elected annually by ballot at the annual general meeting.

The club shall be managed by a committee which consists of not less than _____ elected persons and of not more than _____ co-opted persons.

_____ of the elected members of the committee shall retire annually by seniority but shall be eligible for re-election after an interval of _____ year(s).

4.4 The committee shall appoint a Chairman, Secretary and Treasurer and such other officers as they deem necessary.

4.5 The committee shall meet at least four times a year.

4.6 The committee shall have power to co-opt as additional members such persons as, in their opinion, are able to render special service.

4.7 The duties of the committee shall be to safeguard the interest of members by providing the premises, leadership and finance and by encouraging members to take a full and active part in the running of their club, by devising methods of achieving the object of the club exercising with the members a general oversight and assisting in the development and extension of activities.

4.8 Nominations for election to the management committee shall be submitted in writing, countersigned by the person nominated, not less than seven days before the annual general meeting.

Accounts
5. The Management Committee shall cause to be kept proper accounts of all the monies belonging to the club and presented to the annual general meeting of the club.

Annual General Meeting
6.1 A general meeting shall be held within fifteen months of the previous meeting. Not less than twenty-one days notice of the meeting shall be given. Any person desirous of submitting any matter for discussion shall give not less than seven days notice to the member of the management committee nominated for this task. Those entitled to vote shall be those present at the meeting who are members defined in clause 3.

6.2 General meetings may be convened at any time by the management committee and shall be convened by them on receipt of a requisition signed by _____ members.

Model Constitution for a Youth Club

Constitution (see Note 2)

7. The above constitution shall only be altered by resolution passed by a two-thirds majority of the members in general meeting. Notice of proposed amendments to the constitution must be given in writing not less than twenty-one days before the general meeting. No alteration shall be made to the constitution which shall cause the club to cease to be a charity by law.

Dissolution

8. In the event of the club being dissolved any property remaining after satisfaction of all its debts shall be put at the disposal of _____

Notes

1. The Management Committee should be a joint adult and club members' committee in which case members, both adult and club members, are elected at the Annual General meeting.
2. Clubs are recommended to apply for charitable status if they own any property or are liable for payment of rates without remission.

Charitable status confers several privileges, including exemption from income duty and a reduction in the payment of rates. The OBJECT clause given above has been approved by the Charity Commission and the Board of Inland Revenue and should therefore not be altered in any way, including the punctuation.

Other clauses in the above are recommendations only and can be varied in detail to suit circumstances. It is recommended, however, that none of the clauses should be entirely omitted.

Drafted by UK Youth and reproduced with their permission. Contact: Youthwork Resources and Information Manager, UK Youth, 2nd Floor, Kirby House, 20–24 Kirby Street, London EC1N 8TS Tel: 020 7242 4045; E-mail: info@ukyouth.org.uk; website: www.ukyouth.org

13 TAX AND VAT

Tax and VAT can seem a daunting subject, especially when all you want to do is work with young people and keep your club afloat. Giving general advice on tax and VAT is equally difficult because the situation is so complex. It is complicated because (a) not all income is taxable; (b) there are different types of organisations; (c) there are different types of taxes to consider, and (d) because for every rule there seem to be 10 exceptions.

We have a duty to pay tax, whether or not we are asked to by the Inland Revenue or Customs and Excise. If we get it wrong the penalties can be severe. Not knowing the law is no excuse.

Youth clubs enjoy no special tax exemptions or advantages. If you are not careful, unexpected liabilities arise and income is lost. The same rules generally apply if you are a company or an unincorporated association, although registering as a charity can bring savings (for example you should not pay Corporation Tax) and you can easily reclaim tax made on tax-effective donations (Gift Aid).

As far as fundraising is concerned, the two main areas to worry about are direct tax and indirect tax (i.e. Value Added Tax – VAT). This chapter gives a quick outline on each and how they apply to your fundraising. It also has a brief look at how to get the most from your donations through Gift Aid.

You may well need to take specialist advice, especially at an early stage. For example, if you are planning a major fundraising campaign, you may go over the VAT threshold for the first time. That will affect not just that appeal but all your other activities as well. Or if you organise an event which generates a surplus, the profit may be taxed (usually to Corporation Tax) and there is the chance that either VAT will need to be levied on the price charged or, just as bad, VAT incurred in mounting an event will not be recoverable.

In general, direct taxation is kinder to the voluntary sector than indirect taxation. The sad fact is that the change of taxation policy over the last 20 years or so has resulted in a shift away from direct taxation to indirect taxation, so that many groups in the voluntary sector are paying taxes which they were not paying some years ago. Further, those taxes are 'hidden' in that they are invariably a tax on the cost of mounting an event.

A word of warning: fundraising is not itself a charitable purpose, and can never therefore be a primary purpose trade of a charity.

DIRECT TAXATION

What tax reliefs are available to charities?

If you are a charity you can qualify for various tax reliefs. These include:

- Exemption from Income Tax, Corporation Tax and Capital Gains Tax.
- Investment income is exempt from tax so bank and building society interest can be paid gross.
- Charities receive a mandatory 80% relief from the Business Rate (contact you local authority about this). This can be increased to 100% at the discretion of the local authority.
- Charities can reclaim tax on some donations paid by tax-payers (see below).

However, the two most complicated areas are those dealing with trading profits accruing to a charity and the profits of a lottery conducted by a charity.

The Trading exemption

The law states that there is an 'Exemption from tax in respect of the profits of any trade carried on by a charity, if the profits are applied solely to the purposes of the charity and either:

- the trade is exercised in the course of the actual carrying out of a primary purpose of the charity;
- the work in connection with the trade is mainly carried out by the beneficiaries of the charity.'

Primary purpose trading

What are the primary purposes of a charity? Well, each charity is different. In order to discover what are the primary purposes of your charity, look at the objects clause in the constitution or governing instrument of your charity. In the event of a school for instance, the objects are the advancement of education, so that the trade carried out by a charitable school would be the delivery of education in return for school fees. In a research charity, the primary purpose trade would be the sale of the results of research undertaken by the charity.

Where youth projects are concerned, it is difficult to see how a primary purpose trade can be carried on, except for membership fees or something like the running of courses designed to improve the conditions of young people and to assist in their spiritual, moral and physical development. The mounting of such courses for a fee, and the levying of membership fees for a youth club, would both count as primary purpose trading in these circumstances and would thus be exempt.

Basically, if you are thinking of trading (i.e. charging for any service) get professional advice before you start, rather than just hope that the trade will qualify.

A trade carried on by the beneficiaries

The other exemption covers things like workshops for disabled people in which goods are produced for therapeutic or training purposes and are then sold to the public in order to continue the training or therapy. In the case of youth projects, young people may be trained in a skill and then carry out that skill by way of a trading venture as part of the actual training. People on college courses often have to serve some time in the real live situation (for example catering students will be required to prepare and serve food for the public as a part of their course). In this instance, the trade is not part of the primary purpose of the charity, but because the work is mainly carried out by the beneficiaries of the charity it will be exempt.

However, be very careful to work out exactly who are the beneficiaries of the charity. For example, a charity may be established to relieve the elderly and carry out that purpose by providing gardening services to them. The work may be carried out by young people but the fees charged will not be exempt in this situation simply because the work is carried out by young people – they are not the beneficiaries of that charity. Again, an excursion to the governing instrument of your charity is the starting point.

Occasional fundraising

Because active fundraising events (as opposed to street collections and similar events) are undertaken to make a profit, there is always a risk that the event might be classed as the conduct of a trade (remember that mere fundraising is not a charitable purpose). However, to help charities, the Inland Revenue has published an Extra Statutory Concession, which is intended to remove the uncertainty in respect of these events, and to exempt the profits arising from tax.

There are various elements which are required for a fundraising event to be exempt. Firstly, it must be an event which is clearly organised and promoted primarily to raise funds for the benefit of the charity. Social events which happen to make a profit do not fall within the exemption. People attending or participating in the activity must be aware that its main object is the raising of funds.

An excellent leaflet issued jointly by the Inland Revenue and Customs and Excise (CWL4 *Fundraising events: exemption for charities and qualifying bodies*) gives some examples of events which might be held for the purposes of raising funds:

- a ball, dinner dance, disco, or barn dance;
- a performance – such as a concert, stage production, and any event with a paying audience;
- a fete, fair or festival;
- a bazaar, jumble sale, car boot sale, or a good-as-new sale;

- a game of skill, a contest, or a quiz;
- a dinner, lunch or barbeque.

For an event to be exempt, it must be part of a limited number held in any financial year. Eligible events are limited to 15 per financial year of the same kind of event held in the same location. Where charities hold 16 or more events of the same kind in the same location during any one financial year, none of the events are eligible to be exempt.

Some events do not qualify for exemption:
- Where the event is part of 16 or more of the same kind (see above).
- Events which are not organised primarily and promoted for fundraising purposes.
- Events which are organised and promoted for another purpose (for example an AGM).
- Asking the public for money through street collections and the like.
- The activity of selling goods is not an event, and therefore is not eligible for exemption, even where the proceeds and received by, or donated to, a charity. Where sales of goods take place within a qualifying fundraising event it is covered by the relief and zero rating may apply in particular circumstances. Further information is available in the leaflet CWL4 (see below).

Once the event is held to fall within the exemption, then all profits generated by that event should be covered (so long as the activity is a necessary part of the event). So, admission charges, the sale of refreshments, raffle tickets, programme sales and advertising revenues will all be exempt – the key is, as with these examples, that the sales do not constitute a separate profit-making activity, since they cannot stand alone.

CWL4 Fundraising events: exemption for charities and qualifying bodies

This leaflet is issued by the Inland Revenue and Customs and Excise is available from the website: www.hmce.gov.uk, or by contacting the tax and VAT authorities listed at the end of the chapter.

Income from Lotteries

There are two kinds of lotteries which are exempt from taxation.

Small lotteries incidental to exempt entertainments

Exempt entertainments are bazaars, sales of work, fetes, dinners, dances and similar events which are limited to one day or extend over two or more days. These are exactly the kinds of events which are exempted from tax on their profits as small local fundraising events (see above). Key features of such a lottery are that there is a cap on the amount of money which might go to private gain, and none of the prizes in the lottery shall be money prizes. In addition, the tickets can only be sold at the entertainment, and the result must be declared during the entertainment.

Societies' lotteries

Societies' lotteries are lotteries which are promoted, among other things, for charitable purposes, for support of athletic sports or games, or for activities of a cultural nature. They must be registered with the local authority when total ticket sales are less than £20,000 (or the Gaming Board if total sales are over £20,000), and the net proceeds – after deducting proper prize money and proper expenses – are applied to the purposes of the society. The Gaming Board sets out the maximum proportion of the gross proceeds of the lottery which can be distributed as prizes, and the maximum proportion of the gross proceeds which can be spent on administration. Further information on lottery regulation is available from the Gaming Board of Great Britain enquiry line: 020 7306 6269; website: www.gbgb.org.uk

The profits in both cases must, of course, be applied for charitable purposes for the tax relief to be available.

The chief issue in qualifying for the exemption is to ensure that the lottery to be conducted falls within the conditions set out for it under the terms of the Lotteries and Amusements Act 1976. This is frequently amended as the National Lottery develops, so it is always necessary to check that your information is current. This is another occasion when a professional adviser should be consulted before the lottery is advertised and the tickets printed.

VAT

Value Added Tax (VAT) is a tax on goods and services (or supplies). These can range from petrol to computers to membership fees. VAT is possibly even more complicated than direct tax and if you get it wrong there are strict penalties.

There are four categories of VAT
- **Standard rated** supplies are taxable and attract VAT at the standard rate (currently 17.5%).
- **Zero rated** supplies are also taxable and liable to VAT but at 0%. This means that although this income is considered to be taxable no VAT has to be accounted for.
- **Exempt supplies** are specifically exempt from VAT and do not attract a VAT charge. Exempt income is not taken into account when deciding whether you have to register for VAT.

- Certain forms of income are entirely **outside the scope** of VAT so VAT is not chargeable. Again such income is not taken into account when deciding on registration.

The basic position is that you must register for VAT if the annual value of your VATable supplies (i.e. those which are standard rated or zero rated) exceeds or is likely to exceed the registration threshold (£54,000 in 2001/02). Please note, this does not include exempt supplies or supplies outside the scope of VAT. Therefore, if your only income is from subscriptions and joining fees (which are exempt from VAT) then you will not have to register for VAT. However, if you land a company sponsorship worth more than £54,000 a year, then you must register, and the sponsorship will be a full rated supply. Alternatively, if you have five different areas of full rated or zero rated income and they total over the threshold (even though individually they are less than the threshold), you will have to register.

In other words, you need to bear two things in mind:
- VAT is only charged on your standard rated supplies. (For the registration test, ignore exempt supplies and those outside the scope of VAT.)
- VAT registration only becomes necessary if VATable (i.e standard or zero rated) supplies exceed the threshold in one year. Therefore, if they are less than the threshold in the period, you don't need to register. The threshold test is applied to any twelve month period, not necessarily your financial year or the tax year.

The next question is: 'How do I know which supply falls into which category?' The following is a general list, although do not treat it as fail-safe. There are, unfortunately, lots of exceptions to lots of rules so each case needs to be approached differently.

Standard rated
- Sponsorship
- Hire of equipment and facilities to non-members (but see under 'exempt')
- Catering
- Sales of goods (but see under 'zero rated')
- Vending machine income
- Bar sales
- Telephones
- Gaming machine income
- Profit making competitions (but see under 'exempt')
- Sales of assets/equipment

Zero rated

- Books, magazines and handbooks
- Programmes and fixture cards
- Cold take-away food
- Sale of donated goods by a charity
- Young children's clothing

Exempt

- Continuous hire of facilities
- Lotteries and raffles
- Other lettings
- Competition fees (where all proceeds are returned as prizes or when provided by non-profit distributing bodies)
- Interest and insurance commission
- Fundraising events

Outside the scope

- Donations
- Grants
- Insurance settlements
- Compensation payments

In practice, much of your grant income will be outside the scope of VAT. Occasional fundraising should be exempt from VAT. However, if fundraising becomes more regular and starts to contribute a substantial proportion of your revenue, it will probably become VATable.

The consequences of registering

Once you register, you will have to charge VAT in the future on all full rated supplies at the standard rate (for example on catering) and do a quarterly VAT return to Customs & Excise. The good news is that you can 'offset' some VAT you have to pay against the VAT you charge. But the other point to note is that you may well have a range of activities some of which may be exempt from VAT, some full rated and some outside the scope. In any case, you will probably need a VAT specialist to help you, at least in the early stages.

When planning your fundraising, it is worth thinking about the VAT situation. If you are planning major building alterations, is there a way of recovering some or all of the VAT? Will your fundraising mean you go over the VAT threshold anyway? Is there a way around this (such as organising payments so that you do not receive more than £54,000 VATable income in any one financial year)?

TAX-EFFECTIVE GIVING

In one sense all donations to charities and voluntary organisations are tax-effective in that the organisation in receipt of them is unlikely to have to pay income or corporation tax on them. But some donations to charities are even more tax-effective because the charity in receipt of the donation can recover the income tax on the donation thereby increasing its value by around 30%. There are procedures to follow, but they are not that complicated.

> **The value of tax-effective giving**
>
> Assume someone makes a Gift Aid donation of £100 a year to a charity. To have given this amount, on current basic tax rates (22%) the person would have needed to earn £128.20, of which £28.20 would have been paid over in tax. The charity can then reclaim the £28.20. In other words, tax-effective giving increases the amount available to the charity by nearly a third at no extra cost either to the donor or to the charity.

Gift Aid

Gift Aid has made tax-effective giving simpler to administer. A single Gift Aid declaration can make all a tax-paying individual's payments to a particular charity, whether a one-off gift or regular donations, eligible for tax relief. This can be administered as long as:

- The donor completes a Gift Aid declaration which is then kept by the charity. The declaration can be as simple as a sentence included on the donation form, for example '❏ Please tick here if you would like Anytown Youthful Charity to reclaim the tax on this and all future donations you make★ ★In order for us to reclaim the tax you have paid on your donations you must have paid income or capital gains tax (in the UK) at least equal to the tax that will be reclaimed (currently 22p for each £1 that you give)'. The donor then signs and returns with their donation, or it can be a dedicated document (see box).
- The charity records an audit trail to link a payment to the donor. The charity needs to record each payment separately and be able to show the Inland Revenue how much each individual donor has given.

Further information is available from the Inland Revenue at www.inlandrevenue.gov.uk or by contacting Inland Revenue FICO (Trusts and Charities), St John's House, Merton Road, Bootle, Merseyside L69 9BB Tel:0151 472 6036/6037; Gift Aid helpline: 0151 472 6038/6056

Model Gift Aid declaration

Gift Aid declaration

Name of charity: _____

Details of donor

Title: _____   Forename(s):_____   Surname:_____

Address: _____

_____

_____

Postcode: _____

I want the charity to treat
* the enclosed donation of £
* the donation(s) of £   which I made on ____/____/____
* all donations I make from the date of this declaration until I notify you
   otherwise
as Gift Aid donations

* *delete as appropriate*

Signature _____   Date ____/____/____

One Gift Aid declaration can cover all future donations, although the individual can cancel this agreement at any time. There is also a limit on the level of benefits a donor can receive (around 2.5% of the value of total donations up to a limit of £250.

A sponsored run, for example, could attract a further 28% (on 2001/2002 tax rates) to the donated income if:

- all the sponsors are tax payers
- all sponsors complete or have completed a Gift Aid declaration
- the charity can prove that they have made the payment.

With good record keeping charities can reclaim tax on almost any donation, however small, as long as the donor is a taxpayer.

CAF and other vouchers

If someone gives you a donation using a Charities Aid Foundation (CAF) voucher – or another charity voucher – you cannot reclaim any tax on these. This is because the donor has already made a Gift Aid donation to CAF and CAF have then reclaimed the tax it. Tax cannot be reclaimed twice (unfortunately!).

CONCLUSION

You need to make sure that you get paying taxes right. The Inland Revenue or Customs & Excise won't be swayed by the fact that your committee is made up of willing volunteers who did not know the law. If tax is due then tax is due and you will have to pay it. This chapter should have alerted you to the main areas of possible concern. The message is that if you are not sure get specialist advice and get it early. DSC is grateful to Kate Sayer of Sayer Vincent for her help with this chapter. Sayer Vincent can be contacted on 020 7713 0709; website: www.sayervincent.co.uk

---

Useful contacts

Inland Revenue – for Corporation Tax
Look under 'Inland Revenue' in your local telephone directory and contact your local office
Website: www.inlandrevenue.gov.uk

Inland Revenue FICO (Trusts and Charities) – for tax-effective giving
St John's House, Merton Road, Bootle, Merseyside L69 9BB
Tel:0151 472 6036/6037; Gift Aid helpline: 0151 472 6038/6056

Customs and Excise – for VAT
Look under 'Customs and Excise' in your local telephone directory and contact your local office

Gaming Board of Great Britain – for lottery regulations
Enquiry line: 020 7306 6269; website: www.gbgb.org.uk

The Directory of Social Change publishes *A Practical Guide to VAT for Charities* by Kate Sayer.

The book is available from the Directory of Social Change: Tel: 020 7209 5151; website: www.dsc.org.uk

---

USEFUL ADDRESSES AND SOURCES OF INFORMATION

Here are some general sources of information and advice. Several chapters in the book also contain addresses of useful contacts for that particular subject.

General information

The National Youth Agency
17-23 Albion Street
Leicester LE1 6GD
Tel: 0116 285 3792
Minicom: 0116 285 3788
Fax: 0116 285 3775
E-mail: info@nya.org.uk
Website: www.nya.org.uk

Youth organisations

British Youth Council
2 Plough Yard
Shoreditch High Street
London EC2A 3LP
Tel: 020 7422 8640
Fax: 020 7422 8646
E-mail: mail@byc.co.uk
Website: www.byc.org.uk

National Council for Voluntary Youth Services (NCVYS)
2 Plough Lane
Shoreditch High Street
London EC2A 3LP
Tel: 020 7422 8630
Fax: 020 7422 8631

UK Youth
2nd Floor, Kirby House
20-24 Kirby Street
London EC1N 8TS
Tel: 020 7242 4045
Fax: 020 7242 4124
E-mail: info@youthclubs.org.uk
Website: www.ukyouth.org

Publications and training

Directory of Social Change
24 Stephenson Way
London NW1 2DP
Tel: 020 7209 5151
Fax: 020 7391 4804
E-mail: books@dsc.org.uk
Website: www.dsc.org.uk

A free booklist can be obtained by:
- viewing and printing from the DSC website
- contacting DSC's publications department

DSC publishes a range of fundraising guides, including directories of grant-making trusts. Several chapters of this book also contain details of useful publications. Other publications that may help readers of this guide include those listed below. Prices were correct at the time of going to press, but may be subject to change.

- *The Complete Fundraising Handbook*, Nina Botting & Michael Norton, 4th edition, 2001, £16.95
- *The Complete Guide to Creating & Managing New Projects*, Alan Lawrie, 2nd edition summer 2002, c.£12.50
- *Finding Company Sponsors*, Chris Wells, 1st edition, 2000, £9.95
- *Promoting Your Cause*, Karen Gilchrist, 1st edition, 2002, £10.95
- *Writing Better Fundraising Applications*, Michael Norton & Mike Eastwood, 3rd edition spring 2002, c.£14.95

DSC also runs the largest programme of training courses, seminars and conferences in the UK voluntary sector. For a copy of the latest training guide, contact the training department on 08450 77 77 07, e-mail training@dsc.org.uk or visit the DSC website.

Law and finance

The Charity Commission (for England)
Harmsworth House
13–15 Bouverie Street
London EC4Y 8DP
Tel: 0870 333 0123
Fax: 020 7674 2300

Liverpool office:
20 Kings Parade
Queens Dock
Liverpool L3 4DQ
Tel: 0870 333 0123
Fax: 0151 703 1555

Taunton office:
Woodfield House
Tangier, Taunton
Somerset TA1 4BL
Tel: 0870 333 0123
Fax: 01823 345003

Website: www.charity-commission.gov.uk

Inland Revenue for England, Wales and Northern Ireland

Inland Revenue FICO (Trusts and Charities)
St John's House
Merton Road, Bootle
Merseyside L69 9BB
Tel: 0151 472 6036/6037; Gift Aid helpline: 0151 472 6038/6056
Website: www.inlandrevenue.gov.uk

Customs and excise
Website: www.hmce.gov.uk

Corporate support

Business in the Community (BitC)
135 Shepherdess Walk
London W1V 8EP
Tel: 0870 600 2482
Fax: 020 7486 1700
Website: www.bitc.org.uk

Business Community Connections
14 Northfields
London SW18 1UU
Tel: 020 8875 5700
Fax: 020 8875 5701
Website: www.bcconnections.org.uk

Environment

Council for Environmental Education
94 London Street
Reading RG1 4SJ
Tel: 0118 950 2550
Fax: 0118 959 1955
Website: www.cee.org.uk

Shell Better Britain Campaign
King Edward House
135a New Street
Birmingham B2 4QJ
Tel: 0121 248 5903
E-mail: info@sbbc.co.uk
Website: www.sbbc.co.uk

Europe

England Office of the European Commission
8 Storey's Gate
London SW1P 3AT
Tel: 020 7973 1992
Fax: 020 7973 1900/020 7973 1910
Website: www.cec.org.uk

European Union website:
http://europa.eu.int

European news and information website:
www.europe.org.uk

National Lottery

Website: www.lotterygoodcauses

Awards for All
1st Floor, Reynard House
37 Welford Road
Leicester LE2 7GA
Tel: 0845 600 2040 (for application information)
Website: www.awardsforall.org.uk

Community Fund
St Vincent House
16 Suffolk Street
London SW1Y 4NL
Tel: 0845 791 9191 (for application forms and preliminary enquiries)
Fax: 020 7747 5299
E-mail: enquiries@community-fund.org.uk
Website: www.community-fund.org.uk

New Opportunities Fund
Heron House
322 High Holburn
London WC1V 7PW
Tel: 0845 000 0121
Textphone: 0845 602 1659
Website: www.nof.org.uk

Websites

www.citizensconnection.net
www.do-it.org.uk (volunteering)
www.thesite.org.uk
www.youthinformation.com
www.youth.org.uk

GEOGRAPHICAL INDEX OF FUNDERS

ALPHABETICAL INDEX OF FUNDERS